DATE DUE

GAYLORD			PRINTED IN U.S.A.

From the Sands to the Mountain looks at change and continuity in the San Juan Southern Paiute Indian community. Surrounded by the Navajo and Hopi tribes, the San Juan Paiutes now number only two hundred, clustered mainly at Willow Springs and Tuba City, Arizona, and at Navajo Mountain, Utah. Overlooked by the federal government for the last several decades, in competition with the Navajos for land and water, the San Juan Paiutes have nevertheless persisted as a distinct group politically, socially, and culturally. The unique circumstances of the San Juan band, together with its relationship to other Southern Paiutes, make their case a particularly important one for the study not only of tribal politics but also of simple egalitarian societies in general. Essentially in agreement with previous authors who have emphasized the disruption of traditional Southern Paiute life that occurred with the arrival of non-Indians, forcing adaptation to a new socioeconomic environment, Pamela A. Bunte and Robert J. Franklin also find clear continuities in social and political processes that deserve more attention.

Pamela A. Bunte is professor of anthropology at California State University, Long Beach. Robert J. Franklin is professor of anthropology at California State University, Dominguez Hills.

Studies in the Anthropology of North American Indians

Editors
Raymond J. DeMallie
Douglas R. Parks

FROM THE SANDS TO THE MOUNTAIN:

Change and Persistence in a
Southern Paiute Community

**Pamela A. Bunte and
Robert J. Franklin**

**University of Nebraska Press
Lincoln and London**

The paper in this book meets the
minimum requirements of American
National Standard for Information
Sciences—Permanence of Paper
for Printed Library Materials, ANSI z39.48–
1984

Bunte, Pamela Ann
    From the sands to the mountain.
    (Studies in the anthropology of North
American Indians)
    Bibliography: p.
    Includes index.
    1. Paiute Indians—History.
2. Paiute Indians—
Social conditions. 3. Indians of
North America—Arizona—History.
4. Indians of North America—
Arizona—Social Conditions.
I. Franklin, Robert J., 1952–
II. Title.
III. Series.
E99.P2B86   1987   979.1'00497
87–25507
ISBN 0-8032-1189-9 (alk. paper)

Contents

List of Tables

List of Maps and Figures

MAPS

FIGURES

Acknowledgments

The impetus for this study came from previous works by the authors: an Indiana University Ph.D. dissertation (Franklin 1984) and a report submitted on behalf of the San Juan Southern Paiute Tribe to the Federal Acknowledgment Branch of the U. S. Bureau of Indian Affairs to document the tribe's federal acknowledgment petition (Bunte and Franklin 1984). Although many of the data and ideas presented in this volume derive from these previous works, the material has been extensively updated, revised, and reworked.

The study was based in large part on data obtained from research projects funded by the Administration for Native Americans, the Phillips Fund of the American Philosophical Society, New Mexico State University Mini-Grant Program, Indiana University Department of Anthropology Field School, Native American Rights Fund, and DNA-People's Legal Service. We especially wish to thank the Native American Rights Fund, which contracted with Dr. Veronica E. Tiller Associates of Washington, D.C., to carry out a documentary search in the National Archives. This generated a major segment of the federal archival materials used in the study. Dr. Omer C. Stewart also provided important archival materials from his personal files and from the Denver Federal Archives and Records Center.

Mrs. Marie Lehi and Mrs. Anna Whiskers, San Juan Paiutes from Willow Springs, pointed out and described the properties and uses of many San Juan food and medicinal plants. Dr. Richard Spellenberg, botanist at New Mexico State University, identified and provided scientific names for our field specimens.

We wish to thank the many people who have read and commented on earlier versions of this study, especially: Richard Stoffle, Omer Stewart, Irene Barrow, Kim Gottschalk, Terry Reynolds, Martha Kendall, Harold Schneider, James Vaughan, and Charles Bird. Special thanks are extended to Wallace E. Hooper, who oversaw preparation of the final copy, and to John Billovits and Rhoda Winters who drew the maps and figures.

Most importantly, we should like to express our gratitude to the San Juan Southern Paiute people for their unstinting hospitality and friendship over the past six years and also for their painstaking help in assembling the data that form the basis of this book. Without their sponsorship and help this study could not have been done.

Finally, we wish to note that the authors' names are given in alphabetical order, not in order of their respective contributions; this work truly has been coauthored.

INTRODUCTION

In undertaking this study of the San Juan Southern Paiute Tribe, we have sought to provide a sociopolitical history and ethnography of this community. Other studies have dealt with Southern Paiute history (Euler 1966; Stoffle and Dobyns 1983) or have analyzed aspects of present day life (Knack 1980), but this is the first that seeks to make the connection between the political and social processes at work in a modern Southern Paiute community and this community's social, economic, and political history. Previous authors have emphasized the disruptions which took place with the arrival of non-Indians and the consequent adaptations that Paiutes were forced to make in the new social and economic environment. All Southern Paiute societies have changed greatly during the past one hundred and fifty years, but at the same time there are clear continuities in cultural tradition and social and political processes. In connecting the present with the past, continuity and discontinuity are equally important and both form the basis for our study.

Throughout this study, we refer to the San Juan Southern Paiute community as the San Juan Southern Paiute Tribe. "Tribe" is not intended in any anthropological sense and does not have any theoretical status in the analysis. Rather, we are following a convention established in federal policy discourse. In this sense, tribe in most cases implies an Indian community that can establish its continuous existence as an autonomous polity throughout history to the present.

Order and Content of the Study

Since the San Juan Paiute Tribe is only one of several Southern Paiute tribes, we must understand the San Juans in the larger context of Southern Paiute society, culture, and history. Chapter One outlines the historic experiences and sociocultural background that the San Juans share with the other Southern Paiute groups as well as those that are unique to the San Juan community.

The second part of this introductory chapter is devoted to a discussion of theoretical considerations. We reexamine the theories of political organization that have been used in the past to describe Great Basin societies and present our own perspectives, which we feel are better able to account for all of the available information.

In Chapters Two, Three, and Four, we present the internal and external social, economic, and political history of the San Juan Southern Paiute Tribe from the earliest historical accounts dealing with their land and the group itself up to the present. In this study, we seek to understand change and persistence in the internal workings of San Juan society over historical time. At the same time, we examine the conditions to which the San Juans as a people have been compelled to adapt in their effort to maintain corporate tribal identity and hold onto the remnants of their collective estate.

Chapter Two has two main goals. First, it reconstructs the major elements of San Juan sociopolitical organization and land use as they existed just prior to Navajo and Mormon entry into the area in the 1860s and 1870s. This provides a crucial starting point for the analysis of change and continuity that follows. Second, it presents the course of San Juan history from the earliest Spanish exploration in 1776 until 1900, on the eve of the establishment of the first federal Indian agency within the San Juan Southern Paiutes' aboriginal lands. Chapter Three analyzes San Juan internal social, economic, and political history between 1900 and 1970 against the background of their nonofficial, local level external relations with American Indian tribes of the region. Chapter Four examines the course taken by San Juan official relationships with the federal government from the first decade of the twentieth century to the present.

Chapters Five, Six, and Seven provide a description of the contemporary situation and a look at new directions the community is taking. Chapter Five examines three important areas of modern San Juan culture: language, religion, and kinship. It also looks at the manner in which their culture serves to distinguish them from other American Indian groups both ethnographically and in terms of their own and their neighbors' concepts of ethnic identity. Chapter Six presents current social and political organization and attempts to show how the group's political life is an outgrowth of more general social and economic relations that bind the San Juan Paiute people together as one corporate tribal community. Chapter Seven looks at what the San Juan Southern Paiutes are presently doing to shape their own future as well as the various forces that may influence their choices.

1

SOUTHERN PAIUTE SOCIETY

The Southern Paiute People

The San Juan Southern Paiutes live on lands presently under the supervision of the BIA Western Navajo Subagency at Tuba City, Arizona. Although the San Juans are a very small group in comparison to their Navajo and Hopi neighbors (current genealogical and demographic data put their population at approximately 190), their numbers are within the range of other Southern Paiute groups, such as Kaibab or the five bands of the Paiute Indian Tribe of Utah. Their two major communities are at Willow Springs and nearby Tuba City, and at Navajo Mountain/Paiute Canyon. There are also a number of outlying households or household clusters, notably the cluster of families headed by Paiutes who live on the White Mesa Ute Reservation, near Blanding, Utah. Although these latter families live a distance from the two major San Juan communities, they continue to plant at Paiute Canyon in the Paiute farming area.

Culturally and in terms of social organization, the San Juan Paiutes are closely related to other Southern Paiute groups, and somewhat more distantly to the Southern Utes, such as those of the Ute Mountain and Southern Ute Tribes in southern Colorado. Southern Paiute traditional mythology, rituals, language, and other lifeways are markedly similar from Willow Springs, Arizona, to Cedar City, Utah, and down to Las Vegas and Moapa, in southern Nevada (see map 1).

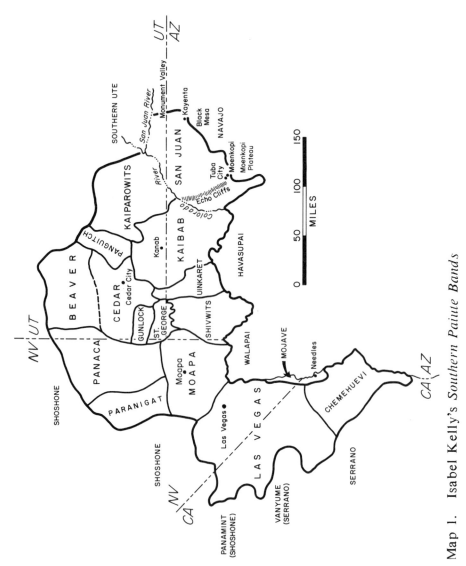

Map 1.   Isabel Kelly's *Southern Paiute Bands*

The Southern Paiutes form an ethnic group (sometimes referred to by themselves and others as the Southern Paiute Tribe or Nation) that is composed of several internally cohesive tribal communities scattered over four western states. Some of these tribes, or "bands" as Kelly (1934, 1964) and others call them, are federally recognized and have reservations. This is the case for the Chemehuevi of southern California, the Moapa and Las Vegas Paiutes of southern Nevada, and the Kaibab Paiutes of northern Arizona. In Utah, the so-called "five bands" north of Kaibab were among the few tribes of Indians actually subjected to the termination policy of the 1950s. They have recently been reinstated as one recognized group under the name of the Paiute Tribe of Utah (see Knack's 1980 study of household structure and economic situation). Other groups are not federally recognized; that is, there is no official relationship between the federal government and these tribes as polities. These include the San Juan Southern Paiutes and the Pahrump Paiutes of Nevada, who have no reservation lands clearly set aside for them. The widely scattered locations of these present communities reflect the geographic extent of Southern Paiute occupation at the time of Spanish exploration in the eighteenth century and Anglo, especially Mormon, settlement in the mid-nineteenth century (see Kelly 1934; Stewart 1942; Euler 1966; Stoffle and Evans 1976; and Stoffle and Dobyns 1982 and 1983).

These Southern Paiute tribes act and staunchly consider themselves to be politically autonomous. It is nevertheless the case that close social, political, and economic ties have been maintained among them throughout the historic period and probably before (Stoffle and Dobyns 1982 and 1983). Thus, Kelly (1964:33) noted: "As early as 1901, for the celebration of a 'Cry,' some 300 men and women assembled--Paiute from the Kaibab, St. George, Moapa, Cedar, San Juan, and Kaiparowits groups, as well as some Shoshoni from western Utah." In recent decades, such social occasions as powwows, round-dances, and funerary rituals have typically drawn participants from all four states.

The historic unity of Southern Paiutes as a whole, as well as the persistent internal cohesion of the individual Southern Paiute tribes, has been maintained in the face of adverse circumstances. As Spicer (1971) pointed out, external pressures are an important factor in the unity and persistence of any social or political group. Southern Paiutes in general have faced a number of problems in competing with their neighbors that have tended to exacerbate their own as well as outsiders' perceptions of ethnic differences. Although interethnic conflict has historically occurred between Southern Paiutes and other Indian groups, especially Utes and Navajos, as well as with Anglo settlers, the common problems faced by all Southern Paiutes in their relations with the federal bureaucracy are equally important for understanding the case of the San Juan Paiutes.

Although the Southern Paiute tribes together form a culturally and socially homogeneous group with substantial numbers, their needs and interests, and even their identity as one ethnic group, have until quite recently not been adequately recognized or dealt with in a unitary fashion by agencies of the federal government. Moreover, where the government has recognized the presence of Southern Paiute groups, its policies have often favored local non-Indian interests.

The Moapa Paiute Tribe of Nevada was the sole Southern Paiute group that was recognized in the nineteenth century and received a portion of its former lands as a reservation; but by 1875 the reservation had dwindled to 1,000 acres unusable for farming, a circumstance caused at least in part by local white expansionist pressures (Stoffle and Dobyns 1983:131-37). In the 1950s, federal trust status of the four recognized Utah bands was terminated (68 Stat. 1099); the fifth band, Cedar City, was not then recognized. This took place even though at that time many, if not the great majority, of their leading members could not speak English very well and all tribal members had little chance of socioeconomic advancement in the closed, predominantly Mormon rural economy of southern Utah, where prejudice has long been a serious political and economic barrier facing Indians (see Knack 1980, and Stoffle and Dobyns 1982 and 1983). Termination of these bands resulted in a significant loss of their tribal land base to outsiders and even deeper impoverishment for many individual members.

In 1982, following a concerted campaign conducted by all of the Southern Paiute tribes to exert pressure on the government, an all-Paiute BIA field station was established at Cedar City, Utah, to deal exclusively with the concerns of Southern Paiutes. Previously, the various federally recognized Southern Paiute communities were under the jurisdiction of several agencies, frequently sharing agency services and budgets with other, non-Southern Paiute tribes. As a result, officials often had little knowledge of, or interest in, the particular needs shared by Southern Paiutes as a whole, and sometimes exhibited complete ignorance of the identity of the Southern Paiutes as a cultural group.

Within this century-long climate of federal neglect, Southern Paiutes were generally left to manage as best they could in a harsh local economic and political environment with little or no federal intervention to protect or foster their interests. During the later decades of the nineteenth century, many Southern Paiutes literally starved to death when their water sources and farmlands fell into the hands of whites and even wild plant and animal resources were depleted by cattle grazing and other Anglo economic activities. According to Stoffle and Evans (1976:188-89), the demographic consequences of resource depletion for the Kaibab Paiutes were catastrophic: the population dropped from 500 or more to about 80 between the mid-nineteenth century and 1907, when they were finally given a reservation.

For much of the present century, while conditions have been less harsh, Southern Paiutes in all groups have had to fit themselves into the local economic context as best they could. For the most part, Paiutes have served as an underemployed pool of unskilled rural labor, often harvesting for others the produce of lands they once farmed themselves. That members of both federally recognized and unrecognized Paiute groups continued well into this century (in some cases even after the 1940s) to exploit at least some wild foods and medicines, despite their depletion, and even lived seasonally in traditional Great Basin style brushhouses, is less a sign of cultural persistence than a sign of their exclusion from the regional economy and from the more valued land and water resources.

Federal neglect of all the Southern Paiutes has played some part in producing the problems that currently face the San Juan Southern Paiute Tribe. The general situation of powerlessness among Southern Paiutes tended to generate a climate of ignorance among federal officials, and until the establishment of the Cedar City, Utah, field station, Southern Paiutes considered themselves passed over by the BIA in favor of larger, more powerful tribes.

However, there are important differences between the situation faced by the San Juans and that faced by other Southern Paiute groups. One major factor is that the San Juan Paiutes' problems arising from neglect appear to have had relatively little to do with local white interests. Except in the Tuba City area for a brief period in the second half of the nineteenth century and in a peripheral, though mischievous, way with regard to the Paiute Strip controversy of the 1920s, local Anglos appear to have shown little interest in San Juan Paiute territory.

The most serious problem for the San Juan Southern Paiutes has been competition with Navajos over resources. Unlike other Southern Paiute groups, whose resource competition difficulties began at an early date, the presence of a rapidly expanding Navajo population in the Western Navajo Reservation and the encroachment on Paiute lands and water that followed became a serious problem for the San Juans only in this century.

Moreover, for the San Juans, federal neglect in the sense of action or inaction that harmed or sacrificed Paiute interests in favor of those of other groups is of even more recent vintage than Navajo encroachment. The recent period of negative policy (1922 to the present) followed a period of relatively benign federal policy (1888-1922) during which the existence of the San Juan Paiute Tribe, their land tenure in the Western Navajo Reservation, and their social needs were recognized by the Indian Service and other agencies.

Unlike the other Southern Paiute groups, the San Juan people's contact with non-Paiutes was (and still is) almost entirely with the surrounding Navajos and other Indians rather than with Anglos. This fact alone has produced significant differences between the historic experience of the San Juans and that of other Southern Paiutes. Although subjected to social and economic pressure by the surrounding Navajos, permitted and perhaps to some extent encouraged in this by federal policy, the San Juans have persisted as a distinct group politically, socially, and culturally.

Southern Paiute Sociopolitical Organization Reconsidered

The unique historical circumstances of the San Juan Paiute Tribe make it an important case for students of modern Indian ethnicity and federal Indian policy history. The San Juan case is equally valuable for the study of Southern Paiute politics, both aboriginal and postcontact, and for the general study of political systems in egalitarian societies.

Since its publication in 1938, the description of Southern Paiute and other Great Basin societies that has become the standard for both scholars and lay people is Julian Steward's *Basin-Plateau Aboriginal Sociopolitical Groups*. In this work,

Steward reconstructed postcontact Southern Paiute society as it existed at approximately 1870 in the Las Vegas and Pahrump area of southern Nevada. He also proposed a general model of Great Basin society that attributed social and political organization to conditions in the physical environment. Although Steward was neither the first nor the last to interpret Great Basin societies from this perspective, he provided the most coherent, compelling, and influential formulation of this view. The use of Great Basin sociopolitical organization as a cornerstone to his two widely known theories, cultural ecology and multilineal evolution (Steward 1955), greatly contributed to the impact this viewpoint has had on later scholars' assumptions about Great Basin peoples and small-scale egalitarian societies in general.

According to Steward's model, Southern Paiute economy and society were determined by the environment in which the people lived and the level of technology available to them. The aridity of the land, the scattered resources, and a reliance on seed gathering all interacted to produce among Great Basin societies a mobile, fluid population that did not have strong ties to any social or political group larger than the family nor to any special land area.

Of particular importance is Steward's claim that the Great Basin Indians were an exception to his 1936 generalization (quoted in Steward 1938:258) that "all peoples in an area of low population density have some form of politically autonomous landowning band, which is greater than the bilateral family." In the conclusion to his work on the Great Basin Indians, he stated:

Western Shoshoni, probably Southern Paiute, and perhaps some Northern Paiute fall outside the scope of the previous generalizations, which were too inclusive. They lacked bands and any form of land ownership. The only stable social and political unit was the family. Larger groupings for social and economic purposes were temporary and shifting. The radical departure of these peoples from the band patterns, however, is explainable by ecological factors not previously encountered. It has been shown that the unusually great economic importance of seeds largely restricted the economic unit to the family. Communal enterprises did not always aline the same families, so that there were no large groups having political unity. It has also been shown

that the peculiar occurrence of certain foods, especially
seed species, entailed interlocking subsistence areas
which militated against land ownership. [Steward
1938:260]

Bands, for Steward, were corporate groups whose members
"must habitually have cooperated in a sufficient number of
economic and social activities under a central control to have
acquired a sense of community of interest" (1938:181). Bands
also characteristically held a territory with recognized
boundaries (1938:252, 258). For Steward, Southern Paiutes had
little in the way of communal activities and no sense of
community land ownership.

Steward based these conclusions on his model of Great
Basin ecology. He believed that the primary subsistence
strategy of the Las Vegas and Pahrump Southern Paiutes in
Nevada, like that of the Western Shoshonis, was seed gathering
(1938:232, 234). Land ownership and group cohesion were
unlikely to develop since families might be in a different area
each year, reflecting the erratic availability of plant foods
(1938:254). Although he noted that the Southern Paiute
practiced some horticulture, he felt that "this modified their
ecology only in minor ways" (1938:235). According to Steward,
land ownership existed, but only at the individual or family
level, the paradigm examples being small, noninheritable plots
of horticultural land or family-owned groves of mesquite
(1938:183). For him, there was no corporate ownership of a
more inclusive land base.

Steward variously described the largest Southern Paiute
sociopolitical unit as either the family or the village. Although
he felt that the family was "the only stable social and political
unit" (1938:260), in his description of Southern Paiutes he
referred repeatedly to their village organization (1938:181,
252). He apparently reconciled this ambiguity by concluding
that the village was a group of families wintering together for
only one winter, having "little cohesion, except the possible
bond of [kin] relationship" (1938:185), in effect, dismissing the
village as temporary and ineffectual.

Although Steward's work remains important, some of his
findings must be reinterpreted in light of new information
bearing on Southern Paiute ecology and economy in the
precontact and early historic periods. There are three points in
particular where more recent information on ecology and
economy differs from Steward's account. First, the semidesert

environment, when properly managed, was probably much richer than was previously thought. Also, riverine irrigation and other forms of farming appear to have played a major role in the aboriginal and early historic economy of Southern Paiutes in Nevada and Utah. Finally, cooperation at the community level and between communities was an economic necessity in many hunting and gathering activities.

Steward emphasized the aridity of the land and the poverty of the people, but the Paiutes' environment may not have been nearly as limiting as he believed. He described Southern Paiute land as generally "a succession of arid mountain ranges and aggraded, sage-covered desert valleys," adding that:

> Some horticulture was probably practiced by all Southern Paiutes, but it seems to have been a minor supplement to hunting and gathering and contributed little to their prosperity. Fremont . . . described the Paiute of the Muddy and Moapa Rivers as barefoot and nearly naked predatory Diggers. [Steward 1938:180]

Historical investigation suggests that the Southern Paiutes utilized a number of land management techniques to increase the quantity and availability of collected desert plants and animals. For example, mid-nineteenth century Mormon accounts recorded the Paiutes' habitual practice of burning brush and grasslands to stimulate new growth, thereby benefiting humans directly by increasing seed production and indirectly by increasing forage for game animals (Stoffle and Dobyns 1983:76-78). There is also evidence that Paiutes deliberately propagated wild plants, notably mesquite and wild grapes, by transporting seeds from their original sites to other suitable locations. In addition, certain wild seed plants, especially mentzelia, chenopods, and amaranths, were also cultivated, usually requiring a minimum of labor from the Indian farmer (Stoffle and Dobyns 1983:60-63). Contemporary non-Indians, with the notable exception of botanist Edward Palmer (1878:603; cited in Stoffle and Dobyns 1983:62), simply ignored these cultigens as weeds.

Early explorers and settlers were well aware of Paiute cultivation when it involved such familiar crops, as maize, beans, and squash, and their accounts make it clear that Southern Paiutes in Utah and Nevada once farmed extensively and produced a surplus that could be used in trade (Stoffle and Dobyns 1983:49-60). For example, in 1826, Paiutes farming near the confluence of the Virgin and Santa Clara Rivers in southwestern Utah offered the explorer Jedediah Smith and his men maize and pumpkins in exchange for pieces of iron (Brooks 1977:58; cited in Stoffle and Dobyns 1983:51). From the late 1840s and early 1850s, when the Mormons first arrived in southern Utah and Nevada, until the early 1870s, already well into the era of white settlement, there were numerous accounts of Southern Paiute maize cultivation throughout the region using riverine and spring irrigation systems as well as dry farming, and on fields as large as 100 acres or more (Stoffle and Dobyns 1983:50-56). As ethnohistorian Richard Stoffle concluded (Stoffle et al. 1982), the Southern Paiutes of Nevada and Utah in the early historic period must be seen as farmers and foragers who dominated the desert environment rather than being dominated by it.

Perhaps more importantly for our understanding of ecological influences on sociopolitical organization, Steward was not aware of the extent to which Southern Paiute hunting and gathering practices required cooperation above the household level. Some of the best evidence for this comes from Steward's own consultants' statements. For example, in his discussion of pine nut collecting, an important food source in this region, Steward noted two significant facts. First, he reported that it was the job of the village chief to announce when the nuts were ripe (1938:182). Second, he stated that:

> Permission to gather on a tract was readily extended to families which owned tracts in areas where the crop had failed. Thus, Shoshoni at Ash Meadows were often invited to pick on the Spring Mountains, and, when the Spring Mountains crop failed, Paiute were invited to pick in the Shoshoni Mountains. [1938:183]

Steward wrote of family owned tracts, but the properties of pinyon pines would make that type of ownership unlikely. In contrast to mesquite groves, which are very productive from year to year and which, at least prior to contact, grew in small, widely separated oases, pinyon pines grow continuously over large areas and are productive only one or two years out of seven (Stoffle and Dobyns 1983:63; Thomas 1973). Because entire pinyon pine areas were productive one year but not the next, communities were encouraged to develop reciprocal use agreements to offset the unreliability of the resource in their own area. This would have required the community as a whole to maintain collective rights in pinyon tracts, thus militating against individual or family ownership that might conflict with community needs.

Not surprisingly, communities guarded their use-rights jealously, expecting fair return for shared use. Steward noted that shared use was by explicit invitation. He also recorded that trespass (uninvited use) could provoke verbal exchanges, fights, and even the threat of witchcraft on the part of rightful owners (1938:183).

Since this type of exchange necessarily took place every year, a widespread information network must have existed so that each village group could be kept abreast of the locations of ripe pine nut stands and also so that reciprocal use agreements could be worked out and maintained between groups. Steward's data suggest that this information network was one of the primary responsibilities of the village chiefs, who had to inform the village group when (and probably where) the nuts were ripe (1938:182). The role played by village leaders is another important indication that corporate ownership of resources was involved. Our own oral historical study among the Southern Paiutes in Utah and Arizona supports this interpretation. We were also told that such invitations were extended by local leaders to neighboring groups for both deer hunting and seed collection as well as pine nut picking.

Steward's description of sociopolitical organization among the Southern Paiutes was based not only on his understanding of their ecology and economics, but was also influenced by his understanding of politics in egalitarian societies. Like many students of political systems before and after him, notably Meyer Fortes and E. E. Evans-Pritchard (1940), Morton Fried (1967), and Elman Service (1975), Steward believed that leaders in egalitarian societies did not exercise coercive authority, especially the ultimate exercise of authority, the penalties of death or banishment, and that therefore governmental institutions in such societies were fundamentally different from those in nonegalitarian or hierarchical societies. He concluded that Southern Paiute leaders lacked such authority and it seems clear that he was correct. Because of this observation--and his belief that there was no sociopolitical organization above the household level in Southern Paiute society--Steward concluded that Southern Paiutes lacked governmental institutions altogether.

He was aware, however, that the Southern Paiutes had

leaders and recorded features of leadership which suggest that governmental institutions were more elaborate than he believed:

> From informant testimony, Paiute of the Pahrump and Las Vegas regions were never unified in a single band. AH named a succession of three Las Vegas chiefs (towin'dum): Patsadum, who died many years ago; then Tasiu'dum, who also died many years ago; then A:udia', who was recently killed. For the region of Ash Meadows and Pahrump he named Takopa (who was probably born at Las Vegas and died at Pahrump about 1895). Takopa's main function was to direct the festival. ChB added that when Mojave raided Las Vegas people, Takopa might assist them, perhaps even taking command.
>
> Informants from both Pahrump and Las Vegas regarded Takopa as chief of "all the Southern Paiute" but could name no function of his which did not involve dances or transactions with the white man. Benjamin, a veteran scout of the United States Army, who had lived at Tule Springs near Las Vegas, succeeded Takopa in his position. [Steward 1938:185]

We should add that in describing the Las Vegas "festival" mentioned in the above passage, Steward (1938:184) noted that it lasted three or four days; that it terminated in mourning rites; that it was planned and directed by a chief who announced it six to eight months in advance; that the chief made speeches while the festival was in progress; and that visitors came from the local Paiute communities at Beatty, Ash Meadows, Pahrump, and Las Vegas, and other Indians even came from as far away as San Bernardino, California.

In sum, Steward's data suggest the presence of important governmental institutions among Las Vegas and Pahrump Southern Paiutes. It seems especially clear that chiefs and possibly subchiefs as well existed among the Paiutes in the southern Nevada area and that the chiefly office had well defined duties and spheres of authority. Most notably, the chief had the authority to direct large social and religious undertakings like the festival, as well as the authority to make "transactions with the white man" and lead his people in war against other Indian groups (Steward 1938:185). In many ways, the functions of the Southern Paiute chief as described by

Steward were similar to the external political functions
Florence Ellis (1951) ascribed to the Southwest Pueblo position
of "outside chief," also called variously "war chief" or "war
priest."
  Nevertheless, other questions concerning the nature of the
political community remain unanswered. One question concerns
the nature of community decision making processes. We know,
for example, that decisions were made that affected access to
community resources, but we also know that the chief probably
did not have the independent authority to make them. We do
not know whether the largest political unit was at the level of
the local community (Steward's village) or whether it was
somewhat larger, as information on chiefs and subchiefs seems
to suggest. Finally, although Steward suggested that kinship
was an important organizing factor in larger sociopolitical
groups like the village, the nature of early historic Southern
Paiute kinship organization is still largely unknown. Although
Las Vegas and Pahrump sociopolitical organization is beyond
the scope of this study, a discussion of the types of political
processes generally found in egalitarian societies proves useful
to any attempt to describe the sociopolitical organization of a
Southern Paiute community.

Politics in Egalitarian Societies

Politics in egalitarian societies consists of fundamentally the
same relationships that are found in hierarchical societies. In
all political systems, power, as a relationship between individuals or groups, is reciprocal. As one theorist has stated,
"both members of the relationship act in terms of . . . the
controls that each has over matters of interest to the other"
(Adams 1975:22). In relationships between followers and
leaders, followers have control over at least one matter of vital
interest to the leader or group of leaders--their support--so that
followership is the ultimate source of an individual's ability to
exercise leadership powers. Based on this power relationship,
individual members or subgroups allocate the power to make
decisions for the community, to represent it with outsiders, and
so forth, to an individual leader or a leadership group.
Although it is commonly thought that the difference between
egalitarian and nonegalitarian political systems rests in the
type and manner of powers that are allocated, much more
important is the degree to which all members of the society

exercise equivalent controls over matters of interest to their fellow members and to their leaders. It is the latter factor-- itself in large part determined by the economics of production and exchange--that ultimately determines whether members will have equal or relatively equal access to the decision making process in their community (see Schneider 1974 and 1981).

Examples of leaders or leadership groups in small-scale egalitarian societies include those often identified as the headman, spokesperson, or council. Headmen or spokespersons, like leaders in all societies, have a certain constellation of powers allocated to them. The actual domains of community life over which a leader will have authority differ from society to society. For example, while in the United States the federal government does not have authority over religious matters, in many societies religion is an integral part of the leader's duties. As long as we can point to a consistent group of powers held by each subsequent leader, we can consider the leader to hold a leadership office.

Although the withdrawal of support by the followers is always a possibility, it is nevertheless the case that in many egalitarian societies leaders retain the support of the com- munity, and thus the powers allocated by their constituency, for lengthy periods. As Adams (1975:34) indicated, these individuals have "special capabilities and controls" that are recognized as such by the community. They also tend to have the same skills in molding public opinion and keeping followers that skilled politicians in Western democracies have. Leaders are chosen by the community for these very skills and capabilities.

Leaders are not the only or even the most important mani- festation of authority found in egalitarian society. Consensual decision making, which in some sense at least is a basic process in all human societies, is the mainstay of politics in small- scale, egalitarian societies (see Adams 1975:62, 215; Giddens 1977:338-40; Schapera 1956). The consensus unit involved in such decision making may be formal or informal and is usually composed of all adult members, all adult males, or a group of elders.

Schapera, in his analysis of political organization in South African societies (1956:85), discussed such consensual decision making in two hunting and gathering societies, the San Bushmen and Bergdamas. The men of each local band gather nightly around the central fire to discuss group affairs: the following day's hunting; moving camp; burning the brush; organizing initiation ceremonies; trading and visiting with neighbors; and arranging to protect their land from aggression or to seek retaliation for previous hostilities. As a point of comparison between informal decision making of this type and decision making in more complex societies, Schapera (1956:217) also concluded at another point that "maintaining territorial boundaries," "resisting external aggression," and "the organization and direction of cooperative enterprises often involving the whole community" were three functions "common to all forms of government."

Although small-scale egalitarian societies do have leadership offices with well defined (albeit to us sometimes unusual) constellations of duties, in most cases decision making is a group, rather than individual enterprise. Thus, the leader is in Schapera's (1956:86) terms often the "executive officer" and representative of the group rather than the head decision maker. In discussing the Cherokees' "white political division," which took charge of domestic affairs in the town or village, Fogelson (1977:190) noted that decisions were arrived at by a council of elders which debated the matter until consensus was reached. During these meetings, the "peace chief," the head of the white division, "played a moderating role by exercising considerable diplomatic tact in subtly steering discussion but never appearing self-assertive."

In looking at the San Juan Southern Paiute community in the present day and in the historic record, we discover similar patterns of political leadership and consensual decision making. As was apparently also the case in the Paiute communities of southern Nevada, historic and modern San Juan political leadership has been characterized by limited powers but highly respected moral authority. The Paiute leader's role within the community closely parallels that of Fogelson's tactful and moderate Cherokee "peace chief." However, the Paiute leader has also exercised powers relating to external affairs, some of which in the past resembled those associated with the Cherokee office of "war chief" (Fogelson 1977:190-91). External duties appear, in fact, to be more central to the leadership office in San Juan society. All other political powers, including the power to make decisions affecting the community's internal and external affairs, are exercised by a council of elders, who in the present day at least include all mature members of the tribe both male and female.

The way in which the community itself is organized varies

considerably in small-scale, egalitarian societies. Kinship in particular is generally recognized as a more important organizational factor at the community level in small-scale societies than in larger, more complex societies. Nevertheless, its role should not be exaggerated. Even in small egalitarian societies, there are always some members of the group who are not consanguineally related and at the same time there are always some kin who are members of other communities (Schapera 1956; Mair 1962:15). Moreover, while the ideology of group relations may stress the importance of kinship, actual community relations typically exhibit other processes as well. On the other hand, while complex societies like our own are thought of as impersonal, in fact kinship relations as well as personal networks of friends often play an important role in political process.

While San Juan society today is to a large degree organized along the lines of a particular system of kinship relations, it has not always been so. In this study, we will be looking at kinship and political community in San Juan Paiute society, as these have changed in response to changing conditions and have also come more and more over the course of recent history to be considered by community members to be one and the same.

2

SAN JUAN
SOCIOPOLITICAL
ADAPTATIONS IN THE
PRERESERVATION PERIOD,
1776–1900

Midnineteenth Century Sociopolitical Organization
And Land Use

Determining the internal organization of a traditional society
without the benefit of contemporary ethnographic observation
is at best a somewhat doubtful enterprise, destined to contain
important gaps and probably inaccuracies as well. In the
following analysis, we have worked from two sources--
conventional historical documentation and Indian oral
historical accounts. The first type was produced by contemporary witnesses, but for their own purposes and
occasionally with considerable ethnocentric bias. Moreover,
prior to the 1860s, such evidence is relatively sparse. The
second source, while it often provides greater insight into
internal organization and intertribal relationships than the
first type, consists of accounts passed down by word of mouth
and recorded in permanent form only many decades after the

events in question. In addition to our own field interviews, we make use of other sources of recorded oral history, notably the ethnographic work of Isabel Kelly (1964:167-74) and Omer Stewart (1942), both of whom worked with the San Juan Southern Paiutes very briefly in the 1930s.

In reconstructing mid-nineteenth century San Juan life, four areas are discussed: territory; land use; leadership and decision making; and sociopolitical groups and modes of group formation. Each of these aspects of early San Juan society is important from the standpoint of later sociocultural change. Although considerable change has occurred since this early period, certain elements of community life have proven much more susceptible to change than others. San Juan Paiute territory and land use, in particular, have evolved considerably over recorded history, even during the era preceding Navajo and Mormon entry. On the other hand, there is a structural core of San Juan sociopolitical organization, especially the kinship system and political institutions of leadership and collective decision making, that has persisted in recognizable form through many decades of change. We believe that this core of institutions, at least in its broad outlines, is common to the early nineteenth century cultures of all Southern Paiutes. It thus represents a conservative force that has channeled and constrained the San Juan people's political and economic adaptive choices, even as it has served as a potent tool enabling them to persist as a people.

Territory

The issue of territory is an important one for understanding both sociopolitical organization and economics. The extent to which the San Juans can be shown to have had territorial boundaries recognized by themselves and their neighbors is one indication of their sociopolitical autonomy and corporateness, in this as in any other era. At the same time, territorial boundaries and historic territorial rearrangements reflect changes in intertribal relations throughout the historic period. Finally, we must attempt to establish the San Juan Tribe's pre-1860 land base in order to achieve a clear conception of the economic and social changes that occurred when Paiutes began to lose access to resources within this land base.

Both Kelly (1964:167 and map 1 opposite p. 1) and Stewart (1942:233, map 2), working from 1930s Southern Paiute testimony including that of San Juans, assigned a virtually identical aboriginal territory to a Southern Paiute sociopolitical entity they called the "San Juan Southern Paiute Band." Modern consultants, which included not only San Juan Paiutes but also several knowledgeable Kaibab elders, consistently described these same pre-1860 territorial boundaries. Those whom we interviewed did not appear to have been aware of either Kelly's or Stewart's publications and their accounts can be taken as independent corroboration.

A version of Kelly's map of Southern Paiute band territories (Kelly 1934), which shows the San Juan territory along with the territories of other Southern Paiute bands, is reproduced as map 1. Important locations within the San Juan Tribe's historic occupation zone in Arizona and Utah are shown on map 2.

Kelly described the aboriginal San Juan tribal estate as follows (1964:167): "roughly, the area extended from Monument Valley to the Little Colorado and from the San Juan River to Black Mesa and Moencopi Plateau, without including either of the latter." However, as Mormon accounts (Cleland and Brooks 1955:280, 282; Ivins 1875) and modern consultants indicated, and in fact as Kelly herself pointed out (1964:171), San Juan Paiutes organized hunting expeditions outside of this territory, particularly in the San Francisco Peaks area, near Flagstaff, Arizona, and north of the San Juan River in Utah. We were also told that periodic wild seed gathering took place in House Rock Valley, beyond the Colorado River, as late as the early decades of the present century.

The resources of the San Francisco Peaks area, especially the deer, appear to have been used by many local tribes. In any event, the San Juan people used this area without considering it to be theirs exclusively. This also appears to have been the case in the Henry Mountains and the Bear's Ears area, north of the San Juan River.

When San Juans gathered seeds at House Rock, they did so as the result of an express agreement with the Kaibab Paiutes living in the area. In return for allowing Kaibab Paiutes to gather seeds on the Kaibito Plateau in the summer, the San Juans could gather at House Rock in the fall. According to our consultants, the host group in either case would sponsor a round-dance for their visitors. Round-dances were one of the mechanisms used by Southern Paiutes to cement the social and political ties between local groups upon which reciprocal resource use agreements were based.

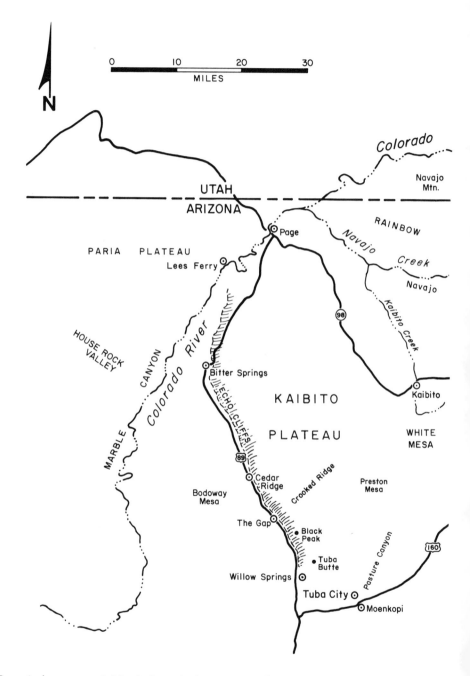

Map 2.   Arizona and Utah Lands in the Region of San Juan Occupation

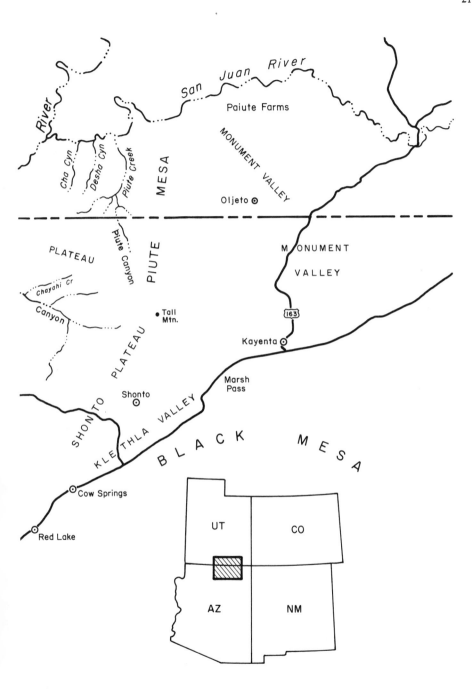

Because they brought unrelated young people together, such dances also resulted in marriages, creating ties of affinal and later consanguineal kinship across local group boundaries. Of the several marriages that occurred between Kaibab and San Juan Paiutes during the nineteenth and early twentieth centuries, more than a few can be traced directly to round-dances and other social visiting between the groups.

In her treatment of Kaibab Paiutes, Kelly made note of "exchange visits" (1964:23) in which Panguitch and Cedar Paiutes were permitted to exploit "the local terrain," but she did not mention the San Juans. She did, however, record "occasional marriage with Panguitch, Kaiparowits, and San Juan Paiute in former times" (Kelly 1964:99). In fact, one woman named *Muvwi'ait* ("No Nose"), whom she listed as having lived in the House Rock area (1964:20), is said by modern Kaibab Paiutes and Willow Springs San Juans to have been a San Juan woman from the Cameron area who married among the House Rock Paiutes. Her place in Kaibab and San Juan Paiute genealogies links many Willow Springs residents, including the present San Juan tribal spokesperson, with leading families at Kaibab.

During the pre-1860 period, there is some historical evidence of territorial boundaries and boundary change. The journal of the Spanish explorers, Fathers Dominguez and Escalante, who led the first Spanish exploration of Ute and Southern Paiute lands, described the Paiutes living in the vicinity of Navajo Mountain as a separate local entity on a par with the other local communities of Utes and Southern Paiutes identified elsewhere in Utah and Arizona (Chavez and Warner 1976:101-109). They indicated that the Colorado River was their western boundary, in keeping with Southern Paiute oral tradition, but assigned the southern area near present Tuba City and Moenkopi to Havasupai occupation. Based on information from other sources, especially Hopi oral histories cited in the second part of this chapter, it appears that the San Juans had begun to occupy this southern section by at least the 1830s but that the Havasupais only gradually retreated from it in subsequent decades. According to the Spanish explorers' description of intergroup relations, the San Juan people were already in conflict with the Hopis in 1776. Modern San Juan consultants have stated that early Hopi-Paiute conflict arose out of competition for fields and water in the Moenkopi Wash area. All of this suggests that the pre-1860 territorial boundaries described by Southern Paiute consultants were actually the result of San Juan expansion southward in the eighteenth or nineteenth century.

U.S. Army correspondence of the late 1850s reveals that the Navajos recognized a defended territorial boundary between themselves and the Paiutes at Marsh Pass, near present Kayenta (see Walker 1859a). This was the major geographic entry point between the Navajo settlements in the Canyon de Chelly area and pre-1860 San Juan-occupied lands. Marsh Pass lies on Kelly's eastern aboriginal San Juan Paiute boundary at the northern end of Black Mesa.

Land Use

Turning to questions of land use and economics in the mid-nineteenth century, modern consultants, like those interviewed by Kelly and Stewart, indicated that the San Juan people practiced three major modes of food production to exploit the lands then in their possession: hunting, wild plant food collection, and farming (see Kelly 1964:168-72 and Stewart 1942:240-56, 335-38). This section focuses on the types of plant and animal foods that were used by the San Juans and the land areas associated with them. In later sections, we examine certain aspects of social organization relating to land use, including land tenure, community members' access to collecting and hunting areas, and the sociopolitical organization of economic activities.

Tables 1, 2, and 3 list respectively important wild animals, wild plant foods, and plant cultivars used by San Juan Southern Paiutes, and known locations where they were produced and/or harvested prior to and in many cases after Navajo and Anglo settlement. The information in these tables comes from Kelly (1964:170-72), Stewart (1942:240-45, 250-56), and from our own ethnobotanical research with modern San Juan Paiute consultants.

With the exception of maize and squash, the tables include only those plants that could be identified scientifically through collected specimens. In the case of some wild plants, equating the Paiute term with a single species or even genus may be misleading. Certain Paiute plant terms, notably terms for seed plants such as *wa'iv*, *warav*, and *pas(i)*, refer generically to groups of plants with similar features and uses, even though only certain varieties were available for identification.

Table 1: Game Animals Utilized by San Juans, Circa 1860

English Name	Paiute Name	Ecological Zone/Location
Large Game:		
Deer	*tuyuy*	High pine forest: Coconino and Kaibab Plateaus, Navajo Mountain and region north of the San Juan River.
Antelope	*waants*	High grasslands: Kayenta, Kaibito Plateau, Antelope Hills (north of Flagstaff).
Mountain sheep	*nax(av)*	On heights above Page to Navajo Mountain; Skeleton Mesa.
Elk	*paruy*	Paria Plateau (outside of San Juan territory).
Small Game:		
Cottontail	*tavuts*	All zones.
Jackrabbit	*kamuts*	All zones.
Porcupine	*yunguputs*	High pine and pinyon-juniper forest.
Rat	*kaatsits*	All zones.
Badger	*unaputs*	High pine and pinyon-juniper forest.
Beaver	*pangwits*	Navajo Mountain.

Table 2: Wild Plant Foods Used by San Juans, Circa 1860

Botanical and English Name	Paiute Name	Ecological Zone
Seeds:		
Agropyron sp.	*paxankw*	High grasslands.
Amaranthus palmerii	*kumut(ʉ)*	High grasslands, and lower elevations.
Atriplex canescens	*tønøv*	High grasslands.
Chenopodium spp.	*warav*	Multiple zones.
Descurainia sp. (tansey mustard)	*ak(ʉ)*	Oasis areas.
Helianthus annuus and sp. (sunflower)	*akʉmp, akʉmpiruats*	Oasis areas, some high grasslands.
Juniperus sp. (juniper or cedar)	*wa'ap(ap)*	Pinyon-juniper forest and high grasslands.
Muhlenburgia pungens	*tangwawa'iv*	High grasslands.
Oryzopsis hymenoides (ricegrass)	*wa'iv*	High grasslands.
Pinus edulis (pinyon nuts)	*tʉv(a)*	Pinyon forest.

Botanical and English Name	Paiute Name	Ecological Zone
Seeds:		
Portulaca oloracea	*tuupu'iv*	Around fields.
Quercus sp. (acorns)	*tømup*	Paiute Canyon.
Sporobolus airoides	*mønup*	High grasslands.
Sporobolus contractus	*kwakwe'iv*	High grasslands.
Berries and fruit:		
Fragaria sp. (wild strawberry)	*tuvwiis*	High pine forest.
Lycium pallidum (coyote berry)	*shuna'up*	Desert lowlands and near fields.
Lycium spp.	*u'up*	Desert lowlands.
Prunus sp. (chokecherry)	*tønøp*	Canyon oases.
Rhus trilobata (sumac or squawberry)	*iis*	Oases.
Rosa woodsii (?) (wild rose)	*ts'ampiv*	Canyon bottoms and oases.
Vaccinium sp. (blueberry)	*kainap*	High pine forest.

Botanical and English Name	Paiute Name	Ecological Zone
Other Plant Foods:		
Agave (agave or century plant; stalk base baked and eaten)	*yaant*	Desert lowlands and canyon bottoms.
Allium sp. (wild onion)	*wichas*	Multiple zones.
Opuntia sp. (and other varieties of cactus; leaves and fruit eaten)	*manav, yuavip*	Desert lowlands.
Orobanche sp. (broomrape)	*tu'u*	Near oasis farmlands.
Stanleya pinnata (greens eaten)	*tɨmar*	In fallow fields.
Typha latifolia (cattails; roots and heads eaten)	*tø'iv*	Oases and marshlands.
Yucca baccata (broadleaf yucca; fruit eaten)	*wiisiv*	High grasslands and lower elevations.

Table 3: San Juan Cultigens, Circa 1860

Cultigen	Paiute Name	Cultivation Techniques
Zea mays (maize)	*kumwi* (specific color names also)	pot- and ditch irrigation; dry farming.
Cucurbit sp. (squash)	*naxɨrɨs*	same as corn.
Amaranthus caudatus	*kumut(ɨ)* *akakumut(ɨ)*	broadcast, irrigated same as corn.
Helianthus annuus (sunflower)	*akɨmp*	broadcast or self-seeded; no irrigation.

The large game animals--deer, antelope, and wild sheep-- have largely disappeared from the Western Navajo Reservation area, allegedly because of Navajo overhunting and competition with grazing livestock. However, many of the wild plant species listed, although apparently much scarcer on the Western Navajo area than they once were, are still collected by the San Juans, forming a minor part of their diet. All of these wild plant varieties were still being collected sporadically within the last fifty years. There are a number of individuals, particularly in the south where gathering seems to have persisted the longest, who have a broad knowledge and practical experience with gathering and processing traditional plant foods and medicines. The specific techniques used by the San Juans in food collection and production, preservation, and preparation are virtually identical to those that have been recorded in the ethnographic literature for other Southern Paiute groups utilizing the same or similar resources. (See Kelly 1964, especially the treatment of Kaibab food production and other technologies, pp. 39-86; Stewart 1942:240-66, 327-30; see also Stoffle and Dobyns 1982, chap. 4 and 1983, chap. 4, which contain the most complete ethnohistorical accounts of Southern Paiute horticulture and wild plant management.)

The most important zone for the collection of many wild seeds, including grasses, chenopods, artemisia, and others, begins at approximately 5000 feet above sea level. At this elevation are found the plateau grasslands and scattered juniper woodlands of House Rock Valley, the Kaibito Plateau, Klethla Valley, and the Kayenta-Monument Valley area.

In addition to these seeds, this zone was also at one time inhabited by large antelope herds, hunted by the San Juans using trap corrals and other techniques (see Kelly 1964:171). In the 1950s, a Navajo showed archeologist Milton Wetherill a wingtrap corral on Skeleton Mesa, indicating that it dated to 1890 and was used by Paiutes to capture wild sheep (Wetherill 1954). The editor of Plateau, the journal in which the report was published, added in a note: "Similar brush corrals have been reported near the Hopi Buttes, Kinnikinnick Ruin, and on Anderson Mesa southeast of Flagstaff, and on Gray Mountain west of Cameron" (Wetherill 1954, editor's note, p. 116). In these latter areas, the game pursued would more likely have been antelope and possibly deer. Kelly also reported San Juan antelope hunting "upstream [southeast] from Cameron," and on the Kaibito Plateau (1964:171).

Desert lowlands, areas below 5000 feet located in the Page area and in the vicinity of the Colorado and Little Colorado Rivers, provided some small game and various plant foods, including cactus leaves and fruit, and berries, especially the various *Lycium* species called in Paiute, *u'up(i)*. More importantly, however, sunny slopes and canyon bottoms in this zone also supplied sweet *Yucca baccata* fruit and agave (century plant), the stalk and base of which were pit-roasted, pounded, and dried as cakes. Some agave roasting pits have been located at Willow Springs and others are said to exist closer to the areas near the river canyons where agave grows. According to consultants, only a man born in the summer was permitted to tend the roasting agave.

Pinyon-juniper forest, between 5000 and 7000 feet, is found within San Juan territory in the Cedar Ridge area and across broad stretches of the Kaibito, Shonto, and Rainbow Plateaus. Paiutes also had access to pinyon forest in the Bear's Ears area, north of the San Juan River, and on the South Rim of the Grand Canyon, outside their occupation zone (see Kelly 1964:171). Pinyon-juniper forest provided two crucial food sources, deer and pinyon pine nuts, as well as wild sheep, porcupine, badger, and other game animals, and other plant resources, including an important medicinal and sacred plant, *k'oap(i)* or wild tobacco (*Nicotiana attenuata*).

High pine forest, starting at approximately 7000 feet and composed of ponderosa pine, and other conifers at higher elevations, is rare within the San Juan historic occupation zone, the major such area being located on the heights of Navajo Mountain. San Juan Paiutes also utilized the high forest zone in the San Francisco Peaks area and the Paria Plateau, north of House Rock. Besides game, this zone supplied certain plant foods, notably wild strawberries and blueberries.

Throughout the San Juan Paiutes' pre-1860 occupation zone are scattered many oases with permanent or seasonal sources of water and soil suitable for farming. These include sites along the San Juan River and its tributaries, in the Paiute and Navajo Canyon system, in the marshy land nearby Kayenta, and finally the series of springs and wash flood plains along the Echo Cliffs from north of Cedar Ridge to the Moenkopi Wash area by Tuba City. Oral history and nineteenth century documentary sources indicate that Paiutes grew maize and other crops in many of these areas. Most of the known nineteenth century family heads were each associated with several specific field sites, suggesting that farm land was abundant and that Paiute farmers used a long or short fallow system, seldom planting the same field in successive years. Oral histories make mention of irrigation works, especially in Paiute Canyon and the Willow Springs and Tuba City area. Both Kelly (1964:170) and Stewart (1942:254) recorded the use of diverted stream or spring water to irrigate fields. It is not clear, however, how extensive or intensive the use of irrigation was prior to Mormon and Navajo entry. Before 1860, only one documentary source attests to San Juan Paiute farming (Hafen 1947:95).

By the early twentieth century, Paiute-built irrigation works and other improvements at Willow Springs and Paiute Canyon were relatively complex and must have involved a considerable labor investment. In addition to oasis farming, San Juan horticulturists periodically opened dry farming areas in likely places in other zones, and continue to do so today.

Sometime in the late nineteenth century, according to San Juan oral history, Paiutes began to herd livestock--sheep, goats, and cattle. One San Juan, whose affidavit was taken by the Navajo Tribe in their Indian Claims Commission case (Dick's Sister 1961), indicated that during her childhood, the 1880s approximately, the Navajo Mountain San Juans were acquiring sheep from Navajos living in the vicinity of Tall Mountain, about 10 miles southeast of Upper Paiute Canyon. She implied that herding began at that time or shortly before. She stated that Navajos had moved into the Tall Mountain area only recently, and added that the Paiutes "used to gather wild grains for food, also, they hunted wild animals."

However, one historic source, the Mexican governor of New Mexico, Jose Antonio Vizcarra, recorded that he encountered a group of Paiutes with goats in 1823 in the region just south of Paiute Canyon (Brugge 1964). It is not clear whether these goats represented a permanent herd, thus contradicting Paiute oral tradition, or whether the animals were intended for immediate use, having perhaps been acquired from the Navajo group that Vizcarra's soldiers had been vigorously pursuing at the time of the encounter.

Leadership and Decision Making

In the mid-nineteenth century and earlier, both documentary and oral historical evidence indicate that the San Juans made decisions and acted as a corporate group for political and economic purposes. In the mid-nineteenth century, there were hunting and gathering activities that involved the tribe as a whole. External relations between the San Juans and other regional groups in the pre-1860 period provide other examples of collective decision making and action. We have already noted that the San Juan and neighboring Kaibab Paiutes exchanged usufruct rights to gathering sites. This relation persisted from early in the nineteenth century until the first decades of the twentieth, according to a number of consultants. The San Juans were also involved in intertribal alliances and warfare. Thus, for example, a continuous state of hostility appears to have existed between the Hopis and the San Juan Paiutes from 1776 to the 1860s. According to one Hopi traditional account, in the early nineteenth century the Paiutes actually destroyed the Hopi village of Moenkopi and kept the Hopis from reestablishing fields there for several decades thereafter until the Mormons arrived and helped bring peace to the area ("Information Concerning Hopi Problems" 1939:11). In a Havasupai traditional story recorded by Spier (1928:378), and in U.S. Army correspondence dated 1859 (Walker 1859a and b; Simonson 1859), there are indications that the San Juan Tribe was at war on separate occasions with Havasupais and Navajos.

In both cases, these sources also recorded that a Paiute leader met with his counterparts in the other tribes and reached peace agreements with them.

In historic times, from at least the 1870s to the present, most forms of collective action, including seasonal movements, dances and funerals, social control, and in the past, even warfare, were initiated through a form of consensus group decision making which we call the "council" and which the San Juans call the *shuupara'ap* ("meeting") or *niavishuupara'ap* ("leader-meeting").

For the latter half of the nineteenth century, the historic record and San Juan traditional accounts yield specific instances of council decision making indicating the type and extent of its powers. In one case at least, a council exercised coercive force. The white trader Joe Lee (1974:29, 34) claimed to have witnessed in Paiute Canyon a collective decision to mutilate a man's foot because he had committed rape-incest against his sister.

Unfortunately, little evidence beyond the most general information exists for the period prior to 1860. Stewart noted (1942:300) that the San Juan Paiutes had a "council," and that its powers were not limited to war. He also indicated that the San Juans, unlike the three other Southern Paiute groups in his study, allowed women to participate in council meetings. Kelly did not describe San Juan political process, although she did describe several specific incidents in which community assemblies among the aboriginal Kaibabs chose and replaced "chiefs" (1964:26-30). At one point, her consultant's statements imply that the community could collectively exercise the death penalty in cases of murder: "Sometimes the father or brother of the deceased killed the murderer; when, as usual, the latter fled, 'all the people planned to kill him when he returned'" (1964:27).

The tribal leadership office we call the "chief elder" is the second major persistent political institution in historic and modern San Juan political life. The San Juan tribal leader's position has historically revolved primarily around relations with outside groups. This complex of external powers and responsibilities is exemplified in the pre-1860 period by the reported Paiute-Havasupai and Paiute-Navajo peace agreements cited above, in which a (possibly the) Paiute leader appeared to play a crucial role as tribal representative and negotiator. In the period following 1860, the tribal leader figured

prominently in San Juan relations with Anglos, including
federal agents, as well as with other Indian communities.

The San Juan people, like other Southern Paiutes and many
other North American Indian peoples, believe strongly that no
single person can legitimately hold coercive authority over
another. Despite this limitation of their powers, chief elders
have historically exercised considerable influence in internal
tribal affairs through their moral authority. Tribal chief
elders are often described as having a special relationship with
the supernatural which sets them apart from other tribal
members including other elders. *Pak'ai*, a late nineteenth and
early twentieth century chief elder, is said to have died and
been resurrected, to have had visions of the hereafter, and as a
living man to have walked with a visiting "angel." Alfred
Lehi, his successor, made cryptic prophecies, some of which the
San Juan people believe have only now begun to be fulfilled.
The present day tribal leader has prophetic dreams and waking
visions in which she hears the guiding voice of *Shɯnangwav*,
whom Paiutes name in English God or the Great Spirit.

Oral history recorded by Stewart, Kelly, and ourselves
indicates that while nineteenth century leaders held no
coercive authority within the tribe, they were attributed very
specific leadership duties in internal tribal affairs. One
traditional duty that has apparently lapsed in the present
century is the morning speech. At sunrise, San Juan Paiute
leaders used to shout out long monologues to the households
residing together in the camp. They would give general moral
instructions, for example, that people should share meat with
other families. They would also announce the hunting and
gathering activities that the group would take part in that day
and the days ahead, activities that had presumably been
planned in council. Among the San Juans, the leader
occasionally led hunting and gathering activities, although
often other elders with special practical or magical expertise
would lead, as for example in the hunting of certain big game
animals, like deer and antelope. Even war leadership could be
allocated to someone other than the chief elder on an ad hoc
basis.

Kelly described patterns of local settlement leadership in
aboriginal Kaibab that closely parallel accounts provided by
modern San Juan consultants. For example, she stated that
among the Kaibab "a 'big' chief . . . addressed the people
every morning" (1964:26-27). Kelly cited not only cases from
her own consultants but from Edward Sapir's unpublished

notes as well. Her description indicates that although Kaibab leaders also lacked coercive authority, in disputes or crimes it was often the leader who would suggest appropriate settlements, for example that an indemnity be paid the relatives in cases of accidental homicide.

In the second half of the nineteenth century and in the twentieth century, we are able to identify a continuous succession of tribal-level leaders beginning with Patnish in the 1860s and possibly 1850s. Oral history provides general information on the duties and activities of leaders prior to 1860 and also mentions the names of several early leaders. Unfortunately, there is not enough information in traditional accounts of this early period to permit us to identify reliably any of these figures as tribal leaders, rather than influential tribal elders or perhaps local leaders.

Omer Stewart (1942:345) recorded four "names of old leaders" among the San Juans: *Avinʉav* ("Makes gurgling noises while reclining" [because of gas]), *Tønacha'a* ("Ram," or "Male sheep"), *Machʉkats* ("Has a beard"; known in Navajo as *Daghaa'i*. "Whiskers"), and *Kwiøn*. Of these, at least one, *Machʉkats*, was a leader of merely local importance in the southern area in the years after 1860. *Avinʉav*, the father of *Machʉkats*, may have been a tribal leader in the first half of the nineteenth century. According to oral tradition, he made morning speeches and led at least some San Juan people in seasonal economic activities and in war. There is no information available concerning the size or nature of the group that he led. *Tønacha'a* was the father of *Pak'ai*, mentioned earlier. It is not known whether *Tønacha'a* held the chiefly office as his son did or not. The fourth leader named by Stewart, *Kwiøn*, is unknown. *Kwiøn* may not be a name at all since it resembles *(ku)kwoin*, the Southern Paiute kinship term for "mother's older brother" with the possessive pronoun "my" attached to it.

In addition to the individuals mentioned by Stewart's consultants, there were other nineteenth century men who are remembered as leaders in the north, around Navajo Mountain and Paiute Canyon. Toward the end of the nineteenth century, when the north had begun to become more autonomous as a result of Navajo expansion, a figure named *Napa(')ats* emerged as a leader. (The intended sense of this name is forgotten; depending on which variant of the name is taken, the Paiute means ambiguously: "Foot," "Has no foot," or "Has a really big foot.") By the end of the nineteenth century, he was succeeded

by *Muupᴂts*, known best to outsiders by the Navajo translation
of his name, *Nascha*, "Owl."

In the early nineteenth century, a group of families moved
into the Navajo Mountain area from across the Colorado or San
Juan Rivers. Shortly after 1900, a large proportion of this
group, together with other San Juans, left the Navajo
Mountain-Paiute Canyon settlement group to farm at Paiute
Farms and graze livestock in Monument Valley. Many of these
in turn moved to White Mesa and Allen Canyon, Utah, and
Towaoc, Colorado, where they lived under the tribal
jurisdiction of the Ute Mountain Ute Tribe.

During the nineteenth and early twentieth centuries,
however, this group appears to have been accepted as part of
the San Juan Tribe and its leading members were influential,
especially in the northern area. Two of these leaders were
Pangwits ("Beaver") and *Panashiaxar* ("Shining One"); it is not
clear whether they were co-leaders, leaders of separate
subgroups, or successive leaders. Comparison of genealogies
given in Southern Paiute by San Juan consultants with the
genealogy that Dick's Sister provided through a Navajo
interpreter in her affidavit (Dick's Sister 1961) suggests that
Pangwits was the Paiute leader known to the Navajos as
Ba'azchin(i), "Born for him."

Sociopolitical Groups and Group Formation

By the end of the nineteenth century, two semiautonomous
territorial divisions of the San Juan Tribe had emerged: the
northern area settlement group, in the Paiute Canyon-Navajo
Mountain area; and the southern area settlement group whose
movements and land use, although at first less restricted than
in the north, still had their focus in the Willow Springs area.
Omer Stewart remarked on these two subgroups and supplied
their Paiute names which remain with some slight variation the
same today (1942:237): the "Tatsinunts," or *Atatsi[nᴂngwᴂ]tsing*,
"People of the Sands," living in the south; and the "Kaiboka-
tawip-nunts," or *Kaivyaxarᴂrᴂ[tᴂvwipᴂnᴂngwᴂ]tsing*," (Navajo)
Mountain People," living in the north. For a brief period, from
the turn of the century to approximately 1918, there was also a
short-lived third settlement group in the Monument Valley area
with farms at Paiute Farms, the "People of the Wild Oats
Place" or *Wa'ivᴂxarᴂrᴂtsing*.

In addition to these two territorial subdivisions, localized,
land holding, ambilineal descent groups had also begun to

crystallize in the early decades of this century around the remaining irrigated farm lands in the Paiutes' greatly reduced land base. The formation of corporate descent groups occurred first in the north, where pressure on farm lands was greatest, and then in the south. The Paiute-held farming sites in both the north and the south are presently subdivided into areas belonging to particular ambilineages. Land tenure and inheritance are governed by membership in these ambilineal groups.

Oral and conventional historical data indicate that these two levels of sociopolitical organization did not exist as such in the mid-nineteenth century. Throughout the nineteenth century, Paiutes appear to have moved freely from one resource area to another within the lands they occupied. This suggests that tribal members in general enjoyed free access to any and all resource areas within the community's total occupation zone. Such open access appears to have been accorded tribal members even in the case of irrigated farmlands. While some groups, notably the kin groups of *Muuputs* in the north or *Machukats* at Willow Springs, seem to have farmed only in the north or south, no Paiute farming areas, including those of Paiute Canyon and Willow Springs, were restricted at this time either to local residents or to members of particular families.

Tribal members' relative freedom of access to land and resources during the mid- and even late nineteenth century is illustrated in certain historic cases of movement. The San Juan leader, Patnish, and his followers were at one point identified with the Navajo Mountain area (Dellenbaugh 1962 [1908]:167-68). Later observers located them near the Mormons' Moenkopi Mission far to the south (Ivins 1875; Brown 1875-1877). According to Joe Lee (1974:9), in his boyhood (c. 1881) many San Juans who farmed in the south in the summer would winter with their stock near Navajo Mountain. In the 1890s, it was still possible for a substantial group of these southern area farmers to move north and open fields in Paiute Canyon (Lee 1974:29), although this last movement apparently soon after led to disruption in the northern community. As noted in our discussion of land use, farming land was relatively abundant prior to Navajo and Mormon entry. It is not surprising then that there were few restrictions on tribal community members' land use.

In the period before the emergence of descent group and territorial subdivisions, the tribe itself acted as an economic and residential group on a much more frequent basis. In the mid-nineteenth century, the tribe cooperated seasonally for autumn pinyon gathering and deer hunting. As a result of these and other collective economic activities in the fall and the quiet season of winter that followed, the tribe camped as one group for extended periods.

In addition to modern consultants, Kelly's San Juan Paiute consultant, Joe Francis, a southern area resident, offered telling evidence concerning seasonal residence patterns in this early period. Francis, an old man in the 1930s, stated that when he was a child, his family and at least fourteen other "camps," whose male heads he named, spent the winter together at *Tuukwarʉr* (1964:169). Kelly incorrectly identified the place as Shinumo Altar. There are two hills named *Tuukwarʉr* ("Black Hill") in San Juan country, one known in English as Tuba Butte and the other as Black Peak. Both are located immediately northwest of Tuba City, Arizona, not far from each other on the sandy southern reaches of the Kaibito Plateau, known in Paiute as *Atatsiv*. Francis' statements may be taken to imply that the community camped at *Tuukwarʉr* on a yearly or at least a very frequent basis. Modern consultants suggest that, although *Atatsiv* was a popular wintering site well into the twentieth century, other sites, notably Page, Kayenta, Cameron, Kaibito, and even Dennehotso, located beyond Kayenta, were also periodically used as wintering sites by the San Juan Tribe at this time.

Among the fourteen names of "individuals with camps" at *Tuukwarʉr*, five are known: "Tɨnɨsta (ram)," or *Tønacha'a*, "with his several children"; "Napacɨ," or *Napa(')ats*; "Paguicɨ," or *Pangwits*; *Chaiyaxai*, a Paiute whom Navajo oral testimony placed at Navajo Creek in the 1860s at a site known in Navajo by the same name (Brewer 1937:57); and "Panakarɨ, who later moved to Paiute Canyon," and who may have been *Panashiaxar* (both are variants of the same adjective, *pana-*, "shine"). Four of these five were from the Navajo Mountain area, even though this winter encampment was located in the south. All five figure prominently in oral tradition, and four are remembered as leaders of some sort, suggesting that the "camps" they each headed were larger than mere nuclear, or even extended family households.

Although we may assume that at least some San Juan families would have decided not to camp each year with the rest, it is nonetheless clear that winter encampments during this period represented a pattern of residence and close social interaction at the level of the San Juan Tribe itself. Moreover, Francis' account, like the evidence cited above, indicates that whatever subtribal social groups existed midcentury, these groups' movements and resource use were not restricted by any boundaries except at the maximal level of tribal territory.

Kelly's description of the breakup of the San Juan winter encampment in the spring is consistent with the view that this settlement group brought together members from all parts of the San Juan territory. She wrote, apparently quoting her consultants: "As the snow melted, camp was broken and the people scattered--'some toward Cameron, some toward Navajo Mountain, some to Tuba; they went anywhere'" (1964:169).

This seasonal residence pattern of dispersal in spring and early summer deserves some further explanation. In contrast to the situation today, in which Paiutes' farms are all clustered into a few restricted areas, available field areas in the mid-nineteenth century were widely scattered over their territorial range. In what may seem a paradox to conventional wisdom, the farming season for the San Juans, and probably for other nonriverine Southern Paiutes like the Kaibabs, may well have been the time of year when smaller subtribal kin groups were the most isolated from the main group. Although she did not specifically cite farming as a factor, Kelly (1964:22-24) noted a similar annual cycle at Kaibab: "People from practically all parts of Kaibab territory forgathered at the communal grounds [primarily the Kaibab Plateau] . . . during much of fall and winter"; then "with the approach of summer, the people returned to what they considered home base . . . their privately owned springs." To summarize, farming dispersed the San Juan Tribe into smaller residential groups, perhaps extended family households, whereas large game hunting, pinyon gathering, and the gathering of certain seeds, especially grasses, all appear to have united the tribal community as a production team and a residential group.

Despite the changes that San Juan sociopolitical organization has undergone, there is one constant thread throughout--the Southern Numic kinship system. The San Juan variant of this system has features that differentiate it sharply from Hopi and Navajo kinship: 1) *all* of ego's known second- and first-generation ascendent collateral kin are merged with the grandparents and the parents' siblings, respectively; 2) second- and first-generation descendent kin are merged in a similar fashion, since these terms are all self-reciprocal; and, finally, 3) all of ego's known same generation collateral kin are merged with siblings. This merging of distant with close kin goes hand in hand with a stringent incest prohibition, forbidding marriage or sexual intercourse with any known blood relative. Since this system with its merging principle and the attendant incest rule was also present in at least some other Southern Paiute communities, at Kaibab (Kelly 1964:121-30; Bunte Fieldnotes 1978) and the five Utah Paiute groups (Knack 1980:53), it is doubtful that the unusual historic conditions affecting San Juan society can be held responsible for their kin term system or their broad incest prohibition.

These features have helped make the system a powerful ideological framework within which members of present day San Juan Paiute kin groups and even members of the tribe itself may conceptualize and validate their ties of social, economic, and political solidarity as ties of close kinship. These features would also create problems for modern San Juan sociopolitical groups, particularly at the ambilineage level, if they were the sole criterion of group membership, since by themselves they include people whom group members might wish to exclude. Necessarily, kinship is not the only factor determining modern group membership.

The role of kinship in mid-nineteenth century sociopolitical organization is unclear. Traditional genealogies, admittedly underrepresentative for this early period, indicate that the tribe itself was composed of more than a dozen separate consanguineal lines. While kinship solidarity may therefore not have served to create a sense of corporate identity, as it does in modern sociopolitical groups from the level of the ambilineage to that of the tribe itself, kinship ties would certainly have been an important resource for individuals seeking to make use of kindred networks within and across groups for economic or political purposes. Many of the movements that have taken place between farming areas in the nineteenth and early twentieth centuries have utilized such consanguineal ties as well as ties by marriage. For example, when in the 1890s *Pak'ai* moved with other farmers in the south to Paiute Canyon, he began to farm next to his classificatory brother, *Muupʉts*.

Leaders in particular must have taken advantage of affinal and consanguineal relations and in fact the kinship alliances created by leaders in this early period greatly influenced the structure of the descent and land tenure system that grew up in the period that followed. *Muupʉts*, who apparently succeeded *Napa(')ats* as local leader at Navajo Mountain, first married one of his predecessor's daughters. After their move to Paiute Canyon, *Pak'ai's* son, *Tangwats*, married another of *Napa(')ats'* daughters. *Muupŧts* and *Pak'ai* perhaps sought to solidify their constituency in this manner. Intentionally or not, *Muupŧts* also insured that his descendents, who later became the Owl ambilineage, would hold much of the land formerly farmed by *Napa(')ats'* kin in Paiute Canyon.

External Relations, 1776-1850

At this point we turn to primary historical sources to trace the history of relations between San Juan society and members of other societies during this early period. The documentation includes the accounts of Hispanic explorers and officials as well as oral histories from local Indian groups. As the sparcity of Hispanic accounts would imply, encounters between the San Juans and non-Indians during this period were sporadic and limited in scope. Neither the Spanish nor the Mexican government that followed were ever able to establish a permanent presence in northern Arizona. Both Hispanic and Indian oral historical accounts indicate, moreover, that within their territorial area at least, the San Juans had little or no interaction with Navajos during this period. In the area of the Moenkopi Wash, the approximate southeastern limit of permanent San Juan occupation by the end of this period, there were, however, significant relations between the San Juan people and two other Indian groups, the Hopis and the Havasupais.

Spanish and Mexican Period Hispanic Accounts, 1776-1830

In 1776, Fray Francisco Atanasio Dominguez, with the aid of his religious subordinate and close friend, Fray Silvestre Velez de Escalante, led an expedition through the lands of present day western Colorado, central and southern Utah, and northern Arizona, meeting a number of Ute and Southern Paiute communities along the way. Father Escalante's journal of this exploratory journey has appeared in a definitive translation commemorating the bicentennial of the expedition (Chavez and Warner 1976; see also an earlier edition, Bolton 1950). The explorers made regular astronomical sightings and recorded landmarks and terrain along their route. It was thus possible to trace their route with great accuracy (Chavez and Warner 1976, editor's introduction, p. xix). Moreover, they brought with them Ute interpreters, and recorded carefully the names of different groups, as well as customs, language differences, and other information.

On November 8, 1776, after doubling back from their exploration of Utah and upon fording the Colorado River at a place subsequently called the Crossing of the Fathers, west of Navajo Mountain, the party of Spaniards and Indian guides travelled some six leagues, or fifteen and three quarters miles, taking what they described as "a well-beaten path" along the southern edge of the Rainbow Plateau southwest of Navajo Mountain and north of the Navajo Canyon system (Chavez and Warner 1976:102-103). That day they "found many tracks of Indians" as well as numerous tracks of wild sheep.

The next day, November 9, the party lost the trail and wandered some five miles along the northern rim of Navajo Canyon looking for a crossing point before coming upon "some camps of the Payuchi Yutas, who border on the Cosninas [upland Yumans, presumably the Havasupais]" (Chavez and Warner 1976:103). The term "Payuchi" is a Spanish rendering of the Southern Numic term now used for all Southern Paiutes, *Payuts(i)* or *Payuch(i)*. Many other place names, personal names, and names of Ute and Paiute groups in this journal are also recognizably Southern Numic. In several cases, these names correspond to terms identified in later historical records or in anthropological studies.

On November 9 and 10, the two fathers and two Utes spoke with these Indians, who were apparently extremely suspicious of the explorers. Despite the Paiutes' diffidence, Dominguez and Escalante were able to record a number of interesting points in their journal regarding these people. First, in their summary of all the tribal groups they met, they listed the "Payuchi Yutas" as a separate division among the several divisions of "Yutas," or Utes, which they encountered, suggesting a measure of political and/or social autonomy (Chavez and Warner 1976:101-102). They noted, however, that these Payuchis spoke "the Yuta [Ute] language in the same manner" as the "Yutas Cobardes," or Cowardly Utes. The latter division included all of several other Southern Paiute groups encountered by the Spaniards on the other side of the Colorado River. Within the Southern Numic continuum of related dialects, the various dialects of Southern Paiute remain more closely related to each other than to the dialects of Ute. In their summary, the explorers also described the encampment of Yutas Payuchis, or Paiute Utes, encountered on November 9 and 10 as "the westernmost Payuchis," and stated explicitly in the journal entry for November 7 that the Payuchis' occupation zone extended eastward from the Colorado River, or more precisely from the ford where the Spanish crossed this river (Chavez and Warner 1976:101). Dominguez and Escalante apparently intended the term Payuchi to refer only to Paiutes living in the historic occupation zone of the San Juans, whom they thus distinguished from Southern Paiutes in general.

Dominguez and Escalante discovered in their talks with these Paiutes something of their relations with neighboring Indians. Their journal indicated that the Payuchis "border on the Cosninas," or Havasupais, whose home territory the explorers placed "very close" and to the south (Chavez and Warner 1976:103ff.). The Paiutes told Dominguez and Escalante that the Cosninas were then in the mountains gathering pinyon nuts. In a later entry, the journal implied that the "mountains" in question were the San Francisco Peaks or perhaps the Grand Canyon's South Rim (Chavez and Warner 1976:107). That the Paiutes kept track of the Havasupais' whereabouts in this way suggests a degree of close and presumably friendly contact between the two groups. Dominguez and Escalante seem to have assumed that the two groups visited each other on a regular basis (Chavez and Warner 1976:106). The Payuchis also apparently told the explorers' Ute interpreter that they had hostile relations with the "Moquis," or Hopis (Chavez and Warner 1976:103), although no explanation for the "great enmity" between the two groups was offered or implied. Hostile relations or no, the Paiutes were able to direct the Ute interpreter to "two trails, one toward the Cosninas [Havasupais] and the other to El Pueblo de Oraibi in Moqui" (Chavez and Warner 1976:104). Where there are roads, we may also presuppose there was social interaction and even trade.

According to the journal entry for November 11, these trails were more than mere unmaintained footpaths. Upon leaving the vicinity of the Paiute encampment, the explorers caught up with the lost trail and descended into Navajo Canyon. They wrote that their descent was made easy because the Paiutes had built the trail up "with loose stones and sticks" and on one stretch of it had even built "a stairway of the same, more than three yards long and two wide." These improvements bespeak the importance of the road and of the interaction that took place along it. They also imply permanent occupation of the area, since such an investment in labor would have been an unlikely one for temporary occupants.

The party of Dominguez and Escalante then travelled south across the Kaibito Plateau, passing just to the east of present day Tuba City, and finally arriving at the Hopi Pueblo of Oraibi on November 16 (Chavez and Warner 1976:104-109). In the Tuba City-Moenkopi area, their journal entry of November 14 stated that they came upon a "small farm and camp of the Cosninas," located according to the editors' note in Pasture Canyon, only a few miles northwest of present day Tuba City (Chavez and Warner 1976:107).

Father Francisco Garces, another Spanish missionary-explorer stationed at the Mission San Xavier del Bac at Tucson, in the summer of 1776 passed through the Tuba City-Moenkopi Wash area on his way to and from Oraibi and the other Hopi pueblos (Coues 1900:354-59, 392-406). Although Garces did not encounter Paiutes--his route did not take him farther north than Moenkopi Wash--his journal entries corroborate much of the information on local Indian groups reported by Dominguez and Escalante.

In the Tuba City area, Garces reported a "rancheria of Yabipais," or Yavapais, "that should have as it were 30 souls" (Coues 1900:356). It seems clear from other information supplied by Garces that this settlement was located in the Moenkopi Wash or close by. His account of distances travelled place it some 13 and a half leagues, or 35 miles, west-northwest of Oraibi (Coues 1900:356-59, 392-403), roughly where Tuba City and Moenkopi stand today. Four miles east-southeast of this Yuman settlement on a mesa above the wash itself Garces found a "half-ruined Pueblo," which he wrote was named "Muqui concave," apparently his hispanicized version of Moenkopi (Coues 1900:357-58, 393-95). These Indians, whom Garces identified as Yavapais, another upland Yuman group closely related linguistically to the Havasupais, may well have been members of the same Havasupai, or other Yuman group whose gardens and homes the Dominguez-Escalante party passed by four months later. According to Garces' "Yabipais," a Moenkopi Wash garden area, adjacent to the nearby uninhabited Hopi pueblo, belonged to Hopis from Oraibi who commuted there to tend their crops (Coues 1900:356-58).

While he did not meet any of the "Paiute Utes" encountered by Dominguez and Escalante, Garces was apparently told of

Utes and of their warlike relations with the Hopis of Oraibi and its daughter village, Moenkopi. Like Dominguez and Escalante, Garces was shown two roads, only this time it was Hopis who gave the directions and the two roads led one to "the Yutas" and the other to Garces' Yuman settlement (Coues 1900:392-93, 396-97). Garces also learned, it seems from the Yabipais, that "the Yutas, enemies of the last two Pueblos [Oraibi and Moenkopi], live on one and the other side of the Rio Colorado in the very confluences (*juntas*) of the two rivers that compose it" (Coues 1900:395). If it is the junction of the Colorado and the San Juan Rivers that was meant here, then these Utes were almost certainly the "Yutas Payuchis," or Paiute Utes. Garces stated, somewhat earlier in his journal, that "the Yutas . . . live north of Moqui and are enemies only of this pueblo of Oraibe and of the Moqui concave [Moenkopi]" (Coues 1900:392-93).

There is no mention in either Spanish account of Navajo use or occupation in the lands to the west or north of the Hopi villages. However, Dominguez and Escalante were told by a Hopi Tewa that the Hopis "were currently engaged in a cruel war with the Navajo Apaches, and that these had killed and captured many of their people" (Chavez and Warner 1976:111).

In the journal entries reporting the fathers' talks with various Hopi leaders, Navajo was used on almost every occasion as the diplomatic lingua franca (Chavez and Warner 1976:109-11). This bespeaks long-term relations between the Hopis and Navajos. The Navajos were in any event living at this time as far west as Canyon de Chelly and thus near enough to the Hopi villages to make war or trading and social visits as they do today.

After a gap of almost fifty years, the journal of the Mexican governor of New Mexico detailed the events of an expedition he conducted in 1823 against a group of Navajos. Jose Antonio Vizcarra was chasing a band of Navajos led by a man named Juanico with the intent of punishing them for alleged attacks on Mexican homesteaders living along the Rio Puerco in New Mexico (Brugge 1964:224-25).

On this expedition, Vizcarra encountered Navajos east of the Hopis' First Mesa and in its vicinity (Brugge 1964:231-32). He also pursued Juanico's group over the country north of the Hopi villages, eventually capturing a good deal of their livestock but not Juanico or his followers. During this chase, Vizcarra ran into a group of Paiutes with goats near the north end of White Mesa, north of Hopi and not far from present day Shonto, in Arizona (Brugge 1964:237-39). As they were not the ones being chased, there is no reason to think these Paiutes were not native to the area.

Apparently without giving any warning, Vizcarra's men attacked the Paiutes, killing four men and taking seven captives with the intention of selling them as slaves in New Mexico. However, when the fighting stopped and they realized that they had been fighting Paiutes and not Juanico's Navajos, the captives were released. Vizcarra explained his mistake by stating that he had believed that only Navajos had goats. Taking Vizcarra's explanation at face value, Brugge considered this as evidence that these Paiutes "had already become acculturated to the Navajo way of life" (1964:226).

Since herding has come to be an important symbol of Navajo ethnicity for Navajos and for Americans at large, Brugge's acculturation argument is not surprising. It should be pointed out, however, that by the nineteenth century many Southwestern Indian groups had become at least part time livestock herders, whatever their precontact mode of making a living may have been. Sheep and goats in particular are not much of an indicator of Navajo cultural or social identity, since Hispanics and many other Indians, including the Paiutes' neighbors, the Hopis, all herded. Later records indicate that the Utes of Southern Colorado similarly kept substantial herds of sheep, some of which were undoubtedly acquired from Hispanic settlers in the same manner as the Navajos' (for example, ARCIA 1885:384-85).

There is, of course, no assurance that the Paiutes encountered near Shonto were actually herding goats on a permanent basis, that is, that the goats had not been acquired in trade from Navajos, Hopis, Utes, or Hispanics for immediate consumption, or that the Paiutes had not actually stolen them from any of the above parties, and especially from Juanico's vulnerable group. In any event--Vizcarra's and Brugge's respective theories of ethnic identity notwithstanding--Vizcarra and his men quickly realized once the shooting was over that they had attacked Paiutes and not Navajos; presumably, they were aware of cultural or linguistic differences that overrode the fact of the goats' presence.

According to Brugge's account, Vizcarra's second in command during the expedition, Colonel Francisco Salazar, also encountered a group of Paiutes, this time near the junction of the San Juan and Colorado Rivers. This area, north of Navajo Mountain, is now the core grazing area of the

Paiute Canyon/Navajo Mountain San Juan people. According to other sources, including one Hispanic account to be dealt with shortly, the river canyon bottoms in this area were at one time used for Paiute farming. This land also was later to become an exclusive Paiute Reservation called the Paiute Strip.

If Vizcarra's account provides clear evidence that people identifiable as Paiute were then occupying the Shonto and Navajo Mountain areas, the evidence cannot be so construed in the case of Juanico's group. As Brugge himself comments, "the Navajo were constantly retreating, scattering, and vanishing into hideouts" when chased by soldiers (1964:225). This was likely a temporary flight into the edge of another group's territory, not long-term occupation.

The journal of Antonio Armijo (Hafen 1947), chronologically the next available source, although lacking in descriptive detail, is more useful in determining relative locations of Navajos and Paiutes during this period. Armijo was not conducting a military campaign against any Indian group. In fact, he stated that he was passing through Navajo territory at a time of relative peace (Hafen 1947:91). Armijo also provided what appears to be the earliest historic documentation of San Juan Paiute farming.

In 1829, with a group of New Mexican traders, Armijo led the first pack train over what was to become the Old Spanish Trail through Paiute country to southern California (Hafen and Hafen 1954). His route through the area with which we are concerned proceeded through northern Arizona from the Four Corners area to the Crossing of the Fathers and was roughly parallel to the Utah-Arizona border (Hafen 1947:94-95, esp. editor's notes). According to Armijo's diary of this journey, the last community of Navajos encountered was two day's travel *east* of Chinle Creek (beyond the eastern edge of map 2). Seven days after passing this last Navajo settlement, on November 30, Armijo recorded the following entry: "At the water hole of the Payuches: three Indians were found, no trouble ensued, and it was necessary to scale a canyon for which purpose we had to carry the baggage in our arms" (Hafen 1947:94). The editor, Hafen, identified this as "Piute Canyon, or . . . Upper Crossing Springs near the canyon." The present day upper crossing trail descends right into the irrigated farming area in upper Paiute Canyon held by the descendents of *Miiupɨɨts*. Armijo's group may thus have passed directly through the Paiutes' present fields. This fact may shed light on the otherwise cryptic journal entry that follows.

The next day's entry, for the first of December, describes Armijo's movement down the canyon bottom from the site of his party's descent. He wrote: "At the lake of Las Milpitas ["the little corn patches"]. On this day we had to work our way down the canyon" (Hafen 1947:95). Upon descending into Paiute Canyon, or whichever one it was, Armijo apparently discovered Paiute corn fields and perhaps what may even have been a water-impoundment dam (his "lake") holding either the water of Paiute Creek or more likely spring water from the canyon wall.

Indian Oral Historical Accounts, 1830-1860

San Juan Southern Paiutes' present day oral histories concerning interethnic relations mirror their two-hundred-year-old statements to Dominguez and Escalante. Families whose ancestors lived in the Tuba City and Moenkopi Wash area recall stories of friendly relations with the Havasupais, who are said to have come in the summers to trade with the San Juans at Willow Springs. A major product the Havasupais had to offer was pressed and dried cake made from agave which they gathered, roasted, and preserved in the Grand Canyon area. Round-dances and song contests were held from which Paiute-Havasupai intermarriages resulted. According to tradition, certain of the dance songs that San Juan elders sing today were first learned from the Havasupais at these dances.

K elly appears to have been told similar accounts in the 1930s:

West of the Little Colorado were the friendly Havasupai, with whom the San Juan hunted deer on Coconino Plateau and with whom, it was said, they intermarried. J [Joedie/*Akamanaxwats*] thought there might have been Apache in the area north of Flagstaff; he had heard that there they once fought the Havasupai and Paiute. [Kelly 1964:168]

In their portrayal of Paiute-Havasupai relations as entirely friendly, however, Paiute accounts should be compared with Spier's (1928) Havasupai oral history, discussed below.

With Hopis, on the other hand, relations during this period are remembered as hostile. At the same time, trade and other relations may also have occurred. The following story told by

San Juan elder Marie Lehi refers to events that occurred in the time of *Avin*ᵤₐᵥ, Marie Lehi's great-grandfather. It serves to indicate the climate of uncertain relations between the two groups:

> Her [Marie Lehi's] mother used to tell her stories that Hopis used to steal too much, too. The Hopis and the Navajos used to steal too much. The Paiutes used to get the blame for it. At that time there were some Hopis stirring up Hopis. Her mother's father's father, this happened to. Way back. As he was going digging under the ground, I guess he saw a rabbit-hole in there. These Hopis, they came as he was bending over, as he was trying to get the rabbit, these Hopis they sneak on him. They were poking him with sticks in his butt. And then, they say, as he got that rabbit and they wanted a trade, they wanted to take that rabbit away from him. He got lots of rabbits and the Hopis took them all away and gave him piki [the Hopis' paper-like corn flour bread]. They gave him that kind in trade. This happened near here or by Coppermine. [Bunte and Franklin Fieldnotes, July 24, 1981, with translation from the Paiute in abbreviated form by one of Mrs. Lehi's granddaughters]

Sources of Hopi oral history that bear on this time period and region echo the San Juans' contentions that prior to the period of the Navajos' Long Walk and Mormon settlement there were no Navajos in the Moenkopi-Tuba City area and that Hopi-Paiute relations were hostile. One early source of such testimony, albeit an indirect one, is found in Western Navajo School Superintendent Walter Runke's repetition of testimony given him by Moenkopi Hopi Pole Hongeva in an October 27, 1914 letter to a Professor Gregory of Connecticut:

> Pole says that his grandfather was named Tuba who claimed the present site of Tuba, but on account of the almost constant treachery of surrounding Paiutes and Utes then living near Tuba (he says there were no Navajoes near then), this Hopi named Tuba invited the Mormons to come and live here for purpose of protection against the marauding Paiutes and Utes. Grandfather Tuba lived for some years here under the protecting wing of the Mormons and later moved down

to the present site of Moencopie. . . . He says that he
thinks he was married when he was about 26 to 28
years old and that about four to six years before
married [sic] was the time when any number of Hopis
made a permanent home at Moencopie . . . that would
make the year 1889 the year when any considerable
number of Hopis made a permanent home at
Moencopie. [Runke 1914]

The same account, with some additional details, was
offered by Hopis in two reports submitted to the BIA in 1939.
At the time, BIA officials were meeting with Hopi and Navajo
delegates to reach a settlement of Hopi and Navajo claims in
Land Management District Six and the Moenkopi area. The
first report, entitled "Information Concerning Hopi Problems,"
was not definitely attributed to a Hopi source although it was
apparently submitted to a BIA official, Charles Rachford, by
Hopi Tribal Council delegates on December 4, 1939. The
second, "History of Moencopi and the Hopi Land Claims," also
submitted to Rachford in December, 1939, was attributed to
"the Moenkopi delegate," at that time, Roger Honahni.   Both
reports cite specific Hopi individuals from whom traditional
accounts were apparently collected.
    The first of the two reports, besides corroborating the story
told previously to Runke, adds an interesting episode of
"Paiute treachery" dating to long before the 1870s:

In 1911, a very old Hopi, named Quavaho, died. His
children remember that he told them that when he was
14 or 15 years old, Paiutes captured the pueblo above
Moencopi [the ruin of Posiolelena], destroyed the town
and killed all the people. Two boys escaped who fled
to Oraibi. This must have occurred between 1830 and
1840. (Honahni and Numkena) [surnames of Moenkopi
Hopis].
    In the early 1870's Chief Tuba rebuilt the village
under the protection of the Mormons, who had settled
at Tuba City. By 1873 Moenkopi was well established
and has been continuously occupied ever since.
["Information Concerning Hopi Problems" 1939:11]

The belief that Tuba could not resettle Moenkopi until the
Mormons arrived to protect the Hopis from the local Paiutes
and that there were no Navajos in the area as late as the

1870s was reiterated in accounts ascribed to two Moenkopi Hopis, Frank Tewanemptewa and Pole Hongeva, in the second report ("History of Moenkopi and the Hopi Land Claims" 1939:1, 3). Louis Numkena, Sr., a Moenkopi Hopi leader, recently repeated the same account of early warfare with Paiutes and the resettlement of Moenkopi under Mormon protection (in Courlander 1982:122-24). Again the Hopis claimed that no Navajos were present at that time.

If Hopi oral history is correct, Paiutes lived near Moenkopi as early as the 1830s and were numerous and aggressive enough to prevent Hopi exploitation of Moenkopi Wash. This hostility appears to have been symptomatic of a permanent San Juan expansion southward and was not simply parasitic raiding. The destruction of Moenkopi and the massacre of its inhabitants would seem not to have been the work of opportunistic raiders. Rather, it appears as though the Paiutes sought to monopolize local resources--water and farming land according to contemporary Paiute consultants--by edging Hopi competitors entirely out of the Moenkopi Wash area. Reports that the Paiutes completely proscribed Hopi farming at Moenkopi for thirty to forty years thereafter lend support to this interpretation.

Leslie Spier's *Havasupai Ethnography* (1928) contains accounts of Havasupai oral history as told by his consultant, Sinyella. The latter made a number of references to dealings with Paiutes, but it is not always clear which groups were involved.

In one incident, Sinyella related that when he was eight years old, a group of Paiutes from north of the canyon took up residence with Walapais after fleeing from an encounter with Mormons. Later they traded goods and exchanged brides with the Walapais (Spier 1928:360, 362). The geography suggests that these were Shivwits, or perhaps Kaibab Paiutes, not San Juans.

Later, in an account of peace talks between Apaches, Yavapais, and Havasupais at Oraibi, the Havasupai leader was reported as saying: "The Paiute have been enemies for a long time; they have come and fought us. The Paiute chief came over and said he was not going to fight us anymore. He said they would be good friends to the Havasupai" (Spier 1928:378). These latter Paiutes were almost certainly San Juans, since no other Southern Paiute group would have been involved in warfare in the region surrounding Oraibi. Although San Juan oral history does not recall war with the Havasupais, such may

well have resulted from the San Juan Tribe's southward
expansion into lands that were occupied and farmed by
Havasupais as well as Hopis. Traditional San Juan accounts
recorded by Kelly (1964:168, quoted above) and ourselves, do
indicate that Paiutes and Havasupais may once have fought
Apaches in the area north of Flagstaff, Arizona, a point that
may have some bearing on the peace talks reported by Sinyella.

Sinyella's story also provides an illustrative example of the
early Southern Paiute leader's role. As with the Paiute whose
acts as spokesperson for his people were described in this story,
one of the leader's primary duties was to serve as tribal
representative in dealings with other groups, in matters of war
as well as peace.

Adaptations to Mormon and Navajo Expansion, 1850-1900

By the mid- or late 1850s, the United States government had
begun to take an interest in northern Arizona and the peoples
living there. Not long afterward, the Mormons and Navajos,
both undergoing rapid territorial and demographic expansion,
were also poised on the edge of the San Juan Southern Paiutes'
occupation zone. The government was ready to expand its
influence in territories previously occupied only by the San
Juans and their Hopi and Havasupai neighbors. The Navajos
and Mormons were looking for new lands to settle in. This
part is concerned with the events surrounding the initial entry
and eventual expansion of these three groups into San Juan
lands during the second half of the nineteenth century and
with the adaptations the San Juans undertook as a result. The
first section provides an overview of the historical trends
operating during this half-century. The two sections that
follow it are detailed accounts of the events surrounding the
groups' initial entry in 1850-1870, and the period of actual
settlement from 1870-1900.

An Overview, 1850-1900

To the east of the San Juans, the United States government and
the Navajos were locked in a struggle to halt Navajo expansion
in northern New Mexico Territory (Reeve 1974; McNitt 1972).
During the period of the Navajo Wars and Colonel Christopher
("Kit") Carson's Roundup of the Navajos, between 1859 and

1868, groups of Navajos scattered throughout San Juan territory. They were constantly on the move and seeking to escape the army (Bartlett 1932; Reeve 1974; see also McNitt 1972, Lawrence Kelly 1970, and Thompson 1976, for background on the Navajo Campaigns, the Roundup and Long Walk, and the four years of Navajo exile at Bosque Redondo, New Mexico). This initial diaspora was attended by both friendly and hostile interactions between Paiutes and Navajos, apparently depending on the character of the Navajo groups encountered.

After their release from Bosque Redondo, the 1868 Navajo treaty granted the Navajos their first reservation, 3.4 million acres straddling the New Mexico-Arizona territorial line (Enders 1971:23). However, Navajos soon moved in large numbers into areas outside this reservation "despite efforts by the territorial and national governments to restrict them to the land established for their use and occupancy by the Treaty of 1868" (Young 1961:255).

The major impetus behind Navajo territorial expansion appears to have been their remarkable population growth. Between their return from the Long Walk to Bosque Redondo in 1868 and the beginning of the twentieth century, their population doubled from some 10,000 to more than 20,000 (ARCIA 1865-1900; see also Underhill 1953:223). Nor has their population ceased to expand in the present century. The on-reservation population alone in 1978 was 142,000. Under this pressure, territorial expansion in some direction was probably inevitable.

The government attempted to deal with Navajo expansion and avoid a repetition of the long and costly Navajo Campaigns that preceded the Long Walk by instituting a series of Executive Order reservation expansions (Enders 1971:23-33; L. Kelly 1968:16-36). Because of resistence on the part of Euro-Americans in New Mexico, also expanding their settlement and land use at this time, expansion of Navajo Reservation lands was confined largely to the areas west of the New Mexico line. This point is made clear by the dated Executive Order reservation expansions on map 3, "Navajo Reservation Lands" (see also Kammer 1980:66-67). Thus, the official expansion of Navajo reservation lands took place largely in areas occupied not by Euro-American settlers but by other Indian groups, the Hopis, the San Juan Southern Paiutes, and probably the Havasupais as well.

During the period of the Navajo Campaigns and later,

while the U.S. government was slowly becoming aware of the San Juan Paiute Tribe's existence, Mormons began to explore the San Juan territory and eventually settled in the 1870s where Tuba City and Moenkopi are today. North and west of the Colorado River, Mormons had already subjugated virtually all of the other existing Southern Paiute communities and thereby set in motion the political and economic processes that would reduce these Indians to utter poverty by the early twentieth century (Euler 1966; Stoffle and Evans 1976; Stoffle and Dobyns 1982 and 1983). Soon after the Moenkopi Mission and pioneer colony were founded, Mormon and other white traders began to set up trading posts among the Navajos, Hopis, and Paiutes, some of which have continued to operate to the present day.

In the early 1880s, Mormons also began to settle the area of Utah just north of the San Juan River and the 1884 Executive Order area. Not long after, Colorado cattlemen began to expand their operations here also. As this area was apparently the territory of other sociopolitical groups of Paiutes and/or Utes--there is some confusion and even controversy as to local Indians' ethnic affiliation--Anglos in this newly settled area were plagued by Indian cattle theft and raids. Paiute and Ute resistence to white settlement in the area culminated in the locally famous "Posey Wars," led by Polk and Posey, leaders of the San Juans' Paiute neighbors, the group that came to be known as the Allen Canyon Paiutes or Utes (Thrapp 1942; Parkhill 1961). Open conflict between Indians and Anglos in this region of Utah, San Juan County, continued until Posey's death in 1923 and played an indirect role in the Paiute Strip controversy of the 1920s and 1930s.

The Mormon farmers and cattlemen living in Tuba City, Moenkopi, and surrounding areas were forced to abandon their homesteads by 1904 as a result of the government's condemnation of their property in 1902-1903 (Lee 1974:55; Young 1961:258). The government purchased their improvements for a mere $48,000 when it established the Western Navajo Agency and School at Tuba City.

All three food production strategies utilized by the San Juan people prior to 1860 were directly or indirectly affected by Navajo and Mormon economic activities within the Paiute occupation zone. San Juan Paiutes were compelled to give up many traditional material economic activities and intensify others. They also adopted ways of producing food and other forms of wealth that they had not utilized before, at least on any permanent basis. During the last decades of the nineteenth century, San Juan Southern Paiute material economics underwent a great qualitative and quantitative transformation, one that would lay the groundwork for social changes still to come.

Between the 1860s and 1900, the Navajos expanded their grazing activities, and presumably their hunting as well, into the grasslands and pinyon-juniper woodlands of the Kaibito Plateau to the south of the Navajo and Paiute Canyon systems. In the region surrounding the Mormons' Tuba City colony both Navajos and Mormons grazed large numbers of stock. As a result, by the beginning of the twentieth century the San Juans were beginning to abandon seed collection (with the notable exception of pinyon nuts and certain wild fruits, such as *Lycium* or *u'up*). Consequently, the San Juan people gradually came to depend primarily on farming and on trade with whites and other Indian groups to supply their need for carbohydrates and other nutrients previously provided by wild vegetable foods.

Because of competition for grazing with Mormon and Navajo livestock, as well as overhunting, large game--antelope, deer, and wild sheep--all but disappeared from San Juan territory. Although San Juan Paiutes continued to hunt large game outside their territory, such as on the Coconino Plateau north of Flagstaff, or in the Henry Mountains north of the San Juan River, they were probably also under pressure to make up a deficit in animal protein. As a result, by 1890 the San Juan people had all adopted livestock management as a major component of their material economy. By the 1880s, in the northern part of the San Juan Paiute Tribe's nineteenth century occupation zone, the initial symptoms of conflict and competition with Navajos for grazing lands had already begun.

While alternative wild food sources were gradually becoming scarcer and the San Juans were becoming increasingly dependent on cultivated foods, in the final quarter of the nineteenth century the Navajos and Mormons were also exerting pressure on San Juan farm lands, forcing Paiutes to farm fewer acres more often and probably more intensively. Although we know little about historic San Juan farm sites in the Navajo Canyon system, and therefore cannot infer that Navajo expansion played any major role here, San Juan oral histories suggest that these were the first farming areas abandoned to Navajo expansion.

In the south, around the modern Paiute farms of Willow

Springs and in the Moenkopi Wash area where Paiutes historically farmed, the record is clearer. In the period between initial Mormon settlement in the 1870s and the last full decade of the Mormon presence in the 1890s, Paiute farming areas in Moenkopi Wash and along the Echo Cliffs south of Willow Springs were lost, apparently to Mormon expansion. After the Mormons left, all lands in the Moenkopi Wash not used by the new agency and school were parcelled out to Hopis and Navajos. Although Paiutes were farming the Moenkopi Wash when the Mormons first settled there, after 1900 they would never again farm further south than Willow Springs. One Navajo oral history (quoted below) suggests that Navajos may also have been partially responsible for the loss of some Paiute farmlands in this southern area.

Basketry, produced by women, became ever more important in the nineteenth and twentieth centuries as a resource that could be traded to whites for flour, coffee, and other goods (Bunte 1985). Oral traditions also maintain that the Paiutes acquired their first herds of sheep and goats by trading water-jugs and ritual basketry to the Navajos. Although basketry production for trade is most significant in the twentieth century, it appears to have seen its early beginnings as an important sector of the San Juan economy in the 1870s and 1880s.

During the latter half of the nineteenth century, written records provide the first glimpse of internal decision making and tribal leadership in the context of specific historic events. Also for the first time, primary historic sources make mention of individual San Juan Southern Paiutes by names that can be identified in modern genealogies. From these individuals, who number among them nineteenth century leaders such as *Pak'ai*, virtually all living members of the group can trace bilateral descent.

The Foot in the Door, 1850–1870

The Army, The Navajos, and the San Juans, 1850–1860

The first Anglo-European account dealing with Southern Paiutes east of the Colorado River is a short but revealing statement in the journal of Dr. P. G. S. Ten Broeck, a surgeon with the U.S. Army stationed at Hopi in 1851–1852: "I saw three Payoche Indians today. They live on a triangular piece of land, formed by the junction of the San Juan and Colorado of the West [the Colorado] . . . " (quoted in Schoolcraft 1860:82-83; reprinted in Euler 1966:70). This is in the area north of Navajo Mountain where the Paiutes had been encountered by Vizcarra's second-in- command, Salazar, some thirty years before. Their presence at Hopi suggests that San Juan Paiutes were engaged in some sort of nonhostile relations with the Hopis at this time, probably trade.

During this period Anglo-Americans as yet knew very little of the region in which San Juan Paiute territory was located, which only a few years earlier, in 1846, had come into the possession of the United States (Reeve 1974:298). This was obviously the state of affairs in 1855 when the Meriwether Treaty was made with the Navajos. The following year, Governor David Meriwether of New Mexico Territory wrote to the Commissioner of Indian Affairs on December 30, 1856: "As no other people inhabit the country west of the established claim of the Navajos and the Utahs [the Utes of Colorado and northern New Mexico], and east of the Colorado, I have assigned it to those Indians" (quoted in Reeve 1974:292). Soon after, the Navajo Campaigns led the U.S. Army deeper into the region.

In 1860-1861, Brevet Lieutenant Colonel Edward R. S. Canby launched a military expedition against the Navajos, who at that time were located to the east of Marsh Pass and Black Mesa, known to the U.S. Army respectively as Puerta Limita (more correctly, Puerta de las Lemitas) and Mesa de la Vaca. According to historian Frank McNitt (1972:392), "Again on the basis of information he had received, Canby believed that if the main body of Navajos were to flee toward Marsh Pass, he would have them entrapped, caught in nearly impassable country with nothing on the other side but Paiutes, who were said to be hostile to the Navajos." On November 8, at the close of this initial campaign, Canby reported: "We . . . found to our bitter disappointment that all the statements and reports upon which we had relied were erroneous; that the Pah Utes were not at war with the Navajoes, and that the Sierra Limita [Marsh Pass] was no barrier to their further flight" (quoted in McNitt 1972:401-402).

The ultimate source of the "statements and reports" of hostilities between Navajos and Paiutes that Colonel Canby made the basis of his strategy appears to have been a report submitted by Captain John G. Walker bearing on his reconnaissance mission to Black Mesa and Marsh Pass in

September 1859. His report contained the following passages:

> 13th--Marched this morning with 20 E. down the valley
> 4 miles to the mouth of a cañon entering from the west
> which is known by the name of *La Puerta Limita* [Marsh
> Pass]. In this cañon which is of considerable length
> there is said to be several lagunas [lakes or pools] and
> good grazing and is the home of a band of Pah-Utahs. . .
>
> Beyond the *Mesa de la Baca* there are one or two cañons
> mentioned by my [Navajo] guide as having water and
> grass, but they are within the Pah-Utah country with
> whom the Navajos have been at war for sometime past.
> [Walker 1859a]

Walker indicated that his Navajo guide was the source of the
information that the lands west of Marsh Pass and Black Mesa,
then known as *Mesa de la Baca*, were "Paiute country" and that
the Navajos were not on friendly terms with these Paiutes.
According to oral history, the San Juans farmed and gathered
seeds in the Marsh Pass-Kayenta area. If they defended this
boundary against Navajo encroachment, as Walker's guide
seems to have implied, it may have been to prevent livestock
damage to wild plant resources and especially to cornfields.

A letter from Major John S. Simonson at Fort Defiance to
Lieutenant John D. Wilkins, Acting Assistant Adjutant General
at Santa Fe, dated three days after Walker's reconnaissance
report and a second report from Captain Walker also enclosed
with Simonson's letter confirm that the information supplied
by Walker's guide concerning Paiute occupation and relations
between Paiutes and Navajos was correct. However, they also
suggest a good reason why the Navajos may not have been
afraid to enter Marsh Pass during Canby's campaign a year
later. Simonson wrote:

> Also herewith is forwarded the Special Report of
> Captain Walker in relation to the movements of the
> Mormons with the Indian tribes. Not a doubt exists that
> this tampering with the Indians, is to the prejudice of
> the citizens of the United States, and the intent of the
> government.
>
> A *Pah-Ute* [emphasis Simonson's], who visited the Indian
> Agent here, informed me of the proposed council at

Sierra Panoche [Navajo Mountain], and expressed himself anxious to attend it, in order (as he says) to bring about a peace with the Navajoes; he said the Mormons had baptized him into their church. . . . [Simonson then states that he attempted to talk the Paiute out of joining the Mormon Church or attending the council.] Much more was said of the same tendency, and he promised he would not attend the Mormon Council, his manner however contradicted his promise, and I have no doubt he will present himself and induce as many Navajoes as he can to be present also. Every prominent man among the Navajoes has heard of this Mormon Council, and doubtless some will attend it. [Simonson 1859]

In his second report, Captain Walker stated that during the reconnaissance mission:

[M]y camp was visited about eighty miles west of the mouth of the Cañon de Chelly by a party of Pah-Utahs, one of whom could speak the Navajo language, and gave the following statement to my Navajo guide in presence of the interpreter. --That the Mormons had deputed them and some others who had gone on to the Cañon de Chelly, to meet the Navajos and to make peace with them--that they (the Mormons) were anxious to see peace established between all the different tribes between the Colorado and Rio Grande, and by that means to resist the encroachment of the people and government of the United States, the natural enemies of the whole Indian race--that unless they resisted us that we would soon have their entire country--that they (the Mormons) would assist them with arms and ammunition to do this--That in order to carry these views fully into effect, the Mormons have sent them (the Pah-Utahs) to invite the Navajoes to meet them and all the different bands of the Utahs & Mohaves at the Sierra Panoche, a mountain some seventy or eighty miles east of the Colorado and about forty miles south-east of the junction of the Rio San Juan and Colorado Chiquito [Walker here, as elsewhere, confuses the Little Colorado with the Colorado]. This council is to be held about the middle of October next at which time the Mormons are to distribute arms and ammunition to the various tribes represented in the Council who will join the alliance.

That this statement is substantially true I have every reason to believe as the Pah-Utahs to confirm their story exhibited various presents from the Mormons such as new shirts, beads, powder, etc. I was further confirmed in this opinion by meeting the next day a deputation of Navajoes on their way to Sierra Panoche to learn the truth of these statements, which had been conveyed to them by a Pah-Utah Indian whom I saw in the Cañon de Chelly afterwards who had been sent as a special envoy from the Mormons to the Navajoes. [Walker 1859b]

Walker's and Simonson's reports suggest that the Paiutes living at Sierra Panoche or Navajo Mountain *were* at war with the Navajos but may have reached some kind of peace agreement as much as a year in advance of Canby's campaign. Whether or not the Paiutes ever got the peace agreement that they wished for, the Navajos, army officers, and possibly Mormons as well, clearly recognized the Paiutes living west of Marsh Pass as an autonomous polity with which other groups could be at war or make peace. The reports of movements of deputations between the central places of both tribes, Navajo Mountain and Canyon de Chelly, are one confirmation of this.

Both Simonson and Walker take special notice of one Paiute man whom they apparently believed played a leading role as the Paiutes' representative to the Navajos. While he cannot be identified, this person may well have been a tribal-level leader among the San Juans at this time, possibly the Patnish the Mormons name in later accounts, who was reputedly a friend of the Navajos. Walker describes this unnamed Paiute as a "special envoy" from the Mormons. If he came from Navajo Mountain, it is unlikely that the Mormons had any control over the choice of representatives. More likely the Paiutes sent someone whom they could trust. Interestingly, Simonson's report stated that this Paiute did not just come to speak with Navajo leaders, but also took time to speak with Walker and Simonson, when he met them, and "visited the Indian Agent" at Fort Defiance. One might well expect of a responsible leader that he would first wish to size up the Mormons' adversaries before his people committed themselves to either side.

Early Mormon Encounters with the San Juans, 1859-1870

Between 1859 and 1870, Jacob Hamblin conducted the seven expeditions to Hopi (and later to the Navajos as well) that were to lead to the founding of the Moenkopi Mission and Mormon settlement of the area in the 1870s (Creer 1958). There are several primary sources available for these expeditions, including Mormon pioneer Thales Haskell's journal of the second expedition (Brooks 1944) and Little's biography of Hamblin edited from interviews with him in 1881 (Little 1971 [1881]).   Hamblin, as well as most of the Mormons accompanying him, were familiar with Paiutes and to a limited extent with the Southern Numic language through their earlier experiences in the Southern Utah Mission. Also, at least the first four of these expeditions were accompanied by Paiute guides from groups associated with that mission (Creer 1958:9-16; Corbett 1952:151, 171-75, 183, 207).   These expeditions ought, therefore, like the previous Spanish and Mexican period expeditions, to have provided documentation for the location of Paiute land use, settlements, or other signs of occupation. However, their usefulness is limited, in part because of the pioneers' minimal knowledge of northern Arizona.

The first expedition, which set out in the fall of 1858, appears to have encountered no Indians east of the Colorado River until the Hopi village of Oraibi (Little 1971 [1881]:58-63). The second expedition, in the winter of 1859-1860, crossed the Colorado at Ute Ford west of Navajo Mountain and passed over the Kaibito Plateau to Oraibi. On this journey they encountered Paiutes and Paiute camps at several locations, but no Navajos or Hopis until Oraibi. Two days and fifty miles from the Colorado, according to Haskell, the party camped and "Bro. Hamblin and Pierce went onto a high rock and struck up a big light thinking to raise some Indians. In a short time four made their appearance. Said there was plenty of water at their camp which was only about a mile from us" (Brooks 1944:79). Hamblin recalled this encounter in his interviews with Little and specified that the Indians were Paiutes (Little 1971 [1881]:64-65).   The next night the expedition made camp 22 miles further on: "2 Indians came to camp. Said there was plenty of water at their camp a short distance to the right of the trail" (Brooks 1944:79). In the entries for the next two days, November 7 and 8, Haskell revealed that the "Indians" encountered all along were Paiutes (note that only Paiute interpreters were brought along) and that the boundary to the

Navajo occupation zone was some 30 miles northwest of Oraibi:

> Monday 7th [November]--Commenced packing at
> daylight. Soon discovered *another Piute* [previous entries
> simply mention "Indians"] coming. He led out and we
> followed about a mile and a half to water where four
> or five of them were camped. We traded for some
> antelope meat and took breakfast. Remained in camp
> and let the animals rest. . . . Plenty of water in a rock
> basin good, and plenty of wood at this place.
>
> Tuesday 8th--One Indian volunteered to go with us.
> Took breakfast, packed up, and started. Traveled 18
> miles and camped at Kootsen tooeep [Paiute *ku'utsian
> tɐvwip*, "my father's older brother's/younger brother's
> child's country"]. Indians said that we had better keep a
> good lookout for our animals as we were in the Navijoe
> country. [Brooks 1944:80; emphasis added]

This indication of entry into areas where Navajos were
present, or at least a threat, occurred by Haskell's reckoning
only 30 miles from Oraibi (Brooks 1944:80), beyond or at the
edge of the San Juans' pre-1860 territory (see map 1).

Southern Paiute ethnohistorian Robert Euler wrote that
Haskell's account provides "no indication whether the Paiutes
were resident there or merely on a trading mission to the
Hopis" (1966:71). While this appears to be true superficially,
closer study confirms that these Paiutes were local residents.
The Paiutes apparently told the Mormons that the region
surrounding one camp site was the home country of a kinsman.
At the previous day's camp, the Paiutes had apparently been
hunting the antelope that were then plentiful in the area,
something nonlocal Paiutes could only have done with local
community members' permission. The Paiutes also consistently
showed themselves knowledgeable about water sources and
other features of the environment.

Upon arriving at Oraibi, Hamblin, the expedition leader,
asked Haskell and another Mormon named Shelton to remain a
year among the Hopis as missionaries (Brooks 1944:81).
Throughout his stay at Hopi, which lasted only four months,
Haskell reported the frequent comings and goings of Navajos,
who often traded not only with the Hopis but with Haskell and
Shelton as well. Haskell also recorded that he saw a number of

Paiutes there trading in February of 1860:

> Saturday 18th--Several Piutes came in to trade for blankets and provisions. I traded for a piece of buckskin and made me a whiplash.
>
> Sunday 19th--Piutes still in town. They invited me to go to their camp but I did not go. . . .
>
> Tuesday 21rst--Lots of Piutes in town today. Had a long talk with the chief. He showed very friendly disposition. . . .
>
> Thursday 23rd--Spent the day writing and to the Piutes. Br. Shelton is trying to learn some to write. . . .
>
> Monday 27th--Wrote back Journal. Excitement between Oribes and Piutes. Had an invitation to talk to them. Discovered that they were about equally to blame. Told them that it was better to live in peace with one another which they seemed to believe. [Brooks 1944:93]

This source suggests that a large number of Paiutes had camped near Oraibi to trade or that they had made a short trading expedition from a winter encampment not far off, perhaps in the Tuba City area. Buckskin seems to have been a major trade item. Even today, Kaibab and San Juan Paiutes come to the Hopi villages to trade buckskins that they have prepared in the traditional fashion. In this incident also, the Paiute leader again appeared in the role of spokesperson with leaders or representatives of non-San Juan groups. Finally, Haskell related a disagreement between the Hopis and the Paiutes. He reported telling the two groups "that it was better to live in peace," and may have been referring to an earlier state of actual conflict.

The third expedition met no Navajos between the Colorado River and Oraibi until the party was attacked near present day Red Lake, Arizona, in November of 1860 (Little 1971 [1881]:65-73). According to U.S. Army records, Canby had pursued--and lost--the Navajos through Puerta Limita/Marsh Pass only a few weeks before. This coincidence would tend to confirm a connection between the Navajo Campaigns and an initial Navajo push into Paiute territory in 1860.

Apart from the accounts of Hamblin's expeditions, which

prove to be of limited value for San Juan ethnohistory, accounts of events on the western side of the Colorado during the 1860s also shed some light on San Juan activities. In 1864, the Paiutes and Utes in areas previously settled by Mormons began to resist the Mormon presence. For three years they "waged guerrilla warfare against the settlers from Sanpete County to the south of Kanab [areas just west and north of San Juan territory in Utah and Arizona]" (Corbett 1952:258). Jacob Hamblin attributed this state of hostility to the fact that the settlers' livestock grazing and other activities had destroyed the Indians' wild plant and animal resources causing them to suffer increasing hunger and demoralization (Little 1971 [1881]:87-88). San Juan Paiutes, with Kaibab Paiute and possibly Navajo allies, appear to have joined in this guerrilla warfare, perhaps in sympathy with their Southern Paiute relatives and friends of other bands but almost certainly also out of opportunistic self-interest.

Early in January 1866, two Mormons, Dr. James M. Whitmore and Alexander McIntyre, were killed at Whitmore's ranch at Pipe Spring, near the present Kaibab Paiute Tribal Council building. At first Navajos were blamed for the raid. Hamblin, in his 1869 journal (quoted in Corbett 1952:267), claimed to have aided a dying Kaibab Paiute some time after 1866 who told him that a San Juan Paiute leader named "Patnish" had led him, another Kaibab Paiute, and several young Navajos on the 1866 raid. Later records make it clear that Patnish was the leader of the San Juan Paiute tribal community from at least this period until his death in the 1870s.

A series of incidents followed during the next several years that shed some light on this alleged combined San Juan-Kaibab-Navajo raid. Reports of these incidents also recorded the character of ongoing relations between the San Juan chief elder and the leaders and members of the Kaibab Paiute band. In 1871, on his return from a meeting with Navajo leaders at Fort Defiance in an effort to get the Navajos to stop raiding the Mormons, Hamblin met a group of San Juan Paiutes by the east side of Ute Ford:

> When we arrived on the cliffs before crossing the Colorado, the Piutes living in the Navajo Country [sic] came to me and said as they had taken part with the Navajos in raiding on our people, they desired to have a good peace talk. They were about thirty in number. . . .

Arriving at Kanab, we found all well. Everybody appeared to feel thankful for the success of our mission and the prospects of peace. The Kanab Indians [now the Kaibab Tribe] also congratulated us on our success.

Some of the Piutes from the east side of the river accompanied us home. They spent much of the night in talking over [with the Kanab Paiutes] events that had taken place during the previous three years. They said they had not visited each other much during that time. [Little 1971 (1881):104, 106]

Not long after this, according to Hamblin's biographer Corbett (1952), Patnish and a group of thirteen Paiutes from the San Juan territory came to Kanab:

Patnish came to Kanab looking for Jacob. When he found him he asked for a horse and other things such as tobacco, meat, and ammunition; and if he could get them he would go back and preach peace, but if not, he would preach more raids and perhaps blood. His request was refused and the chief left in a surly mood.

Jacob and Brother Young dispatched a letter to Erastus Snow [L.D.S. Church president] asking for immediate reinforcements. They told Brother Snow that they were afraid Patnish and his men would try to steal some stock when they started back; that one of Patnish's men told them that Patnish would remain another day to see Coal Creek John [a Kanab Paiute]. They hoped something could be done to put the quietus on Patnish if he attempted to drive off any stock. They believed that Patnish's object was to see if he and other lawless fellows could make successful raids. [Corbett 1952:314]

Powell's Grand Canyon exploration party was in Kanab at this time. Later, Fredrick Dellenbaugh, a member of the expedition, wrote:

I had as yet seen none of the natives of the locality. They were now very friendly and considered harmless, thanks to Jacob's wise management. The only Indians the settlers dreaded were some renegades, a band of

Utes and Navajos, collected by a bold and skillful chief named Patnish, whose "country" was south of the Colorado around Navajo Mountain. He was reputed to be highly dangerous, and the Kanab people were constantly prepared against his unwelcome visits. He had several handsome stalwart sons, who dressed in white and who generally accompanied him. Though Patnish was so much feared, I do not remember to have heard that he committed any depredations after this time. [Dellenbaugh 1962 (1908):167-68]

Dellenbaugh met Patnish in 1872, when he came visiting with Captain Frank, the young chief of the Kanab Paiutes. He described him thus: "Old Patnish came in occasionally. Though he did not look particularly dangerous his eye was keen and his bearing positive. Nobody would have interfered with him unless prepared for a fight to the finish" (1962 [1908]:250).

This series of events and encounters involving Patnish and the San Juans, and the way Anglo contemporaries interpreted them, requires comment on several points. First, Patnish's actions as a chief elder illustrate the outside representative's role characteristic of this office, especially as it is exemplified by later and more readily identifiable San Juan leadership figures, such as *Pak'ai* and Alfred Lehi. Patnish met with Mormon leaders as well as leaders of the Kaibab Paiute community and was seen dealing with foreign affairs up to and including matters of war. In later years after peace had been established, San Juan Paiute leaders would carry on relations with outsiders that involved anything from labor contracting with whites to the organization of intertribal trading and gambling.

These events also demonstrate the close ties that existed between the San Juans and Kaibab Paiutes, between ordinary members of the groups as well as between their leaders. The sense of contemporary accounts of linkages between San Juans and Navajo warriors is less clear.

Although there is no clear evidence that Patnish participated in any raids, it is quite possible that a San Juan Paiute might have organized raids involving Navajo warriors as well as Paiutes. The frequent pattern of temporary alliances between Utes and Navajos for the purposes of raiding, even against other Navajos, is discussed by historian Reeve (1974:41-59). Interestingly, in 1866, at about the time of Patnish's supposed raid on the Whitmore ranch at Pipespring, the Indian

Service superintendent for Utah, F. H. Head, wrote:

> Black Hawk, a somewhat prominent chief of the Utah
> Indians, has been engaged for more than a year past in
> active hostilities against the settlements in the southern
> portion of this territory. His band consisted at first of
> but forty-four men, who were mostly outlaws and
> desperate characters from his own and other tribes. . . .
> His band, from what I consider entirely reliable
> information, now numbers one hundred warriors, one-
> half of whom are Navajoes from New Mexico. [ARCIA
> 1866:128]

Such mixed war parties were anything but unusual, and far
from being political or social mergings of tribal communities,
are to be seen simply as alliances of convenience among groups
or individuals, based purely on political and economic self-
interest. In the following section, Moenkopi Mission leader
James Brown's account of a later incident involving Patnish's
men indicates that no understanding existed between the San
Juan Paiutes and Navajos living in the general Moenkopi area.
Whatever may actually have been the case, Hamblin clearly
thought that Patnish was the one who organized the raiding
party and that Kaibab Paiutes were involved as well.
Ironically, from the Mormons' viewpoint, if Patnish's alliance
with the Navajos did occur, it may well have been an outcome
of the Mormons' own attempts in 1859 to get the Navajos and
San Juans together to talk peace. Patnish may even have been
the Paiute envoy the Mormons had the Paiutes send to talk
with the Navajo leaders.

A final point to consider is the question of Patnish's
identity. If he could be placed within the genealogical
framework of present day San Juan society as somewhat later
figures, such as David Lehi/*Pak'ai* or Ruben Owl/*Nasja/
Muuputs*, can be, this would extend San Juan internal political
history, and in particular the succession to tribal leadership,
that much further into a murky past. Unfortunately, all
solutions to this problem are speculative. The name could be an
English rendering of the Paiute *pa'(a)nish*, meaning "big" or
more commonly "loud," quite an apt description for the
historical Patnish. Living San Juan Paiutes recall no one by
that name, not surprisingly considering that Patnish was
described as "old" in 1870 (Dellenbaugh 1962:250). The name
may also have been an English alteration of a known Indian

name. *Pangwits*, the Paiute leader from Navajo Mountain, was apparently also known to the Navajos of this period by the name *Ba'azchin(i)*. Both names, especially the latter, bear a superficial resemblance to "Patnish." It is equally likely that *Pa'nish* was a name the Kaibab Paiute community gave to someone remembered by a quite different name in his own community. If that were the case, any one of a number of prominent men of that generation might have been Patnish, including *Pak'ai's* father, *Tønach'a*, or *Machʉkats'* father, *Avinʉav*.

San Juan Encounters with the Navajos in the 1860s

While historical sources provide a great deal of information bearing on when and for what reasons the Navajos first entered San Juan territory, Navajo and San Juan Southern Paiute oral histories of the Long Walk period have recorded specific interethnic encounters that resulted from the Navajos' flight out of their homelands to the east. The oral history of both groups suggests that some of these encounters were friendly while on other occasions hostility and even bloodshed resulted.

San Juan people whose ancestors lived in the Paiute Canyon and Navajo Mountain area recall that around 1864 a few families sought refuge with Paiutes from Kit Carson's soldiers. These Navajos, according to tradition, were hidden in Paiute Canyon until the soldiers left the area. According to another story, *Tuutaʉts*, grandmother of Angel Whiskers and great-grandmother of Maryann Owl, and *Yaxats*/Washington Dutchie, the younger brother (or perhaps cousin) of Priscilla Dutchie, were mistakenly captured by Carson's troops. Friendly Navajo captives untied the two children at night and allowed them to make their escape, tiptoeing their way out from among the sleeping Navajo captives and troops.

A number of other stories from the period of the Navajo Campaigns emphasize the Paiutes' fear of more warlike groups of Navajos who were also wandering through their lands at this time. Until the region became more peaceful during the 1870s, groups of Paiutes out hunting or gathering are said to have kept their campfires small for fear of Navajo attacks. Stories from Paiutes whose ancestors lived in the south recall the actions they took to defend their homes. For example, Paiutes used to keep watch for Navajo bands from Tuba Butte and other promontories. The following account is an especially well loved traditional story of Paiute revenge during the Long Walk period. An apparent allusion to this story in Omer Stewart (1942:346) suggests that he, too, was told a version of it. Conflict with Hopis also figures in this account:

> There were two old people from Page who were visiting. Hopis killed them. The Paiutes killed and scalped a Hopi woman. [Alfred Lehi's] uncles, *Taatøts* ["White Hair"] and *Taʉnkwar* ["Buckskin"] were war chiefs then. Paiutes from Navajo Mountain came down. Navajos killed them. They [the Navajo Mountain visitors] had told the Willow Springs people when they would come back from gathering but they didn't come back. A runner ran out to where they were supposed to be, checked, and ran back to tell the leader. The leader told the two war chiefs. They held a council and decided to go on the warpath against the Navajos. One of the war chiefs sang a song to bewitch the Navajos [the narrator sings the following; the nonsense syllables of the refrain are omitted]:

> *Maikwa apʉivyayʉpatʉm. ka piaxakʉ'ngwa';*

> *Maikwa o'om parʉxay, maikwa achʉ'ʉm tuukwingwa';*

> *Maikwa o'om piaxakʉy, maikwa o'om kach*
>   *tuukwi'ngwa', apʉivyayʉpantʉm*

> [I] say thus, [you] who will fall asleep, you are not hard to beat;
> [I] say thus, your arrow is limp, say your bow you cannot draw;
> [I] say thus, your arrow is hard for you, say thus, your arrow you cannot draw, [you] who will sleep.

> As they were going along, a coyote crossed their path; they caught the coyote and took it with them. Then they went a little farther and a Navajo crossed their path. They took him with them, too. They cut the coyote open and the Navajo too. They got the coyote's heart out and the same to the Navajo. They exchanged their hearts. These war chiefs really knew what to do: the whole tribe of Navajos went crazy. The Paiutes

killed all those Navajos. Then they built a shade house.
They made a plan. They hung up the Hopi lady's hair
and the Navajos' hair and they had a victory dance and
songs. That was the end of the war path. All the
Indians were dancing naked. This was a story [Alfred
Lehi] told. [Bunte and Franklin Fieldnotes, summer
1982]

This story seems to suggest the presence of a separate war
leadership office, perhaps on the model of the Puebloan war
chief/priest (see Ellis 1951). Other accounts from this period
indicate, however, that the chief elder normally dealt with all
external matters, including war. The incident recounted in the
story may instead have involved a temporary allocation of
leadership authority, perhaps of the sort that occurred in the
hunting of large game when it was felt that another elder
possessed special skills needed for a particular job. It is also
possible that Alfred Lehi, to whom consultants attributed the
story, was simply aggrandizing the roles played by his own
kinsmen.
    There are a number of published sources of Navajo oral
history that are particularly revealing about encounters with
San Juan Paiutes in the 1860s. Brewer (1937) recorded "The
'Long Walk' to Bosque Redondo as told by Peshlakai Etsidi."
In his remembrances of his family's flight from the army,
Etsidi recalled the Navajo Canyon area, south and west of
Navajo Mountain, as part of a long itinerary that was
otherwise generally outside the area of historic San Juan
occupation. In this brief mention, he implied that Paiutes were
then the occupants of Navajo Canyon. For example, Etsidi
related (Brewer 1937:58): "In the spring we moved into a
canyon not very far away; the canyon was called Tchah Yah
["arm pit"; Chaiyahi is a branch of Navajo Canyon close to
Navajo Mountain], because of a Paiute who had a sore under
his arm and lived there." Isabel Kelly's consultant, Joe Francis,
listed *Chaiyaxay* as one of the Paiute family heads who joined
the winter encampment on *Atatsiv* (1964:169).
    The Navajo Community College at Tsaile has published a
collection of oral histories entitled *Navajo Stories of the Long
Walk Period* (Roessel 1973). Narratives told by Navajos whose
ancestors passed through Paiute country during the 1860s
described encounters of various kinds. For example, a Navajo
Salt Clan member from Navajo Mountain, Longsalt, and a
Shonto man, Nelson, both recounted stories of conjoined

Paiute-Ute attacks on Navajos in the lands south of Navajo Mountain during the 1860s (Roessel 1973:169, 174-77). Another account of San Juan Paiute-Navajo relations during the 1860s, that of Littlesalt, also a Navajo Salt from Navajo Mountain, mentioned no hostilities and in fact echoed Navajo Mountain Paiutes' accounts of the Long Walk period (Roessel 1973:159-68). Littlesalt stated that one of his late "grandfathers" was befriended and fed by Paiutes living at Navajo Mountain. He recounted the flight in 1863 from Carson's troops northwest from the Navajo farmlands east of Hopi into the plateau and mountain land of the northern part of the San Juan occupation zone. Paiutes were encountered everywhere in this area, near present day Page, along the Colorado River, and in Paiute Canyon.

Son of Old Man Hat, in his autobiography recorded by Dyk (1938), remembered two encounters with Paiutes that occurred after the Long Walk period, when Navajos began to settle in San Juan territory on a more permanent basis. The second encounter, which occurred by Paiute Canyon in 1884, will be discussed in a later section. The first took place just after 1868 on the northwestern side of Black Mesa. This area by Kayenta, Marsh Pass, and Black Mesa was apparently the first place incoming Navajos occupied on a permanent basis. The local Paiutes appear to have willingly permitted Son of Old Man Hat's family to stay there: "Mostly Paiutes lived along the foot of Black Mountain, and in the summer at Another Canyon we lived with them" (Dyk 1938:10). Son of Old Man Hat, then a small child, made friends and played with the Paiute children there. The amicable tenor of many early encounters between the two ethnic groups suggests that the first stages of Navajo entry into Paiute territory did not seriously affect the Paiutes' accustomed use of resources.

Another reminder of the early historic San Juan presence as recorded in Navajo tradition is reflected in Navajo toponymy. The sense of most Navajo toponymic references to Paiute occupation is not usually to be found in the literal meaning of the names themselves but in the traditional accounts for the names: Navajo place names often record notable individuals or events from oral history.

The name *Ba'azchini* ("Born for him," where Paiutes presently farm in Upper Paiute Canyon), for example, was recently explained thus by a Navajo from Navajo Mountain:

A Paiute man had two wives, and at a place where they

had made a camp, the Navajos said among themselves
that a Paiute woman was about to give birth. Some of
the menfolk went to where the woman was. As they
were approaching the woman, one of the Paiutes met
them and told them to stay away. As they stood there,
and as they looked to where the woman was about to
give birth, one of the Paiutes was standing on the
woman's womb trying to push the baby out. The
Navajos tried to enter the brush corral, saying that
wasn't the right way to treat a woman about to have a
baby; but, still, they were pushed aside. Then the
woman gave birth; and soon the second wife went into
labor. So, in one night two women gave birth for one
man. [Roessel 1973:168]

According to her affidavit, collected by the Navajo Tribe for
its Indian Claims Commission case, Dick's Sister/Ʉnap, a
Navajo Mountain Paiute, testified through a Navajo interpreter
that *Ba'azchini* was her father's father (Dick's Sister 1961).
Contemporary genealogies indicate that *Ʉnap*'s paternal
grandfather was *Pangwits*, already noted as an early leader on
the local or tribal level. Polygyny among the San Juan Paiutes,
and indeed among other groups of Paiutes as well as Utes,
seems to have been associated primarily with important men.
Pak'ai is said to have had three wives, although perhaps not all
at the same time. The storyteller's account of Paiute childbirth
practices does not correspond to any known custom and should
perhaps not be taken at face value. As an example of ethnic
stereotyping, however, this account illustrates the degree to
which contemporary and historic Navajos have considered
Paiutes to be culturally foreign.

According to one recent oral history, two names of sites in
Navajo Canyon, *Nii'tsi'įį*, and *Ch'aayahii* (respectively, "Raw
Face" and "Under Arm"), are references to early Paiute-Navajo
warfare:

At the place called *Ch'aayahii* the Navajos shot one of
the Paiutes that was a second lieutenant in his
underarm with an arrow. That was how the place got
its name *Bayoodzin Bi' Ch'aaya Biishi* ("Paiute Killed by
Wound Under His Arm"). . . . Then one of the Paiutes
was shot in the cheek by a Navajo. That is how the
place got its name of *Nii'tsi'įį* ("Raw Face"--in Navajo
Canyon). [Roessel 1973:173-74]

Note, of course, that Peshlakai Etsidi's first hand account (in Brewer 1937) of how Chaiyahi got its name was quite different, suggesting that modern attitudes towards Paiutes have influenced oral traditions.

Finally, the area called in Navajo *Ba'adowei*, English Bodoway, west of Cedar Ridge, is said by Navajos to have been named after an early Paiute leader (Roessel 1973:174; Van Valkenburgh 1941:14). According to people at Willow Springs, this was *Pa'atoxwai* ("Tall" or "Long" in Paiute), who was an ancestor of the present tribal spokesperson and lived at Bodoway Mesa and Cedar Ridge. However, he is not remembered as a particularly important figure in San Juan oral history.

Adaptations to the Navajo and Mormon Presence, 1870-1900

The Mormons' Moenkopi Wash Settlement in the 1870s

During the period of settlement in the Moenkopi-Tuba City area, beginning in the 1870s, the Mormons came into much closer contact with the peoples living in the region surrounding Tuba City, and their writings reflect the greater accuracy and detail of their knowledge. Mormon pioneers in the 1870s recorded several accounts that describe the early years of Mormon settlement at Moenkopi and Tuba City and their relations with local Indians. Richest in descriptive detail are Volume Two of Cleland and Brooks' (1955) edition of John D. Lee's diaries and James S. Brown's autobiography (1971 [1900]) and journals (Brown 1875-77).

Lee spent the period from June 26, 1873, to March 13 or 14, 1874, in Moenave, a spring-fed farming area along the Echo Cliffs about halfway between Willow Springs and present day Tuba City. During this period, Lee was in quasi-exile, seeking to escape prosecution in Utah for his role in the Mountain Meadows massacre, twenty years earlier. Lee's journal entries tell of a daily exchange of services, goods, and social visits with the Hopis and Paiutes living and farming in the vicinity of the Moenkopi Wash. The Hopis were Tuba, his wife, and his brother-in-law, "Taltee." Lee also found Paiutes farming at Moenave and other springs in the area. The Paiutes mentioned by Lee were "Shoe" or "Shew," his wife and family, "Pocky" and his wife, as well as three other unnamed Paiute families who hunted for Lee's family when he was away (Cleland and

Brooks 1955:310).

As Navajo ethnohistorians Brugge and Correll pointed out (1973:183-84), Lee at first referred to his farm's location as "Moencroppa," probably his version of Moenkopi, until his entry of August 21, 1874, when he suddenly and without explanation began to call it "Moweeyabby" or variants of that name (Cleland and Brooks 1955:287). The reason for the change may be inferred from the fact that Jacob Hamblin, who was familiar with the area, visited him on that day for the first time. "Moa Ave," was the old, and apparently etymologically correct name for Moenave: the name still appears on older U.S. Geological Survey maps. Moa Ave resembles the Paiute word for mosquitoes, *mooavi*, and may have originated with local Paiute farmers, as did the name, Moapa, or "Mosquito water," a Paiute farming area in southern Nevada that was also colonized by Mormons. In many Mormon colonies, the Mormons' use of flood irrigation led to outbreaks of malaria, to which local Indians proved especially susceptible (see Stoffle and Dobyns 1982:110). It is probable that the Mormons adopted the Paiute name for this place since, as Lee's account indicates, only Paiutes were farming there when Lee arrived.

Lee's initial reference to Moenkopi, recorded upon his arrival to the area and before he actually settled there, implies that he believed it to be a settlement of Hopis, Paiutes, and Navajos, living side by side and farming together, the leader of which was the Hopi, Tuba (Cleland and Brooks 1955:270). In subsequent journal entries, Lee spoke of the Navajos as having a separate village. At one point in giving directions Lee located this settlement 18 miles up the valley from Tuba's camp at Moenkopi (Cleland and Brooks 1955:314, 318, 320). This may have been on or near the present site of Red Lake, Arizona, today a Navajo farming area. Throughout the 1870s and 1880s, the Navajos probably had no permanent settlement much closer than this to the Moenkopi-Tuba City farming area (see discussion below of Brown 1971 [1900]:470; and Welton 1888, also quoted in Brugge and Correll 1973:191).

San Juan Paiutes, on the other hand, were farming at several locations in close proximity to both Mormon and Hopi farms. According to Lee, at least one Paiute, named Pocky, had fields at Moenkopi, and perhaps lived close by Tuba's family. The Paiute Lee named Shoe had fields at Moenave, using the same irrigation water as Lee, and also at other, unidentified springs near Moenave, possibly including Willow

Springs.

In addition to farming, Lee made mention of other San Juan economic activities and types of land use. He referred in passing to San Juan Paiute deer-hunting on the San Francisco Peaks and the South Rim of the Grand Canyon (Cleland and Brooks 1955:280, 282). Lee also described San Juan manufacture of water jugs woven from sumac and waterproofed with pinyon pine pitch gathered on the South Rim. Interestingly, he noted that Paiutes wove these jugs primarily as trade items for the Navajos, suggesting the emergence of the basketry trade that was to become an important, new source of income for Paiutes in later decades (Cleland and Brooks 1955:269).

Of the Paiutes who figure in Lee's journal, only Pocky can be identified with an historic San Juan Southern Paiute figure, *Pak'ai* ("Bobs along": *Pak'ai* was afflicted with arthritic hips and walked with difficulty). Also known as Lehi or David Lehi in English, *Pak'ai*, was distinguished in later historic accounts as chief elder of the San Juan Tribe. During his long life, he cultivated fields at several other sites besides Moenkopi, including Government Spring, just north of Willow Springs, and *Akanukwit*, a spring by the old Tuba City cemetery (also noted as a San Juan farming site used by Joe Francis' father in Kelly 1964:169).

If there was any lingering feeling of hostility between the Hopis and the Paiutes, Lee was apparently not aware of it. It is clear, however, that both Paiutes and Hopis distrusted and even feared the local Navajo settlement. On September 4, 1873, Lee recorded that Tuba and Taltee stopped by to ask him to move in with them at Moenkopi so that "the Navajos would not be so apt to steal." Taltee repeated the request two days later. Lee noted at the same time that the Paiute, Shoe, was very much worried by the possibility of a Navajo attack. On a different occasion, one of the Paiutes who hunted rabbits for Lee's family informed Lee that his two brothers and his wife had been killed by Navajos, although this was probably not by members of the local group (Cleland and Brooks 1955:293-94, 310).

A year and a half after Lee left Moenave, another Mormon pioneer, Anthony Ivins, recorded an encounter with Patnish and a group of Paiutes near Moenkopi (Ivins 1875). In his journal entry for October 30, 1875, Ivins wrote: "We travelled 8 miles to the Mo-an-coppy. The party of Indians who were with Pahtnish and who camped near us last night [thus 8 miles from

Moenkopi] went on West hunting, Pahtnish travelling with us to the Moancoppy." This incident offers information concerning two important aspects of San Juan politics at this time. First, in separating himself from the rest of his group and proceeding on with the Mormons to their destination, Patnish may have been acting in accordance with his responsibilities as chief elder. At the same time, this implies that in keeping track of the Mormons and maintaining his relationship with them, Patnish was performing tasks that he and his people saw as more important and perhaps more central to the role of chief elder than any guidance he may have exercised in such internal group activities as hunting. Second, Patnish and his followers, whose movements earlier sources had associated with the Navajo Mountain area, were here shown camping in and utilizing lands in the southern section of the San Juan occupation zone. For Patnish's people, this association in different accounts with areas that were later to become separate settlement areas within the tribe tends to confirm that no south-north subdivision existed at this time. Concerning Patnish in particular, his active presence in both north and south may likewise mean that he was a tribal, rather than simply a local leader.

James S. Brown was called to the Arizona Indian Mission at Moenkopi in 1876, starting in March, and again in 1877, from the end of January to the beginning of August. Although he spent a good deal of this time at Oraibi or at Navajo and Zuni settlements near the New Mexico-Arizona border, he also stayed at the Moenkopi Mission much of the time, dealing with Navajos, Hopis, and Paiutes. He noted Tuba's presence at Moenkopi and mentioned other Indians farming there, but did not specify their numbers or tribal affiliation. Only one Navajo camp is mentioned, "Chief Hustelso's . . . up the Moencoppy Wash . . . about twenty-five miles" from the mission (Brown 1971 [1900]:470). "Hustelso" may have been the Navajo *Hastíí (li)Tso* ("Mr. Big"), whom Brugge and Correll (1973:177) believed was an early resident at the site of Tuba City itself.

In the months of May and June, 1877, an incident occurred at the Moenkopi mission that again brought Patnish into the limelight, this time as in the Ivins journal in association with Paiutes living the Tuba City area. The incident illustrates in concrete fashion the workings of San Juan consensus group decision making during this period. The context in which it occurred also suggests that local San Juan residents were dissatisfied with the Mormons' increased presence in the Moenkopi Wash.

Brown's journal entries tell the story:

Tuesday 8th [May]--continued [sheep-shearing]; and some Piuts came down Wednesday 9th--the work of shering was continued. H.O. Fulmer went to camp; I sent word for the Brethren to gard their stalk [stock] for . . . the Piuts was mad and thretend to steal. . . .

Saturday 12th--I continued my studes, in the afterpart of the day Peacons [a Navajo leader] son came saing that his father had sent him to tell us that Patnish the Pieute chief had died; and that the Pieuts was mad and Thretend to mak a raid on ower stalk at the Moanycopy and if they could get stalk without sheding Blood they would be satisfied but if not they would have Blood and stalk

My friend Hustelso [the local Navajo leader] and others said that they thout we had better go down and hav us come back to their camp agane and stay as long as we pleased;

So we pact up as spedly as posable the Navajoes asisting us in evry posable way they could; and one of them acompaned us home wher we arived just after dark and Found the people getherd for prears. I notified them of what was up.

And for the first time on this mission caled out a gard and sent E. Nels and W Johnson to Notify Lees and P nelson at willo Springs to gether their stalk and come as soon as they could. [Brown 1975-77]

Although the Mormon settlement was tense, no attack occurred. On the 17th of May, Brown wrote:

2 piutes came in with Brused heads, and said that in their council they had bin devided 6 in favor of pease with the mormons 5 in favor of Raiding on us at the Moanycopy and they Broke up in a fight and the five went to get the Utes to join them in Raiding upon us, wilst the others come to Notifiy us of the danger and

they prepared to stay ner us for protection; we still keep gard and herd stalk. [Brown 1975-77]

Through the months of May and June there were references to precautions taken against Paiute attack. However, hostilities actually appear to have been averted as of the 24th of May: "Warm and pleasant the frendly Piuts came in, and we agan let all the dry stalk Run but hurded the horses and milk stalk." Of this, Brown's autobiography stated briefly (1971:469): "we had a talk with some of the Piutes, and the threatened trouble was averted."

Brown's account of this episode provides important information about Paiute political decision making. At each level of the modern sociopolitical organization, from locally residing ambilineages up to and including the tribe, decisions regarding group policy or social control of group members are made through a process of lengthy discussion of issues at a public council meeting. While most members of the group, including children, are present and lend more or less of their attention, it is only the elders who actively participate in discussion. On those occasions when a substantive decision actually comes out of the discussion, it must receive the unanimous concurrence of all adults, not just the community's elder members, in order to be implemented.

While something similar to the modern council process was certainly operating in Patnish's time, there appears to at least one significant difference: the role of gender. Only men are mentioned in Brown's account of the Paiute "council" (compare Stewart's indication of both male and female council participation, 1942:300). Today, women speak up on an equal footing with men at all levels of political decision making, including the tribal level. In the last fifteen years, apparently for the first time in Paiute history, even the position of tribal elder has passed into the hands of women.

In Brown's time, another factor may also have operated to increase male elders' influence in San Juan politics. In the 1870s the San Juan Tribe had been at war off and on for decades with just about every other local ethnic group except the other Southern Paiute communities. The San Juan Tribe's political organization therefore could be expected to have been much more militarily oriented than in later years after peace had been established. The outbreak of fighting between factions which Brown reported, and the belligerent words and actions of Patnish and other Paiutes reported by various sources in this period, are one indication that aggression and aggressiveness played a major role in political process. If so, one might reasonably expect women to have had less status and less access to decision making and positions of authority than was the case in later years. Today there are strong informal sanctions against the expression of anger or aggressiveness in public life: even angry words are extremely rare at council meetings.

A second important point also emerges. If Brown's report was accurate, only eleven men actively participated in the council discussion. Because there were so few taking the elder's role, this would seem to indicate either that the council did not involve the tribe as a whole, or that the position of elder was more restrictive than in the present century. The latter possibility would imply that San Juan society was less egalitarian than it is today, and not simply in terms of gender relations.

The first of the two explanations seems the more likely. Since the season was late spring, most San Juans were probably at their farming areas, preparing their fields for planting. Many, if not most, of the San Juan people would have been residing too far away to take part easily in this meeting, despite the importance of the issues discussed.

This may well explain Brown's mysterious reference to "the Utes" whom the losing faction threatened to fetch "to join them in [r]aiding" the Mormons. Those whom Brown understood to be Utes may simply have been San Juans farming in other areas within San Juan territory, especially in the north. *Pangwits* and *Panashiaxar*, and their kin who had joined the San Juan Tribe after immigrating from the north and who habitually farmed in the San Juan River system and in Paiute Canyon, may even have been identified as Utes by San Juan people in the south. Dick's Sister, a Navajo Mountain San Juan resident, appears to have identified her own ancestors from this group as Utes as late as 1961 (Dick's Sister 1961). San Juan testimony today indicates that this kin group, or some part of it, may actually have come from the Kaiparoits Plateau west of the Colorado, within the territory of Kelly's Kaiparoits Paiute Band (1934, 1964; see map 1).

To determine the relative accessibility of positions of authority in the 1870s and today, we may compare the ratio of elders to community population size, with the caveat that eldership is only partially a function of relative age and that we have no information on population breakdown by age group before the twentieth century. Estimates of the Paiute population in the Moenkopi Wash area run from 30 (Welton 1888) to approximately 100 (Michie to Acting Adjutant General, July 13, 1892; quoted in Brugge and Correll 1973:193). When describing the 1881 summer-winter transhumance of Paiutes farming in the Tuba City area, Joe Lee (1974:9) stated that on the trail north to Navajo Mountain "herds and flocks and family units were strung out for several miles." This suggests that more than 30 people were involved, especially since not all local farmers took part in this seasonal movement. If the larger estimates are more or less correct, then a quorum of eleven male elders out a local seasonal population of 100, or 11%, is about the same proportion that we find today. Out of 60 tribe members residing in the southern area settlement near Tuba City in 1983-1984, 8 males were acting as tribal elders (13%). Assuming--not unreasonably--that there was a fairly equivalent age distribution in both periods, we may conclude that whatever the status of women might have been, men's access to positions of power in internal decision making has not changed substantially since the 1870s.

Turning from questions of internal organization to the topic of intergroup or foreign relations, the San Juans were also depicted in Brown's account as a group whose capacity for military action was sufficient to frighten a well armed, though at the time still small, Mormon population, numbering 25 in 1877 (Brugge and Correll 1973:187). The Navajos, also, despite their apparent eagerness to please the Mormons, did not offer them any protection. In fact, Brown reported in his May 12 entry that the Navajos urged the Mormons to return to their own settlement, perhaps because they wished to remain neutral. The distance between the Navajo camp and the Moenkopi Mission, some 25 miles according to Brown, would have meant that any protection or assistance, other than advice, which Hustelso might have extended to the Mormons would necessarily have exposed Navajo people and stock to San Juan reprisals. In any event, Paiutes clearly had their own policies that were not shared with the Navajos. If there had ever been an alliance involving Patnish's San Juan followers and these Navajos, it was not operating at this time.

Major John Wesley Powell and the San Juan Tribe

During the early period of Mormon settlement and just prior to it, Major John Wesley Powell, the explorer and ethnologist, was conducting research on the Great Basin Indians, including the Southern Paiutes. Although he visited most of the San Juan Paiutes' cultural congeners in the Great Basin during the late 1860s and early 1870s, including several other groups of Southern Paiutes, Powell himself apparently never visited the San Juan Tribe on the other side of the Colorado River.

The only members of Powell's Colorado River expeditions to visit the San Juans or meet one face-to-face in San Juan country were Walter Powell, the major's cousin, and Jacob Hamblin, who on their return from a side trip to Hopi in the fall of 1872 hired a San Juan Paiute at Moenkopi to guide them part of the way back. Walter Powell noted in his journal (Charles Kelly 1948-1949:469) that this "Pah-Ute" had a "cornfield in which there were a lot of melons, squashes and pumpkins were [sic] growing. A fine spring coming out of this cliff watered it finely." According to Walter Powell's estimate of distances travelled, the Paiute guide's garden and spring lay some 23 or 25 miles from Moenkopi along "a line of cliffs breaking back toward the north," presumably Echo Cliffs. As Powell and Jacob Hamblin resumed their northward itinerary from this farm site after stopping to lunch on baked "punkin" and other foods supplied by their guide, Powell noted (Kelly 1948-1949:469): "Looming up in the distance are the peaks that stand guard over the Thousand Wells, but they seem to recede as we advance." The Thousand Wells are a group of water pockets, natural bedrock catchment basins and pools, from which present day San Juan Paiutes in the *Atatsiv* area water their horses and cattle. These pools lie on the northeastern slope of that prominent segment of Echo Cliffs known as Hamblin Ridge, which stretches southward from the Gap to a point just north of Willow Springs. Hamblin Ridge would thus appear to be the "peaks" mentioned by Walter Powell. From his description, this Paiute farm must have been at Willow Springs or at another nearby spring along the cliffs. Since according to Powell the Paiute guide was lame and resided at Moenkopi, he may well have been the arthritic *Pak'ai*.

The next day near the Gap Powell found "the remains of 2 or 3 wickiups" that he identified as belonging to Navajos because of signs of sheep-herding (Kelly 1948-1949:470). As no

Navajos were present, it is also possible that this was a Paiute camp of the sort that the San Juans made in the Gap area well into the 1950s. In a 1941 BIA publication on Navajo geography, the anthropologist Van Valkenburgh characterized this area as "a favorite camping place for the small band of Strip Piutes who are remnants of Padawa's [Bodoway or *Pa'atoxwai*] old band" (1941:28).

In 1873, Major Powell and George W. Ingalls, Indian agent for the Moapa Paiute Reservation in Nevada, served as Special Indian Service Commissioners and conducted an investigation into the status of the various groups of the Great Basin region, including Northern Paiutes (Paviotsos), Shoshonis, Utes, and Southern Paiutes. The purpose of this investigation was to ascertain the locations of Indian tribal communities and determine their political organization and intertribal relations so that a system of agencies and reservations could be set up for them without exacerbating intertribal conflicts.

The *Annual Reports of the Commissioner of Indian Affairs* from the second half of the nineteenth century, both prior to, and to a certain extent after, Powell's and Ingalls' inquiry, reveal that there was a great deal of confusion as to the identification of the various ethnic and political groups of the area. Southern Paiutes, in particular, were erroneously subdivided into as many groups as Anglo folk terminologies and variant spellings of the word, Paiute, could permit: Piedes, Pai-Utes, Pah Utes, Piutes, etc. Powell's and Ingalls' investigative visits to the various groups culminated in their report to the Commissioner of Indian Affairs published in 1874 (Fowler and Fowler 1971:97-119).

Unfortunately for the San Juan Tribe, Powell and Ingalls, by their own admission, did not look into their situation personally but instead relied on hearsay:

There is a small tribe of Pai-Utes in Northern Arizona, on the east side of the Colorado River, known as the Kai-an-ti-kwok-ets, which was not visited by the commission. This little band lives in a district so far away from the route of travel that your commission did not think it wise to occupy the time and incur the expense necessary to visit them in their homes. . . .

The Kwa-an-ti-kwok-ets, who live on the eastern side of the Colorado River, are nearly isolated from the other tribes, and affiliate to a greater or lesser extent with the Navajos. [Fowler and Fowler 1971:103, 107]

There are several indications that suggest the hearsay information included in the commission report was inaccurate. First, the population figure given for the San Juan Paiutes, 62, is an underestimate and does not agree with other sources for the same period, including other government accounts.

Another indication is Powell's and Ingalls' use of the term, "Kwa-an-ti-kwok-ets," to refer to the San Juan people. As Powell himself noted elsewhere (Fowler and Fowler 1971:38), Southern Paiutes conventionally referred to sociopolitical groups in terms of their territorial affiliation, using what Powell aptly called a "land-name." "Kwa-an-ti-kwok-ets," or more correctly *kwaiantukwats* ("person from the other side") is not a proper territory name, but rather a term used to refer loosely to any group living beyond some natural barrier. The San Juan people themselves occasionally refer to Paiutes on the other side of the Colorado River by this term. The use of the term by Powell and Ingalls suggests that they obtained their information on the San Juans in garbled form from someone familiar with the Paiute language, perhaps Jacob Hamblin, Powell's long-time guide. The Kaibab Paiutes, who may well have given Powell or Hamblin the term in the first place, even today frequently refer to the San Juans by the term *kwaiantukwatsing* as well as by the two subcommunity land-names that Stewart first recorded (1942:237).

It is also likely that the statement that the Paiutes on the east side of the Colorado affiliated with the Navajos derived from stories related by Hamblin or other Mormons concerning Patnish's 1866 mixed war party, as discussed earlier. However, the possible existence of such a mixed war party tells us very little about the actual political or social relations between the two tribes.

Powell's prestige was such that his summary dismissal of the San Juan Tribe may well have discouraged government officials from taking a closer look at the San Juans and their relations with local groups, at least for the remainder of the nineteenth century. In a similar fashion, his influential opinions appear to have postponed the establishment of a federal relationship with the Kaibab Tribe during the same period, with disastrous consequences for Kaibab Paiutes (see Stoffle and Evans 1976:186-88).

San Juan Life and Competitive Relations with the Navajos, the 1880s

While the Mormons were expanding their farm and livestock holdings in the Tuba City area, increasing numbers of Navajos were also filtering into the Kaibito Plateau region just to the north of Tuba by way of their initial settlements along the Klethla Valley. During the 1880s, there is evidence to suggest that, although the San Juans were not yet forced to restrict their movements because of Navajo settlement, relations between the two groups were becoming more strained because of increased Navajo resource utilization, particularly in the northern half of the San Juan occupation zone.

Joe Lee, the grandson of John D. Lee, was witness to events in San Juan history from the early period of Mormon settlement at Moenkopi until well into the first half of the twentieth century, after the Mormon settlers had left what was to become the Western Navajo Reservation. In 1946, at the age of 73, Joe Lee dictated a short sketch of his life to Gladwell Richardson. While this account contains minor historical inaccuracies, it also provides sensitive insights into local Indians' experiences of this era.

During his childhood in the 1870s and 1880s, Joe Lee was able to observe first hand the daily economic life of the San Juan people. In 1876 at the age of three, he moved with his family to Willow Springs, near the old Willow Springs Trading Post a mile or so below the Paiute farms (Lee 1974:8; note the mention of the Lees' homestead in Brown's May 12, 1877, journal entry quoted above). According to Lee, when he was a child, "Havasupai, Piute and Navajo Indians lived around Willow Springs, Moen Ave and the ancient Hopi village of Moenkopi. Before I was ten years old the 'Supais moved back to Grand Canyon country, their traditional homeland" (1974:8). This date, 1883, appears to be the latest recorded for Havasupai occupation in the Moenkopi Wash area.

As a child, Lee learned both the Navajo and Paiute languages by playing with Indian children. The fact that he spoke Paiute is corroborated by living San Juan and Kaibab Paiutes who knew him as "Joedie," or, in Paiute, *Chuuri*, when he was the proprietor of the Gap Trading Post. His close relationships with both Paiutes and Navajos makes his testimony particularly useful.

With evident fondness, Lee recalled from his childhood and

youth several Paiute individuals and their families as his "special friends" (1974:9): Lehi, One Eye, Chief Nasja from the Tuba City, and his older "brother" from Navajo Mountain, also named Nasja. Lehi was almost certainly David Lehi, or *Pak'ai*, from whom are descended the numerous Lehis at Willow Springs as well as several other families in that area. Although "One Eye" has not been identified elsewhere, either in other documents or in San Juan oral accounts, Lee stated elsewhere (1974:34) that One Eye was the father of a well-known figure, Dora Nelson, from whom a number of Navajo Mountain San Juan Paiutes are descended. The elder Nasja was the same local Navajo Mountain leader whose son, called by Navajos and Anglos alike by a Navajo name, Nasja Begay, led Cummings and Wetherill to the Rainbow Bridge in 1909. Nasja's English name was Ruben Owl in later BIA documents. Precisely who the non-Navajo Mountain Nasja, referred to by Lee as "Chief Nasja," was is unclear. Because the Paiutes pronounce the Navajo word, Nasja, as *Nacha*, it is possible that Lee was referring here to *Pak'ai*'s father, *Tønacha'a*, and that either he or Richardson simply mistook the unfamiliar Paiute name for the very well-known Navajo name. If this is so, then Lee's reference to "Chief Nasja" may mean that *Tønacha'a* was at one time a tribal level leader.

In 1880, when Lee was seven years old, he ran off with a group of San Juans from the Tuba City area who were making what he implied was a regular movement of their livestock to winter pastures on the northern side of Navajo Mountain:

> Each Fall Piute families around Tuba City gathered up their horses, cattle and sheep, moving north into Utah to winter at Navajo Mountain. This meant a trip of more than 100 miles across the wildest canyon country imaginable. . . .

> In November 1881 I was with Chief Nasja's family when they packed up for winter quarters. I wanted to go with them and he took me up on his saddle. Herds and flocks and family units were strung out for *several miles* when Father came along. Finding me with Chief Nasja he inquired about it. Nasja asked if it would be all right to take me along with his family. [His father absentmindedly gave permission]. . . .

> We went through many canyons to Navajo Mountain,

camping between it and Little Navajo [a hill northeast of the mountain]. When the first big snow threatened, the entire family group moved around by Glass Mountain down into Bridge Canyon. Their camp was pitched in a great cove right close to the natural bridge [Rainbow Bridge]. We stayed there warm and snug all that winter. The stock spread loose to the Colorado River and through side canyons. A brush fence [this is current practice in Paiute sheep and cattle herding in that area] across the main canyon kept untended stock from straying out. By the time Mother found out where I was, deep snow covered the country and she couldn't send for me. [Lee 1974:9; emphasis added]

It is not clear from Lee's account whether he believed that most or even all of the Paiutes living at Tuba City took part in herding and the associated transhumant life-style at this date. No other historic descriptions of San Juan economic life in the 1870s or 1880s, such as those of Lee's grandfather and Indian Agent Welton discussed below, made any mention of Paiute livestock in the Tuba City area. Willow Springs area Paiutes state that in this period, the time of *Pak'ai*'s prime, some kin groups at least, including that of *Machʉkats* living at Willow Springs, owned only a few donkeys and cows and no other stock. A San Juan tradition recounts that *Pak'ai* himself received a cow and bull from what Paiutes describe as an angel. However, according to the affidavit of Dick's Sister (1961), when she was a girl in the 1880s the Paiutes at Navajo Mountain were trading woven water jugs and wedding baskets with Navajos living by Zilnez Mesa, or Tall Mountain, for pottery and sheep.

As noted earlier, this pattern of transhumance and free movement from north to south described by Joe Lee also indicates that Paiutes shared their lands in the Tuba City and Navajo Mountain areas, so that they must have been perceived as a unitary estate held by, and available to, the tribal community as a whole. At the same time, the division into northern and southern settlement areas, which so influences economic cooperation and associated group decision making in the present century, had not yet crystallized as a structural feature of San Juan sociopolitical organization.

By the end of the 1870s, the Mormons were also seeking to expand into the geographically isolated southeastern corner of Utah, just north of the San Juan River. Before creating a shorter passage through Hole-in-the-Rock from western Utah (see the historical accounts of Miller 1959 and Reay 1980), they conducted an expedition through San Juan territory in 1879, laying out a possible passage in that direction. The expedition travelled from Lee's Ferry south along the Mormon road west of the Echo Cliffs to Moenkopi and then northeast through present day Cowsprings, Marsh Pass, and Kayenta to cross the San Juan River beyond the Paiute occupation zone east of Bluff, Utah.

Near present day Dennehotso, on what would have been the extreme eastern edge of the San Juan occupation zone, the group encountered a Paiute camp and a Navajo camp near the same water source, according to the "Camp Records" kept by the expedition (quoted in Miller 1959:24). The journal of the head scout, Kumen Jones, contains the following entry concerning the encounter:

> An incident occurred before reaching the Chinalee [Chinle Creek, not shown on map 2] showing the tact of our captain. Upon passing a large camp or village of Pahutes, one of their number (later known as Peeagament), came blustering out and demanded $500.00 before the train would be allowed to proceed through his country. The Captain's being the first team, a short stop was made to try and pacify the old fellow. A few mild explanations were attempted, the only effect being to cause the old man to press his demands in a higher key. Noting this Smith ordered him out of the way, and proceeding some distance, struck camp for dinner. The captain quietly passed the word around camp that it would be the right thing to give the Indians a little something to eat, or other small gifts such as tobacco, etc. Especially the small children were to have something to eat, but no one was to give the noisy old fellow anything or notice him in any way. The result soon made the wisdom of this course apparent as the Indians old and young were all jolly and friendly, and the old man was a psychological study. [Jones' journal, p. 4; quoted in full in Miller 1959]

In this account, some twenty years after the first bands of Navajos moved into what had been the eastern fringes of the San Juan's pre-1860 territory, the Navajo presence had not yet limited the range of San Juan occupation. Dennehotso, according to oral tradition, was an important seed gathering site, as well as a site where aphis sugar was collected from the cane that grew there in marshy areas (see Isabel Kelly's descriptions of this food product, 1964:46, 171). Although there is no other record of an individual named *Piaxam'ini*, the name, meaning in Southern Paiute "One usually having sugar" seems a likely one given the presence of the aphis sugar cane.

Although Paiutes and Navajos were able to camp here side by side in peace, events elsewhere in Paiute country suggest growing tension in their relations. In 1879, two prospectors were allegedly killed by Indians near Monument Valley. At this time, the San Juan Tribe was not under the supervision of an Indian agent. Galen Eastman, the Navajo agent at Fort Defiance, reported the account of the murder that he had received from Navajos in the area northwest of his reservation:

> "Eshke be Clunny" ("Boy with many horses") one of my head men, and son of my head chief on the west--("Ganado Mucho" a most excellent Family) reports that while on a trip recently to the Big Colorado River a Navajo friend in whom he believes implicitly residing also in that vicinity--says, being at a "Piute" lodge 30 days ago--Saw a Black mule (large) and 3 other pack mules etc. taken by said "Piutes" from two white men who were murdered by said Piutes for their plunder. And the Navajos express a desire that said Piutes may be looked after by the "Great Father" for such occurrences are quite to [sic] frequent in that vicinity (60 miles thereabout above Lees's Ferry on the on the Colorado) and the said Piutes often endeavor to lay the blame upon the Navajos. [Eastman 1880]

It by no means clear whether the San Juans did indeed kill the miners or were simply given the blame for it by the local Navajos who reported the incident. Some thirty years later, Hoskinini Begay, son of *Hashkeneini*, a leader among the Navajo immigrants living in the vicinity of Kayenta, told a similar story to Mrs. Wetherill, the Kayenta trader (Gillmor and Wetherill 1934:95), with the additional statement that "the Paiutes told them that they had been using Paiute water to which they had no right." On another occasion, Hoskinini Begay told anthropologist Byron Cummings that he and another Navajo had killed the men, but only by accident (Cummings 1952:8-9). Depending on which version was true, it may well have been the Navajos who endeavored to lay the blame on the Paiutes when they reported the killings to Eastman.

Agent Eastman had a running feud with Thomas V. Keam, a trader at Keam's canyon near Hopi who was recommended at least twice as a replacement for Eastman (McNitt 1962:166-85). In 1882, on the basis of statements against Keam made by a Philip Zoeller, Eastman accused the trader of "influencing" the Paiutes to murder prospectors (Eastman 1882). Keam answered the accusations with affidavits from Indian agents and others. The competition between the two men was exacerbated by the fact that both were interested in rediscovering the dead miners' strike.

This episode in agency politics would be of little interest to our subject were it not that these affidavits include accounts of an expedition to Paiute Canyon with Navajo guides to retrieve the stolen mules and other property of the dead prospectors. Indian Agent Alexander Stephen's account of this expedition and other events surrounding the murders is the most detailed:

> In the month of July 1880 Captain F. J. Bennett, Navajo Agent [Eastman was removed and then reinstated during this period], came to this place [Keam's Canyon] and held a council with the Navajoes and Moquis concerning matters in dispute between the tribes. During this council some Navajoes who live close to the Pah Ute country, near the San Juan River, reported to Captain Bennett that two Americans had been killed by the Pah Utes during the winter of 1879 and that the Pah-Utes had mules and firearms belonging to these men. Captain Bennett instructed those Navajoes to obtain possession of the Americans' property and bring it to Mr. William Keam who would reimburse them. . . .

> Shortly after the council those northern Navajoes brought here and left with Mr. William Keam two mules, a rifle and a revolver, which they reported to him as being everything belonging to the Americans . . . They claimed to have paid, in way of barter with the Pah-Utes for this property, the amount of Thirty-five dollars. . . .

> In January 1881 Aaron Stull and Robert Reese came to this post. Stull told me that he lived with Mr.

Mitchell [H. L. Mitchell, a Colorado cattleman and father of one of the murdered prospectors] and had been sent for the above mentioned mules.

With Reese I had some former acquaintance and he and Stull told me all the particulars which Mr. Mitchell had been able to gather from the Indians concerning the murder of his son and Meyrick.

It corroborated the story told to Captain Bennett by the Navajoes, namely, that they were killed by Pah-Utes, about a hundred miles North from here, after having made a mining location.

Stull and Reese, on the suggestion of Mr. Mitchell, now wished before returning to Colorado, to make a search for the location of it from the South. They proposed, if I would furnish them assistance, that they, Mr. Mitchell, myself, and Mr. Keam would share the proceeds of the venture. In this I agreed and furnished them fresh horses, provisions, and a Navajo guide. Stull had previously been in the Pah Ute country. . . . On the fourth evening from here they camped on the brink of a Canon occupied by Pah-Utes, some of whom came into their camp, one of them wearing Meyrick's [the other murdered prospector] shot belt as recognized by Stull. The guide I sent with Stull & Reese had met a Navajo friend whom he induced to accompany them, as he understood the Pah-Ute language and knew the country. During the evening these two Navajoes overheard the Pah-Utes discussing a plot to murder the two Americans and their guide. The Navajoes managed to inform the Americans of this danger, and by wary and prompt movement effected a safe return to this place. [Stephen 1882a]

In this deposition, Stephen tacitly recognized that the Paiute community and its territorial holdings were socially and politically separate from the Navajos and their holdings. One indication of this is his assumption that the Paiutes would have attacked and killed not only the Americans but also the Navajos accompanying them. Moreover, he referred to the area surrounding the Paiutes' canyon as "the Pah-Ute country."

According to San Juan oral history, during the 1880s they

began to have problems with Navajo stock, especially horses, which were permitted to wander into the area between Paiute Canyon and Navajo Canyon and into the Paiute Mesa area east of Paiute Canyon. In an effort to halt these incursions, the San Juans built and maintained a long brush fence from the rim of upper Navajo Canyon all the way to Tall Mountain.

In his autobiography, Son of Old Man Hat told of an 1884 incident that appears to be related to these incursion problems. The date for this incident, estimated by Navajo ethnographers Shepardson and Hammond (1970:31), is significant since the area that includes Paiute Canyon was made reservation land by an Executive Order in the same year (see map 3). In this encounter, a Paiute, whom Son of Old Man Hat named "Nabahadzin," while herding his own horses attempted to prevent Son of Old Man Hat's step-father from herding sheep down into Paiute Canyon. Nabahadzin is the name that Navajo Mountain Navajos use today to refer to the nineteenth century Paiute leader, Napa(')ats. Napa(')ats reportedly told the step-father that the canyon was not for Navajos, and the two men then "quarrelled and cussed each other" (Dyk 1938:111-12).

Several details in this passage from Son of Old Man Hat's narrative corroborate testimony collected from San Juans at Navajo Mountain. The Navajo family was moving from Tall Mountain along "Lower Valley" (perhaps the location now called in English Sage Valley, located on Piute Mesa), to the trail that goes down into Paiute Canyon from Piute Mesa. This was during winter so that few if any Paiutes would actually have been in the wet canyon bottom itself; the Paiutes primarily used the canyon in the summer for farming and in restricted areas for grazing. Although most Paiutes would have probably been in the vicinity of Navajo Mountain rather than at Paiute Canyon, Napa(')ats and members of his family group often wintered on Paiute Mesa, east of Upper Paiute Canyon. According to Paiute oral tradition, during the late nineteenth century the Paiutes occasionally shot at Navajos to prevent them from letting livestock down the trail during the summer when corn was growing in the canyon.

The Moenkopi Wash Land Squeeze, 1880-1900

In the 1880s and early 1890s, Indian Service Inspectors and others made recurrent visits to the Tuba City area to

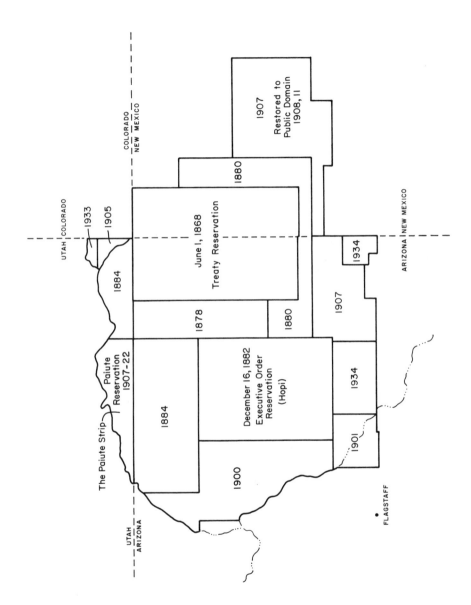

Map 3.　Navajo Reservation Lands

investigate the relations between the Indians and the Mormon settlement. In some instances, documents for this period indicate that Mormons were encroaching on San Juan farms and water resources. As a by-product of their investigations and early attempts to expand the federal government's influence over the local Indians, federal officials also gradually became more aware of the San Juan presence in this southern reach of their occupation zone.

The first of these inspections was conducted by C. H. Howard in 1882. Howard recommended reserving the Moenkopi Wash and surrounding area for the local Indians' exclusive use, a suggestion that would wait some twenty years before being implemented.

In two of his reports he made reference to Paiutes living in the lands north of the 1882 Executive Order Moqui Reservation and west of the Navajos, but he was not aware of their presence in the Moenkopi Wash. For example, in his report to the secretary of the interior, H. M. Teller, dated November 29, 1882, he stated:

> The Pah-Utes come over from Utah, especially renegade criminals, and roam at will. Once establish and mark the boundaries of this new Reservation and the incursions of these outside Indians, most of whom are the wildest and most unmanageable tribes, can be restricted and their bad influence upon the Navajos effectually checked. [Howard 1882]

Ironically, shortly after Howard's reports were completed, Agent Stephen wrote to inform him that Paiutes were farming in the Moenkopi Wash: "We found Oraibis, Navajos, and even a few Pah-Utes farming peaceably together" (Stephen 1882b).

In 1888, Special Indian Agent H. S. Welton visited the Moenkopi area. His reports to the commissioner of Indian affairs gave a much more detailed account of Paiute occupation in that area, one which was also consistent with Mormon accounts from the previous decade:

> On my recent visit to the Oraibi Moen Copie Settlement, I found Oraibis, Pi-utes and Navajoes *in about equal numbers*. But while the two former are inclined to settle down and work the lands, the Navajoes had sheep, goats and horses, and were roveing [sic] in search of feed therefore. Except some 20 or 30 who are settled in the

Moen Copie wash some *12 miles above Moen Copie*. They dam the wash and irrigate therefrom. . . .

I met with these Navajoes telling them they must return to their Reserve or take lands in severalty [these lands then being public domain]. I talked long with them through their headman "musher."

Having now been on the East South and West sides, I think fully half of the Navajoes are off their Reservation. And doubt the ability of their chiefs to get them back. [Welton quoted in Brugge and Correll 1973:191-93; emphasis added]

During this visit, Welton met with the local Paiutes and discovered that they were in danger of losing their farms and water sources in the area to Mormon settlers. In a second report, he recommended they be given allotments at Willow Springs, site of the present day San Juan farms, and another spring on the north side of the Moenkopi Wash. He provided the locations of the allotments, the names of the allottees, and other details:

While executing your orders of March 27th . . . I found in the vicinity of "Moen Copie Wash" some 30 Pai-Utes. Several of whom had in small crops of corn squash melons &c. at small springs claimed by the whites, but upon which were no improvements. Believing these Indians entitled to the lands they were cultivating, I hired conveyance and made *personal inspection* of the springs and the Indians improvements therat [sic] and would respectfully recommend that the following described lands be allotted in severalty as follows viz.

To *Dog-Eye* or *"Whiskers"* (a Pai-Ute Indian and head of a family) the land bounded as follows

Commencing at a point of red sand rock 4 rods NE of the highest and most easterly Spring of the several known on the offical map of 1887 as "Willow Springs" being about 400 yards south of an open fissure between the two highest and most prominent peaks of a Range known as "Echo Reef" and its southern terminus being 13 miles from Tuba City and 4 1/2 miles N.W. of "Moa

Ava" [Moenave] (see map) and running west 160 rods thence south 160 to the place of beginning and containing 160 acres more or less.

To *Kesh-te-lee* or "Big feet" also a male Pai-Ute and head of a family a tract 160 rods square immediately west of and adjoining the lands of Dog-eye or "Whiskers" and containing 160 acres m. or l.

To "*Kie-de-ne-he*" or "Lehi" a Pai-Ute Indian and head of family the lands bounded as follows

Commencing at a point 4 rods N.E. of the most eastern Spring of the Springs known as Pai-Ute or "Hancock" Springs being in a red sand stone bluff fronting south and about midway between Moah Ava and Moen Copie and 4 miles west of Tuba City in Yavapai County Arizona Ter. and runing [sic] West 160 rods thence South 160 rods thence East 160 rods and thence north 160 rods to the place of beginning and containing 160 acres m. or l. [more or less].

To "Ho-hon-ee" male and head of family as above. One hundred and sixty rods square adjoining to and due south of the lands of "Kie-de-ne-he" or "Lehi" and containing 160 acres.

To "Too-wat-sy" (as above) One hundred and sixty 160 rods square adjoining to and due west of the lands of Kie-de-ne-he or "Lehi" and containing 160 acres more or less.

To "Yah-at-ton" (as above) One hundred and sixty rods square and bounded on the north by lands of Too-wat-sy and on the east by lands of Ho-hon-nee.

The first two allotments as above will embrace all the "Willow Springs" and all the land the springs can irrigate.

The last four allotments will form one section and embrace all the water and arable land at "Hancock" or Pai-Ute Springs. I know of no claimant to these Springs. . . .

At "Willow Springs" is no one but the Indians. Several years ago an English Mormon built a small stone hut there stayed one season and abandoned it.

Later a man named *Graves* also built another stone cabin and drove the Indians away but *he* remained only *one* season and left. . . .

The *two* locations if allotted to the Indians will furnish many good *homes* become thriving Indian villages and be unmolested by any present or future settlers.

Should the Oraibis receive their allotments I consider *these* of equal importance. [Welton 1888]

Apparently these allotments were never approved as no other record of them remains. Nonetheless, this report offers clarification on several points. On the one hand, besides the first actual identification and description of the Willow Springs site by name, Welton identified another site in the same area, Paiute or Hancock Springs on the Moenkopi Wash itself. San Juan oral history indicates that there were also other sites that had been utilized by the San Juans in the area. These may have gone unrecorded, either because they were lying fallow and so were unoccupied, or because they had already been appropriated by non-Indian settlers. All local farming sites would have been especially vulnerable to Mormon encroachment because of the Paiutes' common practice of wintering in other regions, as described by Joe Lee (1974:9), and because of fallowing practices.

In addition, although most of the names of Paiute heads of families appear to be in Navajo and thus were probably given to Welton through a Navajo interpretor rather than in Paiute, several of them are traceable to ancestors of living members of the Willow Springs community. "Whiskers" was probably the Willow Springs Paiute farmer, *Machʉkats*. The Navajo name, *Daghaa'i*, like *Machʉkats* refers to his long beard. One of Stewart's 1930s consultants, Priscilla Dutchie, *Machʉkats'* daughter, was identified by his Navajo interpretor as "Many Whiskers' daughter," or *Daghaa'i Bitsi* (1942:239). Twentieth century grazing documents also referred to her by the Navajo name "Dugai Bitsi," "Whisker's Daughter." "Big feet" may perhaps have been *Napa(')ats*, since this is one sense of his name. Although his descendents live in the Navajo Mountain/Paiute Canyon settlement group, *Napa(')ats* was one of those whom Joe Francis, Isabel Kelly's consultant, stated camped near Tuba City in the winter (1964:169). "Kie-de-ne-he" (Navajo *K'aidiniihi*, or "Bad Hips"), is a name still used by contemporary local Navajos to refer to David Lehi (for example, John Sloan, in Bunte and Franklin Fieldnotes, August 10, 1983). *Pak'ai* or Lehi, had arthritic hips and used crutches, according to those who remember him at Willow Springs. "Too-wat-sy" may have been *Tangwats* ("Tooth person"), often pronounced simply as *Tawats*, *Pak'ai*'s son and the father of Alfred Lehi, a twentieth century leader of the San Juan Paiutes. This name may also simply be *toats*, "son" in Paiute, a term which might have referred to almost any male.

Welton's account of the stone houses built near Willow Springs appears to coincide exactly with oral accounts. One of the stone houses remains there today. According to the San Juans, it belonged to a Mormon who made an arrangement to borrow the field from *Machʉkats* and later gave it back to him when he left. The fact that both the Willow and Hancock Springs farming areas were claimed by local Mormons indicates that Mormons were exerting pressure on San Juan resource use in the southern area.

According to Brugge and Correll (1973:187-89), the population of Mormons in the Tuba City colony rose from 27 in 1878 to 230 in 1885. It appears that the Mormons were attempting to expropriate the lands of the local Indian farmers much as they had done in southern Utah and northern Arizona west of the Colorado in the 1850s and 1860s (Stoffle and Dobyns 1982:104-10). This, rather than Navajo or Hopi expansion in the area, may account for the eventual loss of Hancock Springs and such other sites as Moenave and *Akanʉkwit* in present day Tuba City, where Paiutes had previously been farming.

While it seems clear that the Mormons helped to curtail San Juan farming in the Moenkopi Wash area, at least one Navajo traditional account suggests that Navajos' expansion also exerted pressure on local Paiute farmlands in the late nineteenth century. In 1967, ethnohistorian David Brugge interviewed Alvin Nez, a local Navajo man then 77 years old, who stated:

My mother's family first settled at Willow Springs.

That's where they were living when the school started
at Blue Canyon [the agency school founded in the first
decade of this century]. It was a long time ago when
most of the Navajo were back on Black Mesa and only a
few came to Gray Mountain [near the South Rim of the
Grand Canyon]. On the way to Gray Mountain, they
came to a spring where there was enough water to farm.
They cut a few bushes and made a little farm and then
they went on to Gray Mountain. Later they came back
and found two Paiute men there who also claimed the
place and started an argument over the water. Finally
they came to a decision to fight over this piece of land.
There were two guns there. Whoever survived would get
the land. Finally, they threatened to kill the two
Paiutes and shot at them. After shooting at them, the
Paiutes decided they didn't want trouble and they left.
The Navajos have been there ever since. . . . This was
after Fort Sumner, but a long time before Daghaa'
Łichii ["Red Whiskers," Lot Smith] was killed here at
Pasture Canyon. [Brugge 1967:101308]

Nez dated these events between 1868 and 1892, the date of Lot
Smith's death. Since he claimed to have used this site well into
the twentieth century, it may be one of a handful of Navajo
farming sites in the general Willow Springs area that were
noted in twentieth century records.

As they expanded their cattle production, the Mormons also
came into conflict with local Navajo herdsmen. After the
death of Lot Smith, who was according to Joe Lee (1974:14-15,
29) a particularly obnoxious bully against whom the Navajos
had a legitimate grudge, Lieutenant R. E. L. Michie was
dispatched from Fort Wingate to investigate the matter at the
request of the Navajo Agent at Fort Defiance. His report, aside
from his conclusions concerning the murder--that the Navajo
later known as Whiteman Killer killed Lot Smith, but in self-
defense--contained general observations on the local
populations of the three tribes and their resource utilization in
the Tuba City area:

I understand the Mormons have been there some fifteen
years and now number from twenty to thirty families in
all. The Indians, Navajoes, Paiutes, and a few Utes have
been using that section as far as the Little Colorado
River, especially in the summer months, the Navajos in

large numbers bringing in their ponies and sheep for water and grazing purposes; also doing a little farming, in the way of a few patches of corn at different points here and there. The Piutes probably number a hundred, and the Oraibis from fifty to a hundred during the summer months. [Michie to Assistant Adjutant General, July 13, 1892; quoted in Brugge and Correll 1973:193]

Michie's report is interesting in that he described the Paiute farmers as more numerous in the Moenkopi Wash area than Hopis and also implied that the latter only occupied Moenkopi on a seasonal basis even at this late date.

Joe Lee stated that in 1895 he visited "the Piutes who had moved back permanently to their canyon at Boschini [*Ba'-aschini,* the Navajo name for Upper Paiute Canyon, after the Paiute leader of the same name]" (1974:29). By this date, it appears that Mormon settlement may have finally forced some San Juan people to abandon farm sites in the south. Lee mentioned several names of Paiutes then farming in Paiute Canyon. Among those named were individuals, notably Lehi and "Chief Nasja," whom Lee had earlier described as summer farmers of Moenkopi Wash sites and winter grazers in the north. By 1895, these families appear to have restricted their movements to the northern area, joining those Paiutes--including *Muupʉts,* Lee's "Navajo Mountain Nasja"--who had long farmed in Paiute Canyon.

Lee recalled an incident that occurred somewhat later, in 1897, involving "three Piute squaws" who were enlisted by the Tuba City trader, C. H. Algert, to embarrass a rival, Joel McAdams, known as "Higgs" (1974:35). This tends to corroborate San Juan oral accounts that a number of families, particularly those associated with Willow Springs and Cedar Ridge farm sites, continued to reside and farm in the southern area north of the Moenkopi Wash after the 1890s abandonment of sites in the wash itself.

Lee had the opportunity to witness other aspects of San Juan external and internal social relations during the last decade of the nineteenth century. In fact, he worked off and on in the Navajo Mountain and Tuba City area until at least 1938 (1974:60). Lee recalled a vivid example of the San Juan system of social control and collective decision making, which he dated to the 1890s:

While staying at Boschini, Piutes took one of their

tribesmen called Nahphuts [*Napats* is Paiute for "Foot-
Person"] and burned his right foot almost off in a fire.
After that they called him Nahphuts--Burned Foot. It
was strictly a Piute affair; no Navajos were involved.
Nahphuts had a very pretty sister, Atade L'Zuni, with
whom he used to go off into the canyons for days at a
time when she moved her sheep camp. To Piutes, as
with Navajos, incest was a crime as bad or worse than
murder. Suspicious kinsmen caught Nahphuts, seized
him and powwowed all night and next day. Finally
instead of killing him they concluded to punish him by
burning his foot so he could never walk again. [1974:29,
continued on p. 33]

They did this because "his sister said he was so quick she could
never get away from him" (1974:33).

Napa(')ats, the "Nabahadzin" of Son of Old Man Hat's
account (Dyk 1938:111-12), although his name is similar to the
culprit in Lee's story, was not "Naphuts." Rather, there was
another late nineteenth and earlier twentieth century century
individual, a youth named *Napats*. His younger sister was also
called in Navajo *Ateed £izhoni* ("Young Girl"), as Lee described.
Her actual year of birth was 1900, which suggests that Lee's
story occurred somewhat later. Whatever the time period, this
incident illustrates a collective decision making process that is
identical to that which functions in social control cases among
the San Juan people today. However, in this historic case, the
community was still capable of exercising coercive force,
which it can no longer do under the reservation system.

3

SAN JUAN SOCIAL HISTORY, 1900–1970

An Overview, 1900-1970

Changing Land Use Patterns: The Diminishing Tribal Estate

In the first years of the twentieth century, the Western Navajo Reservation and Agency were established (see chap. 4). This new reservation eventually included all of the area occupied by the San Juans. The Executive Order of January 8, 1900, made the land which included Tuba City, Moenkopi, and Willow Springs part of the new reservation.

At the turn of the century, the San Juan Paiutes in the south farmed at Willow Springs and along Cedar Ridge, just north of the present trading post. In the north, they farmed at Paiute Canyon and in selected sites along the San Juan River system as far east as the Oljeto area, at the site now called Paiute Farms. One source of this information is the report of Western Navajo Agency Superintendent Stephen Janus (Janus 1909a).

Although wild plant foods had declined in importance,

families from the south continued to gather seeds in grassy areas near Willow Springs and also regularly travelled to gathering areas near Kayenta, Dennehotso, Page, Lee's Ferry, Bodoway, and even Houserock Valley, west of the Colorado River. The San Juan people farming in the southern area also kept small herds of sheep and goats to supplement their other subsistence activities.

In the north, stock raising had become a much more important activity to the local San Juans both for trade and food production. While they also travelled long distances, for example, south to Shonto and east as far as Skeleton Mesa, the purpose of these trips was to search for good forage and water for their herds rather than to gather seeds. Moreover, the Paiutes of the Navajo Mountain area had begun to rely on trading post provisions, especially flour and coffee, at a much earlier time than Paiutes in the south. These goods were already an important component in the diet at the turn of the century in the north.

Navajos occupied much of the Western Navajo Reservation in the early 1900s, and the Bodoway-Cedar Ridge area was an important winter grazing area. Superintendent Janus (1909b) noted that: "From Cedar Ridge north and west it takes in the best part of the winter range of a large proportion of the Navajo sheep." Nevertheless, compared to only a few decades later, the Navajo population in the Western Navajo Reservation was still relatively small at the beginning of this century and had not yet completed its expansion into areas occupied by Paiutes.

At the turn of the century there were, in addition to the Paiute farming areas noted above, other areas of land that were more or less exclusively used and occupied by Paiutes. Consultants from the south indicated that *Atatsiv*, the sandy plateau just to the north of Tuba City, was one such area. Roger Honahni, a Moenkopi Hopi, stated in a deposition (1978:113) that his grandfather had a sheep camp in the early 1900s between Preston Mesa and Tuba Butte. Preston Mesa represents the northeastern boundary of *Atatsiv*, while Tuba Butte is located near its southern edge. According to a map of the area drawn by Honahni, this sheep camp appears to have been located to the south of, or perhaps just within, the land that Paiutes presently use for grazing. He stated that "in between there [Preston Mesa and Tuba Butte]" the Hopis of this one Hopi sheep camp were "the only people that used to be in that area with the Paiutes and also down here at Small

Mountains [apparently Castle Rocks]. The Navajos was nowhere in the area" (1978:113).

Another, much larger area of land that was principally used by Paiutes at the turn of the century was roughly bounded by Navajo Mountain on the north, Skeleton Mesa on the east, and Shonto and Navajo Canyon on the south. In a 1902 letter, Matthew Murphy, then supervisor of farming and later superintendent of the newly founded Western Navajo Agency, reported that in one of his agricultural districts, the area that included White Mesa (west of Shonto, Arizona) as well as the lands north and west of it, "There are about 50 Navajos and 80 Paiutes in the portion not visited [the northwest], but none of the Navajos are located there. They [the Navajos] spend the greater portion of the year east of Skeleton Mesa" (Murphy 1902).

In the early 1960s, anthropologist Christy Turner studied house types at Navajo Mountain and also drew conclusions concerning the initial dates of Navajo expansion in that region:

> Statements from Paiutes today are positive that there were no Navajo around Navajo Mountain until the early 1900s. The first entry of a Navajo into the community that I discovered took place in the early 1890s. All informants [including Navajos] agree that Paiutes lived *all around* the Mountain. [Turner (c.1962):21; our emphasis]

Turner's conclusions are supported and expanded by the work of two specialists in Western Navajo ethnography. Jerrold Levy (1962:790) dated the first Navajo settlement in the Kaibito Plateau, an area south of Navajo Canyon, as of the 1880s. From information gathered during her fieldwork with the Navajo Mountain Navajo community in 1938, Malcolm Collier dated the first permanent Navajo settlement there from the 1920s and gave 1890 as the entry date of White Man Killer (1966:18). The family of White Man Killer, who fled Tuba City after the death of Lot Smith, founded the locally numerous Salt lineage, the first Navajo group to settle in the region just south of Navajo Mountain.

Each of the San Juan settlement areas lost farms and grazing land to Navajo competitors during this century, yet the extent and timing of Navajo expansion varied considerably with each group. The Paiutes' land in Monument Valley and in Utah around Navajo Mountain was made part of a Paiute reservation by order of the Department of the Interior on October 16, 1907. This order withdrew the land north of the Utah-Arizona line from the 110th parallel in Monument Valley on the east to the Colorado and San Juan Rivers on the west and north for the benefit of the San Juan Paiutes (Larrabee 1907). Pressure on Paiutes' holdings in Monument Valley may have already begun, however.

Western Navajo Superintendent Janus reported encroachment in the Monument Valley-Douglas Mesa area in 1908, but mentioned Anglo miners rather than Navajos as the parties responsible:

> The Oljeto Paiutes [the Douglas Mesa subgroup] are prosperous and needed no assistance but they need protection in the matter of their lands. . . .
>
> In fact most of the springs and sources of water in that country are now taken up for use in connection with placer mining claims. I was told, however, that the parties taking the water had no objection at present to the Indians using the land to grow corn on. [Janus 1909a]

In addition to miners, white traders also took over water sources. Mrs. John Wetherill, whose husband established a trading post at Oljeto, Monument Valley, in 1908, related in her autobiography that during their first summer at Oljeto, "when the summer rains held off, there was more trouble with forty armed Paiutes who attempted to water their horses at the Wetherill's waterhole. . . . The few Navajos around the post looked on with interest, taking no part in the argument" (Gillmor and Wetherill 1934:84).

Another incident recorded by Mrs. Wetherill shortly after the Wetherills moved their store to Kayenta described her intervention in a range dispute between local San Juan Paiutes and Navajos. Mrs. Wetherill served as mediator in this dispute between the Paiute and Navajo communities:

> One dispute concerned a cow that had belonged to a Navajo and had been killed by some Paiute boys.
>
> "She was a young cow--one of the best we had," said the Navajos.

"It was a poor cow--already down; and unable to get up," said the Paiutes.

For three hours, thirty Navajo and Paiutes sat in the living-room at Todanestya, disputing.

"Give me a horse for the cow and we will shake hands," said the Navajo.

"It was not worth a horse," insisted the Paiutes.

At last Asthon Sosi [Mrs. Wetherill], realizing that they were coming to no agreement, made a suggestion [that they examine the bones of the cow: if they were white, the cow was thin; if yellow, the cow had been fat]. . . .

"It is well," agreed the Navajo quickly.

"You need not send for the bones. I will give you the horse," said the father of the Paiute boys. [Gillmor and Wetherill 1934:198-99]

Southwestern archeologist Byron Cummings, familiar with the area from his interviews of local Navajos and Paiutes, recorded that such disputes were the result of Navajo expansion into Paiute range, then still reserved as a Paiute reservation. He stated that in 1908:

There were then a good many Piutes living on what used to be known as the Piute Reservation extending between the San Juan River and the Utah-Arizona boundary line from the 110th meridian westward to the Colorado River. That was known as the Piute Strip and was a Piute Reservation at that time. A good many Piutes were still living on the Strip and there was continual clashing between the Piutes and the Navajos because the Navajos were continually attempting to go in on the Piute territory and crowd out the Piutes. [Cummings c.1950s; also quoted in Euler 1966:96]

By the early 1920s, the Douglas Mesa subgroup of San Juan Paiutes had emigrated to the lands north of the San Juan

River. Western Navajo Agency Superintendent-in-charge A. W. Leech visited Monument Valley and stated "that the Navajoes are the real users of this land and it is reported that they have *driven the Piutes out*" (Leech 1923; our emphasis). In the same vein, Van Valkenburgh noted the Navajos' takeover of Paiute Farms: "Once an old Piute farming area this land at the San Juan River crossing (shown as Navajo Crossing on McComb's map of 1860) was later taken over by the Navajos" (1941:115).

By the 1920s, livestock herding had become for the southern area Paiutes an essential subsistence activity. Nonetheless, their herds remained small, probably fewer than 100 head for the entire settlement group if figures for the 1930s are also representative of this period. During the 1920s and 1930s, and to some extent even in the 1940s, San Juan Paiutes moved with their herds as far north as Lee's Ferry in the land west of Echo Cliffs. Kaibab Paiutes recall visiting San Juan encampments at Cedar Ridge, Bitter Springs, and in other areas along the western flank of Echo Cliffs well into the 1930s. In the Kaibito Plateau, east of Echo Cliffs, southern area families occasionally grazed their herds as far north as Coppermine and Kaibito in the 1920s.

Following the 1920s, the southern area San Juan people found themselves increasingly less able to range freely with their herds over lands they had formerly used. By the 1940s, their herds grazed mainly in the *Atatsiv* area, between the Echo Cliffs and Preston Mesa, and as far north as Gap and Crooked Ridge.

Beginning in the late 1930s, the Western Navajo Agency began to keep livestock records, which can now be used to compare the size of the San Juan and Navajo herds. The 1937 records for the region that included the southern area San Juan Paiutes indicate that their herds were considerably smaller than those of many of their Navajo neighbors. With these relatively small herds the San Juan people were simply not able to compete successfully for range.

Livestock numbers were given in terms of the number of sheep units in each individual livestock owner's herd. One adult sheep or goat is counted as one sheep unit, while each adult cow is four sheep units, and each adult horse equals five sheep units. The number of sheep units given did not usually include immature animals, nor did it indicate which individual owners herded their livestock together or what proportion of the general population owned livestock. Nevertheless, these records are quite useful for some comparative purposes.

In 1937, the livestock census for the grazing district that includes Willow Springs and *Atatsiv*, District 3, recorded the following information: 445 Navajo livestock owners with 56,514 sheep units, for an average number of 133 sheep units per owner; 36 Hopis with 2609 sheep units, for an average of 72.47 sheep units; and 8 southern area San Juan Paiutes with 210 sheep units, for an average of only 26.25 sheep units (USDA Soil Conservation Service 1940a). In table 4, "Southern Area San Juan Paiute Grazing Records," we summarize the information for 1937 as well as data on subsequent changes in ownership (U.S. BIA Navajo Agency 1937-66). Each southern area San Juan Paiute for whom we have 1937 livestock records is listed along with the number of sheep units the individual was permitted and the number of actual sheep and horses counted in 1937. We note on this table the status of individual grazing permits for the 1950s and 1960s when that documentation exists. This latter information, although incomplete, illustrates what appears to be a continued trend of livestock reduction for San Juan Paiutes.

One might conclude from the limited number of livestock, especially sheep, owned by southern area San Juan Paiutes that Navajo competition had reduced available range, thereby reducing San Juan herds through attrition. The differences between livestock ownership in all three tribes may also simply represent culturally influenced economic preferences. Some Navajos may have taken sheep herding beyond the level of subsistence because livestock were valued for other purposes-- as a symbol of wealth and social prestige, as producers of wool for weaving and for trade, and as a standard of payment for bridewealth and other purposes. Nonsubsistence uses for sheep and goats may simply have been irrelevant for the Paiutes. Interestingly, table 4 demonstrates that San Juan people sometimes kept several horses even when they kept no sheep. While both conclusions are correct to some degree, and probably involve processes that may actually have complemented each other, demographic evidence from this period strongly suggests the presence of increased nutritional stress among the San Juans. This in turn leads to the conclusion that Paiutes had little choice in the matter of herd size.

Testimony provided by Navajos in the context of the ongoing Navajo-Hopi land dispute may help to reconstruct in a partial way the Navajos' regional land use in the southern area during the 1930s. The testimony of two Navajos, Fred Morez

Table 4: Southern Area San Juan Paiute Records

NAME	1937			1950s to 1960s
	Sheep Units*	Sheep	Horses	
Alfred Lehi	62	42	4	1965 gift to Grace Lehi
Dugai Bitsi (Priscilla Dutchie)	10	5	1	same in 1954; deceased (1960s)
Gus Sanni	39	39		deceased (1941); permit cancelled
Joe Norman	30		6	sold 1968
Coni Yazzi	20		4	cancelled 1946(?)
Chee Tonni	15		3	same in 1954; to daughter (1960s)?
Chester Chelester	4	4		same in 1954
Simon Weepea	30		6	deceased
TOTAL	210	90	24	
Paiute Average	26.25			
Navajo Total (District 3),	56,514			
Navajo Average	133.0			
Hopi Total (District 3)	2609			
Hopi Average	72.47			

* One sheep unit equals one adult sheep or goat;
five sheep units equals one adult horse.

(1982) and Henry Billy (1983), indicated that 1930s Navajo livestock movements tended to skirt the area east of Echo Cliffs and south of Gap where Paiutes mainly grazed. Although they described a pattern of seasonal movement in which Navajos, often with large herds, moved from summer grazing areas near Preston Mesa and Red Lake to winter grazing by Bodoway and Cedar Ridge, the Navajo herders apparently only passed through the northern edge of Paiute-occupied land east of Echo Cliffs on their way through the Gap pass. The only Navajos whom they mentioned as having hogans in this area were living right within the pass itself.

Fred Morez (1982:86-88) also located a 1930s Navajo farming site near the present day Paiute Willow Springs farming area. Henry Billy located three 1934-period Navajo farms at Willow Creek and the springs above it. The closest of these farms would have been roughly a mile from the Paiutes' fields towards the south or southwest. These may or may not have been sites where Paiutes once farmed. When he was asked to name more Navajos farming locally, Billy responded: "From here onwards [to the north], only the Paiutes planted there. This was at the end of the land area" (1983:297). This statement suggests that Billy considered there to have been some kind of customary boundary between the two groups' land use areas there.

Sometime in the late 1930s, the southern area Paiutes lost their fields at Cedar Ridge to Navajos and began farming exclusively at Willow Springs. Increased farming may have exacerbated erosion at Willow Springs, which had already begun in the 1920s. To make matters worse, the fields below the main terrace sustained serious erosion in the late 1930s and had to be abandoned. This loss of arable land may help explain the subsequent out-migration of several southern area families to Kaibab and Utah Paiute communities in the early 1940s.

Since 1940, southern area residents have experienced no loss of farming land. On the other hand, some of the grazing land and most of the grazing permits that they held in the 1930s have been lost. (See table 4 for a summary of changes in southern area San Juan grazing permits during the 1950s and 1960s.) In a surprising turn of events, the pressure on southern range appears to have begun easing up slightly in recent years, as many Navajos who formerly grazed in the area have come to prefer living and working in nearby Tuba City.

In the Navajo Mountain-Paiute Canyon area, Navajo

settlement became a serious factor in the 1920s. Although San Juan Paiutes with large herds still moved as far south as Shonto during some summers in the 1920s, the increasing Navajo population closed off this route by the end of that decade. Afterwards, the Navajo population at Navajo Mountain and Paiute Canyon began to increase more rapidly, putting pressure on Paiutes' farming and grazing land. In 1938, for example, Collier counted 135 Navajos (1966:21), while the Paiute population in the northern area was 42 in the previous year (Western Navajo Reservation Indian Census Rolls, 1937; Bunte and Franklin Fieldnotes, 1982 and 1983).

These Paiutes also had herds half the size of their Navajo neighbors'. Table 5, "Northern Area San Juan Paiute Grazing Records," presents comparative grazing data for Navajo Mountain based on the local 1937 livestock census (USDA Soil Conservation Service 1940b), as well as data on subsequent changes in Paiute ownership (U.S. BIA Navajo Agency 1937-1968). In 1937, while the Navajos in District Two, the grazing district that includes Navajo Mountain and Paiute Canyon, had an average of 109.65 sheep units, San Juan Paiutes in that area had on the average only 58 sheep units. This demonstrates that the Paiutes' herds were not as large as those of local Navajos, while a comparison of tables 4 and 5 corroborates San Juan consultants' statements that livestock herding, including cattle, was more important among northern area San Juans than it was in the southern area.

The Navajo resource pressure in the 1930s was limited almost entirely to the area south of the Arizona-Utah line. Collier described the Navajo community as "bounded on the north by Navajo Mountain, on the south and west by Navajo Canyon and on the east by Paiute Canyon" (1966:17). Her map of the area, which located Navajo winter and summer dwellings for 1938, confirms this (1966:15-16). Only one hogan was located north of the line and according to the scale of her map it must have been barely one mile north.

Although northern area Paiutes had some dry farming areas elsewhere, in the 1930s most farming took place in Upper Paiute Canyon. By this decade, the San Juans' farming area in the canyon consisted primarily of three sites. The most southerly of the field areas was in a side canyon while the other two were located a short distance north in the main canyon on the eastern side of Paiute Creek, the main canyon stream. All the San Juan field areas were irrigated from spring flow.

Table 5: Northern Area San Juan Paiute Grazing Records

NAME	1937 Sheep Units*	Sheep	Cattle	Horses	1950s to 1960s
Lester Willetson	162	92	5	10	sold remaining 101 sheep units (1955)
George Willetson	10			2	deceased (1950s)
Dan Willetson	10			2	sold (1965)
C. Lehi (trust)	139	110	1	5	retained (1960s)
Unap	122	66	4	8	sold (1954)
Sid and Merci Whiskers	99	25	6	10	retained (1960s)
Ephraim Whiskers	8	13		3	deceased (1950s)
Dora Nelson	32	17		3	deceased (1950s)
Willie Lehi	25			5	sold (1957)
Redshirt's Mo.	40	30		2	deceased(?)
Redshirt Nelson	5			1	deceased (1950s)
Toby Owl	25			5	retained (1960s)
TOTAL	697	353	16	56	
Paiute Average	58.0				
Navajo Total (District 2)	27,524				
Navajo Average	109.65				

* One sheep unit equals one adult sheep or goat;
four sheep units equals one adult cow;
five sheep units equals one adult horse.

By the 1930s, some Navajos had fields upstream, or south, of the San Juan Paiute area. Although one or two Paiutes also had fields in this more southern section of the canyon, the area was primarily farmed by Navajos who may have begun farming there as early as the 1920s. However, most of this area was without irrigation until the mid-1930s, according to San Juan consultants, limiting the use that Navajos could make of it.

In 1935, the USDA Soil Conservation Service constructed irrigation works in this section as part of the Paiute Canyon Demonstration Project, often simply referred to as the Paiute Demonstration Project:

> There is a rubble-masonry diversion dam in Piute Creek built through the aid of the Indian Irrigation Service which enables the Navajos to use the normal flow of the creek. The water is conveyed by ditches over a distance of about one mile where it is used for irrigation. . . . The Indians are diverting an additionnal 0.5 c.f.s. from the creek at a point some distance above the present diversion, and it is proposed to construct a diversion weir at this point. There are several springs which are supplying an estimated supply of one hundred gallons a minute. It is proposed to develop these springs and utilize the water for irrigation purposes. [USDA Soil Conservation Service 1935:93]

According to San Juan consultants, Soil Conservation Service engineers also helped Indians open dry farm plots in the area immediately north or downstream of the Paiute farming area as a part of the Paiute Demonstration Project. A small number of Paiute fields existed in this area before 1935, but it is not clear whether Navajos had farmed this area earlier. In 1938, Collier reported a case where a Navajo took over a field in this area which had belonged to *Muuputs*: "Owl sold trees [apricot or peach] to Zoli's wife and Zoli took the whole field" (Fieldnotes, 1938; in Navajo Tribe 1985c, exhibit A, p. 4).

After the 1930s, northern area Paiutes also lost their grazing land in Arizona. More recently, Navajos have begun to expand on the Utah side, in the old Paiute Strip reservation. The emigration of a number of Paiutes from the region after the 1940s appears to be a consequence of this land loss, although off-reservation wage labor was also a factor.

Resource competition is still a reality in the northern area. In 1982, the northern settlement group prevented a Navajo family from taking over the field of Grace Nelson shortly after her death, but only with considerable effort.

The history of resource loss has taken a different course in each of the three areas. In the Douglas Mesa-Oljeto area of Monument Valley, the Paiutes were forced to emigrate by the early 1920s. By the 1940s, the San Juan people living in the southern area had already lost most of what they were going to lose. Since that time, the pressure on their resources has eased off so that they have managed to keep Willow Springs farm land and part of their *Atatsiv* range. In the Navajo Mountain-Paiute Canyon area, Navajo settlement began in the 1920s. Real pressure on both the grazing and farming resources of the Paiutes did not begin in earnest until the 1930s. Since the 1940s, resource pressure has continued unabated and is still a problem for the San Juan people there today.

Decision Making and Leadership

Twentieth century San Juan Paiutes have had to adjust to economic and political circumstances that are very different from those of the nineteenth century. Despite changes in their way of life, important elements of nineteenth century internal social and political organization have persisted.

During the twentieth century, members of the San Juan Southern Paiute Tribe have continued to act as a group in many economic, political, and social matters. Community activities resulted from consensual decisions reached at either the local or tribal level. Such decisions dealt with social control, social gatherings, seasonal movements, and, of special import, control of grazing and farming land. Although San Juan consultants tend to stress events that were out of the ordinary and therefore especially memorable to the community, other accounts indicate that the same consensus decision-making processes were applied in more mundane community affairs as well.

Elder kin played a consistently prominent role in consensus decision making. In case after case, elders were seen discussing problems, instructing other San Juan people, and influencing decision making at every level of community organization from the family to the tribe.

In addition to the general duties shared by all elders, chief elders had a specific constellation of duties and powers very similar to those of their counterparts in the past century. The chief elder's most prominent capacity was to act as a specialist in foreign affairs. Throughout the present century, it has been chief elders who have most frequently dealt with Anglos and other Indian groups. Consultants' accounts of twentieth century San Juan leadership also focus on aspects of leadership that are perhaps less obvious to outsiders, including the chief elder's influence in internal tribal affairs as well as the office's special relationship with the supernatural.

Table 6: San Juan Twentieth Century Chief Elders

Name	Location	Level	Decades
Pakai/David Lehi	South	Tribal and Local	1880?-1930
Machʉkats/ Many Whiskers	South	Local	1880s-1910?
Mʉʉpʉts/Ruben Owl/*Naa(n)cha*	North	Local	1880?-1920
Kavii/Paiute Dick	North	Local	1920-1934
Kainap/Alfred Lehi	South	Tribal and Local	1930?-1969
Muvwira'ats/ Lester Willetson	North	Local	1940-1960s

Table 6, "San Juan Twentieth Century Chief Elders," presents the sequence of chief elders in the twentieth century. In this table, the heading "location" refers to primary settlement affiliation. Under the heading "level" we indicate whether a leader was a tribal-level chief elder or only represented one local settlement. As northern and southern areas became more autonomous in the twentieth century, the office of local chief elder emerged to deal with local needs. The heading "decades" indicates the time periods during which the chief elder is known to have exercised leadership, although these dates are generally approximations.

The Formation of Ambilineal Descent Groups

Leadership and decision making have remained surprisingly consistent throughout the twentieth century, and throughout earlier history. This same consistency, however, does not hold for all aspects of sociopolitical organization. Today's landholding ambilineages did not exist until the twentieth century. In this chapter, we describe the gradual coalescence of separate consanguineal groups into descent groups. The two genealogical charts given in figures 1, "Historical Genealogy, Northern Area," and 2, "Historical Genealogy, Southern Area," trace the genealogical connections among modern San Juan descent groups and between these groups and important historic ancestors, many of whom are remembered as nineteenth century leaders.

In general, when land becomes scarce, landholding ambilineages are apt to emerge from multilineal systems, that is, from systems with unrestricted bilateral descent (Otterbein 1964). Such a process apparently underlay the San Juans' development of ambilineal descent groups during the present century. Since land, especially farm land, had become relatively scarce, kin groups gradually consolidated their hold over the dwindling farm land and began to regulate its inheritance carefully. Young couples were no longer free to open up fields in any farming area but rather had to demonstrate their right to it by virtue of one spouse's membership in the appropriate ambilineage. The couple was expected to choose to farm the land held by either the husband's or the wife's ambilineage and reside with that group. Some flexibility was inherent in the system. For example, a husband who decided to farm at his wife's ambilineage's holdings could later return to his own (or the reverse, in his wife's case) and their children could apparently choose to belong to either parent's ambilineage. Nevertheless, twentieth century San Juans had much less choice than their ancestors did in the nineteenth century.

In the Navajo Mountain-Paiute Canyon local community, we can trace the development of three ambilineages throughout

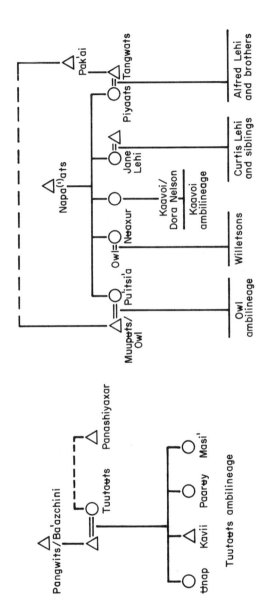

Figure 1. Historical Genealogy, Northern Area

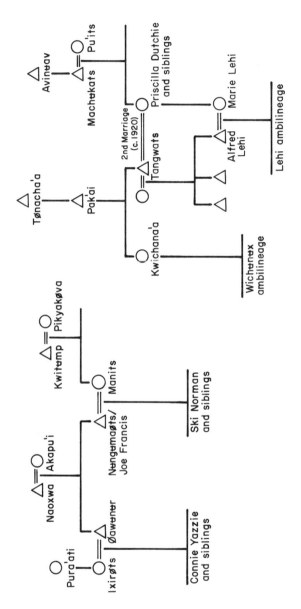

Figure 2.   Historical Genealogy, Southern Area

most of the twentieth century. The *Tuutaħts* group, the *Kaavoi* or Nelson group, and the *Muupħts* or Owl group had all developed ambilineal, corporate properties by the late 1920s. All are traceable to consanguineal groups that existed prior to the turn of the century (see figure 1). The *Kaavoi* and *Muupħts* groups were collaterally related kin groups, through *Muupħts*' marriage to Dora Nelson's maternal aunt, one of *Napa(')ats*' daughters.

Several key marriages between the *Tuutaħts* group and the two other ambilineages have taken place since the 1940s. In particular, two of *Muupħts*' grandsons married into the *Tuutaħts* ambilineage. One married a daughter of *Paarħy* and the other married a grandaughter of *Ħnap*. Moreover, two sons of *Masi'* married women of the *Kaavoi* ambilineage.

Another major reorganization took place when a series of deaths during the 1930s and 1940s in the *Kaavoi* ambilineage left virtually no adult household heads.

At this point, around 1950, all three ambilineages were in a position to consolidate as one. Instead, however, shifts in membership took place, using the possibilities inherent in the flexible ambilineage structure. Despite considerable intermarriage and the breakup of the Nelson ambilineage as a cohesive residential group, there are today still three separate, ambilineally-held sections of farm land in the Paiute area of Paiute Canyon, representing the descendents of *Tuutaħts*, Dora Nelson, and Owl.

The modern situation appears to have resulted from two interrelated processes. On the one hand, a true merger can only take place between unrelated ambilineages. Only in such a case can intermarriages occur, because of Paiutes' incest prohibitions. When members of two groups can intermarry, the children will have rights to use the land of either ambilineage, opening up the possibility for a later merger. On the other hand, ambilineages that are already related to each other through descent from a common ancestor or a set of siblings cannot intermarry. Once separate, they tend to become more rather than less autonomous.

In the northern community, successive generations of intermarriage between unrelated members of the *Muupħts* and *Tuutaħts* ambilineages have brought the two groups together from the standpoint of consanguineal kinship. Nevertheless, one line of descendents from these intermarriages, *Paarħy*'s, is now farming the *Muupħts* land area, while another line of descendents, *Ħnap*'s, remains farming the *Tuutaħts* fields.

Moreover, even the Nelson land area is still held as a collective farming area by Dora Nelson's descendents, some of whom are products of a marriage between members of the *Kaavoi*/Nelson and *Tuutaʉts* ambilineages (see figure 6, chap. 6).

Turning to the south, as figure 2 illustrates, there were three major groups of consanguineal kin at the turn of the century. These were: Joe Francis/*Nʉngwʉmaøts*, his brother *Øawʉnʉr*, and their descendents; *Pak'ai* and his descendents; and *Machʉkats* and his descendents. These consanguineal lines were apparently not yet corporate, landholding groups.

During the first few decades of this century, San Juans in the south farmed at Cedar Ridge, Willow Springs, and a number of other areas. *Pak'ai*, for example, farmed at Cedar Ridge, at a small spring on the northern edge of Willow Springs, as well as elsewhere. The farming land at Willow Springs was apparently not divided up into separate sections by the kin groups at this time. Rather, it appears that it was still possible for anyone to open up new fields.

By the 1940s, however, scarcity of land had become a problem for southern area San Juan Paiutes since the main terrace at Willow Springs was the only irrigated farming area in useable condition. Predictably, this led to the emergence of landholding ambilineages similar to those in the north. Following a series of intermarriages between the major consanguineal lines and population losses in the 1930s and 1940s, most of the southern area San Juan people were consanguineally related by the 1940s. Two collateral ambilineages emerged. By 1950, the land area at Willow Springs was divided between the ambilineal descendents of Alfred Lehi and those of *Wichʉnʉx*, both grandchildren of *Pak'ai*. These two ambilineages have retained possession of their respective sections of Willow Springs and are presently still farming them.

1900-1920

The first two decades of this century saw more official interest in the San Juan Paiutes than any other decade before or after. As a result, federal records give a reasonably complete picture of the San Juans at the beginning of the century.

Soon after the Departmental Order for the San Juan Paiute Reservation was signed in 1907, Western Navajo Superintendent Stephen Janus was asked to report on the condition of the San Juan people. Although his visits to the three major settlements were brief, he managed to observe and comment on both economic and political activities:

I have the honor to report that I have traveled over between 500 and 600 miles of the roughest, driest, and most inaccessible country I ever saw. . . . I have gone where they live, personally interviewed the San Juan Piutes, and taken an actual census of them.

There are 116 individuals in this band: 55 males and 61 females. Of these 30 are adult males and 28 adult females. . . .

These Indians are divided into three groups: Cedar Ridge with 11 families and 40 Indians; Piute Canon with 11 families and 42 Indians; Oljeto with 12 families and 34 Indians.

The Cedar Ridge Indians are 30 miles from here on the road to Lee's Ferry. It is here that David Lehigh [Lehi]--Bahkai [*Pak'ai*]--the accredited chief of all three divisions is at present living. Willow Springs was his old home and there are still two families of his immediate following living there.

The Piute Canon division is about 90 miles north almost at the base of Navajo Mt. and east of it. And I think without doubt in Arizona, and therefor on this reservation.

The Oljeto division is about 30 miles north of the line in Utah, west of the 110th Meridian south of the San Juan River and north of the Arizona line. This is the tract that Inspector Churchill in his report of August 30, 1907, recommended be withdrawn from settlement and entry. This is the most prosperous division of the Piutes. They are two days traveling over the roughest kind of trails from the Piute Canon group of which they were a few years since a part.

It will be seen from the above that the three groups of Piutes are widely separated and it is this fact that has caused delay and difficulty in obtaining any definite information.

The Cedar Ridge band live both at Cedar Ridge and Willow Springs, though latterly most have lived at Cedar Ridge. The families remaining at Willow Springs doing so for the purpose of holding the permanent water, about ten acres of irrigable land and some few peach trees. The flow of the spring here to which the Piutes have the undisputed right is ten (10) gallons per minute. This spring flows directly out of the solid rock high up above the land to be irrigated. . . .

This little holding of the Paiutes is very valuable and necessary to them as the climate is warm enough to permit them raising melons and beans, and always a sure, though under present circumstances, not a large crop of corn. At Cedar Ridge they have to depend on rains which do not always come and besides being nearly 2000 ft higher late and early frosts are the rule.

There are two small stone houses at Willow Springs but these are not occupied except in summer. In winter all the Piutes of this band live at Cedar Ridge, principally on account of the abundance of fuel and water during the winter months, and feed for their ponies.

At Cedar Ridge I counted 55 goats, 11 ponies, and 3 burros, and the Willow Springs families have a small band of goats, 2 ponies and a few burros. Where the flocks cannot be seen it is difficult to get the number as all these Indians are superstitious about counting them.

This band raised a fine crop of corn at Cedar Ridge during the past season, and they derive a small revenue from the manufacture of baskets. They trade corn to the Navajo for mutton.

Most of the year water is very scarce at Cedar Ridge. There are two small springs, each a mile or more from their fields. . . . [Joe Francis's daughter, who was raised here, told us that Paiutes carried water from these springs to their gardens in antelope stomachs.]

Cedar Ridge is on the edge of an extensive winter range [towards Bodoway and the Colorado River] where a great many of the Navajos now have their flocks. In summer, there is no water and they scatter all over the reservation.

The Piutes here live in open hogans and seem to be little troubled with the cold which is sometimes very severe. About seven years ago they tell me they were inflicted with some kind of epidemic during which a large number of them died. Up to that time they had extensive flocks but those were used up at that time in ministering to the sick. The question of providing them with the nucleus of a new flock will be taken up further on. [Janus 1909a]

Janus went on to say of the "Piute Canon Piutes" that he had counted only nine goats and one sheep among them. This small number of livestock probably reflects the Paiutes' reluctance to admit to owning animals that Janus did not personally see, as he himself noted in the south. Most animals were herded above on the plateaus bordering both sides of the canyon, rather than in the canyon itself.

In this report, Janus also mentioned that erosion in Paiute Canyon, apparently caused by "a waterspout" about seven years previous to his visit, had ruined the floor of the canyon for farming. He stated:

These Piutes cultivate a few small patches of corn which they irrigate from a little stream that comes down from springs in a side canon. They can no longer get water from the main stream as the wash is too deep and the side washes too numerous to allow of their going back far enough to get water up on the land.

It is interesting that the superintendent spoke as though the Paiutes had previously been able to use the main stream of the canyon for irrigation. Certainly, the canyon could have supported a larger number of people if that flow were utilized, as is witnessed by the larger area under cultivation since the government constructed more advanced irrigation works in the 1930s. The migration of a number of San Juans from the Tuba City area to Paiute Canyon during the latter part of the

nineteenth century may have overtaxed the farm lands at
Paiute Canyon.

If Paiutes shortened or eliminated the normal fallow period
so that more people could farm the land, this may have caused
the erosion in Paiute Canyon. According to Janus, it was this
erosion that led a number of the Paiute Canyon San Juans to
settle at Oljeto and Douglas Mesa around the turn of the
century. Mormon farmers' expansion in the Tuba City area
during the nineteenth century may have helped bring about the
partial destruction of one of the San Juans' most productive
farming areas, Upper Paiute Canyon, far to the north, as well
as the subsequent split in the northern settlement.

In addition to his description of economic conditions, Janus
recorded an interesting point with regard to political relations
between the Paiute Canyon and Willow Springs/Cedar Ridge
groups:

> Most of the Piute Canon Piutes move over near the base
> of Navajo Mt. in the winter as there is grass there.
> They use the canon in summer to raise corn and melons.
> Chief Lehi [David Lehi/*Pak'ai*] said they would move
> over to Cedar Ridge if he told them to. And if they
> would their chances of making a better living would be
> much better. Not even an Indian could climb up and
> down the walls of the almost worthless canon they live
> in and make a good living. Both they and Lehi were
> favorably impressed with the idea of holding a flock of
> sheep in the Cedar Ridge country. It is my opinion that
> these Indians would be better off almost anywhere else.

Pak'ai probably lacked the formal authority to command such a
move. The reported statement more likely reflected faith in
his own prestige and ability to persuade. More important is
the superintendent's recognition that all three settlement
groups were politically united, with one leader.

Another contemporary BIA account referred to the local
leadership of the Paiute Canyon subgroup. Navajo Agent John
Hunter wrote in 1908 that there were 60 Paiutes living in
Paiute Canyon, with sheep, horses, cattle, corn, pumpkins, and
melons. He then added: "Nasja [the Navajo translation of
Muuputs, "Owl"] is the head Pahute in Pahute Canyon; they
recognize the authority of the United States and trade at Bluff
and Oljatoh, Utah, and Red Lake, Arizona" (Letterbooks of the
Navajo Agents; quoted in Shepardson and Hammond 1970:34).

Oral historical accounts indicate that San Juan chief elders were expected to deal expertly with a broad range of matters from the economic and political to the religious. As economic brokers for the group, San Juan chief elders would arrange economic transactions with outsiders for the whole group. *Muupнts*, for example, in addition to being the political spokesperson for the Navajo Mountain/Paiute Canyon Paiutes, made trips during the first decade of the twentieth century to Richfield, Utah, to trade horses for other stock and for trade goods.

The local chief elder also set up horse races with the Paiutes' Navajo neighbors. Paiutes in the north not only traded horses--many were said to have had sizable horse herds at this time--they were also fond of racing them and gambling on the outcome. Northern area San Juans have pointed out several racetrack sites in the Navajo Mountain area that were used during the first half of this century. Local chief elders, during the first part of the century *Muupнts* and then *Kavii*, were expected to travel to the Navajos and arrange intertribal races.

Pak'ai, as Janus noted, had influence over all three local Paiute communities and thus was a tribal chief elder. Interestingly, present day San Juan oral tradition recalls best the sacred features of *Pak'ai*'s leadership, rather than any particular economic or political activities. This seems to suggest that the leader's relationship with the supernatural may have greater symbolic importance for the San Juan people than leadership in secular matters.

The story of *Pak'ai*'s sacred visions, which appear to have taken place in the late nineteenth or perhaps early twentieth century, is known to many southern area San Juan Paiutes today. The version of the story given below was related by Marie Lehi, the widow of *Pak'ai*'s grandson, Alfred Lehi, and was translated by her granddaughter:

Pak'ai was called Lehi; he was visited by an angel or by *Shнnangwav* [the Paiute deity, see chap. 5]. It happened at Pasture Canyon. *Pak'ai* died and he seen that kind, then he rise again. His relatives were crying, he could see all of them. Suddenly, he was telling, he saw Hell and he was right in the middle of Heaven, too. He knew there was really Heaven, too. He really knew there was Christ and Calvary, they call it, was on the right side. On the left side there was an apple tree.

The apple tree was real great big. If he eats one of the fruits of the tree, he's going into the land where he's never going to return, he's never going to come back to earth. That's what he was told. He was told it wasn't time for him to come, to die yet. He was told to turn back again, to go back to his body or his home. So he was returned, and he came back to life, early in the morning, he said. As he was getting back to his body, his body was really stinky, he didn't want to get back into his body, he didn't want to, he said. His body was scary-looking. He died in the evening or afternoon. He came back to life in the early morning. And as he was getting back to it, his body was stinky. Even though, he got into his body and he could feel some aching. His body was aching, he said. He was sick when he died. For sure, he died over there. His time was up then. [Bunte and Franklin Fieldnotes, July 24, 1981]

Speaking of the same experience on another occasion, Marie Lehi went into more detail about other things *Pak'ai* saw in the next world:

Pak'ai said: They're tracks, sheep tracks, cattle tracks, people tracks, going to death, but none coming back. There's tracks one way, all kinds of dog tracks, cat tracks. There was just a whole bunch of tracks, he said. That's what he said. He told a story like that. He could hear voices, songs. These were the songs he heard [the story-teller sings]:

> *Shakanivwu, shakanivwu ichuxai*
> *Shakanivwu, shakanivwu ichuxai*
> [This white dwelling, this white dwelling, too]

There were all kinds of Indian up there, all nationalities. They were round-dancing. They were far away. He was watching them.

Only chief elders appear to experience direct contacts with divinity. Such stories indicate the special role that leaders like *Pak'ai* played as mediators between the tribe and the sacred realm. *Pak'ai* went to heaven and was sent back to earth to continue living, although presumably now with a spiritual sanction to continue his leadership.

From a comparative viewpoint, *Pak'ai*'s vision displayed a syncretism characteristic of the visions of other nineteenth century Indians who spoke of travelling to the other world during an illness. Handsome Lake, Black Elk, Wodziwob, Wovoka, to name a few, all had religious visions during a high fever. In fact, *Pak'ai*'s experience strikingly resembles the Northern Paiute Wovoka's Ghost Dance vision (Hittman 1973). While this suggests that *Pak'ai* had contact with the Ghost Dance movement, the existence of such stories also indicates how for the San Juan Paiutes, as for other groups, this type of supernatural experience was an important component of secular leadership.

Another story told about *Pak'ai* involved an angel who accompanied him on trips. This angel apparently wore sandals even when it snowed and never needed to eat. Marie Lehi told us: "Every time when they ask him to eat, he say he's already eaten or he's already full" (Bunte and Franklin Fieldnotes, July 24, 1981). According to one story, the angel gave a cow and a bull to *Pak'ai*, the first cattle owned by the San Juans.

These accounts of one San Juan leader's visionary experiences help us understand the awe and respect San Juans felt for their chief elders and may explain their willingness to listen to and follow them in the absence of strong coercive power. In telling us her life story, Marie Lehi recounted that when she was born at Pasture Canyon early in this century, her mother was going to throw her into the water to drown her. *Pak'ai*, however, "said not to do that." According to Mrs. Lehi, it was only *Pak'ai*'s moral influence in the community that saved her life (Bunte and Franklin Fieldnotes, July 24, 1981).

Patterns of social interaction among members at the tribal and subtribal level are equally important for understanding the San Juan Paiute community at this time. In the fall, the tribe continued to camp together for pine nut gathering. Visiting and round-dancing, although not necessarily bringing the entire tribe together at one time, also offered occasions for social interaction and cooperation between members of different San Juan settlement communities. It was through such social and economic activities that old ties were maintained, marriages arranged, and so forth. Marie Dutchie from the southern area settlement met her husband-to-be, Alfred Lehi, who had been raised at Navajo Mountain, when he was visiting the southern area for a round-dance. Her mother eventually arranged for Marie to marry him (Jake, James, and Bunte 1983).

By the beginning of the twentieth century, local areas had also developed an independent community life. In each settlement, San Juan people got together at their farming areas every summer to plant and to harvest, providing the occasion for cooperative labor as well as purely social visiting. Moreover, work with San Juan consultants in identifying past residence sites indicates that from at least 1910, households in both the northern and southern areas tended to camp as one community in winter camping areas.

In the Navajo Mountain region, San Juan Paiutes camped most winters during the second decade of the century in a small area northeast of Navajo Mountain. The families of *Muuputs*, *Kaavoi*, and *Tangwats* (*Pak'ai*'s son), all consanguineally related, camped in separate households with separate structures, yet all were located within 50 yards of each other. Less than a half a mile away, located in two other camps, lived the households of the Cantsees, Willetsons, and Curtis Lehi's family.

These latter households ceased to exist as separate household groups by the early 1930s. Either they left the tribe, as the Cantsees did, to move with the Monument Valley Paiutes to Allen Canyon, or they were incorporated by marriage into one of the main ambilineages. Lester Willetson and Curtis Lehi both married women from the *Tuutauts* ambilineage and resided afterward with that group.

The remaining residential cluster was the *Tuutauts* group. During the teens, the *Tuutauts* group of families spent some winters in the grazing area north of Navajo Mountain apart from the other northern area San Juans. According to modern San Juan testimony, since this group owned the most sheep and goats, lack of sufficient forage prevented them from spending every winter in close proximity to other San Juan camps. Yet even this group camped some of the winters between 1910 and 1920 in the settlement cluster with the other San Juan households.

In this early period, the households living together in winter camps at Navajo Mountain constructed rectangular winter houses of large timbers, characterized by an unusual roof shape, a horizontal ridge pole with gabled roof timbers. According to Stewart (1942:257), this gabled house type was found only among the San Juans and one Ute group.

There was a similar pattern of winter camp clustering in the southern area, where Paiutes often selected areas for winter settlements that were at a distance from their present land area at *Atatsiv* and Willow Springs, perhaps because they had wider options available to them than did the northern area San Juans.

Because of this, we were able to travel with consultants to only one southern area winter settlement, located on *Atatsiv* and occupied around 1917. However, it exhibited the same clustering pattern found in the northern area, being composed of at least three different house sites occupied by members of *Machɨkats'* and Joe Francis' consanguineal kin. The entire settlement was less than one half mile wide.

Near the end of this period, an event of world-wide significance also touched the San Juan Paiute community--the 1918 influenza epidemic. Although the morbidity and mortality rates of this epidemic were high all over the world, certain communities and regions tended to be particularly hard hit (Crosby 1976). High death rates were found primarily in isolated areas where nutrition, medical care, and housing all tended to be of poor quality. When one of these isolated communities was struck by the disease, everyone generally got sick at once. Since such an isolated community could not rely on outside help, there was no one to care for the sick or supply food to nourish them.

The important difference that nursing care could make is underscored by the contrast between the epidemic's effects on the Navajos and Hopis. The Hopis, while they had many ill from the disease, survived with relatively few deaths apparently resulting from the high quality of nursing care provided for them by the Indian Service (Crane 1919; Reagan 1922). The widely scattered Navajos, however, received little nursing care and suffered greatly from the epidemic (Crane 1919; Reagan 1922; Gilmor and Wetherill 1934).

The San Juan Paiutes were certainly one of the most isolated Indian groups at that time period, as Superintendent Janus had remarked. Not only were they without any kind of modern medical care, but their plight also went virtually unrecorded. The only documented deaths appearing in published accounts of influenza fatalities were those of one of *Muupɨts'* sons, the Nasja Begay who was instrumental in the Anglos' discovery of Rainbow Bridge, and his four children, all of whom died on route to Blanding, Utah, and whose bodies were found by Anglos.

It is clear, however, from oral accounts that many other Paiutes died of the flu during the winter of 1918-1919. We mention here only the most reliable cases. *Tangwats'* wife was said to have died during the epidemic. *Tangwats* and an adult son, Alfred Lehi, soon after moved to the southern area while the youngest son, Willie Lehi, born in 1917, was raised from infancy by Dora Nelson, his classificatory aunt. Curtis Lehi's twin sisters died of "sickness" during the winter of 1918-1919. Marie Lehi has spoken to us several times of the flu-related deaths of her brother, *Akavu'its* and his young wife, *Taa.* The couple's youngest son, J. I. Casey, born in 1917, was raised by his uncle, Harry Brooks, and his grandmother, *Ixirøts*, not by his parents, a fact which also tends to link this couple's death with the 1918 influenza epidemic.

The influenza epidemic among the Paiutes had two immediate consequences. On the one hand, since the mortality age distribution of this particular epidemic, unlike normal flu epidemics, was heaviest among those aged 20 to 30 years old (Crosby 1976), the San Juans immediately lost many people in their most productive years. Of particular importance to the future was the probable loss of a proportionally large number of women in their childbearing years.

In addition, a whole subgroup of San Juan Paiutes, the Douglas Mesa Paiutes, moved away at this time. While several sources identify resource competition with Navajos as the ultimate cause of this migration, Paiute oral history indicates that the influenza epidemic also played a contributory role. Superintendent E. E. McKean of the Consolidated Ute Agency, the jurisdiction where the Monument Valley Paiutes ended up, also reported that this group had "left through fear during the flu epidemic" (McKean 1923).

In the San Juan Paiute view, interethnic conflict and the influenza epidemic were not necessarily unconnected events. San Juan people even now tend to explain catastrophic illness as the result of witchcraft, especially episodes of illness that appear to involve groups rather than isolated individuals. Witchcraft or sorcery, for the San Juans and for many other peoples the world over, are an inevitable component of conflict between groups. For Paiutes, disease may be a consequence of deliberate sorcery or may occur simply because conflict causes people to "think bad thoughts." One motif that appears repeatedly in San Juan stories of supernaturally caused disease and death is the idea that a group can escape by avoiding or moving away from the social situations where deaths are occurring. In their own accounts of the Douglas Mesa Paiutes' abandonment of Monument Valley, San Juans imply that the flu epidemic was just one of the natural consequences of the interethnic competition for resources in the area.

The San Juan Paiute Tribe has only recently recovered from the twin effects of the influenza epidemic, the migration and the loss of many young people. However, the Navajos who most likely had mortality rates similar to the Paiutes recovered remarkably quickly from it. The Navajos went into this epidemic with relatively few people in the high mortality age group and quite a few under the age of 20. According to the *Navajo Yearbook*, 62.6% of the population in 1915 was under 20 (Young 1961:326). Therefore, the Navajo growth rate did not slow appreciably (Young 1961:321), although in seeming paradox their population did drop between 1918 and 1920 (Aberle 1974).

The San Juan Paiutes, on the other hand, went into the epidemic having already experienced several decades of resource competition and most likely had either a stable population or were already losing population. (See Janus' reference above to an epidemic which must have hit the southern area San Juans around 1900.) In either case, they would not have had a large number of females almost ready to enter childbearing years. Furthermore, the loss of women of childbearing age in a small population can affect the population growth rates over a much longer period of time and in a more drastic manner than in a large population (James Williams, sociologist and census demography specialist, personal communication, 1982). The San Juan Paiutes, then, entered the 1920s with two settlement areas, rather than three, and with a smaller population in the two remaining settlements as well.

1920-1930

Although the 1918 influenza epidemic may have had long term demographic effects, oral historical accounts of social and economic activities suggest that during the 1920s, San Juan life continued much as it had in the previous two decades. In both the Navajo Mountain-Paiute Canyon and Willow Springs-*Atatsiv* areas, the farming season brought together all local San Juan people. All the Paiutes in the northern area spent much of the summer together at Paiute Canyon planting, caring for, and harvesting their fields. In addition to work-related activities, the local Paiutes took advantage of the summer weather and the relative abundance of food to hold social gatherings near the farm area, notably horse racing and round-dancing.

Moreover, the social ties between the southern and northern subgroups insured that any horse race or dance would be attended by San Juans from the other settlement area. These gatherings offered occasions for the renewal of old ties and, particularly among the young people, for the creation of new ones.

Joe Norman, originally from Navajo Mountain and Paiute Canyon, was one young man in the 1920s who loved to go to dances. He remarked that he would go to dances at "anytime of the year" (Bunte and Franklin Fieldnotes, July 23, 1981). When he was a young man, Paiutes from Willow Springs and even Utes and Paiutes from Blanding used to gather at the dances hosted by the Paiute Canyon households. The sites in Paiute Canyon where dances and races were held in this period were pointed out to us by the Paiutes who presently live there.

Western Navajo Agency Superintendent-in-charge A. W. Leech reported finding four families of Paiutes totalling 48 persons when he visited Paiute Canyon in May 1923. Leach also listed the heads of the four families: "Beluw Nechonie," "Dossonie," "Arvill Lutzin," and "Nasjah" (Leech 1923). Except for Arvill Lutzin these names appear to be in Navajo, suggesting that Leech relied on a Navajo interpreter in attempting to talk with the Paiutes. Modern Paiutes recognize Nasjah as Ruben Owl/*Muupʉts*. "Arvill Lutzin" appears to be a garbled version of "Willetson," and is perhaps Lester Willetson/*Muvwira'ats*.

In the south, the summer farming season brought everyone together at Cedar Ridge and Willow Springs. According to Joe Norman and his wife, Ski Francis Norman, in the 1920s there were several San Juan families who farmed and lived at Willow Springs but who also had unirrigated farms at Cedar Ridge (Bunte and Franklin Fieldnotes, October 19, 1984). Those whom the Normans named as farming in both areas included household heads from each major consanguineal group. These Paiutes stayed with the corn at Cedar Ridge until it was ripe. After it was harvested, they moved back down to Willow Springs where the corn ripened later. In the winter, southern area residents camped together, usually on *Atatsiv*.

According to Joe Norman, there used to be an extensive irrigation system at Willow Springs in the 1920s. It was hand built by the Paiutes themselves and included both the fields on the sloping natural terrace immediately below Echo Cliffs as well as the fields on the next terrace down. However, sometime in the late 1920s, a heavy rainstorm washed out the entire system. It was never completely restored afterward, which probably encouraged further erosion and resulted in loss of productivity.

In the south, as at Paiute Canyon, the summer was a time for visits as well as work. Social gatherings often focused on round-dances, which were held at a site immediately above Willow Springs or at another site on *Atatsiv*, north of Tuba City and near the present Lehi sheep camp. San Juan Paiutes from all areas attended these gatherings. Although Paiutes of all ages enjoyed visiting, unmarried young men especially travelled around to visit and even live for long periods with their relatives.

In the southern area, a number of intermarriages took place between the three major consanguineal lines during this decade. When *Tangwats* and his son, Alfred Lehi, both moved to the southern area soon after the death of *Tangwats'* wife in the influenza epidemic, they married *Machʉkats'* daughter, Priscilla Dutchie, and granddaughter, Marie, respectively. These two marriages helped lay the foundation for the emergence of the Lehi ambilineage in the south in the 1940s and 1950s, since this ambilineage later incorporated both *Machʉkats'* descendents and the field area used by Priscilla Dutchie and her kin. Other unions took place between the southern area consanguineal lines as well. One of these was a marriage later in the decade between Alfred Lehi's younger brother, Joe Norman, and a young woman who was the granddaughter of *Ixirøts* and classificatory granddaughter of Joe Francis.

Norman's account of the events that led up to his marriage to his first wife underscores the authority exerted by elder kinspeople in social matters. Curtis Lehi, Norman's classificatory older brother, brought him down on horseback (they both rode a single horse) from Navajo Mountain in the latter part of the 1920s to marry his first wife, *Kwichʉats*. Lehi had arranged the marriage with the bride's mother's mother, *Ixirøts*, who had raised the girl. Norman's second wife, Ski Francis, a classificatory sister of *Kwichʉats*, was a little girl then and also lived at Willow Springs. Norman's grandfather, *Pak'ai*, his father, *Tangwats*, and his older brother, Alfred Lehi, were of course already living in the southern area when Norman married.

The dense pattern of intermarriage among these southern area kin groups, which involved members of the northern area as well, was one outgrowth of the close community ties brought

about by increased economic interdependence and social
interaction at the settlement level. One purpose behind the
marriages which elders arranged between kin groups may have
been to assure that young couples would have adequate access
to land in a constantly dwindling resource estate. In time,
such marriages resulted in the merging of kin lines and
produced the patterns of ambilineage land tenure that we see
today.

During the first decades of this century, hunting continued
to be an important and frequent communal activity. The close
proximity of households and the frequent interaction among
the members of San Juan Paiute winter settlements allowed the
male elders to plan winter hunts conveniently. According to
oral history dealing with this period and later decades, when
the local chief elder was planning a rabbit or a deer hunt, he
went from house to house to inform the men when it was going
to take place.

As one might expect, rabbit hunts were organized locally
whenever there was a large population of rabbits. The men
used rabbit sticks both for sport and to save ammunition.

Since there were few deer in the reservation area,
communal deer hunts took place off-reservation. In the north,
Paiutes often conducted expeditions to Bear's Ears north of the
San Juan River and west of Blanding, Utah. The men gathered
on a prearranged day and forded the river on horseback. Deer
bones were found in refuse/ash heaps at several 1920s winter
sites in the north, suggesting that such hunts were important to
subsistence even at that date. In the southern area, similar
hunting trips were organized but to the Coconino Plateau north
of Flagstaff. According to William Beaver, the owner of the
Sacred Mountain Trading Post, located 20 miles north of
Flagstaff, Arizona, the late Alfred Lehi once told him that San
Juan Paiutes used to have a deer hunting camp not far west of
the site of his trading post (personal communication 1983). This
camp was reportedly used into the 1940s.

The 1920s brought permanent Navajo settlement to the area
south of Navajo Mountain. Although the number of Navajos
was not great at that time, some Paiute accounts of the period
foreshadow the increased tension that was to come in later
decades. One story described a suspected case of Navajo
sorcery against Paiutes (Bunte and Franklin Fieldnotes, July
16, 1983). In the 1920s, *Unap* gave birth to a stillborn baby,
who died because its head was too soft. According to *Unap's*
descendents, a Navajo witch had killed the child. They told us

that after the baby died and the Paiutes had moved away, a Navajo neighbor came around, walking his horse on the rocks so as not to leave footprints. Some San Juans believe that some Navajo families at Navajo Mountain, especially this man and his relatives, continued to practice sorcery against Paiutes even in recent decades. One San Juan woman suggested to us that this was what accounted for the increase in Paiute deaths in the north during the period between the 1920s and the 1950s.

By the end of the 1920s, Navajos were attempting to expand onto the Utah side of the Navajo Mountain area. One of *Tuutaɥts'* sons, *Kavii*/Paiute Dick, who had taken over the role of chief elder from the aged *Muupɥts*, organized the Paiute men to build a brush livestock fence that ran east from Lost Mesa along the north side of the Arizona-Utah line. The fence was built in part to keep Navajo livestock out of a Paiute spring, named appropriately enough *Kwiakatɥ Paatsipich,* or "Fenced In Spring." Two Navajos in particular used to burn the fence periodically. Their Paiute names were *Paxunap* and *Tuukwatsitɥmp.* Each time the fence was burnt, *Kavii* and the local Paiute men would rebuild it.

In addition to coordinating the defense of San Juan land, *Kavii* had other duties throughout this decade. For example, he conducted horse trading expeditions to the Utah Mormons at Richfield.

1930-1940

During the 1930s, the Navajo Mountain-Paiute Canyon Paiutes spent much of the year, perhaps as much as five or six months, living and farming at Paiute Canyon. Even those who had irrigated or dry fields north of Navajo Mountain generally farmed in Upper Paiute Canyon as well.

Fields in Upper Paiute Canyon were divided into three contiguous, ambilineally held sections. All three remain substantially the same today after fifty years, although certain fields on the extreme northern and southern edges are now in Navajo hands. Furthest south and upstream, the first set of fields was located in a side canyon and watered by the spring *Paxampats* ("Cane Spring"). They belonged to members of the *Tuutaɥts* ambilineage. Bordering this area on the north is the flow from another spring on the main canyon's east wall called *Shɥpɥvats* ("Cold Spring"), used only for drinking water. In the

1930s, the following household heads held fields here: the children of *Tuutants*, that is, *Kavii, Paaruy, Unap*, and *Masi'*; and *Unap*'s daughter, Rose Lehi, the wife of Curtis Lehi. Although Lehi apparently could have farmed his mother's field, located beside those of the Owls, he worked his wife's field instead. Apricot trees he planted there in the 1930s are still alive and bearing fruit.

To the north of this area, on the other side of an eroded clay hill area, the second and third areas are located. These are both on the east side of Paiute Creek in the main canyon and are divided by the flow from *Paatsipikat* ("Water Springs Forth"), marked on U.S.G.S. maps as "Oak Spring." In contrast to the San Juan fields upstream, the soil here was drier and needed relatively elaborate irrigation works to make it productive. The set of fields located south of *Paatsipikat*'s flow belonged to Dora Nelson and her several daughters. Willie Lehi, youngest brother of Alfred Lehi, although not a descendent of Dora, had been raised by her. Later, in the 1940s or 1950s, he inherited the field of *Taaxa*, a daughter of Dora Nelson, and farmed it until his recent death. The most northerly set of fields is located on the same side of the main canyon as the Nelson fields but north of the flow from *Paatsipikat*. These were farmed in the 1930s by the Owls and *Nuaxur*, Lester Willetson's mother. Curtis Lehi's mother, who had farmed here earlier, had left Paiute Canyon for White Mesa, Utah, by 1930.

In addition to these fields, there were several other scattered fields in Upper Paiute Canyon farmed by San Juans. The Willetsons had a second field a distance north of the main area. In 1934, after harvesting that field, Ned Willetson, Lester and *Paaruy*'s teenage son, was thrown from his horse. He was taken to the Owl area fields where he later died.

Because Paiute households and fields in Paiute Canyon were so close to each other, settlement members interacted on a daily basis. While this was especially significant when the majority of the community was in residence during planting and harvesting, it was true even when only some members of each household were left to maintain the fields. San Juans visited each other, were invited to eat at each other's houses, and helped one another out in the fields.

The importance of this social and economic interaction becomes especially clear when we examine dispute settlement. According to two San Juans who lived there in the 1930s, the Paiutes farming in Paiute Canyon occasionally had disputes over irrigation water since some fields shared a common system. One consultant stated that it was the "old ladies" who would argue over water. The major culprit was allegedly *Nʉaxʉr*, Lester Willetson's mother. She apparently tried to use more than her share whenever possible. Although this led to quarrels between *Nʉaxʉr* and the other Paiute water users, social pressure in the community and the strong ties of interdependence among the Paiute households always brought about a quick reconciliation. As Bessie Owl, the paternal granddaughter of *Nʉaxʉr*, stated:

> When she [*Nʉaxʉr*] was hungry, she would calm down when she wants to eat. She used to have to come to the house [of persons she had quarreled with]. *Nʉaxʉr* came to the house to eat. Even when she was mad, she had to eat. They [the other old women] used to talk to her. They used to get mad at each other but they didn't go away. They used to always come to the home and apologize. [Bunte and Franklin Fieldnotes, October 22, 1984]

The interdependence found among San Juan households in the farming settlements was the rule at the winter settlements as well. Information on winter residence locations in the 1930s is particularly complete. For the Navajo Mountain area, consultants located the winter residences of all three ambilineages for virtually every year of that decade. In 1937, Malcolm Collier also noted that there were three Paiute winter residence groups, living in "three separate groups of hogans northeast of Navajo Mountain in the winter" (1966:39-40). Paiute consultants' site locations indicate that these three ambilineages spent several winters out of this decade living within one residential cluster.

Figure 3, "Historic Patterns of Winter Residence at Navajo Mountain: 1928-1950," presents winter residence information for the northern area settlement group for the 1930s and 1940s. In this figure, the winter residence sites of each of the three ambilineage groups are traced on separate time lines year by year and with site numbers. Each site is also located by number on map 4. Figure 3 also specifies for each year whether the sites were located within the same settlement. When the time lines for two or more ambilineage groups fall within the dotted lines, this means the sites in question were part of one settlement cluster. When the *Tʉʉtaʉtʉ* descent

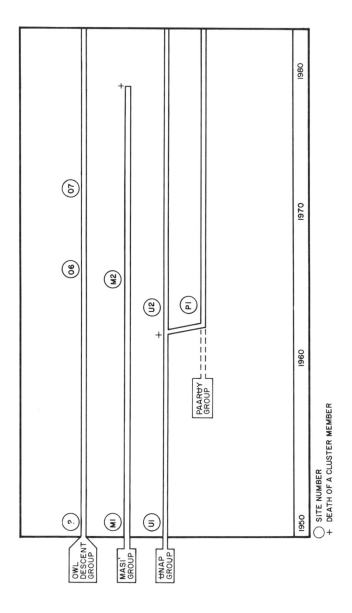

Figure 3.   Patterns of Historic Winter Residence at Navajo, Mountain, 1928-1950

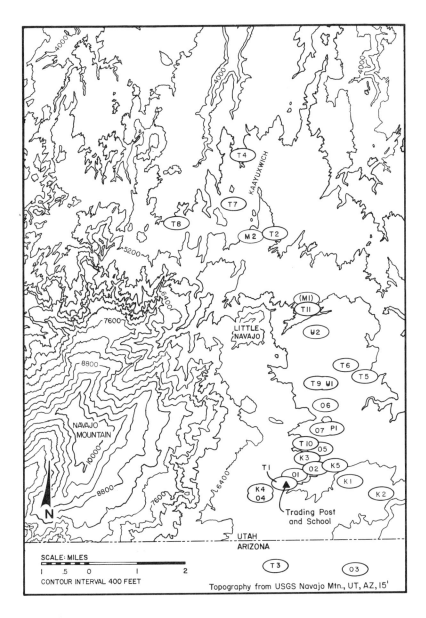

Map 4.   Northern Area Winter Residences, 1928 to Present

group's time line is drawn below the dotted line, this indicates that during that winter or sequence of winters that group did not live in the same vicinity as the *Muuputs* and *Kaavoi* groups.

San Juan winter settlements during this period were composed of two or three camps located near each other. The distance between individual residence sites or camps was usually a quarter of a mile or less and the entire settlement consistently had a diameter of less than two miles. The Paiute households in the winter settlement usually shared the same water source.

During the 1930s and 1940s, residence groups changed winter sites frequently. Several sites were occupied only one winter. Although the physical location of the settlement changed often year by year, the *Kaavoi* and *Muuputs* collateral ambilineages, as figure 3 illustrates, resided in close proximity every winter from 1928 to 1949. The third group, *Tuutauts* ambilineage, often spent the winter elsewhere, because they had a large number of sheep and goats for which adequate forage had to be found. In 1937 they had 322 sheep and goats as compared to 47 for the other two ambilineages combined (see table 5 above; the first seven livestock owners listed were members of the *Tuutauts* ambilineage.) Three large corrals were needed to contain their herd. Since the focal members of this group were not blood kin of the other clusters, the decision to spend winters apart from them can also be explained in terms of social distance and consequent economic independence. Nevertheless, despite these sound reasons for separate residence, the *Tuutauts* ambilineage spent 11 out of the 21 winters included on the chart living near the other two ambilineages. It is less surprising that the *Tuutauts* ambilineage was apart from the other groups ten winters then that they spent over fifty percent of the winter seasons together.

The San Juans' desire to lead a tight-knit community social life is probably the best explanation for this winter clustering pattern. Winter was a season in which the San Juans had time to spend visiting. Gambling games, basketmaking, storytelling, and even doing laundry togther at the water source were all social activities enjoyed by settlement members in the winter. As in earlier decades, male elders in the settlement also organized hunting trips during the winter months.

Even when the *Tuutauts* ambilineage was spending the winter apart from the other two descent groups, certain aspects of the settlement community organization were still in operation. Angel Whiskers recounted an incident that illustrates the cooperation of elders from different ambilineages in enforcing community standards of behavior. The incident occurred at Navajo Mountain in the early 1930s, probably the winter of 1932.

Curtis Lehi was married to the daughter of *Ʉnap* and living with the *Tuutaʉts* ambilineage on the north side of Navajo Mountain (site T2 on map 4). He became jealous of his classificatory brother. Lehi left his wife and her family and went to stay with his mother's classificatory younger sister, Dora Nelson/*Kaavoi*. The *Kaavoi* or Nelson descent group, the Owl descent group, and *Nʉaxur*--Lester Willetson's mother--all lived at the time near the Navajo Mountain Trading Post (O2 and K2 on map 4). *Ʉnap* had a lot of sheep and needed her son-in-law's help herding. She sent her sister's son, Angel Whiskers, to bring Lehi back home to his wife. When Angel came to get him, Dora Nelson "got after Curtis telling him to go away. She was telling him to go back with Angel to his wife. . . . Finally, he agreed to go. They went back on one horse, Curtis in front and Angel in back" (Bunte and Franklin Fieldnotes, October 24, 1984).

This incident indicates the manner in which ties of consanguineal kinship between San Juans at Navajo Mountain operated in daily social life a half century ago. It was from his classificatory aunt, Dora Nelson, that Curtis Lehi sought support when he left his wife. However, rather than side with Lehi against his in-laws, members of a separate ambilineage, and thereby tacitly encourage him in what Paiutes would view as a socially irresponsible course of action, Dora Nelson exerted her influence in concert with the wishes of *Ʉnap* and with the moral standards of the community.

The decision to relocate to a different winter camp after a period of one or more winters at the same site frequently correlated with a death in the ambilineage. In figure 3, a "+" marks the death of a descent group member when it occurred during the winter.

As with the flu epidemic in Monument Valley, San Juans in the north often attributed the sickness or death of one of their members to Navajo witchcraft. An example is found in a story told by one of *Ʉnap*'s granddaughters (Bunte and Franklin Fieldnotes, July 18, 1983). In 1937 or 1938, a San Juan remembered as "Aunt Nellie," probably Nellie Willetson, the teenage daughter of Lester Willetson and *Paarʉy*, fell sick and died two winters later. According to her classificatory

niece, "the Navajos did witchcraft with Aunt Nellie to make
her sick so that they [the *Tuutaɥts* cluster] would move and
then they [the Navajos] could come and steal their house."
These Navajos then allegedly removed *Paarɥy*'s house from the
site, or at least took the largest and best lumber.

In her 1966 monograph based on her field work in 1938,
Collier noted local Navajos' attitudes towards the Paiutes
living in the area. In discussing conflicts among local Navajos,
she stated: "It also seems likely that the proximity of the
Paiute lessens the frequency of disputes among the Navaho
since the Paiute serve, in a way, as scapegoat" (Collier 1966:36).
Elsewhere, she described "the Navaho attitude toward the
Paiute":

> The Paiute are the objects of all kinds of jokes on the
> part of the Navaho whether it is a matter of doubtful
> paternity or bettering an opponent in driving a bargain.
> They are also the first to be accused if anything goes
> wrong. If the wagon tracks have obviously been
> blocked with stones--the Paiute did it. [Collier 1966:40]

These attitudes towards Paiutes doubtlessly reflected the
tension existing in the Navajo Mountain area between the
groups.

In the south, two kin groups, the family of *Akamanaxwats*
and *T'aats* and the group of families associated with Joe
Francis and his dead brother's wife, *Ixirøts*, continued to farm
at Cedar Ridge into the middle 1930s. All southern area San
Juans were also planting at Willow Springs throughout the
1930s. During that decade, Paiutes were still planting on both
terrace levels.

On the natural terrace of fields just below the cliffs at
Willow Springs, there were two main field areas in the 1930s,
separated by a strip of fallow land. In one of these areas,
probably much larger than the other, there were two
consanguineally related groups of households living and
farming side by side. One group included the following
members: *Tangwats* and his wife, *Kanga'av*/Priscilla Dutchie;
Alfred and Marie Lehi; *Para'an*/Chester Chelester; and Connie
Yazzie/*Kwinu* and his wife, Leida Yazzie, like Marie Lehi a
daughter of Priscilla Dutchie. *Tangwats'* now aged father,
Pak'ai, lived and farmed at Government Spring a little to the
north of the two main springs. In the other group of related
households lived: *Øawɥnɥr*'s widow, *Ixirøts*; her sons and

daughters, notably *Kʉ'iv*/Gonah Sani and *Chakwoits*/Harry Brooks; *Nʉngʉmaøts*/Joe Francis and his children, especially *Yuwa'nits*/Harry Francis; and finally Joe Norman and his first wife, *Kwichʉats*/Lucy. These fields were all watered by an impoundment dam and ditch system fed by the more southerly of the two main springs.

The second group of fields at Willow Springs was occupied by *Akamanaxwats*/Joedie, his wife, *T'aats*, their children, including Blue Lee, and *T'aats'* younger brother, *Wiipø*/Sam Weepie. These fields were apparently irrigated by the more northerly of the two springs at Willow Springs. Flow from this spring was also diverted to an impoundment dam and watered fields on the lower terrace, which were farmed by Harry Brooks, Chester Chelester, and Connie Yazzie.

Towards the end of the decade *Wichʉnʉx* and her family began farming at Willow Springs when she married *Yuwa'nits*. After his death, they continued farming his field, located in the fallow land between the two areas described above. In later years, after the family of *T'aats* had departed for Kaibab, *Wichʉnʉx*'s daughters expanded into the land under the northern spring, which her ambilineal descendents now hold today. During the 1930s, Alfred Lehi and Connie Yazzie also had dry farms by the southern tip of White Point, about ten miles north of Tuba City on *Atatsiv*.

The southern area San Juans spent most winters during the 1930s on *Atatsiv*. In December 1937, for example, the Paiutes were living on *Atatsiv* when Omer Stewart visited them in order to interview the older San Juans to complete his Southern Paiute trait list (Stewart 1942). During a week's stay, Stewart interviewed Joe Francis, and Many Whiskers' (*Machʉkats'*) daughter, Priscilla Dutchie. He also spent evenings in Joe Norman's house playing a Navajo gambling game with the Paiutes and some of their Navajo neighbors. The major winter economic activities that he observed were sheep herding and basketmaking (Stewart 1938a:25-27).

So few non-Indians visited the San Juans at that time, that Stewart's visit was well remembered. After a return visit in the summer of 1983, after spending a second week with the San Juan Paiutes, he commented:

> Although forty-six years separated my two visits, old people remembered me and spontaneously offered information about my visit they could not have known except from remembered observations. For example, my

very peculiar camp was described. [Stewart 1984:4]

The importance of basketmaking for the San Juans of the 1930s, which Stewart noted, cannot be underestimated. In the 1930s, Paiutes and Utes were the primary source of supply of the Navajo wedding basket, required for use in many Navajo ceremonies (Steward 1938a and b; Roessel 1983:601-602). Although a typical basket brought only three dollars in the 1930s, basketmaking was the San Juans' principal source of cash income in both the north and south during this decade and for decades to come, enabling them to purchase flour, coffee, and other much needed supplies from local traders.

The 1930s were a time of transition for the local and tribal chief eldership. *Kavii, Muuputs*, and *Pak'ai* all died during this decade. Since Lester Willetson was the local chief elder in the Navajo Mountain-Paiute Canyon area by the early 1940s, it is likely that he had already taken over some of those functions in the 1930s. He was already recognized as a healer. His daughter, Bessie Owl, noted that when Maryanne Owl was a baby in the late 1930s she became very sick. As part of the cure, Willetson laid her on a bed of earth over warm coals to warm away her chill (Bunte and Franklin Fieldnotes, July 23, 1983).

By the middle to the late 1930s, Alfred Lehi/*Kainap*, grandson of *Pak'ai*, was also already becoming a prominent member of the southern San Juan settlement. Stewart (1938a:26) singled Alfred Lehi out, noting that he had an industrious household and had even hired a Navajo boy to herd their sheep.

Alfred Lehi eventually took over *Pak'ai*'s position as chief elder for the tribe as well as that of local chief elder for the southern area. Because of his kinship position, he was well situated for this role. In addition to being the grandson of the former chief elder, he was raised in the north, had lived much of his adult life in the south, and had many relatives in both areas. Furthermore, even in the 1930s Alfred Lehi was contacted by Paiutes from other groups as they were passing through. Dan Bulletts, a Kaibab elder, recalled spending the night with Alfred Lehi's family near Bitter Springs in March early in the 1930s when returning to Kaibab from a trip to Phoenix (Bunte and Franklin Fieldnotes, March 17, 1984). In later decades, Alfred Lehi was to use his contacts with the Kaibabs and other Paiute groups to get jobs for the San Juans and to deal with political difficulties which they faced.

Many Kaibab Paiutes have very clear impressions of the San Juan people from this period. They remember frequent visits between the groups in the 1930s, 1940s, and 1950s (Bunte and Franklin Fieldnotes, August 3-4, 1983). The San Juans used to go to Flagstaff for the 4th of July Powwow every year, where they often ate with the Kaibab Paiutes and sometimes would camp right next to them. In an interview, Kaibab Paiute Gevene Savala (GS) explained how the San Juans appeared to her as a young girl in the 1930s:

GS: But now my first experience with them was when we lived in Flag . . . ah, when we went to Flagstaff for the weekends, like Fourth of July weekend, like I told you, okay?

PB [Pamela Bunte]: Mhm.

GS: And they would come and join us while we were trying to eat something, you know, for dinner.

PB: And they'd camp there with you. But . . .

GS: Aha, well they'd camp in their area, 'cause they had a different area from where we were camping at. But, then, all of a sudden they would appear there [at the Kaibabs' camp] and they'd sit down, down with us to eat whatever we were having. And the older, you know people from here knew, knew about them, I guess, so they never said anything, and they [the San Juans] sat with us and then the younger ones, I guess, were kind of surprised because . . . you don't know that people do this, you know, they just come and they just sit down and join in to eat. And that was an experience

PB: Yeah.

GS: Just out of the blue, you know, somebody comes and sits down.

PB: And just starts eating and talking.

GS: Yeah, starts eating and talking Paiute, you know. And here you thought they were Navajos [because of their dress], but they were Paiutes. [Bunte and Franklin

Fieldnotes, August 3, 1983]

Another Kaibab Paiute, Ralph Castro, also spoke about the Flagstaff Powwow. He mentioned that as a boy in the late 1940s while on his way to the powwow with his family, his grandfather directed him to drive their flat bed truck westward from Bitter Springs to a "dirt road crossroads out in the middle of nowhere." There they picked up San Juan people whom his grandfather introduced as his "great-uncle and uncle, and so on" and gave them a ride to the powwow. Mr. Castro added:

> I never could figure out how my grandfather communicated with them. There's no phones out there, he doesn't know how to write, but he would go out there, and they would be waiting. I could always tell when we were going to do that afterwards, because we'd have to take an empty truck. [Bunte and Franklin Fieldnotes, August 3, 1983]

In addition to the annual powwow, Mrs. Savala also recalled that when U.S. Highway 89 was being built in the 1930s, her grandfather, Tokatop Frank, and other Paiutes worked on the road crews and lived consecutively at three camps along the route with their families. At the camp by Cedar Ridge, the Kaibab Paiutes were regularly visited by the San Juans who lived nearby. The San Juans would often bring meat to share. She remembered in particular that *Kwinu*, a San Juan man known in English as Connie Yazzie, was a frequent visitor. These recollections indicate the regularity of interaction between the two groups as well as its basis in shared kinship and ethnic identity.

1940-1950

The 1940s may well have been the most difficult decade in the twentieth century for the San Juans. During this period, while the Navajo population continued to increase, the San Juan population declined to its lowest point.

The proportion of children to adults among northern area San Juans during the late 1930s suggests that the population there was relatively stable at the beginning of the 1940s. According to available records and other information, there were 42 Navajo Mountain Paiutes with 22 under the age of 18 in 1937 (Western Navajo Reservation Indian Census Rolls 1937; Bunte and Franklin Fieldnotes, 1982 and 1983). However, oral accounts for the 1940s indicate that the death rate accelerated during that decade. In particular, most of the adults in the Nelson ambilineage had died by 1949. One Nelson adult died in the 1930s. Five more died in the 1940s, including Dora Nelson herself. All but one of these, a woman who succumbed to childbirth complications, appear to have died from tuberculosis. *Kavii*/Paiute Dick, of the *Tuutaʉts* group, had also died of tuberculosis in 1934, as apparently did "Aunt Nellie," Lester Willetson's daughter, who became seriously ill in the winter of 1937-1938 and died in the winter of 1940-1941. According to a Paiute census compiled by Navajo Mountain councilman Bert Tallsalt (1954), by 1954 there were only 27 northern area San Juans left and not all of those were living year-round at Navajo Mountain.

Western Navajo census records for 1937 indicate that the population decline in the southern area had already begun its last and worst phase before the 1940s. Of the 35 southern area Paiutes listed on that census, only ten were under 18 years of age (Western Navajo Reservaion Indian Census Rolls 1937). Within a decade, five of them would also die. From consultants' stories, measles and other childhood diseases seem to have been a frequent cause of death in infants and older children in the southern area.

BIA enumerators missed at least one San Juan family in the south, that of *Akamanaxwats* and *T'aats*. In the late 1930s, this family was composed of four adults; however, three of their daughters had already died of unknown, but natural causes, leaving only their youngest child, Blue Lee.

Because so many deaths during this period were disease-related, the decline in population may well have been brought about by increased nutritional stress in the San Juan community. One factor which produced a poorer diet was the Paiutes' increased dependence on trading post supplies, especially flour and sugar. Because of reductions in their agricultural and range land base, however, the San Juans were probably unable to produce sufficient food to support themselves on the reservation, even with the cash income from basketry sales. This situation apparently continued until the late 1960s or early 1970s, when San Juan Paiutes finally began to receive social welfare and donated foods from the local BIA superintendency and other state and federal agencies.

In the first few years of the 1940s, southern area patterns of movement and settlement continued much as they had in the previous decade, despite a declining population. Then about 1942, the Kaibab Paiutes invited the southern area San Juans to join them at Kaibab. Several families accepted the invitation, moving first to Kaibab and later to Utah Paiute communities.

The general superintendent of the Navajo Reservation, S. R. Fryer, wrote to Ben C. Spencer, the supervisor of District 3, apparently in response to Spencer's inquiry about a San Juan request for permission to move to Kaibab:

> This will reply to your letter of March 11 concerning the request of the Paiute band of Indians living on the Navajo Reservation.
>
> There is no reason why these Paiutes may not leave the reservation. However, I'm not in a position to advise them with respect to any rights they would acquire at Kaibab if they were to join that band of Indians [Fryer 1942]

Soon afterward, in 1943, several San Juan households from the southern area moved to the Kaibab Paiute Reservation. San Juan Paiutes today state that these families left the Willow Springs-*Atatsiv* settlement group on account of recurring deaths among their kin. Consultants' accounts indicate that many people at the time attributed these deaths to witchcraft, although it is unclear whether other community members or Navajos were thought to be responsible. Many older members of this group who might have remembered why they left are now deceased. Nonetheless, the economic situation in the south and the lure of off-reservation work must also have been a factor in the decision to leave the reservation community.

According to Kaibab Paiute consultants, "Theodore and Morris [Jake, both Kaibabs,] went over and got them [the San Juans] from that reservation" (Bunte and Franklin Fieldnotes, August 4, 1983). Among the San Juans who moved to Kaibab were *Akamanaxwats'* widow, *T'aats*, and her family; Connie Yazzie and his family; Ski Frances Norman, Joe Francis' daughter; and Joe Norman and his family.

The San Juan visitors were not happy at Kaibab, according to the Paiutes there, and soon moved north into Utah to Gunnison, Fillmore, Delta, Richfield, and other locations to work at beet picking and other jobs that Kanosh Paiutes had arranged for them. Several of the senior citizens interviewed at Kaibab had worked at the same jobs and had joined the San Juans in card playing, hand games, and other pastimes that were popular among the Paiutes.

Several San Juans died while living and working in Utah. When this happened, Paiutes from the Utah and Kaibab communities performed the Southern Paiute Cry ceremony for the deceased. This was apparently the first time that San Juans had taken part in this ritual, which the other Paiute communities had adopted from the Mohaves in the late nineteenth century (Kelly 1964:95).

By 1947, most of the surviving San Juans had returned to Willow Springs. However, this episode started a pattern of seasonal off-reservation labor that persisted through the next two decades. Correspondence retained by the family of the late Alfred Lehi indicates that the Pikyavit family, Kaibab Paiutes who had become leading members of the Kanosh Band in Utah, worked through Lehi to recruit labor for agricultural work with Utah Mormon farmers (Pikyavit 1946). Indeed, during the late 1940s and the 1950s, Alfred Lehi served as the tribe's informal labor contractor. Because a few San Juans acquired cars in the late 1940s, many could work at seasonal jobs off-reservation, returning home to their farms and herds which other family members had been taking care of during their absence.

Economic transactions were not the only form of interaction that Alfred Lehi had with Paiute leaders from other tribes during the 1940s. As early as 1941, he was asked by fellow tribe members to take charge of another matter involving non-Indians:

It all started with [Sam Weepie]. He didn't have his selective service card. *Yuwa'n* [or *Yuwa'nits*, Harry Francis] didn't either. *Chakwoits* [Harry Brooks] didn't have any. These three men told Alfred to take care of it for them, see what he can do for them. And they were told that people who don't have these kind of cards were going to be arrested and put in jail. And he went to, over to the other side to Kaibab or Kanab. The people over there, they made a kind of a, I guess they talked over this, Alfred's concern for his people over here. And he came back to tell these guys that there was going to be a help. There will be help. And from there on, they got their selective service cards. [Bunte and Franklin Fieldnotes, October 20, 1984]

A later incident again demonstrated the usefulness of Alfred Lehi's ties with other Paiute leaders. At the same time, this case suggests the tenor of relations between the San Juans and Navajos in the 1940s. In 1948, Connie Yazzie and Angel Whiskers were involved in a fight with local Navajos. According to Yazzie's affidavit (1948), a Navajo man who later married one of *Wichʉnʉx*'s daughters, choked Angel Whiskers until he passed out.

The Navajos apparently complained to authorities about the fight and a Navajo policeman was sent out to the Lehis' *Atatsiv* camp to arrest Angel. According to Alfred Lehi's testimony in a BIA Field Service affidavit:

[The Navajo policeman] went directly to my hogan and entered without showing any warrant, I then heard him say to Angel Whiskers, "Do you want to go to the Devil? hurry up and get up."

Annie Whiskers my daughter was in the hogan, when she said the policeman jerked Angel Whiskers, he was lying down, dragged him out the door put handcuffs on him. Annie said Angel Whiskers did not hesitate one bit and gave his wrists to the policeman.

About this time my wife [Marie Lehi] said she was coming towards the hogan. . . . [She stated in her own affidavit (La Ree Lehi 1948) that she went to them because she saw the policeman "using unnecesary roughness" and because she thought he was going to beat Angel with a blackjack.]

When I was still at the wood pile I heard the policeman say to my wife, "I am going to shoot your eyes." I looked just as he fired and I saw where the bullet hit the hogan right above the door on the East side. I saw . . . where the bullet hit.

Just as the policeman was reaching for another bullet I rushed toward the hogan where they stood. I told my wife to let the blackjack go which she still held on to.

I told the policeman not to shoot and to behave himself do his duty in a right way. My wife let go then and went back to her basketmaking.

The policeman then said he would have Annie my daughter and La Ree [Marie] my wife tied and hauled on donkeys to jail. [Alfred Lehi 1948]

Alfred Lehi apparently filed this affidavit in support of his own complaint to the Tuba City Subagency concerning the Paiutes' mistreatment at the hands of the BIA Navajo police. Concluding the affidavit, he stated:

The policeman was very unpleasant. They took us [Angel and Alfred] into Tuba City, to the jail. . . . While at the jail the Navajos showed prejudice and unjustness towards us.

I felt very bad and wondered what they had done to my wife as she stayed at home.

This testimony is the truth. I saw [it] myself also [it was seen] by my wife. So please help us.

Anna Whiskers reported to us that the Kaibab Paiutes soon afterward became involved in this incident:

And Alfred, there's another case that he's helped in, the time when Marie was almost shot. He went over to the other side to the Kaibab people to ask for help. The Navajo police almost shot Marie. And after that he started being more a leader [*niavipaxai'ni*, "walk/go around being a leader/chief"]. And when they were living where *Aayuxwitsich* ["They Sit Silently," a site on *Atatsiv*], where they were living up there, they had visitors, Paiutes. Morris Jake [the Kaibab chairman] was there, a person who was always working for us. He came over with a lot of other people. [Bunte and Franklin Fieldnotes, October 20, 1984]

A meeting was held between the Kaibab and San Juan Paiutes concerning the incident with the Navajo policeman. Elma Jake, Morris' younger sister, took notes of the meeting.

Among the San Juans who were present were the southern area elders, Alfred and Marie Lehi, Connie Yazzie, and Anna Whiskers' mother's mother, *Kanga'av*/Priscilla Dutchie. At least one of the Kaibab Paiutes apparently went with the Lehis and Connie Yazzie when they filed their complaint to the Indian Service, since all of the Paiute affidavits were witnessed and signed by Joseph Pikyavit.

After the meeting, according to Anna Whiskers, the San Juans from *Atatsiv* and the visiting Kaibabs went to confront the local Navajo community at a Tuba City Navajo chapter meeting:

> When these Paiutes went down to Tuba City, the Navajos were having, they're having a [chapter] meeting down there, in Tuba City. And these Paiutes, Morris Jake and his group, went into their meeting. The Navajos suddenly closed up their meeting. I don't know what was the meeting about but they suddenly shut it off. [Bunte and Franklin Fieldnotes, October 20, 1984]

Although the San Juans living in the north had been more successful than their southern counterparts in the 1930s, in the 1940s the Navajo population in their area was continuing to increase rapidly and Navajos were beginning to move onto San Juan Paiute land north of the Utah-Arizona border. According to Paiutes who were children or young adults in the 1940s, some Navajos would set the Paiutes' houses on fire when they left them to move to another location for the season. One woman mentioned that this was done sometimes even before the family was out of sight, so that the Paiutes could actually see their home burning (Bunte and Franklin Fieldnotes, July 11, 1983).

According to an account told by a Paiute woman who was a young girl in the 1940s, Paiutes were subject to other forms of harassment. One evening, after her mother and an aunt had gone to the Navajo Mountain Trading Post, she was alone with her grandmother, Dora Nelson, and another aunt, Grace Nelson:

> Some Navajos were playing tricks on us, doing witchcraft trying to scare us off. First, small rocks came in the shadehouse then larger ones. Dora built a big fire and burnt a bundle of sage [to ward off ghosts or witchcraft]. She also burned the bushes around the

avaxan ["shadehouse"]. It started again when the fire died down. It finally stopped when Harry Whiskers, Sr., rode up on horseback. He wanted to marry Grace. [Bunte and Franklin Fieldnotes, June 26, 1983]

Explaining that the scene that followed was full of confusion, the narrator continued:

Dora was talking about the rocks being thrown into the house and how mad she was with Navajos for trying to scare Paiutes away, while Harry, slightly drunk, was asking to marry her granddaughter. Finally, all was settled and Harry went to sleep where his horse was tied up. In the morning, Dora looked all around and there were no tracks anywhere of the person throwing stones. She wasn't scared though, just mad at the Navajos.

This incident took place at a site near a spring called *Tнka'nivyats* in Paiute and *Tseyato* in Navajo (both names mean "cave spring"). The Paiutes used this Arizona camping and grazing area every year in the spring when they were moving their herds from their winter camps in Utah to the plateau above Upper Paiute Canyon.

During the first half of the 1940s, the northern area settlement pattern continued much as it had in the previous decade with three ambilineally organized winter camps. However, by the late 1940s, all four of Dora Nelson's daughters, and Dora herself, had died. By the winter of 1946, the surviving Nelson grandchildren had moved in with the Owls. Although a few years later the Nelsons again moved to their own house at a site near the Owls and attempted to set up separate housekeeping, the 1949 death of one of Dora Nelson's granddaughters in childbirth resulted in the complete disintegration of what remained of the Nelson residence group. Despite the fact that Paiute kin in the other two ambilineages had taken in the children, the school teacher at Navajo Mountain considered the children to be orphans, and sent the school age children off to boarding school in California. According to one of them, the schoolmistress believed that they would simply run away to Navajo Mountain if she sent them to the Tuba City boarding school. The youngest children were given up for adoption by non-Paiutes.

Lester Willetson, who had married *Paarнy* and was living as a member of the *Tнutaнts* group, acted as a local chief elder in

the 1940s and 1950s. San Juan Paiutes remember that he used
to go down to Moencopi to trade buckskins, medicinal plants,
and live eagles to the Hopis. He also used to set up horse races
with the Navajos at the race track near the present day airstrip
south of Navajo Mountain Trading Post, as *Kavii*/Paiute Dick
had done. He was known as a round-dance song leader and
arranged many dances. Finally, Willetson organized hunting
trips. One man who was a young boy in the 1940s remembered
that Willetson would go from house to house notifying the
other Paiute men when a deer hunting trip to Bear's Ears was
going to take place, saying "Let's go hunt in [so many] days"
(Bunte and Franklin Fieldnotes, July 23, 1983).

1950-1970

The 1950s and 1960s were a period of relative stability, in
population as in other areas of San Juan life. Work-related
emigrations out of the community had become, for the most
part, seasonal or temporary. Those who did move away for
longer periods during these two decades retained strong ties
with their kin and settlement groups.

San Juan patterns of residence and movement had
undergone a major change beginning in the early 1950s.
Whereas previously households often stayed only two or three
winters at one place, during the the 1950s and 1960s winter
residences tended to be located in one spot for ten or more
years in succession. In the north especially, winter camps
eventually became the main focus of household life year-
round.

This final section looks at social and economic changes in
the northern and southern area settlement groups in turn. We
discuss cases of tribal decision making and leadership which
involved the two settlement groups as a single community.

In 1950, the San Juan Paiutes at Navajo Mountain were
living in three separate camps. However, the composition of
these camps had shifted considerably from the previous decade.
Figure 4, "Patterns of Historic Winter Residence at Navajo
Mountain: 1950-1980," provides information on northern area
residence groups and their locations for this period as well as
for the 1970s. Site locations may be found on map 4.

The dispersal of the Nelson ambilineage was only one event
leading to the establishment of a new configuration of
residence groups in the settlement. The remnants of the Owl

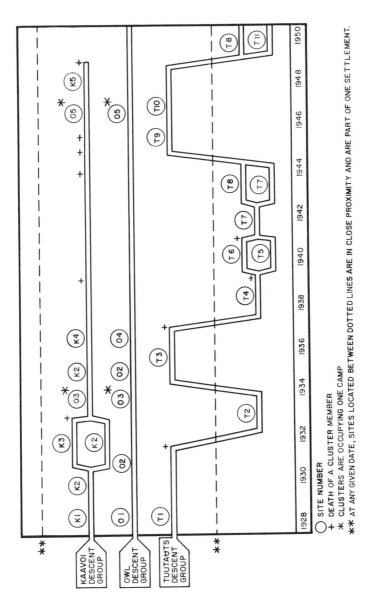

○ SITE NUMBER
+ DEATH OF A CLUSTER MEMBER
* CLUSTERS ARE OCCUPYING ONE CAMP
** AT ANY GIVEN DATE, SITES LOCATED BETWEEN DOTTED LINES ARE IN CLOSE PROXIMITY AND ARE PART OF ONE SETTLEMENT.

Figure 4.   Patterns of Historic Winter Residence at Navajo, Mountain, 1950–1980

residence group, *Muupнts'* daughter Blanche Owl, her childless younger brother, and one of her adult sons, continued to live in the winter at one camp site. Two of her other sons married into * Unap*'s and *Paarнy*'s household groups, of the *Tuutaнts* ambilineage, and continued to share one site until *Unap*'s death in 1962 when they separated from each other to move to new sites. In the mid-1960s, *Paarнy*, her daughter, and her Owl son-in-law joined with the Owls and ceased to be an independent residence group.

Masi', or Mercy, the third *Tuutaнts* daughter, lived at a site apart from her two sisters' households from the 1950s until her death in the late 1970s. As figure 3 indicated for the period 1928-1950, Mercy had always had a tendency to remain slightly apart from her sisters. This may have been because of her marriage to a Navajo, Sid Whiskers, some of whose matrilineal kin were believed to covet Paiute range land in Utah. In a similar but more dramatic case, one of Mercy's sons attempted to bring a Navajo woman to live with him north of Navajo Mountain in 1952. The other Paiutes drove her off, in effect preventing the marriage, because they feared that her kin, too, might eventually use the relationship as a wedge to enter and claim range land. At one point in their ethnography of the Navajo Mountain Navajo community, Shepardson and Hammond indicated that it was common practice for Navajo matrilineage groups to use adverse possession as a strategy for preempting land held by other matrilineages (1970:49).

Although there was no separate Nelson residence group at Navajo Mountain during this time period, there were in fact several Nelson children in residence since Mercy had adopted the three children of her late son, Harry Whiskers, and Grace Nelson. Moreover, the separate *Kaavoi* field area continued to be used only by descendents of Dora Nelson, some of whom were living part time at White Mesa and elsewhere in Utah.

The 1954 census of the Navajo Mountain Paiute community, made by Navajo tribal councilman Bert Tallsalt, presented a fairly accurate picture, omitting only children who were not in school and children of Paiutes who were not residing permanently at Navajo Mountain (Tallsalt 1954). At the same time, the document indicates that Navajo leaders recognized this settlement group as a socially and culturally distinct Paiute community.

In enumerating the members of the northern settlement, Tallsalt divided up the 27 Paiutes on the census into four groups: those that resided permanently in the Navajo

Mountain area; those that traveled back and forth between
Navajo Mountain and other locations such as Allen Canyon or
Blanding, Utah; those that had moved away from Navajo
Mountain to reside elsewhere; and, finally, those that were
away at boarding school. The Paiutes listed as having moved
away from the area, as well as the ones listed as travelling
back and forth to it, had all left either to look for work or
because of marriage. Those still living in the early 1980s have
either returned there or have retained very strong ties to the
group through frequent visiting and continuing to farm in
Paiute Canyon in the summer. The list of those away at school
in 1954 is entirely made up of Nelson children who were sent
to boarding school at Riverside, California, in the late 1940s or
early 1950s.

Shepardson and Hammond, in their study of Navajo social
organization in the Navajo Mountain area, provided
information on the Paiute settlement community as it existed
in 1961, less than a decade after Tallsalt's census:

> Northeast of Navajo Mountain and in Paiute Canyon we
> find clear evidence of early Paiute occupancy. The
> connections of this San Juan Band are with Southern
> Paiutes from across the river. There are possibly three
> original descent lines of Paiutes living here but these
> cannot properly be called lineages in this bilateral
> society. [Shepardson and Hammond 1970:39]

At the time of their field work, there were only 18 Paiutes
living year-round at Navajo Mountain, out of a total
permanent Indian population of 581 (Shepardson and
Hammond 1970:18). These 18 Paiutes were listed in Shepardson
and Hammond's tabular enumeration of all Navajo Mountain
residential groups (1970, table B, "Composition of Camps, 1960-
61," unpaginated). According to this table, Paiutes made up
four of the 46 camps, or household clusters, at Navajo
Mountain, those numbered 34, 35, 36, and 37. The only non-
Paiute member of these camps was Sid Whiskers, married to
Mercy Whiskers and living in camp 37. This table supplies
information on genealogical relations among all adult
individuals owning houses ("hogans") in each camp as well as
their birthdates. This additional information not only makes
clear the close ties of marriage and bilateral kinship existing
within and between these Paiute camps, it also makes it
possible to identify all 18 Paiutes individually. Only one

discrepancy exists between the information in this table and that supplied by modern Paiute consultants. This concerns the relative location of *Paarʉy*'s and *ʉnap*'s households. Shepardson and Hammond listed the two households as separate camps, while San Juan consultants located both households at one site in adjacent dwellings until the time of *ʉnap*'s death in 1962 (see figure 4 and map 4).

Shepardson and Hammond recorded that local Navajos considered the Paiutes to be social inferiors: "The 'People' in Navajo Mountain look down upon the Paiutes as 'not-Navajo.' They are still the butt of mild jokes, as they were at the time of Malcolm Collier's 1938 study" (1970:58). Describing these jokes, they stated (1970:94): "The favorite Navajo Mountain jokes are about Paiutes, such as 'Nasja is your boy friend,' and 'Wochan [Dora Nelson; the Navajo name means literally "Excrement Teeth"] is your girl friend.'"

Like Navajo joking patterns, Paiutes' accounts of Navajo witchcraft during this period also reflect problematic relations between the two ethnic groups. One report of an incident in the 1960s demonstrates that San Juan Paiutes took threats of witchcraft seriously. According to the San Juans, a Navajo made use of *Paarʉy*'s grave to make witchcraft against a San Juan Paiute family (see Shepardson and Hammond's description of Navajos' use of graves and material from graves in witchcraft, 1970:141). According to the family members, a Navajo had placed little sticks on the grave to represent the family members. Interestingly, the Paiutes hired a Navajo medicine man to reverse the witchcraft.

Interethnic conflict in the northern area ultimately stemmed from economic competition. Navajo range encroachment had spread to the area northeast of Navajo Mountain in Utah. Responding to this pressure, Lester Willetson encouraged local Paiute men to rebuild the brush fence that ran north of the Utah-Arizona line between Lost Mesa and Jackrabbit Canyon, the same fence originally constructed by *Kavii* in the 1920s and 1930s. This fence apparently caused much consternation among the Navajos. Madeline Cameron, the trader at Navajo Mountain Trading Post in the 1950s and 1960s, labelled Willetson a "rabble rouser," largely because of what she considered his belligerent opposition to Navajo expansion (Bunte and Franklin Fieldnotes, October 18, 1982). Although he spent much of his time at White Mesa and Blanding, Willetson continued to be a chief elder of the San Juans in the Navajo Mountain-Paiute Canyon area, organizing the community for fence building, hunting trips, and round-dances, until his death in the 1960s.

In the southern area, San Juan Paiute residential and economic patterns also changed. Some San Juans continued throughout most of this period to shift residences seasonally between *Atatsiv* and Willow Springs, but began to remain longer at each winter site. For example, the extended family household which included Priscilla Dutchie, Alfred and Marie Lehi, and Angel and Anna Whiskers used only two winter camp sites during the 1950s and 1960s. Over the course of these two decades and into the 1970s, most households eventually abandoned seasonal movement altogether, and began to reside year-round at Willow Springs, *Atatsiv*, or at two new locations, Tuba City and Hidden Springs.

Consequently, by the 1970s, the southern area households no longer clustered in the winter on *Atatsiv*, but instead came to be dispersed at several sites, each with its own cluster of year-round Paiute household residences. Cars and trucks allowed the various households of the southern settlement to visit each other and continue cooperation in farming and other economic activities in spite of the greater distance between dwellings.

Another factor which encouraged many southern area San Juans to relocate outside of *Atatsiv* was the Paiutes' decreased dependence on sheep herding, partly brought about by reductions in the range land available to them. By the 1970s, only two households, one from each of the two newly emerged southern ambilineages, continued to herd livestock full-time on *Atatsiv*, although ownership and some of the labor involved in herding was shared by other ambilineage members.

Many Paiutes preferred to use cash from basketmaking and other sources to purchase most of their food. In addition, since children from several Paiute families started going to boarding school at Tuba City in the late 1950s and 1960s, some of these families chose house sites in Tuba City or at Hidden Springs by U.S. Highway 89, so that the children could come home on the weekends or even daily.

Members of the southern area settlement group continued to gather together at Willow Springs for planting and harvesting. The farms at Willow Springs were now, however, clearly divided into two ambilineally held sections. Where the families associated with *Machʉkats*' daughter, Priscilla Dutchie, used to farm in the 1930s, Alfred Lehi and his descendents were now farming. Most of the fields that had been farmed by *Ixirøts*' and Joe Francis' kin in the 1930s were now lost to erosion.

However, when Joe Norman and his second wife, Ski Francis, the daughter of Joe Francis, returned from Utah in the late 1940s, they inherited this area. As noted earlier, to the north of the Lehi field area, the descendents of *Wichʉnʉx* had inherited the field farmed by *Yuwa'nits* and later had expanded into the vacant area left by the family of *Akamanaxwats* and *T'aats*, of which only one member now remained, Blue Lee.

Some families or members of families would remain all summer or even year-round at Willow Springs, while others would just come during the periods of intensive farm work. Members of the two households still herding full-time on *Atatsiv* would pasture their sheep and goats on the plateau directly above the springs while they were helping with the farming. Willow Springs became the focal place for Paiute community life in the south. During the summer, southern community adults could visit every day with other ambilineage and settlement members and their children could play together.

As in the north, southern area San Juans also felt that some Navajo neighbors practiced witchcraft against Paiutes. Alfred Lehi is reported to have kept on hand medicine plants to protect himself from witchcraft whenever he visited Navajos. According to his descendents, Alfred Lehi made special trips to Kaibab to gather one medicine plant, which he would rub all over his body before going to squaw dances (Navajo Enemy Way ceremonies) or any other gathering where Navajo witches were thought to be present.

During the 1950s and 1960s, tribal elders from both the northern and southern areas worked together on at least two matters which dealt with the tribal land base. The earlier of these occasions resulted in an "exploration agreement" by which the "Piute Canyon Band Corporation" permitted "oil and gas geological exploration work on our [number illegible] acres, more or less, owned by the Piute Indians and operated by said Corporation" (Piute Canyon Band Exploration Agreement 1952). The San Juans were not federally recognized at this time and the land in question was technically part of the Navajo Reservation, although the San Juan Tribe considered it Paiute land.

This contractual agreement specified royalties to be paid if oil were to be discovered. It was signed by Joe Pikyavit, George F. Nelson, Genevieve Nelson, Alfred Lehi, and Lester Willetson, as well as the representatives of the mining company. Joe Pikyavit, then a Kanosh Paiute, was instrumental in arranging the oil exploration deal. George Nelson was a San Juan Paiute from Navajo Mountain who had married a Koosharem Paiute, Genevieve, and lived in Richfield, Utah. Alfred Lehi was, of course, tribal chief elder as well as chief elder of the San Juan Paiutes in the southern area, while Lester Willetson was the chief elder in the northern area. Since Pikyavit, Lehi, Nelson, and Willetson are no longer living, little information on this arrangement is available other than what the contract itself recorded. Apparently, no oil was ever discovered, although consultants state that test wells were drilled behind Navajo Mountain. Although only northern area land was involved in this agreement, the fact that Alfred Lehi helped to arrange it and signed the contract is an indication that the agreement and the land in question were seen as matters for tribal level representation.

In 1964 or 1965, an archeological project provoked a second meeting concerning the San Juan tribal land base. Sometime in the early 1960s, Anglo archeologists with a Navajo crew began a series of excavations at several Anasazi sites in the Navajo Mountain area. A San Juan Paiute, Jack Owl, also worked on this crew but did not participate in all of the digs. At present, it is not known who was responsible for managing the excavations, although the project may have been associated with either the Glen Canyon Dam salvage archeology project or the Navajo Tribe's Indian Claims Commission case.

The San Juans claim that the Anglo archeologists and Navajos excavated abandoned and even currently occupied San Juan sites, including homes and graves. Alfred Lehi called a tribal meeting at Paiute Canyon in 1964 or 1965. According to his daughter, Anna Whiskers, this meeting was held because of complaints from San Juans at Navajo Mountain:

> I remember that. It was with *Kaaxwats* [Joe Pikyavit, from Kanosh] and *Shaimuni* [Ralph Pikyavit, also from Kanosh]. It was because those Navajos were claiming those old Paiute homes there. Some company, some people somewhere, were digging up graves, where the Navajos were getting paid for digging and claiming that they used to live in [Mercy Whiskers'] cave [a summer dwelling]. That's where they were digging and the Navajos were getting paid for that. It was old Paiute ruins they were doing. And the Navajos were paid so much for that, digging up Paiute homes. [Bunte and Franklin Fieldnotes, October 20, 1984]

According to Anna Whiskers, several southern area residents, including Alfred Lehi, J. I. Casey, and *Para'an* /Chester Chelester, also came to the meeting in Paiute Canyon. Bessie Owl, who attended the meeting, stated that all the Navajo Mountain elders were present. According to consultants, the Pikyavits, Joe and Ralph, brought along an Anglo man from Cedar City. Although no one recalls his English name or his purpose in coming, he was called *Achʉats* in Paiute.

Alfred Lehi took *Achʉats* around to show him grave sites and sites where San Juans formerly lived, much as present day San Juan consultants have insisted on doing with us. According to his brother, Joe Norman, Alfred Lehi "wanted the white man to know about the Paiute country, where the Paiutes were living" (Bunte and Franklin Fieldnotes, October 19, 1984). Joe Norman, who also gave us an account of the meeting, stated that after the Paiute Canyon meeting, *Achʉats* stopped off at Willow Springs on his way back to Cedar City.

More clearly than in the previous case, this meeting dealing with San Juan land involved elders from both the southern and the northern settlement groups and thus was an instance of tribal level consensus group decision making. Alfred, acting as chief elder, called the meeting and then shepherded the Anglo visitor around.

As with *Pak'ai* before him, San Juans seem to remember best Alfred Lehi's sacred leadership and supernatural experiences. According to his family members, he got up every morning at dawn to pray, waking his grandchildren so that they could watch and participate. He taught them the sacred Paiute songs that they had to sing while facing east and making a corn meal offering in special baskets. He spoke traditional, non-Christian prayers before meals and at the beginning of tribal council meetings. Once when she was asked how today's tribal councils differ from those of Alfred Lehi's day, the present spokesperson, Lehi's granddaughter, stated that the prayers that her grandfather used to open meetings made them more sacred and special (Bunte and Franklin Fieldnotes, 1982).

Alfred Lehi is also remembered for his prophecies. Many of these, including the examples cited here, are still current among the San Juans. On one occasion, he is reported to have uttered: "Someday the smallest tribe is going to drive the largest tribe back where they came from." Community members reportedly wondered what was meant by the smallest tribe. Some years later, it occurred to one of Lehi's daughters,

Grace Lehi, that he must have been referring to the San Juan Tribe.

Alfred Lehi is also reported to have prophesied: "Everybody is going to get 'marks'" (*taxwaikyaivyatʉm*, "will be branded/marked"). It is said that these marks will be like scars or brands, but no one knows what the import of this prophecy is.

A final example of his prophecies is the following: "Soldiers are going to turn against their own people; their own children are going to do this." Some San Juans have interpreted this to refer to young educated Navajos who have worked for the Navajo Relocation Commission and are therefore, the Paiutes say, helping turn some of their own older relatives out of their homes (Bunte and Franklin Fieldnotes, June 26, 1983).

According to consultants, relatives and other community members would all listen and "feel scared inside" when they heard him say these things. Without warning and on any occasion, he would apparently go into a trance and begin speaking. Some Paiutes suggested that his prophecies were the result of dreams and drew comparisons between them and the sacred dreams and visions of *Pak'ai*, his grandfather.

In 1969, Alfred Lehi died after falling from a cliff on his way home on horseback from Tuba City. Members of his ambilineage believed that a Navajo living at Moenave had pushed him to his death. Accounts of his funeral in Tuba City demonstrate his significance to both San Juans and non-San Juans. San Juan Paiutes from both the northern and southern areas attended the funeral, as well as Paiutes from Kaibab, Kanosh, Koosharem, and Allen Canyon, as well as Navajos and Anglos. It is said that over 100 cars and pickups followed the hearse to the Tuba City cemetery.

Alfred Lehi's tragic death brought about a change in community leadership which encouraged the San Juans to get involved in external politics with other groups besides Southern Paiutes. While he was alive, the community relied on him to deal with outsiders. But Lehi appears to have preferred not to interact with non-Paiutes, especially non-Indians. This may have helped to isolate the tribe from the federal bureaucracy at Tuba City and from Anglo society in general. His death opened the way for new leaders who were more willing to confront federal officials and enlist the help of white outsiders.

Afterwards, Lehi's daughter went to Kaibab to seek help in

an investigation of the circumstances of her father's death. At the same time, she explained to the Kaibab Paiutes some of the other problems the San Juans were experiencing. As the Kaibabs were more knowledgeable in dealing with the Anglo bureaucracy, they volunteered to help their San Juan relatives find solutions. As we will see in the next chapter, the other Paiute groups also encouraged the San Juans to take advantage of outside professional assistance. This brought about a revolutionary change in the way that external political relations were conducted by the tribe.

4

SAN JUAN RELATIONS WITH THE FEDERAL GOVERNMENT, 1901–1984

The San Juan Tribe and Federal Government, 1901-1935

The founding of the Western Navajo Agency (WNA) in 1901, and the subsequent opening of the Tuba City Boarding School by the Indian Service, brought about in the short run a much closer and more continuous relationship between the U.S. government and members of the San Juan Southern Paiute Tribe. In 1907, the Department of the Interior set aside the San Juans' traditional area in Utah, at that time the only part of their holdings without federal trust status, as an exclusive San Juan Paiute reservation. By way of background, in 1884 this area in Utah, together with contiguous lands in Arizona, had been "set apart as a reservation for Indian purposes" by

Executive Order (ARCIA 1884:252; Hagerman 1932:12; see map 3). While no specific Indians groups were named in the 1884 order, government correspondence of the period suggests that the government had in mind the Navajos as well as the Paiutes since both were known to be be present there. The Utah section of the 1884 Executive Order area was returned to public domain in 1892 (Hagerman 1932:12), although the reason for this decision is not known.

The Western Navajo Reservation, with its agency headquarters at Tuba City, continued to be administered autonomously until 1935, when it was consolidated with other regional superintendencies dealing with Navajos under one superintendency at Window Rock. At the time of the consolidation, the Navajo Tribal Council was already exerting a marked influence on federal decision making in the region. After the mid-1930s, the Navajo Tribe also began to play a much greater and more direct role in the administration of reservation lands and populations, encouraged in this involvement by new developments in federal Indian policy which favored greater tribal self-determination (see L. Kelly 1968).

Following 1935, these administrative changes, together with other factors already present, began to create barriers to communication between the San Juan people and federal administrators. Moreover, unlike the Navajos and Hopis who had become increasingly skillful in their dealings with outsiders, until the death of Alfred Lehi in the late 1960s the San Juan people lacked both the appropriate communication skills and the willingness to communicate with non-Indians that would have made it possible for them to make their viewpoint known to federal officials and the public at large. San Juan Paiutes gradually slipped out of federal awareness during the period from the mid-1930s to 1968, resulting in federal policy decisions that ignored or were even prejudicial to the interests of Paiutes.

The first section of this chapter looks at the record of the government-to-tribe relationship provided by the Annual Reports of the Commissioner of Indian Affairs (ARCIA) for this period. This information, consisting largely of administrative population statistics for the Western Navajo Agency, serves to raise a number of important problems for historical analysis, which succeeding sections seek to resolve. The second section examines the early development of the federal wardship relation between the Western Navajo Agency and the San Juan Tribe, a relation that culminated in the government's recognition of San Juan internal political organization and in the establishment of the 1907 Paiute Strip Paiute Reservation, thereby bringing all of the San Juans' remaining territorial holdings under federal supervision. The third section analyzes the federal documentation produced by the Paiute Strip episode, a sequence of maneuvers involving federal officials, energy interests, local cattlemen, and the Navajo Tribe. In the 1920s and early 1930s, the Paiute Strip Paiute Reservation was arbitrarily restored to the public domain and subsequently was made an addition to the Navajo Reservation. The final section deals with the immediate aftermath of the Paiute Strip episode and the changes in the San Juans' federal relationship that occurred partly as a result of it.

San Juan Paiutes as a Recognized Administrative Population

There is considerable evidence in the federal documentation of this period that the officials of the Western Navajo Agency (WNA) considered the San Juan Southern Paiute Tribe as Paiute and as a separate administrative population from the Navajos and Hopis whom they also served. Throughout the WNA reports and correspondence of this period, officials make mention of individual Paiutes as students at the Tuba City and Marsh Pass schools or mention Paiutes in relation to other administrative matters. Some examples are examined below.

The most obvious, and certainly the most public indication of recognition, is the repeated inclusion of Paiutes in the WNA population statistics. Table 7 lists all WNA population statistics bearing on Paiutes, including published statistics (ARCIA 1906-1936) and unpublished figures (Western Navajo Agency Annual Reports [ARWNA] 1910-1935). In virtually all cases both the published and unpublished Paiute figures were listed under the heading "Paiute Tribe," indicating that the BIA recognized at least the enumerated Paiutes as members of a separate tribal reservation population.

While these population figures should be taken as evidence for a federal relation with the San Juan Tribe, they also raise important and thorny questions for our understanding of San Juan history. The reader will already have noted serious inconsistencies in the ARCIA estimates: they fluctuated wildly in the early years, settled near 200 between 1911 and 1923, but

Table 7:   WNA Paiute Population Statistics

Year	Paiutes listed under WNA, Arizona	Under WNA, Utah
1906	350 (ARCIA:481)	not applicable
1907	25 (ARCIA:173)	" "
1908	200 (ARCIA:185)	" "
1910	113 (ARCIA:61)	" "
1911	200 (ARCIA:54)	" "
1912	200 (ARCIA:73)	" "
1913	190 (ARCIA:49)	" "
1914	190 (ARCIA:77)	" "
1915	190 (ARCIA:63)	" "
1916	190 (ARCIA:74)	" "
1917	150 (ARWNA)	" "
1918	190 (ARCIA:84)	" "
1920	170 (ARCIA:65)	" "
1921	174 (ARCIA:42)	" "
1922	191 (ARCIA:30)	" "
1923	193 (ARCIA:24)	" "
1924	No separate listing (ARCIA:31)	" "
1925	" " " (ARCIA:33)	" "
1926	" " " (ARCIA:33)	" "
1927	30 (ARWNA)	" "
1928	32 (ARWNA)	" "
1929	26 (ARWNA)	" "
1930	25 (ARCIA:36)	" "
1931	No Paiutes listed (ARCIA:58)	" "
1933	32 (ARCIA:115)	" "
1934	32 (ARCIA:124)	4 (p. 149)
1935	Figure for other tribes only (ARCIA:159)	4 (p. 167)
1936	33 (ARCIA:210)	4 (p. 217)

then were absent for a few years only to resurface in the late 1920s considerably reduced. What do these figures mean as population estimates and what do they tell us about the federal relationship with the San Juans?

To be sure, a certain amount of inaccuracy arose from the nature and purpose of the estimation process itself. As Robert

Young pointed out in *The Navajo Yearbook* (1961:312), such population estimates, especially prior to the 1930s, must be understood as administrative attempts to gauge "service populations," that is, particular groups who were served by an agency and had to be budgeted for. Under the superintendency system, which held sway during this period, these figures were based primarily on the records of populations kept by school personnel and thus often underrepresented families with no children in school or of school age (see discussion in census expert W. Kelly's report on the creation of a Navajo Population Register, 1964:25-26). While this may account for some omissions from WNA counts and Indian census rolls during this period, the larger anomalies, that is, the early fluctuation, the sudden gap in the 1920s, and the subsequent reappearance of a drastically reduced population, find their explanation in a closer examination of WNA history and changes that occurred in the Paiutes' government-to-tribe relationship.

The Establishment of a Government-to-Tribe Relationship,
1901-1920

The earliest indication that Indian Service and other government officials were aware that Paiutes were included in the service population of the Western Navajo Agency actually occurred in the last years of the nineteenth century when the agency was still in the planning stages. In his 1898 report to the Secretary of the Interior, Indian Inspector James McLaughlin discussed the proposed agency and school at Tuba City. He wrote: "The village of Tuba City . . . would afford one of the best locations for a large Industrial School for the Navajo, Moqui, and Piute Indians, who live in the vicinity, that could be found in Arizona" (McLaughlin 1898). This recommendation, mentioning all three local tribes, was taken up in subsequent documents dealing with the establishment of the Western Navajo Agency and School (McLaughlin 1899; Jones 1899; McKinley 1900).

With the founding of the new agency, reports and correspondence soon began to mention Paiutes. WNA farming supervisor Matthew M. Murphy noted the presence of 80 Paiutes in one of his farming districts, northwest of Shonto (Murphy 1902). The region described includes Paiute Canyon and the area surrounding it.

In 1905, a series of events began that led to recognition of the San Juan Southern Paiutes as a polity and to their being given the Paiute Strip in Utah as a reservation exclusively for their use. Laura Work, superintendent of the Panguitch school, wrote to the Commissioner of Indian Affairs "concerning the condition of the Kaibab and San Juan Indians, two bands of Paiutes in Southern Utah" (Work 1905).

In a second letter two months later, Work made specific recommendations concerning "the San Juan Pahutes, another band of destitute Indians in the southeastern part of Utah":

> I have at various times placed the needs of these Indians before your office, especially in my annual reports, and will here recapitulate the same, as the matter appears to me:
>
> 1. The land along the San Juan River, secured to the Indians by some means, so that envious cattle men cannot dispossess them;
>
> 2. Water brought on the tillable portions, so that each family can make a home, the mountainous parts being used in common as a range for sheep [she mentioned earlier in the letter that the San Juans had sheep and had learned "the art of weaving" from the Navajos; note that they were no less culturally Paiute in her estimation, and in fact she stated at the same point that they were "nearly related" to the Kaibab Paiutes].
>
> 3. The purchase of a few sheep for each family containing one or more weavers, or a small common herd, to be divided at some future time when its growth shall warrant such division; in my judgment sheep are a necessity toward self-support for this particular band of Indians. [Work 1906]

Soon afterward Work was replaced at Panguitch by Walter Runke, who had served four years as industrial teacher at the Western Navajo School and was himself to be WNA superintendent for several years starting in 1914. In response to a follow-up letter from the commissioner regarding Work's recommendations, Runke made the following report of the San Juan Paiute "band":

> The "San Juans" are located in north-west Arizona and

in south-west Utah south of the San Juan River. I have
learned from fairly reliable sources that they number
about 85.   They are living with and amongst the
Navajoes and have adopted the nomadic live [sic] led by
these Indians. [Runke 1907]

The location and the population estimate ascribed here to the
San Juans echoed Murphy's account in 1902, and thus may
have reflected only the northern area population. Runke's
population estimate also approximated Superintendent Stephen
Janus' 1909 figures for the two northern settlement groups,
Paiute Canyon and Douglas Mesa. It seems clear that, although
Runke recognized the San Juan people as a social and political
group by calling them a "band," he was talking only about San
Juan Paiutes in the north. Lacking the experience he would
later gain as WNA superintendent, he may not have known of
the Paiute presence at southern sites like Willow Springs, Gap,
Cedar Ridge, and the sandy plateau north of Tuba City, or of
the connection between Paiutes in both areas.
    At least two inspections were made of the San Juan
Southern Paiutes to determine their status and needs, the first
by Inspector Levi Chubbock in 1906, and the second by
Inspector Frank C. Churchill in 1907. It was Superintendent
Matthew Murphy who served as guide for both trips to the
Navajo Mountain area. In a letter responding to Churchill,
who had contacted Murphy in regard to the second inspection
trip, Murphy revealed that Chubbock's earlier trip had been
less than successful:

I reached Kanab, Utah, a few hours after you had left
there; if I had met you I could probably have given you
some information in regard to the band which
sometimes lives in Paiute Canyon east of Navajo
Mountain, but which at that time and may be yet, at a
lake [?] that is situated between the San Juan and
Colorado Rivers.

If this is the band you are looking for they are hard
to locate and they will very likely have nothing to say
when you do locate them.

I took Mr. Chubbock to the San Juan last November
to see this band but they would not come in to have a
talk. They ask for nothing but to be left alone. . . .

We would be pleased to have you and Mrs. Churchill
visit Tuba, and I will do what I can to help you to
locate your Indians. [Murphy 1907]

Churchill was able to visit both the Kaibab and San Juan
Paiute bands, and recommended to the commissioner of Indian
affairs that reservations be set aside for both. Acting BIA
Commissioner C. F. Larrabee passed the recommendations on to
the secretary of the interior where they were approved on
October 16, 1907. What became known locally as the "Paiute
Strip" was then withdrawn

from all forms of settlement and entry for the use of
the Paiute Indians, [including] all the vacant public
lands in the State of Utah, bounded as follows:

Beginning at a point where the San Juan River
intersects the 110th degree of west longitude; thence
down the Colorado River to a point where the said river
crosses the boundary line between Utah and Arizona.
[Larrabee 1907]

The order was reformulated to include an additional clause
specifying the southern boundary overlooked in the original
order, the Utah-Arizona line (Larrabee 1908)   In the
accompanying letter, the reservation was specified "for the use
of the Kaibab and San Juan Piute Indians." According to one
elderly Kaibab Paiute, Mabel Drye, an attempt was initially
made to get the Kaibab Tribe to join the San Juans on the new
reservation by Navajo Mountain (Jake, James, and Bunte
1983:48).

Murphy revised his 1906 estimate of 350 Paiutes under his
jurisdiction (ARCIA 1906:481) to 25 in 1907 (ARCIA 1907:173).
Since the latter figure referred only to the southern area
population, this reduction probably reflected a decision,
following Churchill's recommendations, to place the Paiutes in
the north under Utah rather than Tuba City. This situation, in
which the San Juan Tribe found itself under two agency
jurisdictions, was by no means a rare occurrence at this time,
the Navajo and Hopi Tribes being prime examples of multiple
agency jurisdiction during this period.

Because the Colorado River posed a serious hindrance to
travel and communication between the northern San Juans and

their new agency at Panguitch, it was quickly decided that Tuba City would be a better agency through which to channel appropriations for the San Juans living in the north. In a letter to the commissioner, the new Tuba City Superintendent Stephen Janus quoted a letter previously received from the BIA office, dated August 13, 1908, which referred to this decision:

As "the San Juan Paiutes are now abiding on the Western Navajo Reservation and properly under your jurisdiction he [the Panguitch Superintendent] recommends that you [Janus] be authorized to make all expenditures . . . you are hereby directed to make an investigation as to the needs of the San Juan Piutes and transmit a report thereon to this Office . . ." [Janus 1908]

Janus then proceeded to offer his assessment of the San Juan Paiutes' status as a single group and of their needs:

In his report for 1905 my predecessor [Murphy] gave the number of Piutes in the northern part of this reservation as 300, and in his report for 1907 he gives it as 25. I can find no information in this office referring to them but the twenty five referred to are doubtless the Piutes living within fifteen miles of this school at Willow Springs. There are also a few living on Cedar Ridge on the road to Lee's Ferry and the rest are in the extreme northern part of the reservation, some in what is known as Piute Canon, and the rest scattered along the San Juan River, and in the vicinity of Navajo Mountain. I have no information as to the whereabouts or exact number of the bulk of these Indians but doubtless shall be able to find them. From what I can learn of them they are certainly in need of assistance. Those near here are very poor, having no shoes. . . .

But as soon as I can get matters here in running shape, I will make a trip and gather detailed information as is necessary to make the report required.

The report Janus submitted at the beginning of the following year, quoted in chapter 3, reveals that his own 1910 estimate of 113 Paiutes was based on an actual count of 116 individuals he was able to contact in person during 1909.

Moreover, on the basis of Janus' description of San Juan Southern Paiute political organization, it can also be presumed that the local superintendency administration had become aware of the San Juans as a self-governing tribe. Janus' recommendation that the government deal with all three settlement groups of the San Juans through the group's traditional chief, Lehi or *Pak'ai*, most clearly illustrated this recognition (Janus 1909a).

Over the following decade there were scattered mentions of San Juan Paiutes as pupils at the Indian schools and in other matters pertaining to their status as an administrative population. Superintendent C. R. Jeffers' Annual Report (1911), noted that Paiutes and Hopis, as well as Navajos, practiced silversmithing in the WNR and that both Navajos' and Paiutes' advancement in school was "slow." The following year, he reported two cases of scarlet fever at the Western Navajo School at Tuba City, one of which was a Paiute pupil named "Philip" (Jeffers 1912).

Walter Runke's reports and correspondence during his tenure as WNA superintendent made several such mentions. He noted in his Annual Report for 1915, "The jurisdiction is inhabited by three separate Indian tribes; the Navajo, Hopi and Piute, the Navajo being largely preponderant. All three tribes still continue to indulge in their old Indian dances" (Runke 1915b).

Runke was especially sensitive to the mixed tribal population of his reservation, perhaps because of his stint at Panguitch during the period when the BIA was looking for an agency and school for the Kaibab and San Juan Paiutes. In 1915, he requested that the BIA place in his legal jurisdiction the northern-most San Juan Paiutes. While the WNA was to be the agency through which federal funds for the San Juan Paiutes were to be funneled, those Paiutes located at least part of the year on the Strip may have technically fallen outside the WNA's law enforcement jurisdiction. In any event, Runke believed this to be the case:

> I would like to bring to the attention of the Office the matter of placing these Piute Indians under the jurisdiction of the agency. There are several reasons that could be advanced for making it desirable that these Indians be placed under this jurisdiction. These Indians have reserved for them the so called "Piute Strip" located in the state of Utah . . . Their reservation

lies contiguous to the Navajo reservation under my
jurisdiction, and although the "Piute Strip" is specially
reserved for these Indians and to some extent used by
them, they, however, make their home, a large share of
the time, in what is called "Piute Canyon" which is
located south of their reservation lands and on Navajo
lands of this jurisdiction. In fact the only land which
they farm is located on this Navajo reservation, I am
informed. [Runke 1915a]

At this time, that is, between Janus' report in 1908 and the
1918 Influenza epidemic, San Juans were still farming in the
area of Douglas Mesa or Paiute Farms, as well as at other sites
along the San Juan River closer to Navajo Mountain. The latter
sites are located in Utah. During or shortly after 1918, the
combined pressures of the Paiutes' fear of the flu and local
Navajo expansion appear to have forced the Douglas Mesa
group from the farms recorded by Janus in the Oljeto-Douglas
Mesa area (see Van Valkenburgh's corroborative account of
Navajo pressure and Paiute abandonment of Paiute Farms
[1941:114]).

In two letters dated February, 1916, Superintendent Runke
reported that he had hired a Piute, "Joedie" or *Akamanaxwats*,
as a temporary policeman to carry a message in a case
involving a group of Navajo criminals and their leader,
"Taddytin" (Runke 1916a and 1916b). In the second letter,
Runke stated that he chose a Piute rather than a Navajo
because he believed a Piute would more trustworthy,
presumably because a Navajo might more easily side with or be
influenced by Taddytin, himself a Navajo.

In 1915, Runke had referred to his jurisdiction as the
Navajo Reservation. Significantly, in 1919 after five years of
dealing with the peoples under his superintendency, he wrote
to Commissioner Cato Sells to request that the WNA and
boarding school be renamed the "Painted Desert School and
Agency." He wished the change partly because of the problems
of mail mix-up with Fort Defiance and other Navajo Agencies,
but also because, as he stated:

The name, "Western Navajo," for this jurisdiction is
itself a misnomer for the reason that the Jurisdiction is
inhabited not alone by Navajos but we also have a
considerable population two other tribes, namely the
Hopis and the Paiute and a few Utes. It is incorrect

therefore to call the Indians of this Jurisdiction by the name, "Western Navajo." The name does not recognize the fact that there are other Indians on this jurisdiction entitled to equal rights with the Western Navajo. [Runke 1919]

This makes clear the extent to which Runke was cognizant of the San Juans' separate status as well as their rights to reservation lands and agency services. Inspector W. S. Coleman, in his report of the same month, seconded Runke's request and referred the commissioner to Runke's reasons (Coleman 1919). Unfortunately, this suggestion, which might in a small way have encouraged the federal government to maintain its awareness of the WNR's non-Navajo inhabitants through the years of change to come, was never taken up.

At the close of the WNA's second decade, the San Juan people had arrived at what could be called the high point of their federal relationship. To be sure, through the 1920s, 1930s, and even into the present day, the government continued to recognize the Paiutes' presence, especially those living in the south close by Tuba City at Willow Springs, Gap, and Cedar Ridge. In the 1920s, however, a series of events set the federal government's relationship with the San Juan people on a different course from the one it seemed to be taking in the first two decades of the twentieth century.

The Paiute Strip Episode, 1921-1933

In 1921, Leroy A. Wilson of the Paradise Oil and Refining Company, Montecello, Utah, wrote a rapid-fire series of letters to BIA Commissioner Charles A. Burke and Assistant Commissioner E. B. Merritt requesting a permit to drill on the Paiute Strip (Wilson 1921a, 1921b, 1921c). At first he was told that there was no authority to give such a permit (Merritt 1921a). Wilson's third letter, however, met with a more obliging response:

Some of the lands are probably included in those withdrawn from the public domain by order of the Secretary of the Interior of October 16, 1907, supplemented by order of May 28, 1908, for the use of the Kaibab and Paiute Indians and known as the Paiute Reservation. . . . in order to secure any rights in the lands involved, it would be necessary to restore the lands to the public domain in which event they would be subject to the rules and regulations of the General Land Office.

If, in view of the foregoing, you still desire to secure a permit to prospect on those lands, it is suggested that you so advise this Office and the matter will be given further consideration at that time. Mr. Byron A. Sharp, Superintendent of the Western Navajo Reservation, Tuba City, Arizona, has jurisdiction over that part of the Navajo Reservation lying in Utah. [Merritt 1921b]

In March, 1922, Superintendent Sharp was ordered by the BIA office to investigate the Paiutes' utilization of the Paiute Strip reservation. He submitted a report of his findings on June 2, 1922, to the Commissioner of Indian Affairs:

In accordance with instructions contained in Office letter of March 15, 1922, I have made a visit to the Piute Strip, which is under this jurisdiction, and submit herewith a report with reference to my findings.

I am inclosing herewith a rough sketch, showing the outlines of the Piute Reservation, and I have located thereon in red the outline of my trip through a portion of that reservation. The land over which I traveled is a level country and is covered with buckwheat and red top grass, which is excellent for grazing purposes, possibly better for cattle than for sheep.

This particular section, which includes not only the Piute Reservation, but also a large section of the Navajo Reservation, is known as the Monument Valley. . . . The land to the west of Monument Valley is very broken, with deep canyons leading into the San Juan River to the north, but the greater portion of the Piute Reservation is covered with a grass suitable for the grazing of both cattle and sheep. [Sharp 1922]

Unfortunately, Sharp's map is not included with the letter in the federal archives. However, his description of "the land over which [he] traveled," plus the fact that he called it Monument

Valley, carefully distinguishing "this particular section" from
the broken and much less accessible land to the west--that is,
the lands around Navajo Mountain and Lower Paiute Canyon--
all make it clear that he did not visit the large area of the
Paiute Reservation to the west of Monument Valley. This
would imply that he could speak from experience and direct
observation only about the area that had been abandoned by
the Oljeto, or Douglas Mesa, offshoot of the Navajo Mountain
subgroup described by Janus earlier.

This point tends to call into question Sharp's sweeping
conclusions in the rest of his report:

> At the present time I find that there are no Piute
> Indians living on the reservation and that not over *100*
> head of *Piute horses* are grazing on that reservation.
> When the Piute strip was set aside as a reservation by
> executive [actually departmental] order in 1907, I
> understand that there were approximately 86 Piute
> Indians who were to benefit by the setting aside of this
> land. Since this reservation was set aside quite a
> number of Piute Indians have died, others have gone
> farther north into Utah around what is known as the
> Blue Mountain Country [Allen Canyon], and I
> understand have received allotments there. Others have
> moved onto the Navajo Reservation and are living in
> what is known as the Piute Canyon just south of the
> state line between Utah and Arizona. The Reclamation
> Service has recently put in an irrigation project for
> *these* Indians at that point.
>
> Others of the Piute tribe have been absorbed into
> the Navajo tribe. Therefore the Piute Reservation does
> not benefit at this time any of the Piute Indians. . . .
> unless your Office intends to hold the Piute Reservation
> for the *benefit of the Navajo Indians*, I can see no
> objection to throwing it open to settlement. [emphasis
> added]

Sharp crucially misrepresented 1920s San Juan land use in
the Paiute Strip in several ways. First, he depicted what other
observers understood to be the Navajo Mountain subgroup's
transhumant residence pattern, based on a normal seasonal
change of pastures between Arizona and the Strip in Utah, as a
permanent move away from the Strip. The report was also

misleading with respect to the situation in Monument Valley. While Sharp may well have been correct in stating that the Douglas Mesa group had ceased to occupy the area on a year-round basis, the lack of further examination into the conditions under which this abandonment took place leaves one with the impression that the Piutes left willingly, having no use for their reservation and preferring to reside elsewhere. Moveover, he stated that some undetermined number of these Paiutes had been "absorbed" by the local Navajo community, although competitive relations and hard feelings between the ethnic groups would certainly have precluded that. Finally, in light of his conclusion that no Paiutes were then deriving any benefit from their reservation, it is curious that Sharp still conceded the presence of some 100 Paiute horses on it, all apparently in the Monument Valley area.

Sharp's report was submitted at a time when the Department of the Interior, under the leadership of Secretary Albert Fall, later infamous for his role in the Teapot Dome scandal, was pursuing a policy of increased mineral exploitation in federal lands. Not surprisingly, Sharp's distortions, whether the result of mere negligence or a deliberate attempt to please his superiors in Washington, had immediate consequences for the San Juan people and their reservation. Little more than a month later, the BIA commissioner recommended to the secretary of the interior that the Paiute Reservation be returned to public domain. In another seven days, Secretary Fall had approved it (Burke 1922).

Almost immediately, Elsie Holliday, a young Navajo woman just back from the Indian school at Riverside, California, began writing to the BIA as well as to S. M. Brosius of the Indian Rights Association on behalf of her family and other Navajos in the Kayenta area who were interested in the Paiute Strip. Brosius himself was soon putting pressure on the BIA to secure the "Indians'" rights within the restored areas (see Hauke 1922).

As a direct result of Brosius' agitation, WNA Supervisor-in-Charge A. W. Leech was requested to make a second visit to the restored area, this time including the western section. Leech reported his findings:

In compliance with your letter of April 28, enclosing a photostatic copy of a letter addressed to you by Mr. R. [sic] M. Brosius, of the Indian Rights association, I

visited what is known as the Piute Strip, or that portion
of land withdrawn by Departmental Order of October
16, 1907, but recently restored to the public domain, and
am submitting the following report:

I find that there are very few Piute Indians living
within this strip, to be exact, I could only locate forty
eight, men, women and children, mostly the latter, and
these live in what is known as Piute Canyon, well
toward the western portion of the strip. The families
consist of Beluw Nechonie with his sisters and their
families, numbering twelve in all; Dossonie, a widow,
with her son and daughters and their families,
comprising fourteen people in all; Arvill Lutzin
[Willetson?], his wife and son, a family of three; and
Nasjah, father, with his daughters and sons and their
families, comprising nineteen in all. I am not sure as to
the spelling of these names as I am not familiar with
Piute [the names, with the possible exception of Arvill
Lutzin, are not in Paiute but in Navajo, suggesting the
presence of a Navajo interpreter]. I was unable to
locate any other Piutes within the strip, and in fact the
ones mentioned above do not live there all the time, I
am told, but from all indications that is their real home.

I found several families of Navajoes within this
territory, most of whom were the Holliday family. This
is quite a large family, comprising six brothers and
their families, *totaling forty one in number*. There are
several other Navajoes who are transients more or less,
visiting the strip at various times with their flocks, but
I did not succeed in finding them at the time of my visit.
The fact of the matter is that the Navajoes are the real
users of this land and it is reported that they have
driven the Piutes out, and are the ones who are making
the effort to have the land withdrawn from the Public
Domain and restored to the Indians.

I met Elsie Holliday who is the prime mover in the
attempt to have this land restored . . . She is a full
blood Navajoe, a graduate of Sherman Institute age 21.
She informed me that upon her return from school
something over a year ago, the Navajoes who had been
accustomed to use the land in question [illegally since it

was withdrawn *only* for Paiute use at the time] appealed
to her to help them obtain the land, and she says . . . she
had four petitions prepared and secured the signatures
of a hundred thirty-four people, all of whom were
Navajoes. *Seventy-four* of the signers were living at the
time on the strip, but *many* of these seventy-four only
lived there at certain times of the year, while there was
pasture for stock on this land. . . . She circulated these
petitions and sent one copy to the Indian Rights
Association, one to the Secretary of the Interior, one to
the Commissioner of Indian Affairs, and another to D.
W. Strickland, an attorney of Denver. . . .

In summing up the result of my visit to this
territory, I wish to say that it is my opinion that the
strip in question contains very few Piutes, perhaps, so
far as I could learn, no more than those previously
mentioned. There are a few living along the northern
side of the San Juan River who occasionally wander
over into this territory, but do not stay any length of
time. The greater number of Indians who use the land
in question are Navajoes whose homes lie on the *south
side* of the Utah-Arizona state line, but who graze their
flocks a portion of the year on this strip. There is no
way of determining the number of these people as at
one visit there might be a considerable number, and at
another time a very few.

The grazing in this strip is fairly good in some
localities, particularly along that portion known as the
Monument Valley, but there is not much water there.
There is some fair grazing near what is known as
Navajo Mountain, in the western portion of the strip,
and a few small streams afford water, but *not many
Navajoes visit this territory*, and as previously stated, the
few Piutes *within it live in this vicinity*. [Leech 1923;
emphasis added]

Leech's report clarified a number of points that Sharp
clouded over. First, the Navajo Mountain subgroup of San
Juan Paiutes was clearly still located on the western portion of
the Paiute Strip as well as on the Arizona side at Paiute
Canyon. According to Leech, they occupied this western area
exclusively. Their number, 48, was comparable to Janus' 1909

estimate of 42. This figure must be taken as the minimum number of Paiutes living on and/or using the Strip, both because Leech only counted those he could locate and because he himself believed there were other Paiutes, possibly at this time living alongside or north of the San Juan River, who still used the Strip at least seasonally. The Navajos at this time appeared restricted to Monument Valley. Leech's estimate of Navajos living on the Strip itself, 74, may have been too high since he was able to locate only forty-one, all relatives of Elsie Holliday. Leech also indicated that "many of these seventy-four only lived there at certain seasons" and that "their homes [lay] south of the Utah-Arizona state line." While he concluded that the Strip was primarily used by Navajos, his own reported information, in terms of numbers of individuals actually observed and in terms of the extent of Strip lands used, was not clear-cut and could in fact be construed as contradicting his conclusions.

The report also gave a more realistic, although still biased picture of Navajo-Paiute relations. First, Leech recorded second hand information that the Navajos at Monument Valley and Kayenta had driven out the original Paiute inhabitants. This observation was seconded by another contemporary, archeologist Byron Cummings (quoted in Euler 1966:96; Cummings 1952:25), and by an anthropological account written later but based on Navajo oral tradition (Van Valkenburgh 1941:115). Secondly, since Holliday collected only Navajo signatures, it seems clear that she and other local Navajos were not interested in protecting preexisting Paiute rights in Monument Valley, as Brosius and others seem to have thought, but in acquiring these rights for themselves exclusively.

While Leech's report may have been the more accurate assessment of the situation, it, like Sharp's report, also betrayed a tacit bias in favor of Navajo expansion coupled with a remarkable insensitivity to the consequences for the San Juan people. Leech's bias is most evident when we examine the relative weight he assigned to the needs and wishes of the 41 Hollidays (evidently newcomers to Monument Valley) versus that given the 48 Paiutes he was able to contact. The same pro-Navajo bias that was reflected in his interpretation of the figures doubtless also accounts for his inability to draw what seems to be an obvious conclusion regarding the legality of the Navajos' takeover in Monument Valley. While Leach was perfectly aware of the history of conflict between Navajos and Paiutes and also knew that the Strip had been set aside "only for Paiute use" and not for Navajos at all, he apparently saw no connection between these facts and his own responsibilities to all of the Indians under his supervision.

In the reports of both Sharp and Leech one can detect the beginnings of an historically significant change in attitude among WNA officials. There was a movement away from the more even-handed treatment of all three ethnic groups characteristic of officials like Janus or Runke towards a conception of local federal responsibilities as defined almost exclusively by the needs of the more numerous Navajos.

Superintendent Chester L. Walker, head of the WNA during the late 1920s and early 1930s, represented perhaps the clearest case of explicit pro-Navajo bias in local administration. For example, he described the Moenkopi Hopis as "squatters" on the Western Navajo Reservation and their use of Moenkopi Wash, which of course considerably predates that of Navajos, as "encroachment" on Navajo lands (Walker 1930a).

There was another factor operating in Leech's investigation that is equally crucial to our understanding of historical relations between the San Juan Tribe and the government. In describing his visit to Paiute Canyon, Leech admitted that his lack of Paiute hampered communication. The presence of a Navajo interpreter must also certainly have hindered frank communication. In a subsequent interview with Elsie Holliday, however, her fluency in English proved a powerful, if not overwhelming, influence in shaping his opinion of the situation.

As Lawrence Kelly's (1968) analysis of Navajo political development also illustrated, already in the 1920s there had emerged a new type of tribal leadership among the Navajos: young, relatively well-educated spokesmen and women who were familiar with the cultural expectations of Anglos and knew how to communicate and work with government administrators. Among the Hopis as well, many newly emerging political representatives showed themselves well able to manage the flow of information in the policy making process to the best advantage of their community.

During this same period, however, and for several decades thereafter, the San Juan Tribe was represented only by its traditional government. Its chief elders were not always friendly or forthcoming with whites, and in any event they lacked the necessary skills to deal with them on their terms. Throughout Alfred Lehi's tenure, when Paiutes ran into problems with the BIA administration or local Navajos, he preferred to call upon allies among other Southern Paiute communities rather than rely on Anglo administrators. The leaders of other Southern Paiute tribes, although sympathetic to the San Juans' needs and often energetic in their defense, hardly possessed more influence than the San Juans themselves. This perhaps misguided self-reliance worked in concert with reservation administrators' growing preoccupation with Navajo interests to isolate the San Juan Tribe from the federal decision making process. The fact that Navajos, in particular, were able to put their desires and views across so forcefully further worsened the Paiutes' situation over the decades that followed the Paiute Strip episode.

As a result of the restoration of the Paiute Strip to public domain, the northerly San Juan Paiutes were placed under the Consolidated Ute Agency in Colorado. The following letter written by Ute Superintendent E. E. McKean to the commissioner of Indian affairs confirmed this and also provided another perspective on the situation in the Strip, this time from a federal official whose first concern was for the needs of Paiutes and Utes:

I have the honor to advise that since the Indians on Douglas Mesa and Piute Canon have been placed under this jurisdiction, it is my desire to be informed regarding the status of that tract of land formerly known as the Piute Indian reservation lying in Southern Utah. . . . If it is at all possible, I would recommend that the land within the boundaries of this Piute Indian reservation be reserved for Piute Indians now living there and those who lived there in the past but left through fear during the [1918] Flu epidemic. If this can be arranged, it will furnish the Indians with a desirable winter range for their sheep. . . . I have been informed that a certain Navajo woman has interested herself in the Piute country with the hopes of securing it for the Navajo Indians. Inasmuch as the Navajos have a very large area of land, at the present time . . . I believe that a greater good would be accomplished if the Piute reservation could be reserved for Piute Indians only. [McKean 1923]

As noted in the previous chapter, by this time several families of San Juan Paiutes from Douglas Mesa had left for Allen Canyon, where they applied for homestead allotments.

They were the Dutchies, the Cantsees, and others, along with members of Posey's band, whose names appear on later maps of allotments at Allen Canyon and nearby White Mesa (see, for example, White Mesa Allotment Map 1939). Still others of the Douglas Mesa group removed to the Ute Mountain Reservation in southwestern Colorado, to the Koosharem Paiute community at Richfield, Utah, or to the San Juan settlement in the Paiute Canyon-Navajo Mountain area. This first migration should be clearly distinguished from the second wave of out-migrants from the north. The second group included the handful of families from Navajo Mountain that Navajo Councilman Bert Tallsalt listed in 1954 as living at the White Mesa Reservation and at Blanding or as moving between Navajo Mountain and White Mesa. This latter group did not move up there in the 1920s but only in the 1940s and 1950s. These individuals, as Tallsalt's list itself indicates, did not abandon their ties to the San Juan Tribe and, unlike the earlier wave of San Juan emigres, did not benefit from any status in the Ute Mountain Tribe.

Despite this change of agency and the departure of many friends and relatives from the Douglas Mesa group, the members of the Navajo Mountain-Paiute Canyon subgroup of San Juan Southern Paiutes continued to live in just those areas where historical accounts had always placed them and continued within the same tribal organization that Superintendent Janus and others had observed. In 1928, in his report of the Navajo Tribal Council held at Leupp, during which the council discussed the desirability of obtaining the Strip, WNA Superintendent C. L. Walker made reference to the fact that substantial use of the Strip was still being made by the northern San Juan Paiutes, although he called them Utes, no doubt because of their agency affiliation under Consolidated Ute:

> Consequently, we cannot state the exact number who occupy this area. There are twenty-five families [Navajos] who remain within this area approximately the year around, but in the course of a year there would probably be as many as one-hundred families grazing within the area. . . . I might state that there are probably one-hundred Ute Indians occupying this land in addition to the Navajos above referred to. [Walker 1928a]

Some of these "one-hundred Ute Indians" were probably former San Juan Paiutes from Monument Valley who had joined the Allen Canyon community but still continued to use their old homeland, especially for seasonal grazing.

Although the San Juan Paiutes living in the south near Tuba City were not supposed to be subject to the change in jurisdiction, which was at least in the minds of the southern Colorado Ute Agency officials to include only those Paiutes living on the former Paiute Reservation, there is evidence that suggests that for a space of four years, between 1923 and 1927, the Western Navajo Agency may have operated on the assumption that all Paiutes had been removed from their supervision. First, there is the chronological gap in Paiute population statistics in the mid-1920s (see table 7 above). In addition, according to the present Western Navajo Subagency Superintendent Irving Billy, the records at the BIA Navajo Area Census Office, Window Rock, Arizona, continue to list many older southern area residents as "full Paiute Indians . . . enrolled with the Ute Tribe in Utah [sic]" (Billy 1984). It seems likely that these records date from a period of administrative confusion in the 1920s regarding the Paiutes' agency status. As we shall see below, it was primarily the thirty-odd San Juan Paiutes living in the south who reemerged in the late 1920s to be enumerated as members of the "Paiute Tribe" in WNA population statistics.

In the late 1920s, more powerful interests began to apply pressure in their effort to have the Paiute Strip made part of the Western Navajo Reservation for the benefit of the Navajo Tribe. Apart from the newly organized Navajo Tribal Council and WNA Superintendent C. L. Walker, Special Indian Commissioner H. J. Hagerman, appointed to negotiate Navajo Reservation expansion with the Navajos' neighbors in New Mexico, Arizona, and Utah, also took an active role in promoting annexation. As a result, the Strip was again made reservation land, initially by Departmental Order on February 19, 1929, and finally, after some delicate negotiation with local Utah cattlemen, by Act of Congress (June 15, 1933).

While the annexation was clearly to have serious consequences for the Paiutes, since it legitimized further Navajo encroachment, the arguments for Paiute strip annexation which BIA officials and the Navajo Tribal Council used in their efforts to persuade policy makers also exercised a significant influence. In attempting to rationalize the addition of the Strip to the Navajo Reservation, certain BIA officials and the Navajo Tribal Council produced a new and transformed view of Western Navajo Reservation history which, intentionally or unintentionally, suppressed a number of important facts regarding San Juan Southern Paiutes' role in that history while simultaneously revising backward to give the Navajos the appearance of having been a permanent fixture in the region. Since the revised version of local history promulgated by the Navajo Tribe and Commissioner Hagerman afterward became for many people in the government the standard version and the one on which a number of important policy decisions in later decades were based, it is worthwhile examining the language of some of the statements from which this view originated.

Hagerman, for example, made recommendations as to the external boundaries of the proposed unified Navajo reservation in his report, *Navajo Indian Reservation* (1932). He described the Paiute Strip situation as follows:

> **Item 5--Executive orders of May 17, 1884, and November 19, 1892, 2,373,870 acres.--**These orders comprise a vast area of country between the San Juan and Colorado Rivers and the Utah-Arizona line, and another large tract in what is now the northern part of the Western Navajo jurisdiction. That part of the strip between the rivers and the State boundary line which lies east of the one hundred and tenth meridian, known as the Paiute Strip, was restored to entry by the order of 1892. The 1884 order states that the areas withdrawn "are withheld from sale and settlement and set apart as a reservation for Indian purposes." It is apparent on the face of it that in order to clarify the status of these lands, further definitions by Congress as to said status are necessary.
>
> Kayenta is situated in that part of the 1884 withdrawal which is in northern Arizona. Kayenta has for many years been the headquarters of this remote and quite inaccessible country. Near it are numerous prehistoric ruins, and in part of it the famous Monument Valley, extending over the Utah border in the Paiute country. The *Indians* of this region are more remote from contacts with the white civilization than any other *Indians* in the Navajo country. On account of their distance from communication with the outside

world they have probably been neglected. *They* have from *time immemorial* used the Paiute Strip north of them, which will be described in more detail later in this report. [Hagerman 1932:12; emphasis added]

Item 20--The Paiute Strip in southern Utah, containing 498,208 acres.--This strip, lying north of the Utah-Arizona line, west of one hundred and tenth meridian, and south of the San Juan River in Utah, became a part of the Indian Reservation by Executive order dated May 17, 1884, was restored by departmental order dated July 17, 1922.

The statements regarding nonusage of this land by the Indians as contained in the report of Supervisor Leech, as a result of which the land was withdrawn from the reservation [here he confuses Sharp with Leech], were apparently ungrounded, since information obtained after the report was rendered show that it was never vacated or abandoned by the *Indians*, but that they have occupied it constantly as far back as we have any record.

In 1927, after completing a survey of the economic conditions of the Indians under the Western Navajo agency, the present superintendent [Walker], finding the lands of the jurisdiction insufficient for the needs of the Indians, and that the position of a large number of Indians occupying the Paiute Strip was jeopardized by the restoration, started investigations and action to have this land again made part of the Western Navajo jurisdiction. [Hagerman 1932:38-39; emphasis added]

Other than his use of the phrase, "Paiute Strip," and a single vague reference to "Paiute country" in Utah near Monument Valley, the San Juan community and its occupation of the area in question are conspicuously absent from Hagerman's brief history of Indian land tenure in the region. The misleading interplay between omission and mention, between selected, specific fact and over-general characterization (for example, "Indians" versus "Navajos") which emerges from Hagerman's historical summary is especially evident in his discussion of lands in the former Paiute reservation. According to Hagerman, the Strip was reserved in 1884 by

Executive Order and mysteriously restored to public domain twice, once in 1892 and again in 1922, even though it was "from time immemorial" inhabited by generic "Indians." Because this account made specific mention only of the Navajos, leaving the potentially volatile issue of San Juan historic priority and continued occupation unexamined, it could not help but give the impression, never explicitly stated, that it was Navajos who had "never vacated or abandoned" the Strip and who had "occupied it constantly as far back as we have any record." While intentionality is virtually impossible to attribute here with any certainty, it is plain that Hagerman's authoritatively uttered account would go a long way both toward legitimizing Navajo expansion and forestalling any potential controversies regarding the San Juans' rights in the area to be added to the proposed Navajo Reservation.

The Navajo tribal government's arguments yield similar implications when subjected to contextual interpretation. In 1929, four tribal delegates sent a petition to the government conceding that Paiutes still used the Strip, but passed over the question of how and when Navajos came to live upon Paiute land. Among their reasons why the Paiute Strip should belong to Navajos, they included the following:

> Second, That this land was formerly known as the Piute Strip, and that it has, as far back as we have any record, been occupied by Indians of the Piute *or* Navajo Tribes, but that it was withdrawn from Indian Reservation without the knowledge or consent of any *Indians*, and was restored to Public Domain in the year 1922. [Navajo Tribal Council 1929; emphasis added]

The strategic presence of a qualifying "or," coupled with the non-specific "Indians," made it unnecessary to admit the Paiutes had historic priority in the Strip. This phrasing simultaneously permitted the Navajos to use the Paiutes' continued presence there as yet another justification for their claim to the Paiutes' former reservation. As with Hagerman, no mention was made of the actual relations between Paiutes and Navajos in the Strip and surrounding areas.

In 1932, Navajo Tribal Chairman Deshna Cheschillige wrote to Commissioner Charles J. Rhoads urging him to speed up passage of the bill that would make the Strip a permanent part of the WNR. He argued:

Not only have the Navajos used this country but the Piutes have occupied it peacefully side by side with the Navajo long before the white settlers ever came into this country. While the Paiutes were in this country they intermarried with the Navajos and when the Paiutes moved north these mixed people became Navajos and remained so even now several of the families in this section have Paiute blood. This fact seems to me a good argument that these Paiutes and Navajos who have made their homes in this sections should continue to occupy the Paiute Strip. [Cheschillige 1932]

In this version of historic interethnic relations, the uninformed reader could not help but be left mystified regarding the Paiutes' current status and location. In particular, Cheschillige implied that the Paiutes who remained on the Strip had willingly and peacefully incorporated themselves into the social network of the local Navajo community. Promulgation of this story, perhaps as much as any other single factor, has been a major stumbling block for the San Juan Tribe in its pursuit of federal recognition and federal solutions to problems with Navajo expansionism and discrimination in agency services. In later years, when the Navajo Tribe was preparing and arguing its suit for settlement of aboriginal title before the U.S. Indian Claims Commission, the tribe's attorneys and experts used an exaggerated version of this incorporation story to argue that the San Juan Tribe's aboriginal territory should be considered as part of the Navajos'. One instance of this was Navajo land claims expert David Brugge's observation (1964:226) that the San Juan people "had already become acculturated to the Navajo way of life" when Vizcarra encountered them in 1823. In the late 1960s, the Navajo Tribe's attorney of record in their Indian Claims Commission case, Norman Littell, used the Vizcarra journal and other carefully presented sources to argue that the "San Juan Paiute Band" had not ever existed and that all people of Paiute descent on the Navajo Reservation had been socially and culturally incorporated into the Navajo Tribe (Littell 1967:49-59). Until recently, this version of interethnic relations between Paiutes and Navajos represented the only one available to federal policy makers and administrators.
WNA Superintendent C. L. Walker was particularly single-minded in his support of what he perceived to be the best

interests of the Navajos. He was also one of the most vocal proponents of the Paiute Strip annexation, and while the legislation was still under consideration he was called to testify in Tuba City before a special subcommittee meeting of the U. S. Senate Committee on Indian Affairs. In addition to submitting a written statement (U.S. Senate 1931:9461-70), in which he repeated Hagerman's history of the Strip virtually word for word, Walker was questioned orally about the proposed legislation and about Paiutes. His responses are worth examining closely:

SENATOR FRAZIER. How many Indians have you?

MR. WALKER. The last census showed 4,508. Of this number, 4,095 are Navajos, 388 Hopis, and 25 Piutes.

SENATOR FRAZIER. Where do these Piutes live?

MR. WALKER. Scattered among the Navajos and up in Piute Canyon, a distance of 80 miles north of the agency here.

SENATOR FRAZIER. Is that what is known as the Piute strip?

MR. WALKER. On the edge of it; yes, sir.

SENATOR FRAZIER. You are familiar, of course, with the bill that is pending before Congress in regard to the Piute Strip being turned over to the Navajos?

MR. WALKER. Yes, sir.

SENATOR FRAZIER. What do you think about it?

MR. WALKER. I think by all means it should be passed. The land was formerly a part of the Indian reservation and it was withdrawn and cut full of holes for oil, but after finding no oil it has been abandoned by the white people and it is occupied almost entirely by the Indians. It is the last land in that section of the country that is available for Indians and they need land so badly. When they can get that, and it would not cost them anything, it seems to me they should have it.

SENATOR FRAZIER. Who occupies this land now?

MR. WALKER. The Indians and I believe 3 white men, 3 white people, 1 or 2 traders and 1 farmer. [U.S. Senate 1931:9473-74]

Senator Frazier gave Walker every opportunity to tell him whether the Paiutes still occupied the Strip and whether the Strip's annexation would not harm their interests. He asked about the precise locations of both groups, phrasing his questions specifically in terms of *Paiutes* and *Navajos*. Walker answered only--and truthfully--that Paiute Canyon was not part of the Strip and that the "Indians" were the sole occupants of the Strip. While Walker cannot be said to have uttered an unequivocal falsehood, neither can it be said that he answered with the whole truth. Unfortunately, Frazier did not press the matter.

Whatever their intent, Walker, Cheschillige, Hagerman, and the four Navajo councilmen succeeded in promulgating a new view of regional social history, one in which Navajo possession of former Paiute holdings was seen as rightful and of ancient standing. What little knowledge earlier Navajo Reservation administrators had had of the Paiute community, knowledge that Janus, Runke, and others had gone to great lengths to obtain, was soon forgotten. Moreover, because this new history came to be generally accepted by many of those involved in creating and carrying out federal policy in the WNR area, the underlying social realities that accompanied the Navajo presence--the increasing interethnic competition for scarce resources and the continual encroachment which has pushed the San Juan into ever smaller enclaves in the heart of their traditional homeland or out of it altogether--were permitted to take their historic course unhindered and beyond federal awareness.

In the Aftermath of the Strip Episode: 1928-1935

The first victims of the federal government's inability or unwillingness to protect San Juan interests in the Paiute Strip reservation were the members of the Douglas Mesa settlement group, who represent the first wave of out-migration. The Consolidated Ute Agency, however, appears to have made a conscious effort to compensate these Paiutes for their lost land rights by encouraging them to make their homes and apply for allotments either on the Ute Mountain reservation, in Colorado, or with Posey's band of Paiutes in the area of Blanding, Utah. As noted earlier, a number of these Paiutes applied for allotments at Allen Canyon or in the White Mesa area and all but a few came to be enrolled under the agency as Utes, receiving full benefits.

In a 1939 letter to the commissioner of the general land office concerning 45 Indian allotment applications near White Mesa, Utah, as of then still unapproved even though they were filed almost ten years before, Commissioner John Collier made it plain that the BIA considered these allotments as some sort of compensation for the loss of the Strip reservation. He was thus well aware that a tacit trade-off had taken place between Paiute and Navajo interests when the Strip was annexed by the Navajos:

> One very important point should be brought out, namely, that those allotment selections were filed by Paiute, Ute and Pah-Ute Indians [note the BIA's apparent confusion as to tribal groups even at this late date] who did not benefit in any way through enactment of the Utah-Navajo Boundary Act of March 1, 1933, supra. Had they been Navajo allotment selections no doubt the applicants could have been persuaded to remove to the reservation extension and relinquish their allotment selections. Therefore, it is unlikely that any agreement was made to cancel these Paiute, Ute and Pah-Ute Indian allotment selections, which action would have been tantamount to sacrificing their rights for the benefit of the Navajos. [Collier 1939]

In the 1930 agreement to which Collier was referring, a group of cattlemen from San Juan County, Utah, requested in return for withdrawing their objections to the bill giving the Strip to the Navajos that no further homestead or allotment applications be permitted to any Indians in the county (see, for example, Colton 1930; or Redd 1930). Charles Redd and other cattlemen, recalling their recent troubles with Posey, particularly did not want any Paiutes, including the refugees from Douglas Mesa, to receive allotments (see Redd 1931). As a result of this agreement, and due to subsequent pressure from

Utah Congressman Colton and local cattlemen such as Redd, Posey's band of Paiutes and those Douglas Mesa Paiutes who had resettled at Allen Canyon after being driven off the Strip, were very nearly forced out of San Juan County entirely. This development was prevented largely by the BIA's staunch defense, under Collier, of the Allen Canyon Paiutes' rights. Significantly, Navajo Chairman Cheschillige was the only Indian leader who was a party to the agreement with local cattle interests which allegedly sacrificed future Indian claims to land north of the Strip (Walker 1930b).

Those San Juan Paiutes who remained at Navajo Mountain and Paiute Canyon also cannot be said to have benefited from the 1933 Act, and in fact it served only to encourage further expansion into Paiute holdings. As we have seen in the last chapter, a number of sources date permanent Navajo settlement in the Paiute Canyon-Navajo Mountain area only from the 1920s. Douglas Mesa would turn out to be only the first of a series of out-migrations resulting from Navajo expansion in the north.

However serious the loss of exclusive rights in federal trust lands, this was not the only important consequence that followed in the wake of the Strip episode. Those Paiutes who were living in the north and were utilizing the former Paiute Reservation were shifted in 1922 or 1923 to the jurisdiction of the Consolidated Ute Agency, in southwestern Colorado. When the Paiute Strip was returned to the jurisdiction of the WNA, those Paiutes who had remained there came under its jurisdiction. While Paiutes living in the south may not have been officially included in the change of agencies, as was noted earlier, from 1923 until 1927 the WNA administration appears nonetheless to have assumed that the entire tribe had been removed from their jurisdiction. The lapse in jurisdiction, the two year lag between the return of the northern and southern groups to WNA jurisdiction, and, finally, the perennial problem of agency personnel turnover, combined to produce administrative confusion with regard to the Paiutes' status on the eve of what was to be a period of crucial reform in federal relations with local Indians.

The first comprehensive field census of the Indians under Western Navajo superintendency, conducted in 1928 and 1929, took place against the background of these jurisdictional shufflings and the administrative confusion that they created. The 1930s Western Navajo Indian Census Rolls, from the earliest in 1930 to the last available roll in 1937, reflected the local administration's confusion with regard to the San Juans' tribal status and, by codifying it in an official form, set the stage for five more decades of federal ambiguity and neglect.

The 1928-1929 field census and the compilation of the 1930 WNA Indian Census Roll were conducted under the direction of Superintendent C. L. Walker, who had identified the Paiutes living on the Strip as "Utes" because of their agency affiliation (Walker 1928a). In his annual reports for 1927 and 1928, Walker enumerated only the southern area San Juan as Paiutes (1927b and 1928b). The first census rolls reproduced this artificial division between north and south, but with a new twist that further obscured both the ethnic identity of northern San Juan Paiutes and their sociopolitical connections with the southern area community.

The 1930s rolls are divided into three sections by tribe, each section containing the names primarily of individuals whose tribal affiliation is identified as "Navajo," "Hopi," or "Piute." With the exception of a few northern residents, only southern area Paiutes were listed as members of the Paiute Tribe throughout the 1930s. The numbers of individuals listed on the Paiute rolls correspond exactly to the ARCIA Paiute figures for the same years, so it is clear which southern area individuals the published figures represent. It should be noted that several southern area families apparently went uncounted in these rolls. Among those known to have remained uncounted were Blue Lee's family, including himself, his sister, his mother *T'aats* and his father Joedie/*Akamanaxwats*, all of whom then living at Willow Springs, and seasonally at Coppermine, Cedar Ridge, and even off-reservation at Lee's Ferry.

Throughout the 1930s rolls, southern area residents were identified, and thus still federally recognized, as members of the "Piute Tribe." In the north, however, the census rolls present a much different picture. In the 1930 WNA Roll, all northern area residents were identified only as Navajos. Between 1931 and 1934, most northern area San Juan individuals were listed as "Navajo-Piute" or "Piute-Navajo," as if they were of mixed parentage. The exceptions fall into two groups: Paiute Dick and the Lester and Susie (*Paaráy*) Willetson family, who were identified throughout as Navajo; and Mercy Whiskers, Curtis Lehi, his wife, Rose, and son, Joseph, and Willie Lehi, the brother of Alfred Lehi, all of whom were listed as "Piute." With the exception of Mercy Whiskers, all of those labeled "Piute," north and south, were listed together in the separate Paiute section of the 1931-1937 WNA Rolls. All Paiutes labeled "Navajo" or "Navajo-Piute" were included in the 1930s rolls of Navajos.

It is tempting to hypothesize that Superintendent Walker, in his anxiety to avoid any flap over the Paiutes still living on the Strip, deliberately constructed the census rolls so as to make it appear that the northern area San Juans had either disappeared or were incorporated into the Navajo Tribe, as had already been reported by Sharp and Cheschillige. It was ignorance, however, rather than connivance, that underlay the mistaken identification of so many San Juans either as Navajos or as part Navajo and part Paiute. One of the best indications of this was Walker's claim before the Senate subcommittee that the 25 Willow Springs Paiutes enumerated in 1930 lived in Paiute Canyon, when he might better for his purposes have given their actual location, Willow Springs and Cedar Ridge. Another WNA official, BIA Forester William Zeh, made a similar mistake in a 1930 report: "The total Indian population of the Western Navajo is 7,225 Navajos, 381 Hopi and 25 Piutes. . . . the Piutes are practically all living in the Piute Canyon" (Zeh 1930). Although Walker and others in the WNA administration assumed that Paiute Canyon must have Paiutes in it, they did not really know who the Paiutes were or where they were located. As we shall see, this state of confusion was a sign of things to come in WNA census record keeping, and not just with regard to Paiutes.

The different labels assigned the northern and southern area San Juans in the 1930s Indian Census Rolls, "Piute," "Navajo-Piute," or even "Navajo," did not reflect differences in blood quanta, culture, or any other biological or social differences between northern and southern residents. On the one hand, among those identified as "Navajo" or "Navajo-Piute" were northern residents long recognized by outsiders as Paiutes and who had no Navajo ancestry, for example, Dora Nelson or the well-known leader, "Nasja," Ruben Owl/*Muupɨts*. On the other hand, there were Paiutes with known Navajo ancestry, like Curtis Lehi, who were labeled Paiute. There are other indications that the division was purely fortuitous. For example, Curtis Lehi and his family may have been identified as Paiutes simply because he had started school at Sherman Institute as a Paiute before the Strip was restored in 1922 and thus had remained a Paiute in the superintendent's records throughout the jurisdictional disruptions of the 1920s (see Walker 1927a).

The San Juan Tribe and the Federal Government, 1935-1984

The years following 1935 witnessed great changes in relations between the government and the tribes living on the Western Navajo Reservation. During this period, the BIA largely ignored the San Juan Tribe as a political group. As a result, the San Juan people remained economically and politically isolated, unable to take advantage of changes in Indian policy that encouraged tribal self-determination and economic development. As the new governments of their larger neighbors, the Hopi and Navajo tribes, grew more powerful, the San Juan people found it correspondingly less easy to control their destiny or protect their tribal interests.

The first section below looks at changes in Indian policy and local agency administration over the last five decades and discusses their contribution to the San Juan Tribe's current situation in relation to the federal government and the tribal governments of the Hopis and Navajos. The second section examines local officials' changing perceptions of the San Juan people and their role in regional history as these are reflected in federal documents since 1935. The final section traces the events surrounding the tribe's attempts, beginning in the late 1960s, to seek solutions to resulting from Navajo expansion and inadequate federal representation.

Local Federal Indian Relations: From the 1930s to the 1980s

When John Collier was appointed commissioner of Indian affairs in 1933, he inaugurated a new era of Indian policy in which the government sought to foster Indian tribes' corporateness and develop their powers of self-determination (see L. Kelly 1968, chap. 9, "New Deal for the Navajos"). Under the Wheeler-Howard Act of 1934, also known as the Indian Reorganization Act, many reservation groups whose traditional governments had atrophied or had even been dismantled as a result of previous federal policies were encouraged to create constitutional governments. In this period, and increasingly in succeeding decades, these new tribal governments, which include the Hopi Tribal Council, were allowed to exercise limited but important powers of self-government.

The Navajo Tribal Council is one of several modern Indian tribal goverments that were not created as a direct result of the Indian Reorganization Act. Its history nonetheless reflects the policy changes of this period.

The Navajo Council was first created in the 1920s by the BIA as a representative body to approve oil leases on Navajo reservations. Prior to this time, the Navajos had not had a unified government, traditional or otherwise. It seems unlikely that the Navajos would have developed a unified government without the considerable and continuous federal intervention that has occurred over the decades since the tribal council's founding. Nevertheless, the Navajo Tribal Council has almost since its inception thought and acted for itself and what it has perceived as the interests of the Navajo Tribe, and has not been an organization of "yes-men," as some critics have believed (L. Kelly 1968, chap. 11).

In 1935, although Collier himself came to the Navajos to persuade them to accept tribal reorganization under the Wheeler-Howard Act, the Navajos voted to reject it. It was not until 1938, after several years of BIA pressure, that the 1920s council system was finally reorganized and the basics of the present system of tribal self-government created (Kelly 1968, chap. 12; Young 1961:381-82). Since then, the Navajo government has assumed an ever stronger controlling role in many reservation programs and other aspects of the tribe's affairs.

While the San Juans' neighbors were adopting constitutional governments and also gradually gaining stronger representation in federal policy development, federal officials were becoming even less aware of the San Juan people. As we have seen, this was due in part to changes in local officials' attitudes towards Paiutes and Navajos and in part to the fact that the San Juan Tribe's traditional leadership did not have the ability or the desire to attract federal attention. Although no formal decision was ever made, the San Juan Tribe for all practical purposes was no longer federally recognized.

As a result, the San Juan people were never subject to pressures to strengthen ties with Washington or to create a federally acceptable form of government, as were their more visible neighbors, the Navajos and the Hopis. Like their neighbors, the Paiutes could not have been expected to adopt a formal political system on their own without direct and continuous federal intervention. Such a system, whatever its other shortcomings, would undoubtedly have enabled the San Juan Tribe to achieve much needed self-representation at the federal level.

The San Juan Tribe's isolation and its social and economic problems were exacerbated by other changes occurring during this period. One of the earliest and most significant was the 1935 consolidation of the various superintendencies dealing with Navajos into one centralized Navajo Agency, with its main offices in Window Rock, Arizona. Previously independent agencies, including the WNA, became satellite subagencies.

In the introduction to the last separate annual report of the WNA, Superintendent F. J. Scott wrote:

> Since the Western Navajo Agency has been consolidated with the other Navajo reservations, no separate program for the Western Navajo Reservation has been prepared. It is presumed that one general program will be prepared for the entire Navajo area. [Scott 1935]

Under the autonomous WNA program, it had already proved difficult for local administrators to deal fairly and consistently with all three tribal groups under their jurisdiction or take account of the special needs of each tribe. The consolidation in 1935 virtually assured that the San Juan Paiute people, already geographically and socially isolated from Anglo society at large and little understood by local BIA administrators, would be subject to even greater federal ignorance and neglect.

Another factor that has helped to worsen the Paiutes' situation has been the growing political influence exercised by Navajos both through the local agency administration and their increasingly effective tribal government. Since the 1930s, Navajos have become integrated into the workings of the BIA administration of their reservation and now occupy positions at all levels of the local agency bureaucracy. This and other important factors, notably the huge influx of funds into the tribal treasury from mineral leases (L. Kelly 1968:199), have greatly strengthened the Navajo tribal government and expanded its political and economic influence.

In 1940, the BIA Navajo Agency undertook the compilation of a Navajo tribal roll. The Navajo tribal government was not involved in this project and did not accept the 1940 Roll as valid until some 13 years later. William Kelly (1964:2-4), in his analysis of their tribal roll, indicated that the 1928-1937 BIA Indian Census Rolls for the seven original agencies were simply retyped and bound in 1940 to make the original Navajo

Roll. All of those San Juan Paiutes who were incorrectly listed as "Navajos" or "Navajo-Piutes" in 1930s WNA Rolls, were apparently also included in the 1940 Navajo Roll.

In May 1951, the Navajo Tribal Council passed Resolution CM-12-51 empowering an advisory committee to establish a procedure for determining tribal membership. The preamble to this resolution asserted that the Navajo Tribe did not accept the 1940 Roll as official:

> WHEREAS, the Tribe has never acted to define what constitutes a member of the Navajo Tribe, and
>
> WHEREAS, no well-ordered system exists for determining who should be included on the tribal roll, or for investigation of individual applicants to determine eligibility for such inclusion . . .

In 1953, the council passed Resolution CJ-50-53, which, after initial rejection by the BIA, was amended and became tribal law in 1954 (see 1 Navajo Tribal Code, section 501). It established the tribe's present membership criteria and for the first time approved the BIA's census records system as the official Navajo roll. It stated that the Navajo membership includes "all persons of Navajo blood whose names appear on the official roll of the Navajo Tribe maintained by the Bureau of Indian Affairs." This section of the Navajo Tribal Code also provides that "children born to any enrolled member of the Navajo Tribe shall *automatically* become members [emphasis supplied]."

Since 1940, the Navajo Roll has been maintained, corrected, and updated by the BIA at the local subagencies and at the Navajo Area Census Office in Window Rock (W. Kelly 1964:204; Navajo Tribe 1985a:6-10). During this period, other San Juans whose parents were already listed in enrollment records were apparently also automatically added to BIA family sheets and other census records.

The Navajo Tribe has claimed recently (1985a:6-6E, 7) that 107 San Juans (amounting to 55% of the current San Juan tribal membership) are Navajos, since they "appear on the official roll of the Navajo Tribe." According to the San Juan tribal spokesperson and the elders of the tribe, these individuals were included in Navajo census records without their knowledge or consent and therefore should not be considered as legitimate Navajo enrollees. The Navajo Tribe has itself conceded that no one, Navajo or Paiute, ever applied for inclusion on the original 1940 roll (Navajo Tribe 1985a:9). The Western Navajo Subagency census records that might help clarify whether the alleged Paiute enrollments were voluntary or involuntary are themselves in a particularly confused state and have been judged by the U.S. Census Bureau to be among the most inaccurate of any kept by the various Navajo subagencies (U.S. Bureau of the Census 1976:3-4). The Census Bureau found in 1977 that 53.7% of the Navajos listed on the Western Navajo roll could not be located during a special enumeration, and concluded that eight out of ten of those, altogether some 4600 Navajos, were erroneously enrolled (1977:1 and table I, p. 14). Put in this perspective, the accidental misplacement of 107 individuals seems quite plausible.

Whether or not these 107 individuals are to be considered as Paiutes or enrolled Navajos will ultimately be decided by the BIA Branch of Federal Acknowledgement or by the federal courts, since this is one of the major issues facing the Paiutes in their bid for federal recognition. The question of whether Paiutes should be recognized as Paiutes or as something else would never have emerged, however, if it were not for the decades-long history of federal confusion regarding the San Juan people and their history.

Federal Perceptions of the San Juans after 1935

Despite the fact that the San Juan Tribe had no official relationship with the U.S. government during this period, some federal officials and employees continued to single out San Juan Paiutes as a distinct social and cultural group. There are many federal documents from this period that identify particular individuals, families, or other larger groups of San Juan people as ethnically Paiute. They include Soil Conservation Service reports of the late 1930s; the Navajo Agency census records discussed earlier, as well as agency range and agricultural records, all spanning the period from the 1930s to the present; BIA General Assistance case files from the 1970s and 1980s; Indian Health Service records and publications; and records of Indian probate cases involving San Juan individuals that were presented to the Department of the Interior's Office of Hearings and Appeals. We wish to take a close look at two of these documentary sources, Soil

Conservation Service reports and BIA census records, before examining another historic trend in federal perceptions of the San Juan people in the last part of this section.

During the second half of the 1930s, the U.S. Department of Agriculture's Soil Conservation Service (SCS) made intensive studies of conservation needs on the Navajo Reservation. Teams of SCS researchers produced a series of forestry, range, agricultural, and other reports. According to one former SCS employee in the Navajo area, William C. McGinnies (1982:40-42), these studies were "primarily in the beginning aimed at Navajos and the Navajo Reservation." He indicated that Hopis were of "secondary interest as far as the Soil Conservation Service was concerned." Paiutes were presumably even less of a priority. Nonetheless, where reports covered areas inhabited by San Juans they usually made mention of Paiutes and Paiute land use.

For example, the SCS "Summarized Report for the Navajo Project," June, 1935, described the site of the Upper Paiute Canyon irrigation project in the following terms:

> Within the walls of this canyon there has been a great alluvial fill ranging in depth from 10 to 30 feet and varying in width from 1/4 to 1/2 mile. This fill has provided rich farming lands for both the Piutes and the Navajos and many fine peach orchards of considerable age are being cultivated. [USDA Soil Conservation Service 1935:92]

A later report (1937:1) gave the "total Piute population" on the Navajo Reservation as 90, a reasonably accurate number for the San Juan people living in both the north and south at that time. The figure may possibly have been based on firsthand knowledge. During this period, the service conducted the Human Dependency Survey, a house-to-house survey of Indian "consumption groups" living on the Navajo Reservation (see the deposition of former SCS anthropologist Gordon Page [1983]). As their reports indicated, the SCS, unlike Walker and other agency personnel, had a clear idea of the Paiutes' population size and their locations, and made no false distinction between northern and southern residents.

Despite the inaccuracies contained in BIA rolls and other records, the Navajo Agency's census personnel also continued throughout this period to identify at least some San Juans as Paiutes. According to Western Navajo Superintendent Irving

Billy, Navajo Agency records continue even today to list many southern area household heads as Paiutes:

A telephone verification was made with the Navajo Area Census Office in Window Rock, and records reflect blood degree for Marie Lehi, Anna Lehi Whiskers, Grace Lehi, Helen Lehi, Francis Norman, and Joe Norman, to be full Paiute Indians. [Billy 1984]

More surprisingly, many San Juan Paiutes who were not included in the 1930s Paiute rolls *were* identified as Paiutes in later BIA census records (Navajo Tribe 1985a:10001-220 and 13113-96, exhibits). In 1973, the Western Navajo Subagency made a list of the Paiutes living under its jurisdiction. While it implied that some of the individuals listed were "enrolled in the Navajo Tribe," it also clearly marked the Paiutes as distinct from the surrounding Navajo population. At the time, Congress was considering legislation that would provide individual allotments to all Paiutes then living on the 1934 Act Navajo Reservation in Arizona who were not "enrolled" in the Navajo Tribe (U.S. Senate 1972, 1973, 1974; Act of December 22, 1974, in 25 U.S.C. 640d). Apparently in an effort to identify these Paiutes, Western Navajo Subagency census records clerks compiled a list (Hemstreet 1973). It enumerates some 89 San Juan individuals by name, with their addresses and other personal data, including virtually all tribal members then residing on the reservation.

Recently, BIA Branch of Acknowledgement historian William Quinn discovered a group of census records at the Western Navajo Subagency office in Tuba City (personal communication, June 5, 1985, with attached copies of the relevant documents). This group was labeled "Paiute" and kept separate from other records. All but one of these records date from March 14, 1973, less than two weeks prior to the March 27 date of the Hemstreet roll; the one exception is dated January 2, 1973. The dates, together with other similarities, indicate that this group of records may have been used to compile the 1973 Paiute list.

While awareness of the Paiute presence runs like a thread through much of the unpublished federal documentation dealing with the Tuba City or Navajo Mountain-Paiute Canyon areas, it did little to affect the perceptions of federal administrators and policy-makers at higher levels. This becomes especially evident when this documentation is contrasted with published accounts produced by the Navajo Agency during this same period, which tended to reflect the official Navajo tribal view of local Indian populations and local history, especially in later years as the Navajo Tribe became more influential in the running of the agency.

An early example of such an account is Richard Van Valkenburgh's *Dine Bikeyah* (1941), a popular guidebook to reservation history and geography published by the Navajo Agency at Window Rock. Although Van Valkenburgh noted Paiute settlement locations in the north at Navajo Mountain-Paiute Canyon and in the south at Cedar Ridge and Gap, he seriously misrepresented their relations with Navajos and their role in local history. He described the Paiutes as "poverty-stricken" and indicated that they were "dying out," but drew no connection with Navajo expansion in the same areas (Van Valkenburgh 1941:114). Rather, he stated that "the two peoples [were] generally friendly and closely allied." More importantly, Van Valkenburgh implied that the Paiutes were recent immigrants who arrived in the area after the Navajos, who by implication were the real owners of the Western Navajo area.

Later Navajo Agency publications made no mention at all of the San Juans' historic or modern presence. One such account is the BIA Branch of Land Operations' (1974) "Soil and Range Inventory" report on Land Management Districts 2 and 8, the old Paiute Strip including Navajo Mountain. Like other recent conservation planning reports on areas of historic and modern Paiute occupation, this report made mention only of Navajo land use, indicating that Navajo occupation in the Paiute Strip followed directly on the heels of the prehistoric Anasazi (U.S. BIA Branch of Land Operations 1974:2): "Except for possible infrequent brief intrusions by Spanish traders, there is no conclusive evidence that the survey area was entered prior to the advent of the Navajo in the latter 16th or early 17th century."

San Juan Entry into the Federal Political Arena, Post-1968

In the late 1960s and early 1970s, the San Juan Tribe with the help of members of other Paiute tribes began to take an active role in ameliorating the problems that had been created by federal neglect. According to Paiutes living at Willow Springs, it was the death of Alfred Lehi that set this chain of events in motion. Lehi died after falling from a cliff by Willow Springs.

Kaibab tribal official Ralph Castro and Kanosh Band leader McKay Pikyavit, blood relatives of several San Juan families, were called in by the Lehi family to help investigate the death.

Almost immediately, the San Juan people began to work on other community projects as well, with the help and guidance of the Kanosh and Kaibab tribal governments and members of other Paiute communities. At the same time, they also sought and received legal assistance from DNA-People's Legal Services, Inc., in Tuba City. Between 1969 and 1970, San Juan Paiutes were encouraged to enroll in the Southern Paiute Nation's U.S. Indian Claims Commission Judgment Roll. They then sought access to economic aid, including BIA general assistance payments, the state funded donated foods program, and federally subsidized housing. Paiutes were entitled to benefits under these programs but had apparently been denied access to them under the Navajo-dominated local agency administration. Eventually, the San Juan Tribe went to the root of their problems, seeking federal recognition of their tribal government and their reservation rights.

On October 13, 1969, McKay Pikyavit wrote to Kanosh Band's attorney Justin Stewart to report a meeting held at Tuba City regarding the San Juans' applications for the Southern Paiute Judgment Roll. He also asked Stewart to work with DNA attorney Samuel Withers (copy of Pikyavits letter in Stewart 1969). According to Pikyavit, this meeting, held on the previous Tuesday

> was called by Calvin Brice tribal operations officer of Phoenix, Arizona [the BIA regional office] and his assistance Alph H. Secakuku same address. Purpose of the meeting was to see if these indians could be tie [sic] in with this Southern Paiute Claim. In april of this year, they were given application to fill out, which they did. These application were giving [sic] to them by Ralph Castro . . .

Pikyavit also noted another problem that the San Juans had asked him to look into and then informed Stewart of Withers' involvement in the case:

> And then there was this other matter they wanted help on . . . That navajoes were taking over their historial [sic] land, saying that the land belongs to the navajoes and hopi tribe saying the land belongs to the Piaute [sic]

indians of Willow Springs and Navajo Mountain . . . .

    I also got to talked to Samuel G. Withers an attorney for the navajoes and repsents [sic] them the Piautes of Willow Springs and Navajo Mountain and he said it would be find [sic] with him for you to work with him. I told him you would contact him.

In a feature article that appeared in the *Flagstaff Sun* on July 14, 1970, Jeff Stone described the series of meetings and other events which followed this early meeting. Castro and members of Kaibab and other Southern Paiute communities in Utah decided to help the San Juan people to enroll for the Southern Paiute claim judgment, even though the total judgment moneys were limited and the inclusion of the San Juans would mean a monetary loss to the other Paiutes. According to the article:

> Castro began, with help from the Kaibab band, an effort to get Paiutes on the Navajo Reservation included on the roll for the federal [Indian Claims Commission] judgment.
>
>   Paiutes from the Kaibab Reservation, the Cedar City (Utah), Kanarsh [Kanosh] and St. George areas, pooled money for gasoline and came to the Navajo Reservation to seek their relatives [this is corroborated by interview material from Kaibab, Cedar City, and Kanosh Paiutes].
>
>   The incoming Paiutes talked and questioned those who came forward. Many common ancestors were discovered, family histories compared. When the process was completed, 98 were sufficiently identified of Paiute ancestors to qualify for the judgment, *even though the share of each established Paiute was diminished* as each new name was added. [Stone 1970:19; emphasis added]

Under the Southern Paiute Judgment Act of October 17, 1968 (82 Stat. 1147), a roll was prepared to pay for aboriginal land rights as determined by the three claims commission judges. Under category (g), which included those Paiutes who were not members of recognized or terminated tribes, 86 persons of San Juan Paiute descent were enrolled (see U.S. Bureau of Indian Affairs 1968). With very few exceptions, mainly those who filed late or minors who were listed on their parents' applications, almost the entire membership of the San Juan Tribe enrolled and each was later paid a share in the judgment. A number of BIA administrators from outside the Navajo Agency, including Calvin Brice, head of the Phoenix office, were eventually involved in the enrollment and verification of these San Juan Paiutes. The San Juans supplied their addresses as well as detailed information on family histories. Apparently, no BIA official ever questioned the San Juans' claim to be Southern Paiutes.

In addition to the judgment roll project, Castro and the DNA set about trying to obtain social welfare, food assistance, and housing for eligible San Juan Paiutes. They soon discovered that Navajo social workers and administrators were at best indifferent to the needs of the Paiutes residing on the Navajo Reservation. Again quoting from Stone's article in the *Flagstaff Sun*:

> [Ralph Castro] came to Tuba City to check on stories by his elders about kin living on the Navajo Reservation . . . He found the small band at Willow Springs cut off and ignored both by the Navajo and the Bureau of Indian Affairs. . . .
>
> Castro went to work first to establish the existence of the Paiutes with the Bureau of Indian Affairs so that they would be eligible for food supplements. . . .
>
> At first, B.I.A. officials refused to hear of non-Navajos on the reservation. Then some officials took a let-them-alone attitude, saying the Paiutes lived well enough on their customary corn and occasional fruit and meat diet, Castro said. [Stone 1970:19]

According to Castro (Bunte and Franklin Fieldnotes, August 3, 1983), when he arrived to help the San Juans they were receiving no social welfare or economic aid whatsoever. He stated that Navajo officials and social workers were actively hostile to his suggestion that Paiutes might be eligible for services:

> I had a few skirmishes there with them. And this one guy is college-trained, too. He was a Navajo social worker. And he says, "Well, we should, we don't have to

help them. They have no business here. This is our
reservation. What are they doing on our reservation?" I
said, "Well, they were here before the reservation was
formed."

The DNA attorney working with the Paiutes experienced
similar difficulties when he attempted to deal with the Willow
Springs San Juans' complaints of food shortages. According to
a DNA memorandum, Alfred Lehi's widow, Marie Lehi, told
Samuel Withers that "she had been told that they [Paiutes] were
ineligible for BIA General Assistance" (Withers 1969).   When
Withers asked the local BIA officials who was supposed to
provide assistance to the Paiutes, they gave him the runaround.
On December 8, 1969, John Amand, "Director of [the] Navajo
Demonstration Project," told Withers that Keams Canyon, the
agency for the Hopis and at that time also for the Kaibab
Paiutes, should deal with San Juan food shortage problems.
Officials at Tuba City Subagency recognized that the Willow
Springs people were Paiutes, but assumed that they were
therefore ineligible to receive agency services which they
believed were restricted to Navajos.   Withers wrote also that
Keams Canyon disclaimed jurisdiction over the San Juans.
In the same memorandum, Withers reported that Phoenix
BIA Branch Office Tribal Operations Officer, Calvin Brice
"stated frankly that it is the BIA Social Worker, Navajo Area,
who is responsible to see that this emergency is met. General
assistance is available and should be applied regardless of
tribal affiliation." BIA case files indicate that the San Juans
only began to receive general assistance in 1970, apparently as
a result of DNA's pressure, despite the fact that general
assistance had been available to Navajos for decades (Navajo
Tribe 1985a:10425-3112, exhibits; Young 1961:290).   Many San
Juan consultants still believe that Navajo social workers
discriminate against them because they are Paiutes, arbitrarily
cutting off or reducing their payments.   Although the files
reveal that Navajo social workers do identify San Juans as
Paiutes, it is not clear whether identification as a separate
ethnic group actually translates into discrimination.
In 1970, Paiutes at Willow Springs also complained to DNA
that they had been denied access to surplus food commodities
delivered by the state of Arizona for distribution by the
Navajo Tribe.   Eventually, DNA was compelled to arrange a
separate Paiute commodities distribution on a temporary basis
through the Hopis at Moenkopi (Ward 1970; Ward 1971).

Although some Paiutes now receive surplus food commodities through the Tuba City Subagency, many claim that on occasion Navajo employees still refuse to distribute commodities to them because they are not Navajos.

Some time in the early 1970s, the San Juan Tribe, Ralph Castro, and the DNA-People's Legal Service also attempted to get housing for the San Juans, this time with no success. According to Navajo Relocation Commission employee Lou Fox, then working on Indian Health Service water system projects, the Navajo Tribal Housing Authority had decided to assist the San Juans with federally subsidized housing (Bunte and Franklin Fieldnotes, July 15, 1983). Roy Dan, a Navajo official of the Tuba City Subagency who had been employed by the housing authority in the early 1970s, corroborated all but a few details of Fox's account, but stated that the Paiutes and the DNA attorney had originally requested the housing rather than the Navajo Tribe or the BIA offering it spontaneously (Bunte and Franklin Fieldnotes, August 10, 1983). Dan added that he had told the DNA attorney the request for housing would have to be approved at a local Navajo chapter meeting. He claimed that such a resolution was never introduced at a chapter meeting and that since the San Juans were actually happier where they were, the Paiutes let the matter drop. According to San Juan elders at Willow Springs, they did manage to get sympathetic Navajos to initiate the proposal in both the Gap and Tuba City chapters, but only the latter passed a resolution. Yet nothing came of the Paiutes' housing application. The Navajo Tribe has recently claimed that it has no record of any Paiute having ever applied for housing (1985a:20).

It was in 1970 that Castro and the San Juan Tribe made their first efforts to gain official federal recognition. The Paiutes believed that this was the only way to force the BIA and the Navajo Tribe to take them more seriously. According to the *Flagstaff Sun*:

> Work for more BIA aid continued and the effort on behalf of the 98 Paiutes on the Navajo Reservation took a new turn: an attempt to get official recognition from the BIA of the Paiutes as an individual Indian band, including the Willow Springs and Navajo Mountain settlements primarily.
>
> Letters were written by attorneys on behalf of the

Paiutes to the BIA in Washington and a reply received that a "review" was being undertaken. [Stone 1970:19]

In a meeting on May 11, 1970, San Juan families from Willow Springs and Navajo Mountain came together in a tribal council to listen to Castro discuss the issue of federal recognition. The minutes of this meeting, signed by all of the elders present, document the tribe's decision to pursue recognition (San Juan Paiute Tribe 1970).

DNA attorney Withers subsequently sent an inquiry to the BIA in Washington, D.C., concerning the San Juans' recognition. He received a reply on June 12, 1970, from Charles Rovin, Acting Director of Community Services:

We appreciate your letter of May 19 concerning formal recognition of a group of Paiutes in the Willow Springs area and a group from the Navajo Mountain area. We will undertake a review of this question and communicate with you further concerning it. [Rovin 1970]

However, no further communication was received.

On February 13, 1970, Castro wrote a letter on behalf of the Kaibab Tribe to the editor of the Gallup, New Mexico, *Independent* expressing his frustration with the federal government's apparent unwillingness to deal with the San Juan Tribe's many problems. He stated:

The Navajo Tribe and the U.S. Government have taken the Paiute land and given nothing in return. They are trying to force the Paiutes out of what was once their land. Keep it up--you are doing a good job--there is now less than 100 Paiutes left in the area. In a few years, there won't be any left and the Navajo Nation and the U.S. Government can say well done. There won't be a Paiute left south of the Colorado River. To get welfare the Paiutes living in the Tuba City area must be listed as Anglo. The Navajo Tribe has and will be taking money for Page, Black Mesa coal and even taken the Paiute Mountain's name away and now calls it Navajo Mountain. . . .

None of this should come as a surprise, the U.S. Government has done this sort of thing in the past and

now the Navajo Tribe with the U.S. Government's help
has hurt every small tribe that must have them as
neighbors. [Castro 1970]

Soon afterward, Castro left office at Kaibab and has not been
directly involved in San Juan affairs since.

Several years after the San Juans first petitioned the BIA
for tribal recognition, events in the Navajo-Hopi land dispute
had reached a point where several separate bills designed to
resolve it had come before Congress (U.S. Senate 1972, 1973,
and 1974). On December 22, 1974, one of them, the Owens
Bill, was passed into law (see Kammer 1980, for a clear and
insightful account of the events and strategies that led to the
passage of the 1974 act).

Although the San Juans were never officially informed, the
act was designed to quiet Indian title not only in the 1882
Executive Order Hopi Reservation, the so-called Joint Use
Area, but also on all Navajo reservation lands in Arizona
outside boundaries of the Joint Use Area and the 1868 Treaty
Navajo Reservation (see map 3). This latter area is also known
as the 1934 act Navajo Reservation, which was established for
"the benefit of the Navajos and such other Indians as may
already be located thereon" (48 Stat. 980-961). The 1934 act
thus gave reservation rights not only to Navajos but to any
"other Indians" who were there in 1934, specifically the Hopis
of Moenkopi and the Paiutes living in or using Arizona
reservation lands.

Because the Hopis and Navajos were the only two Indian
groups who took part in the negotiation and lobbying that
produced the 1974 act, its primary intent with regard to the
1934 area was to permit the Hopi and Navajo tribes to settle
title for it through a lawsuit in the federal court. The federal
district judge in Phoenix reached a decision on the suit over
the 1882 Executive Order Hopi Reservation, or Joint Use Area,
on February 10, 1977. After the Navajo Tribe appealed the
ruling, the Ninth Circuit Court of Appeals decided in May of
1978 that partition should proceed. The second suit over the
1934 act area has yet to come to trial.

While the authors of the 1974 act were primarily concerned
with Hopis and Navajos, the act also offers two forms of
remedy to the San Juans who live in this area at Willow
Springs, *Atatsiv*, and Paiute Canyon. In the first place, the act
provides for Paiute allotments:

> Notwithstanding any other provisions of this Act, the
> Secretary is authorized to allot in severalty to
> individual Paiute Indians, not now members of the
> Navajo Tribe, who are located within the area described
> in the Act of June 14, 1934 (48 Stat. 960), and who were
> located within such area, or are direct descendents of
> Paiute Indians who were located within such area, on
> the date of such Act, land in quantities as specified in
> section 1 of the Act of February 8, 1887 (24 Stat. 388),
> as amended (25 U.S.C. 331) . . . [25 U.S.C. 640d-8]

Such a procedure, evoking the 1887 General Allotment Act, would prove a less than satisfactory remedy for several reasons. First, many San Juans may not be eligible for allotments. A number of Paiutes were not residing on the reservation in 1974 because economic and other conditions had forced them to live elsewhere. More seriously, the Navajo Tribe has alleged that over one hundred San Juans are enrolled as Navajos. This may well mean that unless the federal government decided in favor of San Juan recognition, these San Juans, most of whom are located in the Paiute Canyon-Navajo Mountain area, would also be ineligible for allotments.

Secondly, division of Paiute farming and grazing lands into allotments would disrupt the San Juan Tribe's traditional corporate land tenure system and hasten the dispersal of Paiute land into Navajo hands. It would provide some individuals with allotments while others would receive none, and no regard would be given to who actually used or wanted to use the land. Allotments would be limited to 160 acres in the case of grazing land, and half that or less for farming land. Even if all San Juans were alloted, it is unlikely that they would be able to retain all the land they are currently using, let alone the land they held in 1934. Individuals would be prevented from selling off allotted lands, and inheritance of allotments would be decided according to Arizona law rather than by the customary land tenure system of the San Juan Tribe (see chap. 6). As a result, allotments would become progressively broken up into smaller, less usable plots, assigned to individuals who might not care for the land or agree how it should be used. Moreover, some land at least would eventually become alienated from San Juan ownership. Because of their broad incest prohibition and small population the San Juan Paiutes are generally forced to seek marriage partners outside the community. San Juan custom and practice works to assure that rights to land remain securely within ambilineage, and thus tribal community boundaries. Arizona inheritance law would open up the possibility that non-San Juan, and even non-Indian spouses and other kin might some day inherit San Juan lands.

Finally, if the San Juans were given allotments and nothing else, this would effectively deprive the tribe of subsurface rights to minerals, water, and so forth, as provided in the 1934 act reservation, automatically assigning these rights to the two parties to the lawsuit over this land, the Hopi and Navajo tribes.

The allotment clause also appeared in all earlier bills designed to settle the Joint Use Area and 1934 area disputes, beginning with the first one introduced by Arizona Representative Sam Steiger in 1972 (U.S. Senate 1972, 1973, 1974). Assistant Secretary of the Interior Harrison Loesch explained the intent of this clause in the following manner: "Also within the boundaries of the 1934 reservation are located certain Paiute Indians whose use dates back to antiquity. Section 6 [of the Steiger Bill] provides for allotments to these Paiute Indians in accordance with the General Allotment Act of February 8, 1887" (Loesch in U.S. Senate 1972:30). The Interior Department and the BIA apparently saw nothing questionable in evoking this long discredited policy of allotment, which many thought had ended with Collier's Indian New Deal reforms. Yet more curious is the fact that no BIA official ever elected to inform the Paiutes of their right to allotments, even though the local BIA was, as noted earlier in the discussion of the (1973) Hemstreet list, apparently already deciding who would and who would not be eligible for allotments. It seems probable that this list was intended to provide the Navajo Tribe with information in the event the Paiutes claimed allotments.

Fortunately, the 1974 act provides another mechanism through which the San Juan Tribe can seek to preserve its rights to both surface and subsurface resources within the 1934 reservation. In its original version, the Owens Bill would simply have partitioned the 1934 act area along lines specified in the text of the bill. However, when it reached the Senate floor, it was noted in debates that such a procedure was unconstitutional. New Mexico Senator Joseph M. Montoya stated: "To take land from one tribe and give it to another tribe is in clear violation of the fifth amendment [seizure without due process]" (Congressional Record, Senate, December 2, 1974, p. 37732). In its final version, as passed on December

22, 1974, the act was revised (at 25 U.S.C. 640d-7) to permit the Hopis and Navajos, as well as "any other tribe of Indians claiming any interest," to sue for title, so that any partition would take place through due process.

This clause gives the San Juan Tribe the option of petitioning the federal district court to allow it to enter into the 1934 act area lawsuit as an equal party, an option they eventually took. To satisfy the language of the 1974 act, however, the Paiutes must show that they are a "tribe of Indians," that is, they must be federally recognized, either through a federal court decision or some other means, such as the BIA Federal Acknowledgement Project.

From 1972 to 1974, and even afterward, the BIA and the Hopi and Navajo tribal governments did not inform the San Juan people that the land on which they were living might well be partitioned out from under them, although all three were well aware of the Paiutes' presence in the disputed lands. Nevertheless, during this period both the Hopis and the Navajos began actively courting the support of the San Juan Tribe in the lobbying battle over Navajo-Hopi dispute legislation.

An article in the Hopi newspaper *Qa'toqti* (1974:1, 8) reported a meeting at Moenkopi on July 1, 1974, between "representatives of the Willow Springs and Navajo Mountain Paiutes" and "Gov. Hubert Lewis of Moencopi and members of the village board . . . to discuss the Hopi-Navajo land dispute and the Navajo attempts to stop passage of the Owens bill in the Senate. Approximately 30 Paiutes were in attendance." The remainder of the article described the strategies that the Hopis and Navajos had adopted in relation to the Paiutes. The events detailed reveal the extent to which both the Navajo and Hopi tribes treated the elders of the San Juan Tribe as representatives of an autonomous tribe with whom agreements could be made:

> A spokesman for the Kaibab Paiute tribe was present as well as members of the other Paiute groups [Willow Springs and Navajo Mountain]. They explained to the village board that representatives of the Navajo tribe had approached them in an attempt to persuade them to go to Washington to lobby for the Navajos against partition legislation supported by the Hopis [the Owens Bill]. But by doing so, the Paiutes stated, they would only end up losing their land to the Navajos. The

Paiutes claim that they had settled in this area long before the Navajo came.

The Paiute representatives also stated that they are "tired of being pushed around" by the Navajos and are through with false statements from the Navajos. They cited an example that they apply for housing by carrying out the required procedure of the Navajo Tribe, but do not get any action [see above]. They claim their forms never reach the screening committee, while Navajos in the area get homes built, with running water and electricity.

Several of the board members agreed that the Paiutes are being approached by the Navajos because the Navajos know that the Paiutes could conceivably testify against them, so the Navajos are doing all they can to get the Paiutes on their side. The Willow Springs and Navajo Mountain Paiutes have never been terminated but are currently not recognized as a tribe, and the feeling in the meeting was that when they do become a unified tribe recognized by the Federal Government with their own constitution and by-laws, that they will have the power and ability to fight on their own against Navajo encroachment. [*Qa'toqti* 1974:1, 8]

According to San Juan elders who were present at the earlier meeting between Paiutes and Navajos described in this article, the Paiutes refused to help the Navajos and instead took the opportunity to complain about Navajo encroachment on their land, as well as the federal social services which they were not receiving (Bunte and Franklin Fieldnotes, July 21, 23, 1983). Several other meetings between the Paiutes and Hopis took place after the first one described here and it seemed to the Paiutes that the Hopis were going to take positive steps to help them. In the end, perhaps because the Hopis' primary goal, the passage of the Owens Bill, had been accomplished without Paiute help, the Hopis stopped inviting the Paiutes to meetings. This left the San Juan elders bitter and mistrustful of both the Navajo and Hopi tribes.

During the past decade, the San Juan Paiute Tribe has continued active pursuit of its goal to obtain federal recognition and protection of its reservation rights. In 1979,

the Kaibab Paiute tribal chairman forwarded to then tribal
chief elder, Anna Whiskers, an inquiry from the BIA
concerning "unrecognized Paiutes." The BIA Federal
Acknowledgment Project had just been established in 1978
pursuant to federal regulations (25 C.F.R. 54, now 83). In
1980, with the help of anthropologist Allen C. Turner, the tribe
filed a preliminary petition for recognition. At this time, the
tribe also sought further legal assistance from DNA-People's
Legal Service with its federal acknowledgment petition, as well
as its continued problems in obtaining badly needed services,
including   housing,   plumbing,   irrigation,   and   road
improvements.

     In the course of investigating Paiute complaints, a DNA
attorney learned that much of the land upon which the San
Juan Tribe currently resides was to be litigated by the Navajo
and Hopi Tribes in their suit over the 1934 reservation.
Eventually this problem was referred to the Native American
Rights Fund (NARF), a nonprofit legal foundation
headquartered in Boulder, Colorado, which specializes in
landmark cases in Indian law. In 1982, the San Juan Tribe
motioned the federal court in Phoenix to allow it to intervene
in the lawsuit. Both the Hopi and Navajo tribes objected,
arguing that the sole remedy foreseen for the Paiutes by
Congress was the allotment clause of the 1974 act. The judge
denied the Paiutes, not on the grounds proposed by the Hopis
and Navajos, but because of the potential delays Paiute
intervention might cause. His decision was overturned on
appeal. The 1934 area case has, as was noted earlier, yet to go
to trial. Meanwhile, the San Juan Tribe and its NARF
attorneys have been allowed to participate in depositions of lay
and expert witnesses, interrogatories, and discovery of
evidence pending a decision on their federal recognition from
the BIA. The Hopi Tribe, apparently after consulting with one
of its expert witnesses, Robert Euler, a specialist in Southern
Paiute ethnohistory (see Euler 1966), later removed its
opposition to the Paiutes' intervention in the suit and their
federal recognition. Hopi Chairman Ivan Sidney recently
stated in the *Arizona Republic*: "We know they [the Paiutes]
were around a long time before the Navajo. They deserve
recognition" (Elston 1985:A2).

     The tribe's recognition petition is also pending. In 1982,
the tribe applied for and received a grant from the
Administration for Native Americans to help finance the
necessary research and documentation for federal recognition.

The final petition was submitted in 1984 and is still under review. At first, both the Navajo and Hopi tribes voiced objection to San Juan recognition. As noted above, the Hopi Tribe reversed itself and now supports San Juan recognition. The Navajo Tribe, using the full weight of its influence and economic resources, has continued to oppose the San Juan Tribe. Its attorneys have submitted several reports (Navajo Tribe 1985b, 1985c, and 1986) and thousands of pages of documentation to the BIA. The sheer volume of materials submitted by both the Paiutes and the Navajos as well as the potential repercussions of the case have caused considerable delays in the BIA federal acknowledgement petition review process.

Over the years since Ralph Castro first offered the official assistance of the Kaibab Tribe, the San Juan Tribe has continued to receive support from other Paiute tribes. Notes taken by Kaibab officials at meetings with the San Juan Tribe, for example, those taken at a meeting at Navajo Mountain on March 12, 1977 (M. Jake 1977), testify to continued support from Kaibab. Both the Kaibab Paiute Tribe (1982) and the Paiute Tribe of Utah (1982) passed resolutions supporting the San Juan Tribe in its federal recognition petition.

The other Southern Paiute tribes have also included the San Juan Tribe in their own projects. For example, in 1976, when the Navajo Tribe applied for public lands in House Rock Valley, Arizona--land which traditionally belonged to Paiutes-- Kaibab Chairwoman Vivienne Jake wrote a letter to the Arizona Bureau of Land Management office which included the comments of San Juan elder *Kwinu*, or Connie Yazzie, and chief elder Anna Whiskers (V. Jake 1976). They and other San Juan representatives had been invited to a meeting at Kaibab where their expressed concerns regarding the House Rock issue were recorded. The other Southern Paiutes also sought to include the San Juans in a project to obtain an all-Paiute agency (see, for example, the inclusion of Willow Springs and Navajo Mountain/Paiute Canyon as communities in the Paiutes' proposal, Southern Paiute Nation [c.1982]).

Throughout the 1970s, Anna Whiskers was recognized as the chief elder for the San Juan Tribe. Former Kaibab Chairwoman Vivienne Jake confirmed (personal communication, 1984) that the Kaibab Tribe had acknowledged Anna Whiskers as the official spokesperson and therefore directed all their official correspondence with the San Juan Tribe to her. She is considered by many Southern Paiute elders from other tribes to be one of the foremost living orators in the Southern Paiute language. Her traditional skills as a speaker contributed greatly to her ability to represent the San Juan Tribe effectively with the influential elders of other tribes. Anna Whiskers is the daughter of Alfred Lehi, until his death the chief elder, and is also the mother of Evelyn Whiskers James, present tribal spokesperson and chief elder. For personal reasons, Anna Whiskers was unable to continue in her duties as chief elder. During the first years of our field work, in 1979 and 1980, she was already phasing herself out as leader in favor of her daughter who has the necessary mobility and moreover has the English skills that are becoming essential for the chief elder's duties. Nevertheless, Anna Whiskers remains extremely influential as a tribal elder.

5

ASPECTS OF MODERN
SAN JUAN
CULTURAL IDENTITY

The San Juan Tribe as a Southern Paiute Language Community

Alliances between the San Juans and other Southern Paiute groups, particularly Kaibab and Kanosh, have long been a major feature on the group's external political landscape. There can be little doubt that the language that these groups share and the conception of a shared cultural identity that accompanies the fact of a common language have been at least partially responsible for this historically important pattern of intertribal, but also intraethnic alliance building between the politically independent Southern Paiute communities.

San Juan Southern Paiutes speak a dialect of the Southern Paiute/Ute language, which comprises a group of dialects that specialists refer to as the Southern Numic branch of the Uto-Aztecan language family. Southern Numic is a geographic and linguistic continuum of mutually intelligible dialects stretching from the Uintah Utes in the northeast through the other Ute and Southern Paiute groups in Colorado, Utah, Arizona, and Nevada, down to the Chemehuevi in California (see map 1 for the location of historic Southern Paiute communities). Linguistic differences among dialects tend to increase with geographical distance. Nonetheless, the Southern Paiute dialects, among which we should probably include Chemehuevi, evidence more uniformity among themselves than with Ute (compare for example the language of the Uintah Ute and Kaibab Paiute texts in Sapir 1930). Since the Kaibab Paiutes figure prominently in San Juan political affairs, past and present, and since their dialect is well represented in the linguistic literature (see Sapir 1930 and Bunte 1979), it is worthwhile comparing it with the dialect spoken by the San Juans as a means of understanding the ways in which language unites localized tribes into one ethnic group while at the same time marking clear boundaries between them as separate sociolinguistic communities.

Historically speaking, there is no doubt that the two dialects are closely related. In many ways, the somewhat archaic variety of Kaibab Paiute studied by Sapir, whose data were collected in 1910 but not published until 1930, more closely resembles the style of speech spoken by the eldest San Juan speakers than it does modern Kaibab Paiute. Although there are noticeable differences between the modern dialects, particularly in phonology and vocabulary, modern Kaibab and San Juan speakers have no trouble understanding each other. We have frequently witnessed Paiute speakers from the two groups communicating in that language with great facility. These have included formal occasions, as at tribal meetings in which a member of the other group was a guest speaker, as well as more informal, friendly visiting between members of both groups. Although speakers of both dialects are aware of the slight differences in phonology, morpho-syntax, and vocabulary described below, they do not find that these impede communication. Usually, however, the speakers of one dialect take care to regularize their speech when speaking to members of other Southern Paiute tribes, avoiding or toning down the most obvious dialectal markers. In our comparison of the two dialects, we use the Kaibab Paiute orthography developed by Bunte in conjunction with Kaibab tribal elder Lucille Jake

(1976), with a few modifications to accomodate differences in San Juan Paiute.

The major differences between Kaibab and San Juan lie in their respective sound systems. For example, whereas San Juan has preserved the phonologically conditioned [s]/[sh] alternation that Sapir recorded for Kaibab, modern Kaibab uses only [s]. The word for "pine pitch" is pronounced *shanap* in San Juan and *sanap* in Kaibab. San Juan is also in the process of introducing its own phonological innovations. One sound change that is particularly noticeable in the speech of younger San Juan speakers is the substitution of [ø], a mid, front, rounded vowel, often with retroflex approximate r-coloring (the sound of "er" in many American dialects of English), for the open [o] found in most Southern Paiute dialects. Unlike modern Kaibab speakers, Sapir's Kaibab consultant, Tony Tillohash, also showed a sporadic tendency to front open [o], as Sapir's (1930) transcriptions of Tillohash's speech showed. San Juan speakers also demonstrate a tendency to reduce Southern Paiute nasal plus stop clusters, as in [mp], [nt], [nts], [nch], [ngk], to simple voiceless stops. An example that illustrates all three dialectal differences described here is the word for "cottonwood tree": Kaibab *soovimp* is pronounced as *shøøvwip* in San Juan speech.

There are very few substantive morpho-syntactic differences between Kaibab and San Juan. One example of such a difference, which bears on the use of the article, amounts to a mere contrast in preferred style. Kaibab Paiute consistently attaches the article to the end of all noun phrases except predicate nominals. San Juan, on the other hand, often omits the article entirely, particularly in rapid or informal speech. Thus, in the Southern Paiute version of the sentence, "I saw the boy," the object case form of *aipats*, "boy," would normally occur as *aipatsi-ung* (boy + article) in Kaibab but may often occur simply as *aipatsi* in San Juan.

A second example of morpho-syntactic differences between the two dialects is a structural rather than a stylistic difference. While Kaibab Paiute has four adverbial subordinate suffixes (*-tsi-*, *-kai-*, *-ka-*, and *-ku-*), San Juan has only three (*-tsi-*, *-kai-*, and *-ku-*). Specifically, the aspectual difference between the Kaibab perfective aspect, *-ka-*, and imperfective, *-ku-*, suffixes is neutralized in the San Juan *-ku-* suffix (see Bunte 1986 for a complete description of subordinate suffixes in the two dialects).

While the two dialects share the vast majority of their

vocabulary, especially those items which refer to aspects of their traditional lifestyle, they differ significantly in the ways they have adapted their vocabulary repertoire to modern Western society and its technology. During periods of rapid social and technological change, language speakers generally adopt one of two strategies in expanding their vocabulary to cover new concepts. They may borrow vocabulary from a language that already has a word for the item in question; or they may use the internal resources of their own language to innovate new terms.

Over the course of recorded history since Anglo-European contact, the speakers of Kaibab have generally opted for the former strategy while the San Juans have chosen the latter. One reason for this is simply that San Juan speakers have not been as thoroughly exposed to English speakers as have Kaibab Paiutes. Thus, for "chicken," Kaibab Paiutes use *tsikinants*, the Paiutized English term, whereas San Juans use *akarapits*, literally "red crow." To cite another example, the Kaibab say *aromovi* (<automobile), *kari*, or even "trucki" when speaking of cars and pickups. San Juans use the word *kwaangutu*, derived from a form of the Southern Paiute verbal root *kwaa* "to race" or "to win (a game or race)," plus the suffix *tu(a)* meaning a place or object for doing something (compare Southern Paiute *karutu* "chair," literally a place to sit on, from Paiute *karu-* "to sit"). Similarly, every part of an automobile, or for that matter many other modern devices, like radios, televisions, batteries, etc., all have San Juan Paiute names deriving from native roots through native morphological processes.

Numerals provide another, more systematic example of the manner in which the San Juans have adapted Southern Paiute to the needs of the modern world. Numbers above a few thousand have never been obtained for the other Southern Paiute groups (see especially J. W. Powell's nineteenth century Southern Paiute word lists in Fowler and Fowler 1971). It seems likely that prior to the modern era, Southern Paiute, like other languages in circumstances where speakers have little need for complex arithmetic accounting, had developed no means of naming very large numbers. Modern San Juans, however, do need these numbers when they talk about the larger social world around them which the modern media, through battery-run radios and televisions, have opened up to them. Consequently, the San Juan people have enlarged the old numeral system in ways that permit the ready construction of numerals referring to tens and hundreds of thousands, and even millions. (For a more complete account see Bunte and Franklin 1983 and 1986.)

Although both Kaibab and San Juan Paiutes speak dialects of the same language, a more generalized description of the two groups as modern sociolinguistic communities would differ in several respects. All Kaibab Paiutes are fluent speakers of English. Moreover, while older adults have a thorough competency in Southern Paiute, many young adults and virtually all children at Kaibab have only a limited and passive knowledge of Paiute. Some can respond in English to their elders' native language questions, orders, and comments. Others are aware only of certain isolated, culturally important vocabulary items. Among the San Juan Paiutes, although there are some community members whose knowledge of Paiute is limited or nonexistent--particularly in a few cases where orphaned children were separated from the San Juan community during the years when languages are learned with facility--the majority of San Juans, including children, are still fluent Paiute speakers. Indeed, the San Juan Paiute Tribe is perhaps the only Southern Paiute community where Paiute is the children's first language.

Because Southern Paiute is the language of all aspects of everyday community life among the San Juans, a number of different genres of speaking are still in use that are no longer common in other Southern Paiute communities. These culturally marked kinds of speech include, among others, genres primarily used in formal contexts, such as myth telling and giving moral instruction, when elders are expected to talk to younger people. Although many elders in other Southern Paiute communities are just as knowledgeable and skilled in these genres, the inability of the younger people to comprehend Paiute, particularly the specialized Paiute used in these contexts, means that there is little opportunity for the elders to perform them. Among the San Juans, however, myths are told and moral instructions are still given to young people on a regular basis and in naturally occurring situations. Because they encode much of the socially recognized body of knowledge regarding right and reasonable behavior in everyday life as well as appropriate ritual behavior, an examination of these genres is essential to any cultural study of the San Juan people. The mythological Coyote tales will be discussed later when we consider religion and ritual. In this section, we will briefly examine a proverb- or maxim-like verbal genre that is a major constituent of morally instructive speech. This genre is called *aikнp* in Paiute.

Aikнp, translated by some speakers as "instructions," literally means a "saying," or more precisely a "saying for" someone, for a person's benefit. One group of *aikнp* relate to highly specific situations and are generally meant to be taken literally. Some of the best examples of this type are the sayings associated with life cycle observances. On certain ritual occasions, elder relatives will talk their younger kin through the ritually prescribed actions and restrictions on action that must be observed during times of passage from one stage of life to another. The elders instruct their younger relatives, explaining how they must conduct themselves henceforward. For each ritually prescribed action or restriction on action there is an associated *aikнp* which encodes the prescribed behavior and which, in most cases, also describes--or more often hints at--the supernatural consequences of noncompliance. Examples of this group of *aikнp* are given in the description of life-cycle observances below.

A second group of *aikнp* possesses a greater generality and at the same time more closely approximates the familiar Old World genres of proverbs and maxims. These *aikнp* refer to general ethical principles, but not through literal prescriptions for conduct. Rather, they do so through the use of metaphoric or other figurative language. Elder kin employ *aikнp* when a junior relative needs to be instructed in proper conduct or reminded of previous instruction that they are assumed already to have received and assimilated. For example, a child, or young man or woman, who persists in sleeping late will be told, "you must wake up and go jogging along, and then a deer skin, antelope skin, and jack rabbit skin will cross your path." This instruction is interpreted to mean that individuals who rise early and go about their proper work will receive things worth having that might not have been expected. Although it literally refers to the fortunes of hunting, traditionally and still in the present an important activity for males, it is used equally well to instruct girls and young women not to be lazy. As in European folklore, a great many San Juan *aikнp* revolve around the value of hard work and early rising.

Aikнp are characterized by certain stylistic and rhetorical devices that enable the audience to recognize them as traditional "sayings." Their use provides a compelling and traditionally authoritative means for moral instruction.

While a number of older San Juans, unlike their

counterparts at Kaibab, have virtually no skills in English, many have some fluency in Navajo in addition to their native language. Intensive schooling did not begin for the majority of San Juans until about 25 years ago. Even today, many older San Juans have few occasions to use whatever English skills they have in their daily lives. Navajo, on the other hand, has frequently been a useful language in the San Juans' dealings with outsiders, as in local trade relations. Many older San Juans have some fluency in Navajo, but this appears to be less common among younger adults. Now that most children receive an education in local Navajo reservation schools, English has also begun to show signs of replacing the native language in Navajo society. Because younger San Juans can now communicate in English for most dealings with their Navajo neighbors, they feel less of a need and have less of an opportunity to acquire the skills in Navajo that their elders may have found useful.

The Southern Paiute language serves the San Juans as an important social boundary maintenance device in their dealings with non-Paiutes. When members of the community are in the presence of outsiders, such as Navajos who do not speak Paiute whom they meet while shopping at Tuba City or buying gas at Navajo Mountain, the San Juans almost unconsciously use their common language as a means of maintaining social distance between themselves and the outsiders.

This is very different from Kaibab Paiutes' language use with outsiders. They are explicitly taught not to speak Paiute around non-Paiutes, explaining that the outsiders might think they were being talked about. In fact, in the middle 1970s, several members of the local Anglo town that borders on the reservation expressed amazement that any Paiutes still spoke the language (Bunte 1979). In recent years, however, there is some indication that the Kaibab attitude towards speaking Paiute in public may have shifted somewhat. For example, at a meeting dealing with a conflict over water rights, Paiutes openly spoke their language in front of local Mormons. Since this was a period of increased friction between the groups, this shift in language norms was intended as a symbolic expression of the Kaibab community's solidarity and independence.

San Juan Paiutes generally treat Navajo visitors with respect and formality. Even a visit by a Navajo neighbor with whom they are on friendly terms is considered a formal occasion and the visitor will probably be offered a chair, even when everyone else is sitting on the ground. Also, the conversation with this visitor will be in Navajo if at all possible, that is, if a San Juan who speaks Navajo is available. Such formality tends to maintain social distance between members of the two groups.

In their dealings with other Paiute groups, language helps to encourage a sense of common ethnicity. Particularly for members of the Kaibab Tribe or the bands of the Paiute Tribe of Utah, the Paiute language has come to be a major symbol of the "Paiute way," as it is often called. Since a great deal of traditional knowledge is encoded in the Paiute language, for example, in the names of medicinal and food plants or in the *aikʉp* discussed above, the symbolic importance of language is great. Perhaps because even San Juan children speak the language, members of the Kaibab Tribe sometimes state that the San Juans are more traditional than themselves. Several years ago, one woman from Kaibab left her granddaughter with the Willow Springs San Juan households for a few weeks so that the girl might be exposed to the traditional Paiute way of life and immersed in a full time Paiute-speaking community.

For the various groups of Southern Paiutes, dialectal differences serve to mark community autonomy. Although they are not usually so impolite as to comment on dialectal differences to a person's face, stereotyped differences often surface in talk about other Paiute communities. Among Southern Paiutes, there are folk classifications of dialects based on areal vocabulary differences. These, however, usually tend to oppose areal groupings of several tribes against one another, or even oppose Utes to Paiutes. Kaibab and San Juan Paiutes, for example, are among the groups which Southern Paiutes recognize as using *s(h)ariits* for "dog" rather than *pungkuts* as do other tribes, particularly in Nevada. At Navajo Mountain, the local San Juans tell an amusing story about a language misunderstanding based on the different Southern Ute and Southern Paiute words for "watermelon" (Southern Paiutes say *piɣarʉka'nʉmp*). A San Juan family was visiting in-laws at the Southern Ute community of Towaoc, Colorado, when their host asked one man to go and fetch a watermelon. Since he did not know what she wanted, he went outside and pretended to look, then stayed there too embarrassed to return until someone came out to get him.

Once dialectal variation is socially recognized among the various groups that make up the larger Southern Paiute/Ute language community, it becomes a symbol for local community autonomy: members of each tribal community take a certain pride in their own speech variety and express a mild contempt for the varieties used by other groups. Yet at the same time, all communities recognize their common language as an important tie among them. In this way, the San Juan dialect helps the people maintain a sense of common ethnicity with neighboring Ute and Paiute groups while at the same time preserving a distinct identity.

San Juan Traditional Religion and Ritual

Most modern San Juan Southern Paiutes are active Pentecostal Christians. Their conversion to Christianity is very recent, for many people within the last 15 years. Perhaps because of this, some San Juans harbor ambivalent feelings about their traditional religious beliefs and practices. However, in the last few years at least, the San Juans appear to be coming more and more to terms with this ambivalence. Although the two have tended to be compartmentalized, there now appears to be an attempt to reconcile traditional religion with Christianity. Because the Southern Paiute traditional religion is still a central part of their life and because it differs dramatically from that of Navajos and Hopis, the beliefs and practices associated with it form a major pillar in the San Juan Paiutes' collective self-definition, separate from Navajos and Hopis but joined with other Southern Paiute groups.

There are at least three areas of traditional Southern Paiute belief and ritual that continue to have great importance for the San Juans. One bears on Paiutes' relationship with the natural world, while another concerns beliefs and ritual practices revolving around culturally recognized life crises. All traditional religious cosmology and ritual among Southern Paiutes, however, is grounded in a third body of tradition, the mythological cycle of stories often referred to as "Coyote tales" or, alternatively, as "winter stories" because by tradition Southern Paiutes will only tell them during the winter months.

These stories take place in the mythical time when human beings emerged into the world. They recount the doings of a variety of mythic figures, most notably the pair of brothers which in the San Juan versions of the tales are both named *Shɨnangwav* and which English-speaking Southern Paiutes often call "Wolf" and "Coyote." Sapir (1930) recorded a large collection of Wolf and Coyote cycle myths as told by his

Kaibab consultant, Tony Tillohash, in 1910; Bunte (1980) contains a modern Kaibab version of another myth. Among the San Juans, there are a number of story tellers who can recount the full repertoire of myths. Out of deference to their greater traditional knowledge, the stories are generally told and discussed only by tribal elders, but younger members of the tribe also appear to be quite knowledgeable concerning traditional mythology. The San Juan versions of the winter stories are substantially the same as those collected from Kaibab story tellers.

While almost all the characters in Southern Paiute mythological tales have the names of animals, they are understood not to be like the animals of today but physically to resemble human beings. The mythological characters are the precursors of their present day, natural world namesakes. Many stories end with a mythic figure being changed into an actual animal, often as a punishment, for example, when Coyote's incestuous desires for his five daughters lead his wife to turn him into the "desert dog" (see Sapir's version of "Coyote and his Daughters," 1930:462-64).

These mythic figures are also understood as divinities. The elder of the two *Shɨnangwav* brothers, in particular, emerges in the myths as a primary deity whose symbolic importance is similar to that of the Christians' Jesus or God. Whatever the situation, Coyote's elder brother always performs the morally and ritually appropriate action or explains the proper behavior for his kin and tribe members to follow. The elder *Shɨnangwav* is thus a model elder kinsman. Interestingly, in Christian prayer, the San Juans also name Jesus *Shɨnangwav*, suggesting an attempt to draw a conscious parallelism between the traditional and Christian belief systems. On the other hand, the younger *Shɨnangwav* brother, Coyote, commits every folly and wickedness imaginable in the traditional moral system. In one story, he wishes evil on his elder brother, thus leading to his death (Wolf is later resurrected). In another, he is lazy and only pretends to hunt for his family, beating his shoes on a rock to make them look worn, but in the meanwhile steals food for himself. Many stories focus on Coyote's sexual misbehavior: he forces his brother's wife to commit adultery with him; he commits incest with his aunt and daughters; and so on. In characteristically humorous fashion, Coyote symbolizes and renders ridiculous every facet of what is traditionally seen as wrongful.

At the same time that the traditional stories set forth both explicit and implicit standards of proper and improper actions and beliefs, they also provide cosmological explanations for the origins of life crisis rituals and prescriptions, for the origins of the Southern Paiutes as a people, as well as for their traditional relationships with the natural environment.

Southern Paiute ethnohistorical and ethnographic specialists Richard Stoffle and Henry Dobyns have documented the sacredness which other Southern Paiute groups attribute to their traditional lands (Stoffle and Dobyns 1982, 1983). The San Juans, like these other groups, feel they stand in a particular kind of sacred relationship to that part of the natural world they see as their territorial homeland. This relationship entails the preservation of traditional knowledge concerning specific places and their culturally appropriate uses as well as knowledge of the appropriate ways to approach the plants and creatures of the natural world.

One of the features that marks each territorial community of Southern Paiutes is knowledge of sacred places within their local territory. Among the kinds of sites that the San Juan Paiutes today regard as sacred are historic round-dance sites, graves of their ancestors, and all sources of water, including springs and seep wells. Each of these sites is hedged around with oral history and traditions that elders are careful to pass on. Even sites that have not been inhabited for generations because of Navajo occupation are well remembered in oral history.

Each Southern Paiute tribal community tells a version of the traditional Southern Paiute origin myth which highlights the sacredness of their own local tribal territory. According to this myth (Sapir 1930:351-59), Coyote once opened a sack that he was given but told not to open. From it emerged all the peoples of the world, last of all the Paiutes. Because they were the last to emerge, the Paiutes remained thereafter in the very country where the sack was opened, a place that depends on the group telling the story. According to the Las Vegas Paiutes, Coyote opened the sack in the Las Vegas Wash area. For them, their home territory lies at the center of the world, where all humans originated. According to the San Juan version of the story, Coyote untied the sack near Page, Arizona, so that they consider the original home of all Paiutes to be in San Juan territory. In this way, the creation myth for each group of Paiutes underscores the special sacred character of their own homeland.

Southern Paiutes treat plants and animals with special

reverence as beings with spirits. Thus, medicinal plants are gathered with care and a respectful attitude. Paiute herbalists speak to medicine plants before they are picked, telling the plant why it is needed. As might be expected from the fact that their traditional deities are the precursors of animals, animals are also held sacred. In the past, San Juan Paiute leaders often derived their sacred power from specific animal spirits. *Machukats*, for example, according to his grand-daughter, Marie Lehi, drew his power for healing from eagle and flying squirrel tutelary spirits. In the San Juan community today, wild animals are still considered to have sacred power. Children are forbidden even to watch the preparation of buckskins. In addition, among modern San Juans as well as Kaibab Paiutes, one commonplace ritual especially evokes and symbolizes Paiutes' sacred relationship with the creatures of the wild. When eating out-of-doors, away from dwellings and thus in the natural as opposed to the human world, many Paiutes will throw scraps of food away from the eating place, "to feed the creatures," as they explain.

Life crisis rituals that mark a change in status are yet another aspect of traditional Southern Paiute religious belief and practice still important in San Juan society today. Traditionally, there were three major life-cycle changes mediated by ritual among Southern Paiutes and Utes: first menstruation, first birth, and death. In the case of birth and menstruation, a woman follows the same ritually prescribed pattern. The *first* time she undergoes these important physical and spiritual events, however, the ritual prescriptions and prohibitions are given special notice by her family and the community so that the special instruction she receives from the elders serves to mark her irreversible change in status.

A Coyote tale collected by Sapir, "Coyote Sets the Parturition Customs" (1930:369-77), tells how Coyote estab-lished the birth rituals which all Southern Paiutes traditionally practiced. In the myth, Coyote has a baby after hanging on to a cedar limb. Then, he goes and gathers wood, builds a fire, and makes a bed of heated stones to lie on. He drinks warm water and makes a scratcher to scratch his head with.

While some traditional birth practices that were observed until very recently are no longer possible because of the circumstances surrounding modern hospital births, other aspects of Southern Paiute birth rituals are still followed among the modern San Juans. For example, since they have begun giving birth at hospitals in the last fifteen to twenty-five years, San Juan women no longer give birth as they once did by holding on to a rope attached to a tree or to a house beam. On the other hand, the San Juans still feel it is important not to drink cold water after giving birth. San Juan elder Marie Lehi told us that if the warm water were mixed with the red mineral pigment *tɨɾwiøp* ("earth paint"), the woman would never afterward suffer from thirst.

It is up to San Juan elders to instruct the person passing through a life cycle change. This instruction was done in the past and continues today using the genre traditionally associated with moral instruction, the *aikɨp*. For example, on the occasion of the birth of a first child, the parturient woman and her husband are told a whole set of *aikɨp* by their elder kin. They will be told, among other things, "Don't eat meat, or you will always be eating every last crumb" and "Don't scratch your hair or touch your face with your hands." If they disregard the latter instruction, it is believed their hair will always be tangled and messy and their face will become prematurely wrinkled (hence the head scratcher). The San Juan husband is assigned specific tasks with other *aikɨp*, as well, such as fetching wood and water so that he will not become a lazy husband later on. The husband is also expected to run east each morning before the sun rises. San Juans in the Willow Springs area explain the alleged sloppiness of one young man as having resulted from his neglect of this latter custom when his first child was born. All of the above ritual practices, except for the use of *tɨɾwiøp*, were noted by Stewart (1942:303-307) and Kelly (1964:96-98) as traditional birth practices among other Paiute and Ute groups.

For the San Juans, marriage and children are an essential step in becoming socially mature. To become an elder or a chief elder, it is virtually essential that one have gone through the ritual stage of first childbirth. The majority of the prescriptions and prohibitions found in the traditional instructions dealing with birth focus on the teaching of self-restraint, self-discipline, and the willingness to work hard. Likewise, Coyote in his backwards fashion teaches the same virtues. These are the virtues required of the socially mature person in Paiute society.

The most important rite of passage for a Southern Paiute woman occurred at the time of her first menstruation. For the San Juans, the ritual prescriptions and prohibitions embodied in the *aikɨp* associated with this life event are still very much a part of the present.

Kelly (1964:94) noted that among the Kaibab Paiutes, "puberty observances for a girl were similar to those associated with childbirth." Just how similar is apparent from San Juan elder Marie Lehi's account of this event in her life, as translated into English by her granddaughter:

> I used to fetch wood and carry it from far away--I was real strong. They used to watch me. I couldn't take a bath by myself or touch my hair with my hands. I had to run as far and as fast as I could to the east to get strong, to stay young, and not to get heavy. At that time, I wouldn't eat meat because I was told that if I ate meat I would lose my teeth before I was old. You weren't supposed to scratch your face or you'd get wrinkles. Women at that time would only eat cornmeal. After I had my first menstruation I would run under the rising sun in the morning. I wasn't supposed to follow any trails or tracks--just run straight east. [Jake, James, and Bunte 1983:47]

Notice that the practices observed by girls at their first menstruation mirror those practiced by parturient women. Some practices characteristic of menstruation, however, are shifted to the husband at childbirth. Because of this parallelism between the female's role at puberty and the male's role at childbirth, the husband's tasks of wood-gathering and running to the east may be seen as a form of couvade. All of these practices, which are still observed among many San Juan families today, were noted as traditional practices among Utes and Southern Paiutes by Omer Stewart (1942:309-12).

As recently as twenty years ago, the San Juans observed the same complex of funerary customs that Stewart (1942:312-14) and Kelly (1964:95) described as traditionally belonging to the Utes and other Southern Paiutes. At the death of a member, the San Juans would wash the body and put *tuvwiøp* on the face. According to consultants, the mourners would then recite "special sayings" over the body and bury the deceased either in the house where he or she died or covered with rocks in a rocky ledge or cave. Occasionally, the deceased would be cremated by burning the house down around the body. Since a house in which a death had occurred had to be abandoned, whether or not the deceased was buried within, the San Juans would often build a small shelter apart from the house for a sick relative who appeared likely to die. The deceased person's possessions were also buried or burned. Even the deceased's horse would often be shot over the grave; at many burials, including those of women, one can still see the remains of the deceased person's horse. Mourners used to color their faces with *tᴜᵛwiøp* and singe their hair. After four days of mourning, the community would go back to everyday affairs.

The San Juans continue to believe that certain susceptible people should not approach or see the dead body, to prevent the spirit of the recently deceased from taking the person along as a companion in death. Susceptible individuals included children, the very old, the sick, and pregnant women. Otherwise, San Juans both past and present have little fear of the dead. They are not afraid to talk about the dead and often visit their graves to pay respects in the years after the death.

Because of transportation difficulties in the past, there were no elaborate funerals or wakes. Every San Juan Paiute in the area would come to see the family of the deceased. When meeting they would embrace and weep over one another's shoulders. Those who lived at a distance would weep together with the family on the first occasion of their meeting after the death, whether a few days afterward or several months. So recent was the custom of the cry-greeting observed among the San Juans that even young adults at Willow Springs can recall this practice occurring in their childhood when San Juan Paiutes from Navajo Mountain would visit for the first time after a death. We have observed this cry-greeting custom carried out at Navajo Mountain when local San Juans met with a family whose daughter had just separated from her husband. Each adult in turn wept over the young woman's shoulder and then over her parents' shoulders.

Some fifteen years ago, when most San Juan families had acquired vehicles and many had become Christians, the tribal community started holding funerals in local churches and burying the deceased in a cemetery, usually at Tuba City. These funerals are organized by the entire tribe and bring together friends and relatives from other Southern Paiute and Ute tribes as well. The first such funeral was held for their leader, Alfred Lehi, in 1969. According to consultants, the church in Tuba City where the funeral was held was packed with Paiutes from the San Juan and other Southern Paiute tribes paying their respects. Lehi's horse was shot, some of his possessions were buried with him, and the rest were burned.

While at one time the other Southern Paiute communities

all practiced funeral customs very similar to those described above, as Kelly (1964:95) pointed out, "Towards the end of the [nineteenth] century, an attenuated version of the Colorado River mourning ceremony reached the Kaibab, via the St. George Paiute." This originally Mohave ceremony, which Paiutes refer to in English as the "Cry" and in Paiute as *Yaxap* ("Cry"), perhaps after the traditional cry-greeting custom, is still performed today by the majority of Southern Paiute communities. At present, it lasts one or two nights and consists of one or two song cycles sung by groups of singers led by a ritual specialist. The song cycles are said to sing the spirit of the deceased along a geographical route through the traditional Southern Paiute land to his or her dwelling place in the next world. During the pauses between songs, the mourners get up and speak their grief for the deceased, talk about what they believe that person stood for, and thank those who are present to pay their respects and give their sympathy. They also talk about the common bonds of Paiute ethnicity that unite those members of the different tribes brought together by the funeral ceremony, often specifically citing language and common religious beliefs as symbols of these ties.

Most San Juan adults have at one time or another been to Cry ceremonies performed by other Southern Paiutes. During the 1940s and 1950s when many San Juans were working seasonally in Utah, several San Juans who died among the Southern Paiutes there were given Cry funeral ceremonies. The San Juans themselves, however, had never organized a Cry. One reason may be that, like the Utes who also do not perform the ceremony, they were reluctant to adopt what was originally a foreign custom. According to one San Juan who has lived among the Utes at various times in his life, there is a Ute story that the spirit of the land east of the Colorado River would not allow the spirit of the Cry ceremony to pass over among the Utes and Paiutes living there.

In May 1983, however, after the death of the youngest brother of Alfred Lehi, an important San Juan elder, the San Juan Tribe for the first time organized a Cry on their own soil. When the San Juans at Willow Springs received news that Willie Lehi had died in Blanding, a Kaibab Paiute who happened to be visiting offered the services of the Kaibab singers. While many younger San Juans had some reservations, the tribal elders, including the deceased's elder brother, insisted that a Cry be organized since the singers had offered their help. Over one hundred Paiute adults were present for the all night singing ceremony, which included not only adult San Juans from every family in the tribe, but also several members of the Kaibab, Cedar City, Kanosh, and Richfield communities. Although many children were brought along, they were kept at a distance from the body. Because the ceremony lasted all night, few were awake in any case. Afterwards, even those who had initially been reluctant were pleased that the ceremony had been held. Several young people taped the singing in order to learn the songs.

While their traditional religion may serve as a link between the San Juans and other Southern Numic communities, it is also one of the most important factors maintaining the boundaries between the San Juan Tribe and non-Paiutes, especially Navajos and Hopis. The beliefs and ritual practices of these two tribes are quite different from those of the San Juan Paiutes. (For information on Hopi religious practices, see Eggan 1950:45-60; Simmons 1942; Frigout 1979; Hieb 1979; and for Navajo religion, see Kluckhohn and Leighton 1946, chaps. 6 and 7; Witherspoon 1977, chaps. 1 and 2; Wyman 1983.) For the San Juans, the contrasts between their beliefs and practices and those of their Navajo and Hopi neighbors are central components in their conceptions of the sociopolitical divisions between the three tribes.

Some aspects of the other groups' ritual practices are amusing to members of the San Juan Tribe and become the basis of Paiutes' ethnic jokes about them. The San Juans and Southern Numic peoples in general have traditionally had very informal customs regarding marriage. On the other hand, they are aware that traditional Navajos pay brideprice to the family of a woman they wish to marry (see Witherspoon 1975:24), and that among the Hopis the bride's family prepares bread and other presents for the husband's family. San Juans joke that "Navajos buy their wives, and Hopis buy their husbands."

The San Juans and other Southern Paiutes as well are amused by Navajos' reputed practice of sorcery and by the traditional fear that Navajos have of the dead, especially of non-Navajo dead. On the other hand, the San Juans are horrified when they believe that Navajos have desecrated San Juan graves for the purposes of sorcery or religious ceremony. According to the San Juans at both Willow Springs and Navajo Mountain, some Navajo neighbors have desecrated Paiute graves and burned former housesites either out of fear of the non-Navajo dead or to use materials from Paiute graves for sorcery. On one occasion, according to consultants, a group of young Paiute men from Willow Springs retrieved and reburied the remains of a Paiute man whose bones had allegedly been stolen by Navajos. Consultants stated that local Navajos had taken the remains to an Enemy Way ceremony, or Squaw Dance, where the Navajos had shot at the bones with a gun. According to Kluckhohn and Leighton (1946:222), this ritual is used to cure Navajos who "have received their sickness from non-Navahos." The category of ritually dangerous foreigners includes whites as well as members of other Indian tribes, like Paiutes, and the living as well as the dead. A Navajo had apparently accidentally come upon the Paiute bones at an eroded gravesite on *Atatsiv*.

The San Juan Kinship System

Every aspect of San Juan community life is in some way a reflection of kinship relations and kinship values. The next chapter looks at modern San Juan kinship organization and its role in the social, economic, and political life of the tribe. In the last part of this chapter, we examine San Juan Paiute kinship as an abstract cultural system of ideas and values. Although this system is an idealization of community life, San Juan people's social perceptions and conduct in community life are both shaped in important ways by it.

When modern San Juan consanguineal kinship terms are compared with the native language terminologies of other Southern Numic groups, the uniformity is immediately apparent. The kin term system of San Juan Paiute and three other Southern Numic dialects for which phonologically reliable records are available is summarized in Appendix II. The terms and their glosses are taken from the following sources: Kaibab (Isabel Kelly 1964:143-52); Southern Ute (James Goss 1967:2); Uintah Ute (Edward Sapir 1913:135; Sapir did not list Uintah terms for parents, children, or siblings). For ease of comparison, all terms have been converted into the orthography used here.

As the table illustrates, all four dialects utilize the same basic set of roots, with slight dialectal variation. From the standpoint of semantics, the gloss for each term is also the same in each dialect. The following features are characteristically Southern Numic: the typical Great Basin four-way distinction in grandparental terms by gender and matri- or patrilaterality (see Steward 1938:286); the use of the same root reciprocally between kin who are one or more generations distant, excepting parents and children; and the extension of sibling terms to both cross- and parallel cousins. Although their phonetic transcriptions are less easy to interpret and may contain inaccuracies, see also the kin term lists recorded by John Wesley Powell in his nineteenth century Kaibab and Las Vegas Southern Paiute vocabularies (Fowler and Fowler 1971:129-30, 152-53) and Omer Stewart's comparative table of kin terms which lists terms for virtually all of the existing Ute and Southern Paiute groups (1942:350-51). These sources, together with those summarized in Appendix II, clearly substantiate that a single system kinship terminology was historically used by all Southern Paiute and Ute speakers.

This terminology and the way it is used in social life reveals a great deal about how San Juan Paiutes conceive of their social world in both intellectual and moral terms. One of the most important properties of the system concerns the merging of distant collateral kin with closer kin under the same kinship terms. This characteristic is most clearly exemplified by the fact that San Juans call all of their known cousins, however distant, by the same terms they use with brothers and sisters.

One indication that siblings and more distant collaterals of the same generation are not just referentially equivalent but socially equivalent as well can be found in Southern Numic incest prohibitions. The San Juans, like other Southern Paiute and Ute groups (Stewart 1942:296; Kelly 1964:121; Knack 1980:53), forbid marriage or sexual activity between all known consanguineal relatives. Among the San Juans, this is carried to the full limit of known blood kinship. San Juan Paiutes have the same abhorrence of incestuous relations with fifth and even more distant cousins as with full siblings. In many cases, individuals have been raised with these cousins in a household and ambilineage setting, and played and shared meals with them as often as with their own siblings.

While it has apparently not been noted in studies of other Southern Numic dialects, in San Juan Paiute this merging property also extends to the terms designating collaterals of different generations as well as those referring to siblings and cousins. As a result, the San Juans call first, second, third, and more distant cousins of their aunts, uncles, and grandparents by the same terms as these closer relatives. The siblings of grandparents are likewise merged. Because each of these terms is self-reciprocal, elder kin address junior kin using the same

term.   In practice, more distant kin tend to be treated
according to their apparent age in relation to the speaker and
his or her close kin rather than any abstract generational rank
in genealogy. For example, genealogically distant kin who are
technically of one's parents' generation but who are actually
closer to one's own age may be simply called by sibling terms.
The terms for senior kin, unlike sibling/cousin terms,
distinguish between the speaker's mother's and father's sides.
In addition to marking the gender of senior kin, all of the aunt
and uncle terms except for *paa-* "father's sister" also distinguish
age relative to the connecting parent. This means that junior
kin have several highly specified groups of senior kin
classified according to gender, relative age, and patri- or
matrilaterality, and that each group potentially includes very
distant kin, very close kin, and several degrees in between.

Although we have observed the same referential property
in kin terms among Paiute speakers at Kaibab, this has not
been verified in other Ute or Southern Paiute groups. Martha
Knack, however, observed the extension of English kin terms
among the members of the Paiute Tribe of Utah, "such as
'aunt' to MoMoSiDa" (1980:53). Her consultants claimed that
this derived from traditional usage.

Because of the trend in San Juan sociopolitical organization
towards the coalescence of kin groups, this merging principle
has important implications for San Juan social and political
life. Even at the level of the tribe itself, the great majority of
members are related and call each other by kin terms. Kinship
creates a common bond that supplements and strengthens those
created by common territory, culture, and history. Kinship
values color patterns of interaction in politics, as well as
economic and social activities.   At the same time, this merging
property works to extend the kinship constituency base of
tribal elders and the chief elder. Many tribal leaders are
classificatory older relatives to virtually every tribal member
one or more generations younger than themselves.

The systematic use of self-reciprocal terms between
classificatory grandparents, aunts, and uncles and their
corresponding junior relatives may also reflect important social
ties. Because these senior and junior kin use the same term
with each other, the kinship system highlights the special
relations of solidarity and dependence that often exist between
kin of different generations in San Juan society, even as the
system may deemphasize solidarity between parents and
children. The San Juan practice of shifting children between

related households and fostering them with childless or aged older relatives works to create these important relationships with nonparental kin even as the kin term system provides a convenient means of speaking and thinking about them.

Together with the cognitive categories that kinship terms help to express, San Juan kinship ideology is also characterized by two important ethical principles. One of these is the principle of solidarity. In San Juan Paiute society, blood relatives are expected to share everything they possess: their time, their economic resources, and even their children.

The solidarity principle and the network of mutual access it implies for San Juans is given symbolic expression in their personal naming practices. All San Juan Paiutes receive at least one Paiute personal name during their lifetimes. As with kinship terms, Paiute names are used whenever community members talk to or about each other. For example, parents and children address each other using personal names as well as kin terms. English names seldom come up in conversation, except when Paiutes are talking to outsiders.

As with the Kaibab Paiute tradition of naming (Kelly 1964:131), there are no rules specifying which kin may give a name, when it should be given, or what kind of name it may be. Rather, any relative may think of a name and an adult may be given a new name as easily as a child. If the receiver's kin and the community as a whole use the name, it sticks.

Every Paiute name calls attention to some action or characteristic which the community found amusing in that person. One man is called *Marɥka-øa*, "American Back." His back appears very long from the rear, the Paiutes say, more like an Anglo than a Paiute. One young girl is called *Nɥkav*, "Ears," because her ears are seen by Paiutes as large and prominent. Sometimes she is called *Sipyara'*, "Peaches," because her ears are said to resemble the shape of these fruit when they are split in half to dry. One elderly woman is named *S(i)ki*, "Cricket"; a person who is a complainer or a gossiper is called "a cricket mouth" (*s(i)ki tɥpaxat*), so the name may embody a criticism she received as a young woman.

Since personal names are always in the nature of group-to-individual teasing or joking, they work to deflate individual pretensions. The use of the name in daily life, and the intimate knowledge such use implies, symbolize the control that the social sphere exercises over the personal in Southern Paiute society. Everyone, no matter how old or respected, no matter whether they are elder or junior kin, can be addressed at any time using their Paiute name by anyone in the community. For the San Juans, this familiarity and mutual access is an accepted feature of everyday community social relations.

Although the ethic of kinship solidarity operates in all situations, the egalitarian familiarity that usually accompanies it holds only in informal social contexts. In formal contexts, a second ethical principle comes into play, the principle of deference for elders. This principle takes the same form in many kinds of formal interaction, both social and political: seniors talk, juniors listen. It is this principle that permits elders to monopolize talk in political decision making. Outside the political process, there are a number of situations in which this deferential relationship between junior and senior kin exerts its influence. As noted above, verbal performances, such as the telling of myths or instructive speech using *aikɨp*, are by custom restricted to tribal elders. Indeed, even when young people do not understand the meaning or import of the *aikɨp*, they will not speak up and ask their instructor for an explanation. Instead, they try to figure it out for themselves or later ask another elder to explain it. Likewise, those bereaved relatives who speak at funerals between songs are also elders. In such circumstances, younger adults will be present, listening attentively. Active roles taken by junior adults in formal contexts like funerals or political meetings are almost always in the nature of background assistance. They prepare food, they keep the fire going if it is cold, or carry on some other unobtrusive, but necessary support activity.

The Southern Numic kinship system is one of the distinctive features of San Juan Southern Paiute society when compared to Navajo or Hopi society, which both revolve around matrilineal descent groups (Eggan 1950:17-138; Shepardson and Hammond 1970; Witherspoon 1975). Where descent groups have existed in Southern Numic and other Great Basin communities, they have usually been bilateral, based on descent traced through both males and females. This was the case among the Utes and Wind River Shoshones (Jorgensen 1980:179) and is the case among the San Juans.

The kinship terminologies used by the Navajos and Hopis are also typologically quite divergent from the San Juan system. Hopi kin terminology is of the Crow type, whereas the Navajos employ an Iroquois type (Shepardson and Hammond 1970:235-36; Jorgensen 1980:176). Both Hopis and Navajos differentiate between cross and parallel cousins, terminologically merging only the latter with siblings. The San Juan

Paiute kinship terminology makes no distinction between parallel and cross cousins, but calls them all, as we have seen, by sibling terms. This is consistent with the San Juans' use of bilateral descent. In the unilineal descent systems of the Hopis and Navajos, when siblings of the opposite sex have children-- who are cross cousins to one another--they become members of different descent groups. In San Juan society, however, all persons who share descent from a prominent ancestor may potentially be members of the same descent group, and are in any event all treated as close kin.

San Juan Paiutes are aware of these fundamental differences. However, they tend to focus on other patterns of kinship behavior as more important indicators of ethnicity. For San Juans, one of the most important differences between Navajo and Paiute kinship behavior emerges from the two groups' differing beliefs concerning individual autonomy and the authority of the group over the individual.

Paiutes who have visited Navajos or who have lived with Navajo in-laws consistently remark that Navajos seem not to pay much attention to what their younger relatives do. In particular, Paiutes believe that Navajos tend to ignore the goings and comings of their kin. Whenever someone is leaving a Paiute household, whether it is a child or an adult, the other household members expect to be told where that person is going and often will ask if no explanation is volunteered. This is consistent with the Paiute approach to kinship solidarity and their tendency to value it above personal independence. They claim that Navajos do not even say goodbye when they leave and instead seem to prefer to slip off unnoticed.

This pattern of interaction among Navajos may result from moral beliefs that Navajos share with other Athapaskan groups. In his study of another group of Southern Athapaskan communities, the Western Apaches of east central Arizona, Basso noted that Apaches consider it impolite to take note of a person's arrivals and departures and related this to their belief that the individual's personal autonomy should not be violated in certain ways (1979:50). Scollon and Scollon indicated that Northern Athapaskans in the Canadian Subarctic similarly avoid saying goodbye or other departure formulas even when speaking in English (1981:26-27). While Paiutes' reports of Navajo behavior make sense in terms of Athapaskan morality, the San Juans seem to perceive this violation of what they consider to be normal behavior as a characteristic lapse in morality among non-Paiutes.

6

THE MODERN SOCIOPOLITICAL COMMUNITY

An Introduction to the Ethnographic Study Group

The San Juan Paiute community with whom we conducted our field research consists of approximately 192 men, women, and children, who participated on a regular basis in tribal social and political life during the years of our field research. As of August, 1983, 108 of these resided at least part-time in the two modern settlement areas, making use of the reservation farming and grazing areas that the San Juans see as their tribal estate.

Our description of modern social and economic organization focuses primarily on this on-reservation community. Appendix III, "Residential Groupings and Resource Use by Household among the Ethnographic Study Group, Summer 1983," identifies household locations and heads and describes important kin relations between members and the heads of their own and other households. For reference, household groups and individual community members will be cited throughout this chapter using the numbers listed on this table. Numbers identifying households will be given in square brackets, for example, household [1]; individuals will be identified by numbers in parentheses, for example, (88).

In 1983, 84 San Juans were not residing either full- or part-time within the two main reservation enclaves. Although less is known about off-reservation tribal members, they do nonetheless play a part in San Juan social and economic life. Nonresident households, and especially the elders who represent them, did not take part in community life with nearly the frequency of on-reservation residents, but all actively participated in the political life of the tribe. Despite the distances that some of them had to travel, nonresident San Juans, regularly appeared not only at tribal political meetings but also at funerals, marriages, and other community social gatherings. At one such get-together, announced in English as a "family reunion," members of every family of San Juans and even several Paiute families from Kaibab and Kanosh gathered at Hidden Springs, a cluster of Paiute homes located by U.S. Highway 89, across from the Hidden Springs Baptist Church. There they ate and played games, including *turukwip*, a stick dice gambling game once played throughout the Southwest. Later that night, young and old participated in a Paiute round-dance (*wнikyap*) to traditional songs sung by two elders from the hosting Lehi ambilineage, (21) and (7).

Nonresident participation in community-wide social and political activities was supplemented by individual and family visits on a more informal basis. Moreover, as is the case in other Indian communities, many individuals and families who were residing off-reservation in 1983 were on-reservation community residents in other years, both during and especially before our field work. Many will no doubt return in future years, while others will leave to marry or seek work outside the reservation.

Nonresidents have no overall affiliation among themselves but rather consist of a scattering of households and individuals from several kin groups who left the San Juans' traditional lands for economic or other reasons, but still maintain ties with their remaining kin and with the tribe as a whole. Some are located in Paiute or Ute communities in Utah and Colorado. Others live among other, more distant Indian groups. Still more reside in households in California cities or predominantly Anglo urban or rural areas elsewhere.

Bearing in mind the strict Southern Numic incest prohibition and the size of the San Juan community, clearly one reason why some San Juans reside outside of the reservation settlement areas is simply that they were forced to go afield to look for a suitable spouse. Social and economic pressures have also been a factor in emigration. Not surprisingly, given past history, the majority of off-reservation residents come from the north. One example of emigration from the north involved the recently deceased brother of (104) who married a woman from the Southern Paiute community of Koosharem, Utah, and lived there in 1983. Similarly, the brother of (61), (71), and (83), met a woman of the Yuma Tribe during a stint in the military and now lives on the Yuma Reservation in Winterhaven, California, with his wife, children, and grandchildren.

Many descendents of Dora Nelson, the single most substantial group of off-reservation residents, left involuntarily as children. Her daughters, grandchildren, and great-grandchildren, once numbered some half a dozen households at Navajo Mountain. In the late 1940s, Dora Nelson died of tuberculosis. At about the same time, others of the women heads of households among her descendents also died, one in childbirth. The BIA schoolmistress at Navajo Mountain removed a number of orphaned Nelson children from the care of the few remaining Nelson adults and from Blanche Owl, the now deceased older sister of (82), who had taken in several of the children. Some of the children were sent to the BIA Indian school in Riverside, California, while others were put up for adoption. A brother and sister were adopted by a Navajo family near Window Rock, on the other side of the reservation from Navajo Mountain. Of all the Nelson group, only (104), her brother, and their classificatory sister, Grace Nelson, the mother of (91), (105), and (108), remained at Navajo Mountain by the early 1950s. Brothers (91), (105), and (108) were raised primarily at Navajo Mountain by Mercy Whiskers, their father's mother. Their mother Grace, now deceased, and (104) soon afterward moved to White Mesa, Utah, where they married members of the combined Ute and Paiute community. While the Nelsons are no longer residing as one group, (104), (91), (105), (108), and more recently other Nelsons, like (84), who have since returned to Navajo Mountain, have continued to use and hold collectively the section of Upper Paiute Canyon farm land that belonged to their ambilineal descent group.

It is a testimony to Paiutes' strong sense of kinship and tribal identity that most of the Nelson children have managed somehow to maintain or later reestablish ties with their relatives and with other San Juans, despite circumstances such as adoption, or marriage to non-Indians, as happened in the cases of four Nelson women who were sent as children to Riverside, California. Individual (84), who now lives at Navajo Mountain, was raised by a white Episcopalian priest at Window Rock but returned as an adult. Another man, adopted as a baby by the Window Rock Navajo couple mentioned above, was told by his adoptive parents that he was "really a Paiute" when he was a young man. In 1980, he hitchhiked to Hidden Springs and soon after at a tribal meeting met his Navajo Mountain relatives for the first time, including his classificatory brother (84), whom he had not seen in thirty years. Although this man was raised as a Navajo, he has been coming to tribal meetings and social get-togethers ever since. Interestingly, his adoptive Navajo parents have encouraged him to reestablish ties with his kin and his natal tribe. Finally, two of the Nelson children sent as girls to school in California, both now grandmothers, returned to the Navajo Mountain Paiute settlement in 1984 and one began farming and herding goats there with her grandchildren.

San Juan Social and Economic Organization

Current San Juan social, economic, and political life is influenced by two major factors. The first is kinship, by which is meant both the pattern of existing relations as well as cultural ideas and values that are an inseparable component of such relations. Kinship is what gives San Juan social life its characteristic tenor, noticeable also in the social life of other Southern Paiute groups, despite great differences in economic and political organization. The second factor is land. The existing configuration of land resources and the uses to which San Juans put them have exerted strong influence on the formation and persistence of sociopolitical groups.

Kinship Organization

In an analysis of economic and social organization within the five modern bands of the Paiute Tribe of Utah, Martha Knack (1980) isolated two levels of kinship organization, the household and the "kindred cluster," or group of related households. As Knack pointed out, cluster households and their members are committed to communal life and mutual support because this is for Utah Paiutes a practical adaptation to a hostile social and economic environment. At the same time, these kinship groups did not emerge in a social organizational vacuum, but instead probably made use of preexisting Southern Numic modes of organization and values that were shared also by the San Juans.

Among the modern San Juans, there are several levels of kinship organization operating in social, economic, and political interaction. These include groups that resemble in many ways the household and kindred clusters of households that Knack identified among Utah Paiutes. The San Juan counterpart of kindred clusters, which we refer to as localized ambilineages or simply as ambilineages, are more than simply coresidential groups of bilaterally related households that provide diffuse support to each other. The members of a San Juan localized ambilineage also hold land in common as a corporate group and cooperate in highly organized economic and sociopolitical activities, many of which center on land tenure and use. Moreover, when San Juans explain their ambilineage affiliation to the group, especially when they make collective decisions allocating rights to land, they invoke shared bilateral descent from one ancestor, or--especially at levels of descent organization above the localized ambilineage-- from a set of ancestral siblings as defined by the kinship system.

Ties of common descent between San Juan elders belonging to different consanguineal groups or between chief elders and the various consanguineal groups in their constituency were probably always a factor promoting tribal unity in the historic past. This type of kindred network, composed of cross-cutting ties linking individuals belonging to otherwise unrelated groups, is still a major political resource for potential leaders in other Southern Paiute tribal communities since there is usually no one kinship affiliation that takes in a majority of the members of these tribes (Knack 1980:87-90).

Among the San Juans, however, historic forces have brought about a much tighter kinship organization, one on the verge of subsuming the community as a whole. The economic and social forces that have compelled San Juan kin groups to fall back upon ever smaller territorial holdings also encouraged consolidation of the several preexisting bilateral lines within the tribe into an ever more centralized ambilineage organ-ization. Through their founders or through later inter-marriage, most members of localized San Juan ambilineages are linked to other ambilineages by bilateral descent at some level of genealogical reckoning. In the present day, a substantial proportion of the tribal membership can trace common bilateral descent from two ancestral siblings, *Pak'ai* and his classificatory brother *Muuputs*, or Owl. While this process of consolidation is by no means complete, and may in fact never be, in the minds of many members the tribe itself has become simply a higher and more inclusive level of ambilineal descent group.

In his comparative description of bilateral descent groups among such North American groups as the Kwakiutl of the Northwest Coast or the Utes and Wind River Shoshones of the Great Basin-Colorado Plateau region, Jorgensen concluded that to be corporate, in the sense of having permanence and a clearly bounded membership, bilateral descent groups must also be "united by some additional criterion, such as unilocal postnuptial residence or collective ownership" (1980:179-80). Corporate ownership of land clearly functions to unite San Juan descent groups. As noted earlier, each localized ambi-lineage holds a particular estate in land and moreover acts collectively to produce, distribute, and consume wealth using this estate.

Common residence is also a factor, although San Juans do not practice any form of unilocal residence. In marriages between tribal members, the husband and wife will reside with the ambilineage and settlement area that are most suitable both to them and to the community in terms of available resources and compatible relationships. San Juans reckon descent bilaterally but may choose to belong to only one group at a time, making descent groups ambilineal rather than simply bilateral. In the case of marriages with non-San Juans, an attempt is usually made to persuade the couple to reside within the community, so that the children will not be lost to the ambilineage and the tribe. The in-marrying spouse is usually permitted to use ambilineage land as long as the marriage lasts, but no permanent rights are acquired. This holds true for San Juans who marry into a different ambilineage also.

While in general San Juans do not discourage marriage with non-community members, most prefer if possible to find a San Juan spouse. This is often difficult, especially in recent years, when many young people are already the products of intermarriages between major descent groups in the tribe. Out of the total tribal membership in 1983, including off-reservation residents, 39 individuals were living in marital relationships, customary or otherwise. Fourteen of those married, 35.8% of the total, were married to another San Juan Tribe member. The remainder were married to members of other ethnic groups: 10 (25.6%) were married to Navajos; 4 (10.25%) were married to members of another Southern Numic speaking community, either Southern Paiute or Ute; 2 (5.1%) were married to Hopis; and 9 (23%) were married to members of more distant Native American groups, or to Hispanics or Anglos.

Some information on kin relations within and among households in the two reservation settlement areas is provided in Appendix III, although the descent linkages that unite groups of households as ambilineages are not described. Figures 5, "Southern Area Genealogy," and 6, "Northern Area Genealogy (with Descent Linkages to Southern Area)," indicate which households are members of contemporary localized ambilineages. At the same time, by tracing historic genealogical connections, these figures illustrate continuity between historic northern and southern ambilineages and their modern reflexes. Both figures also take account of descent linkages above the localized ambilineage level. Dotted lines join *Pak'ai* and Owl (*Muupʉts*). Although their exact biological relationship is now unknown, both are described by present day Paiutes as siblings--older and younger brother--and are said to have referred to each other as such. Classificatory siblingship between ancestors has important consequences for their descendents. Any descendent of *Pak'ai* or Owl considers and refers to both as the same type of kinsman. All their descendents consider themselves to be as closely related as if the two men had been children of the same parents. For example, the daughters of Alfred Lehi call both historic figures by the same term, *(pina-)kʉnu-xwaip*, "late paternal (great-)grandfather." Alfred Lehi's children also think of and refer to the grandchildren of Owl as their older and younger brothers and sisters, and this relationship will continue over the generations for as long as the descendents of both men share the same culture and communal life.

Figure 5 shows the major ancestral linkages that southern area residents use to account for the levels of ambilineal descent groups observed there. They include households, the two major ambilineages, and the settlement itself (virtually all are descendents of *Pak'ai*), which appears to exhaust the levels of group membership that are important in the south for farming and grazing activities, as well as other forms of

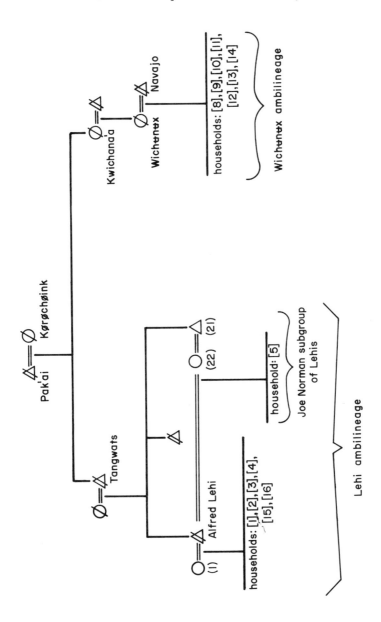

Figure 5.   Southern Area Genealogy

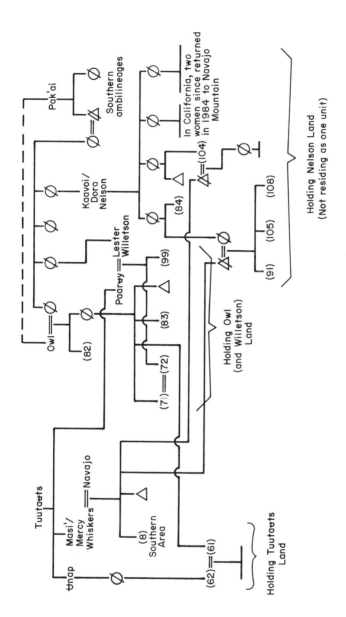

Figure 6.   Northern Area Genealogy (with Descent Linkages to Southern Area)

economic and sociopolitical cooperation. At the first hierarchical level of descent organization above that of the
household, households [8], [9], [10], [11], [12], [13], and [14] are
united as one localized ambilineage through their descent from
Wichнпнx. Likewise, households [1], [2], [3], [4], [15], and [16]
form an ambilineage affiliated through descent from Alfred
Lehi. Both groups hold separate field areas at Willow Springs.
While (22) of household [6] and thus household [5], co-headed
by her daughter, may also be seen as descended from Joe
Francis (see chap. 3), both [5] and [6] are treated as a subgroup
of the Lehi ambilineage. This appears to be the case because
the co-head of [5], (18), is said to be a daughter (out of
marriage) of Alfred Lehi and the co-head of [6] is his younger
brother. Household [7], formed by a single older and childless
man, (23), is dependent on the Alfred Lehi ambilineage,
although he is not a kinsperson of Alfred Lehi. He is,
however, a *Machнkats* descendent and the first cousin of (1),
Marie Lehi, the widow of Alfred Lehi.

In the southern area, the entire settlement group is itself
one localized descent group, subsuming all households with the
possible exception of (23)/[7]. This is because *Wichнпнx* and
Alfred Lehi as grandchildren of *Pak'ai* were classificatory
brother and sister. To date, this type of descent linkage above
the level of the localized ambilineage has had little impact on
economic cooperation and land tenure, both of which are still
primarily the province of ambilineages and individual
households. However, it has had a major indirect effect on the
tenor of social and political life at the settlement and tribal
levels, since both of these originally territorial groups are now
bolstered by an increasing sense of kinship solidarity.

Figure 6 shows descent linkages among household heads in
the northern area, together with linkages to descent groups in
the southern area. Using horizontal winged braces, we have
indicated which household heads--and through them, which
households--are utilizing lands held historically by the three
northern ambilineages, Owl, Nelson, and *Tuutaнts*. These
ambilineages have lost a great deal of their personnel
prematurely and have also through marriage shifted personnel
among the three groups and out of the northern settlement
altogether. Nonetheless, they have retained enough of their
historical distinctness to affect land use and economic
cooperation in the north today.

Individuals (62) and (61), who with their children form household [17], are the sole users of the *Tuutants* Paiute Canyon fields; (62) is the granddaughter of *Unap*. Individual (8), whose mother, Mercy Whiskers, farmed in this area before her death, is married and living in the south with (7), Anna Whiskers. Other descendents of *Unap*'s sisters, Mercy and *Paaruy*, farm in the Nelson and Owl areas. (61), an Owl, recently also opened a field in the Owl area. Number [17] is a large household that is beginning to ramify into sub-households. Most of the Owl area, which includes fields that belonged to the Willetsons, is utilized by households [18], [19], and [24], and less regularly by [20], as well. Note that although Lester Willetson lived and apparently farmed with the *Tuutants* ambilineage during his marriage to *Paaruy*, his son and daughter, (72) and (99), of households [18] and [24] respectively, farm with the Owls, where Lester's mother, *Nuaxur*, also once farmed. The husband of (72), (71), is, after the aged (82), the eldest Owl descendent alive. Except for (61) of household [17], the households farming the Owl land also reside together as one camp, near Lost Mesa, (99) staying with his sister when farming during the summer.

Figure 6 also illustrates the Nelson ambilineage's surprising continuity, despite the dispersal of many of its members in the late 1940s. Nelson descendents continue to utilize Nelson fields in Paiute Canyon, although they reside in various locations. This group, which includes households (84)/[21], [23], [25], [26], and (108)/[27], retains some degree of its former corporateness in that it holds and allocates rights to this land collectively and to some extent cooperates in farming it.

While the northern settlement area does not have the southern area's clearly defined unity as one descent group, its members are all interrelated by blood or by marriage, so that the north is also united by kinship as well as territory. Moreover, there are important ties of common descent that link the two areas. As noted earlier, Ruben Owl was the classificatory brother of *Pak'ai*. Dora Nelson was the classificatory sister of Curtis Lehi and Lester Willetson, and classificatory mother's sister to the children of *Tangwats*, including Alfred Lehi (see also figure 1, p.115). It is not surprising that most San Juans today should conceive of their tribe as a group of consanguineal kin and even as descendents of *Pak'ai* and Owl.

Objectively speaking, the San Juans are more of a territorial than a kin group, but the ideology of kinship and its partial basis in genealogy supports a fundamental assumption that community identity is kinship identity. One reflection of this is the San Juan Tribe's now annual family reunion, called in Paiute *pɪangwɪshuupara'ap*, "kinfolk gathering." From its inception, the family reunion has been a tribal celebration, to which Paiute relatives from other tribes are also invited.

Land and Economics in Community Life

In the production, distribution, and consumption of food and other forms of wealth, every level of San Juan social organization is brought into play, from the household to the tribe as a whole. Economic activities are thus an important aspect of San Juan social organization and a useful illustration of how it works in everyday life.

In addition to kinship, the location and nature of the lands that the San Juans hold also influence patterns of organization and cooperation. The San Juans' farming and grazing lands are now restricted to two areas, one in the region northwest of Tuba City and the other near Navajo Mountain and Paiute Canyon. While both areas are still felt to constitute one tribal domain, the physical fact of discontinuity determines many practical questions such as patterns of residence, everyday economic cooperation, and other forms of frequent face-to-face interaction. Although the two groups of San Juans associated with the northern and southern areas are so cross-cut by consanguineal linkages that they have come to see themselves as one kin group, there is a certain amount of everyday economic and social autonomy in each area growing out of geographical separation and the differing local situations with which residents in each area are faced.

One of the most important ways in which San Juan kinship and economic resources work through daily decisions to produce patterns of community life is to be found in residence. The first part of Appendix III shows the breakdown into household groups in the southern area during 1983. It also locates these households in relation to Paiute farm lands at Willow Springs and the grazing area on *Atatsiv*, as well as other sites, notably Tuba City and Hidden Springs. Where a household is listed with two locations, a seasonal change of residence is implied, normally the result of farming and grazing practices. The second part of Appendix III similarly describes northern households and their residence locations.

A household is defined here as a group that eats its meals

together and sleeps in one house or, occasionally, in two or three adjacent houses. Households may live in more than one structure for various reasons. In household [2], when (9), the daughter of (7) and (8), got married in 1984, a small shack was built besides [2]'s winter hogan at Hidden Springs. Household [3], also at Hidden Springs, maintains what members call a "bachelor hogan," where the young men of the household and visting male relatives sleep during the winter. The women and girls sleep separately in a small, one room frame house next door, for the sake of privacy and probably also because of the stringent incest taboo that forbids much cross-sex touching, especially between classificatory siblings. A woman, for example, is forbidden to step over a classificatory brother's bedding, which would be quite difficult to avoid in a small house where most people sleep on the floor.

A great deal of flexibility exists in San Juan household organization. Some households regularly spend a portion of each year independently in their own house and the rest of the year with relatives in a larger household arrangement. The members of household [10], headed by (36) and (37), live in their own shadehouse at Willow Springs during the summer farming season. Much of the rest of the year is spent in household [9], headed by (36)'s mother, (27). The mother and son group, the tribal spokesperson, (5), and her son, (6), now live with [1], but in the past have lived with (5)'s parents, in [2]. Some households, notably [2] and [14], are independent but move between two seasonal sites.

The personnel structure of households also varies considerably because of the movements of children and young unmarried adults. Children move about between the households of their parents' kin, especially within the ambilineage, in some cases seeming to spend an equal amount of time with each available household. This is not seen as a favor towards the parents but as the parents' duty towards their relatives. Occasionally, mothers express regret that they do not see their children as much as they would like or that they have too little control over a child's behavior because their relatives have them so often. This pattern of sharing children occurs with greatest frequency among ambilineally linked households, and therefore should be seen as another aspect of the cooperative relations that join such groups together.

The duty to share children within ambilineages is often carried further so that it becomes a form of adoption or fosterage. Adopting is linked to other forms of economic interaction besides coresidence. Among the San Juans, as well as other Southern Paiute groups (Knack 1980), parents with several children often give away one or more to be raised by a childless relative or one whose children are all grown. For example, (14), the daughter of (36) and (37), was fostered with (11), a woman in her 40s who has never married or borne children. Individual (11) is (37)'s mother's mother's sister's daughter or, in Paiute terms, her "mother's younger sister." In another case, (4) was given by (7) to be raised by (7)'s unmarried sister, (2). In the north, Blanche Owl apparently fostered one her sons, (83), with her childless younger brother, (82), with whom (83) lived until his uncle's recent death.

Young unmarried adults, like children, often move among their consanguineal relatives from household to household, providing labor and what monetary and other support they can. Most, like the sons of (7) and (8), and virtually all young unmarried women, tend to stay within their ambilineage or at least among relations within one settlement area. In 1983, (16) was living at household [3] in Hidden Springs, away from his home at Navajo Mountain, partly because there were no young men his age at Navajo Mountain. While in the south, he went wherever (3), (15), and another young man, (20), went. They still often travel together as a musical band to perform at tent revival meetings in the area. All four young men are classificatory brothers in the San Juan kinship system. Individual (108), although living at Navajo Mountain between March and August 1983, previously had been staying with [1], [2], and [3], and with relatives off-reservation. When young adults live on a more or less permanent basis with nonparental relatives within their ambilineage or when they regularly visit at times when labor is needed either for farming or livestock, it often reflects an earlier childhood fosterage relationship.

Residence patterns are also influenced by the present configuration of land holdings in both the north and the south and by the relations among households that are associated with land use. The only farming land presently used by San Juans in the south is the alluvial fan below the two springs of Willow Springs. During the agricultural season, the households residing here are all involved full-time in daily farming activities, such as weeding and managing irrigation. Willow Springs farms are divided into two field areas, separated by a strip of presently unfarmed land containing fruit trees, sumac and willow for basketry materials, and asparagus. Each area has an independent water system installed by Indian Health

Service personnel more than a decade ago. Household [2] of the Alfred Lehi ambilineage resides at and farms the fields below one spring. Near their round stone house, (23)/[7] had a Navajo style log hogan, which was dismantled in the summer of 1983. He later built a small frame building further downhill from his previous house. Individual (23), now in his 60s, has a small garden where he grows corn, melons, and squash. Right below the home of [2] is the field farmed by [5] and [6], together with the summer shade of [5] and the round stone house of [6]. Below the other main spring at Willow Springs, to the north of the first, lie the fields tended by households [8], [9], and [10] of the *Wichʉnʉx* ambilineage, and their summer shadehouses.

Willow Springs fields are irrigated primarily by overhead sprinklers fed by two systems of underground pipes that run from tanks at each spring. A few decades ago, one reservoir apparently served a single ditch system for both field areas. Before that, both field areas had separate reservoir and ditch systems, built and maintained by the Paiutes. A wide variety of produce is grown at Willow Springs. Apricots, peaches, grapes, asparagus, and native cultagens, such as *kumutʉ* (primarily *Amaranthus caudatus*), are allowed to grow and self-propagate with minimal seasonal care, mostly irrigation. Willow Springs Paiutes plant corn in bunches of several plants in the typical Southwestern Indian fashion, and intercrop it with a variety of squashes and melons. In 1985, the tribe bought two tractors, one for each settlement area. Before that, fields were either spaded over in the spring by hand or else the Paiutes paid by the hour for a Navajo neighbor to plow the fields with a tractor, often a very expensive proposition. During the growing season, fields are still cultivated by hand with hoes and other tools.

The San Juans who reside in the south also have one grazing area in common, in the sandy plateau of *Atatsiv* east of Echo Cliffs and surrounding Black Peak and Tuba Butte. Although there are Navajo holdings north, east, and south of this area, there appears at present to be less intrusion or pressure on San Juan grazing rights than in previous decades. With the death of some long-time Navajo residents and the removal of their younger relatives to a less rigorous life in Tuba City, Navajos may even be retreating from the San Juan grazing zone. Two households, [1] and [14], are actively involved in year-round management of herds of sheep, goats, cattle, and horses, and a few donkeys. The San Juans now have only two BIA livestock

have only two BIA livestock permits in this area, held by these two households.

While only a few households actually reside in the southern farming and grazing areas and are involved in full-time cultivation or livestock management, production and consumption activities associated with farming and grazing represent an important form of interaction among the households of both ambilineage groups. Appendix 3 provides a schematic summary of patterns of cooperation and produce distribution at the localized ambilineage level. While household [2] of the Alfred Lehi group and [8], [9], and [10] of the *Wichʉnʉx* ambilineage provide continuous farm labor and management, their corresponding households, [1], [3], [4], [7], [15], and [16] in the case of [2] and [11], [12], [13], and [14] in the case of [8], [9], and [10], always gather at Willow Springs for planting and weeding, and for harvesting, husking, and drying ears of corn. Moreover, periodically during the growing season, members of the interdependent households come to Willow Springs by the pickup-full to gather apricots, green corn, grapes, and other produce, each from the appropriate area occupied and managed by households representing their ambilineage. Households [5] and [6] manage their own small fields, consuming all the produce themselves, as does (23)/[7].

A similar situation prevails in livestock production in the south. While the heads of [1] and [14] own the permits, much of the livestock is considered to be individually owned by members of ambilineally related households. These households also provide the labor needed when cattle and horses must be rounded up, branded, and transported to market. A brief description of the livestock operation of [1] will illustrate patterns of kinship interdependence and cooperation in livestock management and production.

The site within *Atatsiv* where the members of household [1] live and have their corrals is called *Chʉkatʉmp* or "Bumpy Rock," after the odd-looking, bumpy black volcanic rocks found nearby. In the early 1980s, the herd of sheep and goats at *Chʉkatʉmp* was still largely in the care of (1), Marie Lehi. Although she is quite active, she is now nearly 90 years old. (2), the unmarried daughter of (1) who has always lived with her, and (4), an older sister's daughter of (2) raised by her from early childhood, now do most the work of caring for the sheep and goats. There is an arrangement that (4) will eventually inherit the herd. Individual (4) was deliberately kept out of school as a child, so that she could receive a traditional upbringing from her aunt and grandmother. Individual (1) is the only San Juan in the south or north who regularly shears the sheep and goats and uses the wool to weave rugs, although others, notably (2) and (4), occasionally weave if extra money is needed.

Sheep and goats are seldom sold (we witnessed the sale of a sheep only once). Instead, they are a primary source of meat, particularly between spring and fall, as lambs and kids grow big enough to be slaughtered. When sheep and goats are butchered, the meat is shared among members of the ambilineage, either by giving away quarters when visiting relatives at Willow Springs and Hidden Springs (visits occur daily when the weather permits) or else at special meals when the whole ambilineage is gathered together. In both forms of meat distribution, [6] and [5], who do not have their own livestock, are usually included with [1], [2], [3], [4], [15], and [16].

The adults of the Lehi ambilineage encourage younger children to make pets of particular sheep and goats in the herd, telling them that this or that animal is theirs. Children single out these animals and their kids or lambs, and care for them with a special affection whenever they come to visit. Although the child receives no other tangible benefit from this symbolic ownership--particularly since there is no cash coming in when the animal is slaughtered and fed to members of the ambilineage, it is made clear to the child and to the people eating the meat that it was this child who provided it. Not surprisingly, this practice upsets many children, especially the first time it happens. Paiute elders say that this is done so as to teach the child at an early age that he or she is expected to share what they have with their kin.

Cattle and horses are dealt with in a different fashion at *Chukatump*. Unlike sheep and goats, which must be watched and herded nearly every day, cattle and horses require relatively little care, except when they must be rounded up for BIA inspection and branding. The San Juans use their own brands as well as BIA range management brands. Because regulations require that adult animals over specified limits be slaughtered or sold, twice a year household [1] and other households of its ambilineage round up their cattle and horses and sell off a certain number animals. For the San Juans, a cattle sale means a significant amount of cash, in 1983 from $250 to $450 a head depending on the weight and health of the animal. Cattle are only slaughtered for meat on very important occasions as when (2)'s older sister's daughter, (17), got married. Interestingly, the cow that was killed for this occasion was (17)'s cow.

In the early 1970s, (2) used her Southern Paiute Judgment Fund payment to buy cattle, establishing the Lehi group's herd. Although (2) owns the permit and bought the cattle, most of animals belong to her nieces and nephews, primarily the sons and daughters of (7). She gave adult animals to them when they were still children. All of the men of the Lehi ambilineage, not just the cattle owners, take part in the work of round-up, branding, and cattle transport. When an individual's animals are sold, the cash goes directly into his or her pockets, as does cash from other sources, such as women's basket sales or the yearly sale of pinyon nuts. Most of this cash, however, will go to provide groceries and gasoline for the household at which the individual is staying. Gas is important since households in the south and north visit other households in their area daily and often visit households in the other area more than once a month. A round trip between Hidden Springs and *Atatsiv*, for example, is roughly 50 miles.

For young men, this economic activity and the cash it brings in are essential to their sense of self-respect. On the one hand, like many Indians in the rural West, they take great pride in their skills as cowboys. On the other hand, since for Paiutes there are few opportunities for even temporary employment on the Navajo Reservation, this cash enables them to be contributing members of their kin groups, rather than dependents.

The horses kept by this ambilineage reflect the same economic pattern as cattle. They are rounded up at the same time and also provide cash, although less frequently and in smaller amounts because of their lesser numbers. The animals that are kept are an important means of transportation, since much of *Atatsiv* is inaccessible except on foot or horseback.

Women have a steady source of cash which is for practical purposes unavailable to men and which tends to make them the primary supporters of their kin: basket-weaving. As Omer Stewart noted fifty years ago (1938a and b), and as others have noted since (Witherspoon 1983:528, caption to fig. 4; Roessel 1983:602), Navajos have long purchased the so-called Navajo wedding basket, essential to traditional weddings and other ceremonies, from either Utes or Paiutes. These baskets are sewn with an awl on coiled sumac or willow rods, using pealed strips of sumac (*Rhus trilobata*) dyed red-brown, black, or left white (the white is often enhanced either by exposure to the sun or by soaking the strips in chlorine bleach). Some Navajos near Willow Springs believe that Paiute-made baskets have special healing properties. San Juan women both at Navajo Mountain and in the south sell every basket they can make. Navajos often come to Willow Springs and Hidden Springs to place orders in advance for several baskets at a time. In addition, wedding baskets are welcomed by some local traders. An indication of the importance and extent of basket production may be seen in the fact that San Juans in the south not only gather local sumac at such nearby sites as Pasture Canyon and Moenave, but also travel hundreds of miles to Utah, to gathering areas near Kanab, St. George, Toquerville, and elsewhere. Moreover, stands of sumac which are ready to harvest are often kept secret by the women of one ambilineage, so that each ambilineage, south and north, has its special sumac reserves. Women are taught as children to clean up carefully the bark and pith from sumac processing, so that other women will not see it and guess or ask where it was gathered.

One local trader, William Beaver at Sacred Mountain Trading Post near Flagstaff, several years ago took an interest in the other basketry patterns and shapes that Paiutes traditionally produced for trade and for their own use. He encouraged the women to weave larger, more carefully made, and, most important, higher-priced baskets (McGreevy 1985). In 1985, the San Juan weavers formed a tribal basketry cooperative to market these "fancy baskets," as they call them. Another, more lucrative market has already opened up for San Juan basketry weavers through the cooperative and through this trader who so long encouraged them.

Residential and economic patterns in the Navajo Mountain-Paiute Canyon area are for the most very similar to those observed in the south, although some important differences also exist. Appendix III offers a general picture of these patterns, which our discussion will attempt to flesh out further.

At Navajo Mountain there are four year-round residence sites. One camp, or cluster of dwellings, is located by Little Navajo, a small peak near the northeastern corner of Navajo Mountain on the Utah side. Although in 1983 only one household, [17], lived there, (108) was in the process of building a house there in the summer of that year. Moreover, two young women in [17] have had children, thereby enlarging it. Another camp, located by Lost Mesa a few miles to the south of the first, consists of four households with separate housekeeping and separate structures: [18], [19], [20], and [21]. [20] also maintained a separate house, north of Navajo Mountain in the same area where before his recent death (82) used to graze his cattle. Household [22], co-headed by (85), a recently deceased Paiute who had been married to a Navajo, resided separately at Rainbow City in 1983. Another Paiute man, a Nelson (84), later married (85)'s widow and adopted the children. Rainbow City is a Navajo housing project in an area a half mile east of [17]'s camp that the Navajo Tribe is trying to develop with federal and Utah state funds channeled through the Utah Navajo Development Corporation.

In addition to households residing full-time at Navajo Mountain, households [23], [24], [25], and [26], which form a contiguous block of Paiute houses and households on the southwestern edge of the Ute reservation village at White Mesa, Utah, are also considered to be part of the northern settlement group. During the summer farming season, all of these latter households reside part-time at Paiute Canyon or Navajo Mountain with the permanent San Juan residents there, coming down for weekends and sometimes for several weeks at a time. Except for the case of [23], who rent their house from the Ute Mountain Tribe, Paiute houses at White Mesa were acquired through Ute spouses, since none of the San Juan co-heads have rights through the Ute Mountain Tribe.

Households in the north do most of their farming in a strip of canyon-bottom land in Upper Paiute Canyon in Arizona. Unlike the south, the Paiute farms here tend to be independent, household-run operations. Households [21], [23], [25], and [26], all descendents of Dora Nelson, are an exception to this. Since with the exception of (84)/[21] these households cannot reside full-time in Paiute Canyon, during the summer their heads and members take turns caring for each other's farms in the Nelson area. While for the most part their agricultural operations are independent, the other Paiute households of Navajo Mountain, as might be expected, freely exchange help in farming tasks that require more labor than one household can supply. For example, in the summer of 1983, household [17] and the authors helped households [18] and [19] harvest their field of alfalfa hay by hand-sickle. In appreciation, [17] received the gift of a truck load of hay.

The grazing area at Navajo Mountain is located east and north of the mountain and is used only by households [17], [18], [19], and [20]. These are the Owls and the descendents of

Tuutaŋts who continue to live at Navajo Mountain rather than off-reservation. Here, too, production tends to be carried out in household groups, although in 1983 two sons of (61) had an arrangement with (82), their classificatory paternal grand-father (actual father's mother's brother) to inherit his cattle in exchange for helping him by looking after the cattle and mending the brush boundary fences that Paiutes still use to enclose cattle for extended periods in pastures north of Navajo Mountain.

The relative importance of households over ambilineages in northern area economic activities is due primarily to the fact that many more households are more involved in farming there than in the south. Because of the isolation at Navajo Mountain, Paiutes there rely much more on corn, dried fruit, dried mutton and goat meat, and other foods that they produce themselves than do southern area families. Recently, some southern households, particularly [3], [11], and [14], have begun to reopen old fields on the lower terrace at Willow Springs and at a third spring nearby. This may result in the breaking down of present patterns of collective work and produce distribution at the ambilineage level so that south and north may eventually come to resemble each other more closely.

Economic cooperation can extend beyond the level of ambilineages and even local settlement groups. One example of this is the new tribal basketry cooperative, which involves women from the entire reservation community. Indeed, every tribal social or political gathering incorporates an important element of economic cooperation, even if it is only the consumption and distribution of food that takes place at tribal meals. However, there is one primary economic activity that involves all levels of social organization in the San Juan Tribe.

Every autumn, usually in October, Indians throughout the Great Basin, Colorado Plateau, and Southwest, go to areas of pinyon and juniper forest to gather pinyon pine nuts (in the eastern part of Southern Paiute country, *Pinus edulis*). Pinyon-juniper forest occurs at elevations between 5000 and 7000 feet above sea level. Each year, only certain regions produce a crop of nuts and the areas and quantities are quite variable. As consultants have demonstrated, by mid-summer one can tell by examining green cones whether an area will be producing that year. With a good information network, one can count on gathering a crop almost every year. In the prehistoric and even well into the historic period, most Southern Paiute groups depended on pine nuts (*tɨɨva*) as a staple food source, so that intercommunity agreements to share information and use rights were crucial to all communities' efficient use of this important regional resource. Nowadays, for the San Juans at least, the nuts have become an important cash crop, in 1983 selling in the Flagstaff area for $1.50 per pound unshelled. We were told that San Juan adults who took part in the harvest gathered and sold between 75 and 150 pounds apiece during the 1983 season--an extraordinarily productive year. We had been shown pine nuts "making," as the Paiutes say, in several highland areas that summer.

During the harvest, San Juan households from both the north and the south usually come together in one tribal camp group in the pinyon area to be harvested. In 1983, families from Navajo Mountain and the Tuba City area camped together in pinyon country near the South Rim of the Grand Canyon. Although the tribe comes together to form a temporary residential unit, it is household groups or ambilineages that act as teams to gather and clean the nuts. The differential patterns observed in farming and grazing between north and south also appear to hold here. For example, household [17] formed one production unit while the households of the Alfred Lehi group who were present formed another team.

While kin groups do the work of production, individuals receive the cash from the sale of their own pine nuts. This is reminiscent of basket production in which female relatives freely take a hand in working on each others' baskets, often putting in a great deal of time, even though only one of them sells it and receives the proceeds. In the case of the sale of pine nuts, as with money from cattle and baskets, individuals often end up spending the money on their households or lending it out to other relatives. In this way, pine nut gathering and sales involve levels of cooperation from the tribe, which camps together, down to the ambilineage and household, which work together and are the eventual recipients of individuals' gains.

Political Process in the Modern Community

The San Juan Tribe is a small and very homogeneous community. Because it is still federally unrecognized, it has never formalized governmental institutions after the Western pattern of the constitutional, bureaucratic state. For these and other reasons, no sharp division exists between politics and other areas of community activity. The authority that community leaders exercise is an outgrowth of authoritative relations created by kinship and traditional religion and morality. The consensus groups, tribal and subtribal, that unite to make political decisions and grant leadership powers are the same kin and territorial based groups that operate in economics and other nonpolitical spheres of social life. While politics overlap many other areas of tribal life, there is still a recognizable and well defined set of institutions and patterns of interaction that constitute tribal government in the modern San Juan Paiute community. These are the subject of this part.

Relations of Authority: The Roles of Elder and Chief Elder

Tribal political meetings belong to a larger category of social contexts, all of which are characterized by two features: the central role of formal verbal performance, and the emergence of asymmetric and authoritative patterns of interaction between elders and juniors. Other examples of formal interaction discussed elsewhere include funerals, men's and women's rites of passage, story telling, and round-dance singing. In meetings, as in these other formal contexts, elder kinspeople monopolize talk using traditionally recognized styles of speech. Juniors simply look on, listening respectfully. According to one Kaibab elder, Dan Bulletts, a parallel institution of traditional eldership also exists and continues to play a major, though informal role in Kaibab Paiute community life (Bulletts 1984).

There are no formal mechanisms for assigning the role of elder to certain community members, just as there is no formal education in the traditional knowledge and verbal skills that are requisite for the role. The community and the individual elder negotiate the authority relationship through an informal consensual process, similar to the process whereby personal names come to be assigned. The word for "leader" in Paiute, *niav(i)*, means literally "name," suggesting that the source of authority is one's reputation in the community. In allocating this type of authority, however, the community follows certain patterns, which can be identified and described.

Subtribal social organization plays a crucial part in the emergence of tribal elders as political and moral leaders in San Juan society, since elders are typically leading members of subtribal kin groups, whether households or larger groups. The exercise of authority at the tribal level is firmly grounded in the fact that the elders' natural constituents are the kinspeople with whom they live and work on a daily basis.

Within households and ambilineages, where economic interdependence is greatest, the deference that is shown to elders is at least partly a consequence of their position as providers. As with the Paiutes in Martha Knack's Utah study (1980), most San Juans, particularly the younger community members, are economically dependent on their kin. In an economic climate that permitted greater opportunity for independence, junior kin might well show less willingness to defer to their elders.

Relations of dependence within subtribal groups do not translate directly into authority at the level of the tribe, however. For example, (2) and (11) are both economic mainstays of their ambilineage, as well as their households. In the context of their kin, both act confidently and with authority. Yet neither appears willing to speak out with other elders in tribal social or political affairs, even though consultants state that they are considered to be elders.

One explanation for their lack of confidence outside the circle of their ambilineage may be that, while both are middle-aged women, neither has ever married or borne children. At the tribal level, community recognition of one's social maturity is essential for the effective exercise of leadership, whether as elder or chief elder. In Paiute eyes, age alone does not confer authority. Among both the San Juan and the Kaibab Paiutes, marriage and the birth of the first child are still considered to be the traditional threshhold marking the passage into maturity, and thus eldership (Bulletts 1984). In both communities, this stricture seems to have relaxed somewhat, although men and women who have never married are still often perceived as not fully adult. The Paiute names of (2), the household head in the example above, and (23), an unmarried elderly man, may reflect this community attitude. Individual (2) is often still called *Na'atsits*, "Little Girl," her name when she was a child, while (23) is called *Aipara*, a name derived from the Paiute term for a young bachelor.

The respect that Paiutes have for someone who fulfills their traditional responsibilities as a spouse, parent, and grandparent, coupled with age and a reputation for wisdom and traditional knowledge, can offset or improve upon one's status as an economic provider to kin. It is this fact of San Juan social and political life that allows aged individuals who retain very little economic influence, such as (1), or (21) and (22), to exert influence on the community in their role as elders, especially at the tribal level. When they speak, whether at meetings, funerals, or other formal occasion, the community shows them especially great respect.

While elders are seen as representing their own junior kin, this does not always mean that the kin group they speak for is the one into which they were born; it can be one that was adopted after marriage. Alfred Lehi was raised in Navajo Mountain, as was his brother, (21). Yet, Alfred Lehi was considered an elder and community leader in the southern group, and only became chief elder and spokesman for the tribe as a whole after demonstrating his effective leadership in the southern area. In a recent case, present day elder (8), although originally from Navajo Mountain and unrelated to most elders in the south, has come to be considered an elder of the southern area Lehi ambilineage, into which he married and among which his children and grandchildren all live.

Outside of tribal level politics, elders are also seen as figures of authority in decision making or other matters that involve only their ambilineage or settlement group. Elders are expected to correct and instruct young people, for example, informally speaking to individuals who are not weeding or otherwise taking proper care of their fields. They are also responsible for moral instruction at life cycle observances within their household and ambilineage.

Whether it is a question of tribal political meetings or subtribal social control and dispute settlement, the collective leadership of tribal elders is a constant feature of all contexts in which authority is exercised. In tribal meetings, where matters concerning every member of the tribe are decided, elders are expected to present before the adult membership of the tribe the point of view of their own households. If the elder is particularly influential, he or she may also speak for the ambilineage or even the settlement area. Any kin constituency will almost always have more than one elder who can speak for it, since most households have Paiute co-heads, and ambilineages and settlement areas are composed of several such households. The fact that one elder speaks for a kin group does not preclude other persons from also doing so if they are seen to be qualified.

In the case of tribal elders from the nonreservation San Juan households, we were not able to observe the exercise of leadership in any other context than at tribal meetings. Members of this group who were married and had children took much the same speaker-representative role for their households, and even for their on-reservation kin, as would elders from the on-reservation group. Non-San Juan spouses were occasionally present at the meetings but did not speak or take part, since they are not considered members of the political community.

The present chief elder, Evelyn James, was formally elected tribal spokesperson at a tribal meeting in 1980. The tribe decided on this formality for the sake of the federal bureaucracy and the Hopi and Navajo tribal governments, because it was felt that outsiders used to formal governmental institutions might otherwise have questioned the legitimacy of her leadership. Mrs. James did not run against anyone else and had in fact been chosen as leader through informal community consensus some time before the meeting where the vote was taken.

What has been said about elders' sources of authority is equally, if not more true of the modern chief elder's position. Mrs. James fulfills most of the socially recognized criteria of maturity. Although still in her thirties, she is a widow with one child and an accomplished speaker, possessing the traditional knowledge that is essential to elders' exercise of authority and participation in decision making. By dealing effectively with outsiders, as she has done over the last several years, and by her visionary religious experiences, she has also shown herself capable of fulfilling the community's expectations of her as a chief elder.

One might expect that a chief elder, who in a real sense speaks for the entire tribe, should also have as broad a kinship constituency as possible. The tribal leader must be able to mobilize much broader support than would be necessary for other elders.

The present tribal leader not surprisingly occupies a central and strategic position with respect to the tribe's social organizational structure. Through her mother, (7), the daughter of Alfred Lehi and great-granddaughter of *Pak'ai*, Mrs. James shares descent with the great majority of tribe members who descend from *Pak'ai* and his classificatory brother, Owl. Since the Nelson ambilineage is collateral to both of the former two descent groups, its members are also counted among her kin. Her father, (8), is a son of Mercy Whiskers, thus linking Mrs. James to the only other major descent group in the tribe, the *Tuutaħts* ambilineage. In each case, Paiute kinship terms merge these more distant kin with close relatives in her own immediate kin group, making virtually the entire tribe her potential kinship constituents.

Although the tribe does not recognize any rule of exclusive succession to leadership, Mrs. James also derives prestige and a certain degree of legitimacy from the fact that she stands in the direct line of descent from several past tribal leaders, especially her grandfather, Alfred Lehi, and her mother, Anna Whiskers, both well remembered and respected recent leaders. She has also inherited their prestigious and useful consanguineal connections outside the tribe to influential members of two other Paiute communities, Kaibab and Kanosh.

Because the chief elder's duties and leadership skills tend to focus on the tribal level--internal matters that involve more than one subgroup within the tribe or external matters that involve the tribe's dealings with the outside world--this office and its special group of powers tends not to come into play in subtribal levels of the sociopolitical process. Nonetheless, because Mrs. James is seen as an impartial and authoritative figure, she is sometimes called upon to help settle disputes that might otherwise be the business of settlement level decision making.

For example, in 1984 there was a dispute over a plot that had belonged to the late Grace Nelson, granddaughter of Dora Nelson. Grace Nelson died in the summer of 1981. During the summer of 1983, (91), (105), and (108), Grace Nelson's three sons, were working Nelson fields in Paiute Canyon. We were told that these fields belonged to (104), an elderly classificatory sister of their mother who lives at White Mesa, Utah. Individual (108) was also working his late mother's field and had her BIA agricultural permit in his possession.

In 1984, (108) temporarily left Navajo Mountain. Since he would not be making use of the plot during the immediate future, he wanted to pass his mother's permit on to another Paiute kinsman so that the plot would not fall into disuse. According to the tribal spokesperson (Bunte and Franklin

Fieldnotes, October 23, 1984), in the fall of 1984 (108) mailed the permit to her asking her to see that a proper decision was made about who would get to use it. Soon after, (84), another Nelson descendent who lives at Navajo Mountain, approached Mrs. James and asked that that land permit immediately be handed him. There were, however, other relatives of Grace Nelson who had potential rights to the field. The field is said to have once belonged to Dora Nelson herself and thus could conceivably be claimed by any of her descendents. Moreover, this was a field that Navajos had recently attempted to take over. Mrs. James believed that besides the Nelsons the northern area settlement and the tribe as a whole would also be interested in seeing that whoever got the field would take good care of it.

Shortly after Mrs. James received the permit in the mail, most of the elders and other tribal members living in the southern and northern settlement areas had gathered at Hidden Springs to plan the tribe's basketry and traditional crafts cooperative. Although it is primarily women who produce crafts for sale, their husbands and male relatives took an active role in helping to set up the association and so were present at the October meeting. The tribal spokesperson had set up the first basketry meeting and was also responsible for dealing with the tribe's economic advisor, who had flown in from the Center for Indian Economic Development in San Francisco. After the meeting, Mrs. James took advantage of the fact that most of the tribal elders were gathered together to speak to them about (108)'s permit and (84)'s request to use it.

The elders and the tribal spokesperson decided that a special meeting should be held to decide what would be done about the permit. Mrs. James, who was asked to preside over this meeting, would set a date and invite the Nelsons as well as all of the elders who lived in the northern area or had some other interest in the plot. In this way, Mrs. James stated, "Everybody will know who has Grace Nelson's land permit . . . Those people will decide who gets the permit." Although (108) later returned to Navajo Mountain and began farming his mother's field again, this case illustrates the chief elder's role as an informal mediator in dispute settlement.

The duties of the chief elder do not just involve tribal politics and the tribal *shuupara'ap*. The chief elder is often called upon to lead and represent the tribe in nonpolitical matters as well. For example, over the last several years, Mrs.

James has been called upon to organize a number of funerals, one marriage within her ambilineage, and the yearly family reunion. In each case, she would meet with or write to the elders representing the various households of the tribe and with them set up a time for the gathering. She was also responsible for getting in touch with those elders of other Southern Paiute tribes who were to be invited. Mrs. James (5) was responsible for arranging the wedding ceremony at a local church when her sister, (17), was married. This wedding drew together households from the north as well as the south, and thus was very much a tribal affair. Along with her mother's younger sister, (11), (5) actually directed the ceremony as it was in progress. In social matters in her own settlement group, (5) also appears to act as a local chief elder, much as her grandfather did. In all these cases, the spokesperson performed duties and used leadership skills like those associated with her political role.

The sociopolitical relations through which authority is granted in San Juan society to elders and the chief elder by their very nature set customary limitations on their exercise of authority. Followers in San Juan society, generally junior kin, show great deference to their spokesperson and elders in contexts where authority is conventionally expected to be exercised. On the other hand, because their powers are implicitly granted to them by their junior constituents and by other elders, the chief elder and elders in general are bound to respect the consensus of the tribe's adult membership and will not act without it.

This is true of both tribal and subtribal level decision making. In social or political contexts where decisions are called for, elders speak privately to the members of their kin constituency first before they speak publicly to represent its views. Similarly, the chief elder will not speak for the tribe in any way that implies she has made a decision on their behalf without obtaining the consent of the entire adult membership, both elders and nonelders. The chief elder and the other elders also have no authority to command adults or use force, even in the context of a meeting. They can only request or persuade. If force were to be exercised, as sometimes it has been in the historic past, it would presumably have to be exercised, or at least approved, by the adults as a group. However, because the elders and chief elder usually represent community consensus, their advice and persuasion bring about compliance. Conversely, because Paiutes recognize that all authority is based on tribal consensus and is created by the same social relationships that create tribal solidarity, the tribal community as a whole holds authority over its leaders. This mutuality of authority, which is instantiated in the specific customary powers that leaders are permitted and expected to exercise, sets very effective limits on the power of both the elders and chief elder.

Although the other Southern Paiute tribal communities now possess formal systems of tribal government, leadership still tends to exhibit this pattern of highly respected, but limited authority, both in formalized tribal government and in the informal, moral leadership exercised by elders in these groups. For example, leaders in the five Utah Paiute bands described by Knack derive their authority from similar sources and operate under similar structural constraints: "Presently, leaders rely on a combination of backing from a large kin group, dynamic personality, and spiritual support" (1980:88). Among Utah Paiutes, according to Knack, this mode of leadership is less effective than among the San Juans, apparently because the kinship constituency principle within Utah band communities promotes political divisions even as it creates unity in subcommunity groups.

The Tribal Meeting or Shuupara'ap

Much of tribal politics takes place in subtribal gatherings and outside of meetings altogether, as when elders informally talk over issues with the kin they represent and with other elders. The public tribal meeting, or *shuupara'ap* as it is known in Paiute, is the most visible realization of tribal political process. It is, moreover, viewed by the San Juans as the only governmental institution capable of making decisions for the tribe as a whole.

Interestingly, while the San Juans often refer to their tribal meetings as *shuupara'ap*, which means simply "meeting" or "gathering," they also have a more specific and technical word that points up the role of leaders, both elders and chief elder, in tribal decision making. This is *niavishuupara'ap*, which incorporates the term for "leader."

Over the last several years, the tribe has regularly met every few months for a political meeting. In the summer, meetings are arranged on a more frequent basis, approximately. every three to four weeks, partly because the unpaved road from Navajo Mountain is much easier to travel at that time of year. Most meetings are arranged and scheduled at the previous meeting. The spokesperson also calls special meetings to deal with unexpected tribal matters.

In the autumn of 1984, the tribe purchased a double wide trailer, which is parked at Hidden Springs and is used for tribal meetings, meetings of the basketry cooperative, as well as the spokesperson's office and the business office of the cooperative. Previously, most meetings were hosted by the southern area and were held at Hidden Springs, although some were occasionally held at Navajo Mountain. Since each meeting is generally attended by between 75 to 125 people, the host settlement would choose a site with a large shadehouse that could accomodate all of the adults attending, such as the shadehouses at the Hidden Springs cluster of houses or the camp of (61) and (62) at Navajo Mountain, both of which have also been used for funerals and other nonpolitical gatherings.

Since food is an integral part of any San Juan gathering, the host settlement group always prepares a large midday dinner at tribal meetings. The San Juan guest families usually provide prepared dishes, provisions of coffee, flour, and soft drinks, or sometimes money as their contribution to the meal. During the summer, later in the afternoon when the meeting is concluded, the young adults and teenagers often set up a volleyball net and play until dark. Older people sit and visit.

The meeting itself usually lasts most of the day and is conducted in two segments, before and after the noon meal. Except for some children, who will be off playing, the tribal members all sit together in a large circle or semicircle facing the tribal spokesperson. At every meeting, a notebook is passed around for those present to sign. The spokesperson later informs the elders by mail as to who was present and what was dealt with at the meeting. Many of the spokesperson's new, nontraditional duties involve writing, especially keeping records for the tribe and maintaining correspondence with nonresident members and those outsiders with whom the tribe has dealings.

The spokesperson begins the meeting by explaining what the tribe is gathered together to decide. In the early 1980s, the tribe began to keep regular minutes, which are read after the spokesperson has opened a meeting. If any outsider has been invited to speak, such as a tribal representative from Kaibab or one of the expert advisors the tribe has hired for ongoing projects, before general discussion begins this person will be expected to give a speech. If the speech is in English, it will be interpreted by the spokesperson, or occasionally by some other interpreter chosen ad hoc.

Then the discussion begins in earnest. If there has been an outside speaker, the spokesperson will lead off the discussion by asking the elders if they have any questions to ask of the invited speaker. The elders will usually interrogate the invited speaker, if he or she is a tribally employed expert. The elders and the spokesperson then begin to speak in turn, starting off by giving speeches that last several minutes each.

Elders spend a large part of their speaking time, especially early in the meeting, setting the stage for a decision. In matters dealing with intertribal relations, for example, elders attempt to provide historical backgrounding for present day relations by referring to or even recounting stories of past instances of such relations as far back as these are recalled in oral tradition. In internal matters, for example, the allocation of land rights within the tribal estate, they generally talk at length about the moral and customary legal setting of the decision, as well as past cases in which a similar decision was made.

It is at this stage that elders' speeches most clearly reflect the highly elaborate and formal oratorical style that is a requisite for political speech making. Political oratory requires firm knowledge of oral history and community legal custom, as well as ability to use *aikнp*, traditional metaphor, and other figures of speech. In fact, many of the same stylistic resources are also used in other formal genres of verbal performance, so that skill in one probably transfers to others. Mastery of this style of oratory should probably be seen as a necessary, but not sufficient criterion for full participation in eldership and its collective exercise of authority at meetings.

When the stage is set, the elders and the spokesperson begin pragmatically to talk through the specific pros and cons of the decision the tribe has before it. When every elder has spoken and the elders and the tribal spokesperson feel they are all in agreement as to what should be done, the spokesperson calls for the tribal membership as a whole to authorize the decision that has been reached. A decision is considered to be made only when the adult membership have expressed their unanimous consent. At present, the spokesperson and the tribe have adopted the Anglo custom of voting by raising hands. Nevertheless, while the spokesperson always counts and records the vote, it is always unanimous. If dissent remains after discussion, the San Juans will simply put the matter aside until a later time. Because anger and spitefulness are strongly censured as foolish and dangerous behavior, San Juan elders seldom argue or confront each other publicly either inside or outside a meeting.

As noted earlier, *shuupara'ap* meetings deal with all matters that affect the tribe as a whole. Over the last several years the tribe has dealt with a variety of internal and external affairs. Tribal meetings have made decisions bearing on the Paiutes' intervention in the Hopi-Navajo land dispute, on tribal economic development planning and potential ways to fund it, and on the federal acknowledgement project.

Tribal meetings have also met to deal with resource allocation issues when these went beyond the scope of the ambilineage or settlement area. For example, in 1984, two of Dora Nelson's granddaughters, who had been living off the reservation since they had been sent away to school as girls, asked the San Juan Tribe if they could come home and have a place to farm and graze sheep in either the north or south. Because farming land at Paiute Canyon and Willow Springs is scarce, any new farm site could potentially prejudice the rights of people already farming there. Moreover, there are other people, especially the young, whose future rights have to be taken into account. Any decision to allocate land in either area therefore requires discussion and approval at the ambilineage or very likely the settlement level. A case involving both areas, as this one did, required a tribal level decision.

In the summer of 1983 and again in the spring of 1984, the spokesperson brought up this issue for discussion among the elders. It was finally decided that the two Nelson women would be welcome in either area. One of the two woman stayed for a while in the south at the camp of household [1] before finally opting to live and farm at Navajo Mountain and Paiute Canyon, her ancestral home. The other is now living at Navajo Mountain but has not yet begun to farm there.

If for some reason they were dissatisfied and wished to go beyond the San Juan community, tribal members could appeal to the Navajo tribal court system, which is now empowered to settle disputes over BIA agricultural and grazing permits. However, members apparently do not see this as a viable option. In fact, to a large degree the San Juans seem to be able simply to ignore the BIA permit system and the Navajo courts. A number of fields in Paiute Canyon and at Willow Springs have never been recorded or given permits by the BIA, although they have been utilized almost continuously since before the permit system came into being.

Nowadays, tribal meetings often serve as an interface between the tribe and the outsiders it employs to deal with land problems, the federal acknowledgment project, and economic development projects. As has historically been the case with chief elders, the tribal spokesperson is given a great deal of responsibility when she acts as liaison with outside experts. She carries on correspondence with them and keeps track of their work after the tribe has approved the project. When, for example, the tribe's attorneys or economic advisors suggest a major new step, the spokesperson must call a tribal meeting and invite the outside experts to speak and answer elders' questions before a decision is made. Although this permits the elders and the tribe at large to keep control of the tribe's external affairs and helps prevent any abuses of the spokesperson's broker or gatekeeper position, it usually surprises outsiders who assume that leadership implies independent decision making.

Subtribal Social Control and Dispute Settlement

The tribal meeting is not an isolated phenomenon in San Juan society. Most cases of social control and dispute settlement that come up in the community are dealt with using the same pattern of consensus group decision making, but at the level of subtribal groups like the ambilineage and settlement. Some examples of such cases reveal the overall similarity between subtribal and tribal decision making.

In the summer of 1982, a young married couple living at Willow Springs had been quarreling and appeared on the verge of breaking up. One day, every adult member of the southern area settlement group who was available gathered at the couple's house. All morning they looked on, while the local household heads talked to the couple. These elders reminded the couple of the duties and responsibilities that spouses owe to each other and that parents owe to children. The elders couched their moral instruction in the form of *aikнp* that are usually spoken to couples who are about to be married or who have just had their first child. These *aikнp* express the expectations that the community has of mature men and women.

In another case, in the summer of 1983, households [1], [2], and [3], and other households from the same ambilineage, repeatedly met together with the rebellious young teenage daughter of one of the household heads. Members of her kin group suspected she had been using drugs and were also concerned because she had quit school. In this case, the elders admonished her partly in terms of the injunctions spoken to young women who have achieved menarche. The basic gist of what she was told was that she should not be lazy and that she should take life seriously if she wanted a long life, and that she should be helpful to her household. In disciplinary cases like this, the parents almost never take sole responsibility for correcting the child. Instead, the elders of the ambilineage and sometimes the entire settlement will deal with the problem as a group.

In addition to *aikнp*, elders weave into their instructive discourse other highly marked and figurative verbal forms. A rebellious teenager may, for example, be told that he or she "laughs at the world" (*tнvwipн kiankнy*) or "is wearing a mask" (*maavн kurunapнxat*). These and many other similar traditional expressions convey more than disapproval. They carry a strong connotation of folly, a dangerous lack of awareness and control, the consequence of which for Paiutes is always seen as a shortening of one's natural lifespan. As with all instructive speech, the junior kin receiving correction are left largely on their own to make sense as best they can of the often mysterious statements of their elders. Paiutes believe that the demand this places on juniors to be active and imaginative listeners helps increase the impact of the message being taught.

Subtribal dispute settlement, as one might expect from its similarity of purpose, follows a similar pattern. Typically, the kinship group involved will hold a meeting, in which elders take leading roles characterizing the problem and proposing appropriate ways of avoiding it in the future. This procedure is used for dealing with relatively important disputes, for example, involving farm plots or grazing areas, as well as relatively trivial matters, such as fights between young people over boyfriends and girlfriends. As with all social control, we were aware of no application of sanctions beyond the threat of group disapproval. Nonetheless, even in cases in which elders themselves are disputants, most community members will make every effort at least to appear to be following the expressed will of their fellow community members.

Under special circumstances, subtribal groups may meet to

discuss matters usually dealt with on the tribal level. For example, when in the summer of 1981 the San Juan Tribe first learned from an attorney of DNA-People's Legal Service that title to San Juan land was to be litigated in the Navajo-Hopi land dispute, this information was first made public at a meeting of southern area households. The San Juans of that group sat around in a circle on the grass near the house and fields of (7) and (8) while the elders asked questions of the attorney through interpreters and voiced their own views. In such cases, the members of the settlement or other subtribal group are not involved in decision making, but simply act as ad hoc representatives for the larger tribal membership that is not actually present.

The Role of Visions and Prophecy in Modern Chief Eldership

In the late 1970s, the present tribal leader, Evelyn James, underwent a period of apprenticeship during which she learned about leadership through helping her mother, Anna Whiskers, in her duties as tribal leader. In 1980, soon after the birth of her son, Mrs. James herself was named tribal leader.

Over the years that followed, Mrs. James came more and more to exercise considerable moral influence over her fellow tribe members and even over tribal elders who are much older than herself. Sometime during 1983 or 1984 she apparently also began to have prophetic visionary experiences, just as had her grandfather, Alfred Lehi, and her great-great-grandfather, *Pak'ai*. She began to have prophetic dreams and even moments of waking contact with the traditional Southern Paiute deity, *Shɨnangwav*, equated by many modern Paiutes in this and other communities with the Christian God and/or with Jesus. Since the Paiutes' new Pentecostalist faith and their traditional religion both emphasize the importance of prophetic gifts, her experiences have validity in both frameworks.

While many San Juans have told us of their own or of others' experiences with spirits of the dead, these are not necessarily usually understood to be sacred visions. True contact with the divine or sacred realm seems historically to have been the exclusive province of tribal and local chief elders. For historic leaders like *Pak'ai* and Alfred Lehi, visions and prophecies stand out in oral tradition, even when many of their secular actions have faded from memory. When Mrs. James began to have such experiences and to describe them to community members, no one seemed surprised; in fact, some elders immediately drew the connection between Mrs. James' visions and dreams and Alfred Lehi's mysterious prophecies. At least partly as a result of her visions, she began about the same time to have much greater confidence in her leadership and to exercise an ever greater moral influence in community affairs.

In the following excerpts from an interview, Mrs. James, describes some of the most important elements in her recent visionary experiences:

EJ [Evelyn James]: I had a dream that really amazed me one night. It was about my experiments [sic] in holding two scorpions. I never held a scorpion before in my hand. I never wanted to hold a scorpion. But anyway, in my dream, said, right in both of my hands that I had two scorpions in each hand. I was holding it. And I didn't even thought about it, you know, the scorpions, I didn't even thought that it might sting me, that I should drop it, I didn't even feel like that. And I looked at the scorpion--I was told from above what I was doing, you know, somewhere the Great Spirit was telling me. Told me that I was holding two scorpions, and told me to look at those two scorpions, and to recognize the scorpions. And I looked at the two scorpions, in the other hand and it was a Hopi, and the other hand I held a Navajo. And the Great Spirit was telling me what I should do. He says, these scorpions you know they're dangerous and if you let them, it's up to you to destroy them, are you going to destroy them? When you destroy them, sure they gonna die. But if you let them go, surely they're going to walk out of your hands. And either way you're going to handle the situation like this. And right in the middle, before I can make my move, before I can do anything else, I thought, it's truth, if I let them go, then they gonna go, if I kill them, both of them gonna die. And right then I woke up. And I was thinking about it, that I was holding a scorpions that described by the Hopi Tribe and the Navajo Tribe.

RF [Robert Franklin]: What exactly did the Great Spirit say to you in your dream? Can you say it the way you actually heard it in your dream? He said it in

English, or in Paiute or in Navajo or Hopi?

EJ: He said it the way that I can understand it very clear. And as I clearly understand Paiute--I didn't hear the voice of it, but I couldn't hear soundings, I couldn't hear the soundings of an English word, any kind of word, but I know that the Holy Spirit, the Holy, that what do you call him, the Great Spirit was talking to me. And I understood it the way he was talking to me.

RF: What is this Spirit's name in Paiute?

EJ: We call Great Spirit *Shɥnangwav*. Or we call him *Tɥvwipɥ Unipɥxat* ["One Who Made the Land/Earth"]. Which means Maker of the World. . . .

RF: You also told me yesterday about your experience when you had to go to the deposition, down to Phoenix, and you were telling me about that.

EJ: When I was, when I heard that I supposed to be taking my deposition, which I have to face the two attorneys of the Hopi and the Navajo Tribe, they ask me questions about all the, all the questions they wanted to ask me, I was kind of very fearful. I couldn't even stand a chance, you know because I'm hopeless, they gonna defeat me. I don't even know very much. And here these recognized tribes, their attorneys gonna question me, and I was feeling, you know, very scared inside. And I didn't even know what to say. And somewhere, along the way, when I was still thinking about it, the Holy Spirit or the Great Spirit spoke to me again. He said not to be afraid. He told me to do this in happiness, because he knows, he told me, that I am a winner. And everything's gonna be all right. And he told me not to, not to be scared all the time and not to handle things foolishly. And so, from there on, I don't feel scared any more . . . I cried when that Holy Spirit or that Great Spirit told me I'm a winner. . . .

I was on top of Willow Springs . . . I went to let the sheep out . . . And I cried, I never felt like this before. I never felt so brave before, never felt so, so strong before. I suddenly felt so strong. I looked around me.

And the Great Spirit said, you're a human, you have a strong bones, strong back-bone. And that's when I found out that somebody that is greater than anybody else is on my side, that I was wasn't alone after all. And after all I wasn't standing and doing this all alone. Somebody else was by my side. And that's where I found, you know, this happiness in doing this. And so I cried, cried all I want to.   [Bunte and Franklin Fieldnotes, October 19, 1984]

Each of these experiences with the divine is of course a reflection of the tribe's current political goals and of Mrs. James' leadership role in the tribe. She focuses on the effect these experiences have had on her personal development as a leader, how they have helped her to discover inner strength and sense of purpose. From the perspective of the tribe, her sacred visions maintain morale in the community and focus support for tribal goals, as well as for Mrs. James' leadership. Many tribal members are frightened by the federal recognition process and by the pending federal court suit. History leads them to mistrust federal institutions and fear the power and influence exercised by the Hopi and Navajo tribal governments. Mrs. James' prophetic experiences give members the sense that right is on the side of the Paiutes and, perhaps more importantly, that the tribe is in control of its own destiny.

For San Juans, visions and prophecy are closely intertwined with chief eldership. The supernatural powers associated with chief elders may in fact be more central to community consciousness than the secular skills and capacities that chief elders obviously need to carry out their duties. The San Juans are not the only group of Southern Paiutes to make this connection. As the following passage from Knack's Utah study shows, supernatural vision is an inseparable component of tribal leadership in these communities as well:

Presently, leaders rely on a combination of backing from a large kin group, a dynamic personality, and spiritual support. For instance, the chairman of the tribal corporation's board of directors [governing all five band communities] is the eldest of a large family of sons, all now married and with families; he traces his decision to assume leadership to a vision which told him he must do so. Two other members of the board of directors are leaders of the Native American Church. The vice-chairman is an extremely dynamic woman, the head of a large family which traditionally dominated the Richfield community . . . The remaining member of the board is the son and social heir of the last recognized Paiute chief, whose position was at least partially spiritual and partially supported by his large family. One young woman expressed the intention to become a leader at some future time, based on a vision she has had of an ancestor who was a renowned chief at the time of Mormon settlement. [Knack 1980:88]

In addition to the importance of supernatural visions, this passage reveals other parallels with the San Juans. One of the most obvious is the importance of the kinship constituency principle. Knack also noted in two cases that chiefly ancestry was seen as prestigious and perhaps even as a source of legitimacy for potential leaders. The role played by the Native American Church and its practitioners in Utah Paiute politics also parallels the role of syncretistic Christianity in the San Juan community. Mrs. James sometimes refers to *Shɨnangwav* as the Holy Spirit and sometimes as the Great Spirit, reflecting the increasingly acceptable integration of both belief systems in San Juan society.

San Juan Relations with Hopis and Navajos on the Local Level

The first two parts of this chapter dealt with the San Juan Southern Paiute Tribe from an inside perspective, describing the beliefs, values, and relationships that characterize San Juan Southern Paiutes as a society. The description of present day San Juan Southern Paiute society would be incomplete without an examination of this group's unofficial social and economic relations with its closest Indian neighbors, the Hopi and Navajo tribes.

There are major differences in San Juan Paiute intertribal relations between the northern and southern areas. For example, San Juans in the northern area have no dealings on an everyday basis with Hopis, while relations between Paiutes and Navajos appear to be markedly more tense in the north than in the south. These differences have to be borne in mind throughout the following discussion.

One of the most important modes of interaction between members of the three groups lies in the area of economic relations. Although most San Juans in both north and south have little to do with Hopis from an economic standpoint, they have important economic relations both of interdependence and competition with Navajos.

As discussed earlier, San Juans in the south have a direct Navajo market for baskets. Although Paiutes in the north do not appear to market their baskets to Navajos directly, it is still the case that the largest proportion of their basketry goes to Navajos, with white traders acting as middlemen. Because this is probably the singlemost important source of cash income for Paiutes, they are very much dependent on Navajos' willingness to buy their baskets.

This interdependence between Navajo buyers and Paiute suppliers is exemplified through a recent incident at a Gap Chapter meeting. The chapter is the lowest level of Navajo tribal government. The Gap Chapter governs an area that in principle at least includes sites occupied by many southern area San Juans. The Tuba City Chapter covers the rest of the San Juans' southern occupation zone. Although the San Juans do not participate in either chapter, they have a few friends and in-laws among the local Navajos who do. According to members of one Navajo family, who live near the Paiute settlement cluster at Hidden Springs and who are friends as well as affines through the marriage of (58) with a Navajo woman from that group, some Navajos proposed at a Gap Chapter meeting that the chapter vote to prohibit the Paiute women of Hidden and Willow Springs from selling their baskets on the reservation. Both the Paiutes and their Navajo in-laws thought this was an attempt to make certain Navajos' baskets more salable. As Roessel pointed out (1983:602), the Navajo Tribe began sponsoring basketry classes for Navajos, increasing the number of Navajo basket weavers on the reservation from fewer than a dozen in the mid-1960s to over one hundred in the early 1970s. The motion was voted down, in part because, as the Paiutes' Navajo in-laws put it, a lot of Navajos in that area believe Paiute-made baskets are the only kind that have special healing properties.

While the wedding basket market may represent an important avenue of economic interdependence, in most other ways the San Juans and their Navajo neighbors are competitors for scarce resources. This is a significant conditioning factor in their interrelations, especially in the north.

One of the most important economic resources in any reservation is the federal relationship. Because of both geographic and social isolation, federal programs are often the main source of employment for reservation Indians. They are also a significant means of dealing with housing and food needs. As has been noted earlier, it was only in the early 1970s that San Juans were able to obtain state and federally funded social welfare and food supplements through the local BIA subagency at Tuba City. To our knowledge, no San Juan has obtained employment through the Tuba City Western Navajo Subagency, even in temporary youth job programs, as local Navajos and Moenkopi Hopis do on a regular basis. Only recently have any Paiutes received federal or state help with housing, and none has done so through the BIA administration. Particularly in the case of employment, which is hard to come by even for Navajos, it is not surprising that a bureaucracy largely staffed by Navajos would give Paiute applications a low priority or even discriminate against them, as the San Juans claim. The employment and services situation is exacerbated at Navajo Mountain where what little federal aid and employment is available is often funneled through the local chapter, rather than the BIA administration.

The San Juans and local Navajos have, of course, also long been competitors for range and farmland. In the south, it appears that such competition has considerably abated due to the growing urbanization of Tuba City. While ethnic competition has prevented the San Juans in the south from gaining access to the greater number of federal jobs that have appeared with the growth of Tuba City, this increase in employment opportunities for Navajos has probably benefited Paiutes indirectly by taking some of the pressure off grazing and farming.

In the north, where urbanization has not taken place and where there is consequently very little wage-labor available locally, grazing and farming remain major sources of livelihood. Consequently, pressure on San Juan resources has continued and may even have been stepped up in recent years. Yet resource competition in the Navajo Mountain area appears to us not to be directed entirely at Paiutes. Conflict and attempts at expansion appear to divide the Navajo community itself into competing descent groups, so that there is considerable disunity among Navajos. Nonetheless, although Navajo interlineage rivalries may have prevented a concerted Navajo takeover of Paiute resources, the San Juans probably

still suffer more serious consequences from resource
competition than do Navajo groups in the Navajo Mountain-
Paiute Canyon area, since they are the least numerous group.
Moreover, as members of a different ethnic group, they cannot
count on support from either Navajos or from the Navajo
political system in handling their problems.

In Paiute Canyon, San Juan farmers have been subjected to
a variety of forms of harassment. Several years ago, there was
an unsuccessful squatting attempt by a Navajo family from
Kayenta in which the San Juan community narrowly avoided
losing a house and irrigated fields in the Nelson field area.
The San Juans from the local settlement group banded together
to induce the Navajos to leave by threatening to take them to
court. In the past, a number of fields within Paiute Canyon
and elsewhere in the north have been lost, allegedly to Navajo
squatters. In addition to the above incident, every summer
Paiute fences have been cut or gates left open so that Navajo
livestock have gotten into their fields and damaged the
growing crops, sometimes completely destroying them.
Although Navajo farms have also been vandalized as part of
ongoing intra- and inter-lineage land squabbles, the San Juans
are particularly powerless to deal with it without federal
support.

The San Juans in the north are also subject to continuing
encroachment on their grazing lands. At present, Paiutes from
the Navajo Mountain settlement group graze almost exclusively
in Utah, to the north and east of Navajo Mountain. In
contrast to the situation with farms in Paiute Canyon, from
Paiute accounts there appears to have been only one Navajo
kin group that has been attempting in recent years to expand
into their grazing area. This group has numbered among its
members two past Navajo tribal councilman from Navajo
Mountain and thus has strong local and tribal political
influence.

Despite the economic relations that are probably the
primary source of friction as well as interdependence between
Paiutes and Navajos, there are intertribal encounters in other
social contexts, mostly church and school, through which some
San Juans have developed friendly ties with both Hopis and
Navajos. Current figures for intermarriage between the three
groups reflect this.

In both the north and south, most San Juan Paiutes attend
Christian church services with Navajos, not only at their local
churches but frequently also at revival tent meetings. In both

the church at Navajo Mountain and the one by Hidden Springs, the bulk of the congregation as well the ministers are Navajos.

While church-going brings Paiutes of all ages together with Navajos, most younger Paiutes have also gone to school with Hopis and Navajos. Most of the younger San Juans who have some fluency in Navajo learned the language in the school environment. Some Paiute children, especially boys, have encountered problems with Navajo prejudice at school, but a number of friendships between Paiutes and Navajo neighbors have also begun there.

7

CHANGE AND PERSISTENCE

In this study we have attempted to describe the San Juan Paiute community as it has evolved over history and as it exists today. Yet the San Juan Tribe is still in a state of change, adapting to changing circumstances and, where possible, self-selecting opportunities that suit members' individual and collective goals and values. In ten or twenty years San Juan political, economic, and social life may very well be quite different from what we see at present, at least in terms of the more superficial aspects.

This final chapter focuses on new directions for change which the San Juan community is on the point of taking. In particular, we examine certain community projects in the areas of political process and economic development which are now in the embryonic stage but which may provide a potent impetus for social, political, and economic change in coming years.

Where are San Juan Paiutes going?

The San Juan Paiute Tribe stands on an important threshold as an Indian community. The outcome of the Branch of Federal Acknowledgment's imminent recognition decision will certainly prove a major factor in determining the future of the tribe. However, whether the decision is positive or negative, life as the San Juans presently know it will continue to change. In what directions, at what speed, and with what consequences for tribe members may only be guessed. It is clear that the San Juans do not want to, and indeed could not, go back to the political obscurity and socioeconomic isolation in which they spent much of the twentieth century. In any event, for the last decade and a half, the tribe's membership has fully committed itself to participation in the wider public arena as the sole effective means of protecting what they have and obtaining what they feel they need.

Since our first visit to the San Juans in 1979, the community has evolved from a group that felt isolated, forgotten, and powerless into a group that has become a part of the national scene and is confidently looking towards the future. During this period, in addition to the federal acknowledgment project and federal land claims lawsuit, they have become involved in projects ranging from a social impact assessment (the Kaiparoits Coal Project in Utah), to a federal economic and political development grant, to a major museum exhibition of their basketry. These diverse projects have entailed intensive interaction on the part of at least some San Juans with outsiders: anthropologists, lawyers, BIA officials, museum curators, and economic development consultants. Concurrent with this onslaught of "experts," the San Juan Tribe's leadership has had to deal with mounting written correspondence, requests for records, and many unfamiliar money management tasks.

By the time this study was completed in 1986, certain directions of change were already clear. In the political sphere, the San Juans had already modified minor aspects of their traditional, customary political organization. Now they also have taken on the project of writing a formal constitution. In the economic sphere, the San Juans were working to form a basketry cooperative in order to seek a wider market for the crafts that had already become the major single source of cash income for member families. In this chapter, we will look closely at these two areas and analyze their actual and potential consequences.

Formalizing an Informal System of Government

In a discussion of problems in American Indian tribal governments, Deloria and Lytle (1983:109) stated:

> The structures, the functions, the technologies, the politics, and even the goals of the white community are in many ways displacing the traditional ways of the Indians. The unanswered question that remains is how much of the traditional Indian culture and values can survive if tribal government continues to develop along these lines.

The San Juans have applied for federal recognition under BIA Federal Acknowledgment Project guidelines (25 CFR 83). This entails that they move from their traditional, informal system of government towards a formalized system that will be acceptable to the BIA and effective in dealing with outside agencies and interests. The San Juans wish, however, to create a constitution and by-laws that will protect and preserve as much as possible the structures and processes inherent in the current system. Given an Indian policy that is presently fairly flexible, and given the fact that their traditional system is still strong, the San Juans have a historically unique opportunity to do just this.

In 1984, the San Juan Tribe applied for and was awarded a tribal development grant from the Administration for Native Americans (ANA) which among other things provided for the formulation of a constitution and by-laws. The formalization process itself is not without dangers and may possibly serve to create problems for the tribe.

These problems fall into two major categories. The first are those inherent in formalizing a nonliterate people's political system based on kinship and informal consensus. Another set of problems involves shifts in traditional authority and leadership relations that are likely to be brought about when the group attempts to mobilize the kinds of skills and abilities that will be required to cope with the federal bureaucracy and other external political and economic interests.

These problems are not hypothetical, since the formalization process and the promotion of new leadership skills have already begun. The San Juans are themselves eager for change to take place. They have long been aware of the benefits and powers that accrue to other tribes, like their neighbors, the Kaibab Paiutes, who have adopted such a formalized structure. At least some San Juans have expressed belief that a formalized government will allow them to deal more effectively with outsiders, especially government agencies. This political development project is thus an example of a planned change that appears desirable to most segments of the society. Nevertheless, the San Juans have not yet fully confronted the potentially undesirable consequences of these political changes.

In the remainder of this section, we will first examine the organizational changes that are already happening or may soon happen, and the specific problems to which these changes may lead. Afterwards, we will discuss strategies for managing change that have been utilized in San Juan and other American Indian societies.

Organizational Changes

The San Juans' political system has recently undergone minor, but potentially far-reaching changes. The most obvious political organizational change has been the addition of what are now called the community representatives. Unlike the elders, these individuals are actually formally selected by local groups. This new institution originated during the writing of the grant proposal to fund the tribe's federal acknowledgment research. The proposal included as part of the tribal oversight process "tribal contact representatives," literate, and therefore younger members from each of the major localized kinship groups who could read preliminary drafts of research reports, communicate the information to the elders and other adults they represented, and forward their comments, additions, and criticisms. By the time the project was complete, the community representatives appeared to have developed a permanent place in San Juan political organization. They form a tribal committee through which other external matters besides federal acknowledgment are channeled before the general membership makes decisions concerning them.

This innovation, and the trend it represents, have the

potential of shifting the locus of power and authority from the elders to younger, school-educated members. It is true that most of the younger members are presently associated with respected elders since they are usually the son or daughter of one. Nonetheless, information is now routed through the representatives who, intentionally or not, control and interpret the information before passing it on.

Another shift in authority from old to young took place during the 1980s when Evelyn James became spokesperson. This new chief elder, despite her relatively young age, has been able to take on all of the traditional duties of the position, as well as all the record keeping and correspondence that the position now necessitates. Early in her tenure as leader, she even took a correspondence course in secretarial skills in order to be able to handle the record keeping required by the BIA which naturally fell to her as tribal mediator with outsiders.

Another major change followed from this increase in paper work--the inception of organized tribal record keeping. Previously there had been no organized record keeping effort. The few letters and other written materials directed to earlier chief elders were usually saved with personal and family papers. Kaibab Paiutes who on occasion attended San Juan meetings sometimes took attendance and wrote minutes, which were also preserved by the San Juan chief elder. The new spokesperson, however, began to keep addresses of all tribal members on index cards arranged in alphabetical order, primarily so off-reservation members could receive notices of meetings, copies of minutes, and such other news as announcements of weddings and funerals. This was the beginning of the codification of the tribal roll. She also began passing an attendance sheet around at meetings for members to sign (later noting attendance on the membership roll) and began assigning certain members the task of taking minutes as well. The latter two innovations she borrowed from the Kaibab Paiutes.

Such a simple change as the recording of membership lists can have important ramifications when it occurs in a society organized in a oral, nonliterate manner. Goody, Cole, and Scribner, leading theorists on the consequences of literacy, recounted that native language record keeping among a group of Vai people in Africa enabled the leadership to acquire a new type of leverage over members. They noted that "application of the Vai script went hand in hand with the

depersonalization of social functions which had previously
depended upon face-to-face interaction backed by normative
rules whose interpretation was open to negotiation" (1977:297).
For example, with writing they could list those who owed dues
or those who lived in a certain geographical area. It also
enabled them to make abstractions that would not have
occurred without the written lists, for example, a summary of
the number of deaths over a certain period and a summary of
the total inactive and active membership for one or more years.

In addition to record keeping, the San Juans will soon
codify much of their customary law and decision making
practices. Such a course should lead to depersonalization of
authority relations in a sociopolitical system that is at present
based on kinship relations and the give-and-take of informal
consensus building.

It may also lead to a decline in the flexibility presently
inherent in the system. Let us take the case of San Juan
Paiute membership criteria and examine it in light of the issue
of flexibility. Although San Juans always knew who were and
who were not members of the tribe, their membership criteria
have never been formally crystallized. Instead, they relied
informally on their knowledge of a person's descent and social
participation. As Goody, Cole, and Scribner (1977) suggested,
informal criteria only work, however, when social functions
depend upon face-to-face interaction. Previously, any San
Juans who moved away, joined other Ute or Paiute groups,
and did not keep up social relations were forgotten by tribal
members after a couple of generations. Since their
participation ceased, memory of the genealogical ties that
connected them to other members eventually vanished also.
For San Juans, consequently, the two criteria came to be
intimately tied together--those people who were known to be
descendents of tribal members were all those (and only those)
who also participated at some level in San Juan community
life.

The act of record keeping, however, allows one to view
descent and participation separately. The heretofore flexible
criterion of participation may either have to be dropped
altogether or redefined and quantified. Record keeping would
allow either solution. As noted above, attendance at tribal
meetings is currently noted on each individual's card. There
appears to be a tendency even now to redefine participation in
terms of meeting attendance rather than the less easily
formalizable types of generalized social participation it has

taken to maintain ties with the community in the past. If participation continues as a criterion for membership, then this opens up the possibility that leaders, or even the majority of members, might begin selectively dropping members who have missed a certain percentage of meetings. In the past, membership criteria have been used by leaders of other tribes in much this fashion to further their own political ends.

On the other hand, if participation is dropped as a membership criterion, it would only be necessary to record births to tribal members to keep an up-to-date membership list. This opens up the possibility of retaining on the roll descendents of members who prior to written record keeping would have been lost, having cut off social relations with the tribal community. Some tribes have felt that it was to their benefit to maintain an inflated enrollment for federal budgetary purposes. However, this can also lead to a situation where a sizable proportion of the enrolled membership bears little allegiance to the goals and traditional values of the original tribal community, which is the case in many tribes today. In any event, the realization of such a potentiality would certainly change the character of the tribal community.

Strategies for Managing Change

There can be no question of preventing change. However, the example of political practice in other American Indian communities suggests that undesired consequences can be avoided or mitigated. This section looks at strategies other communities have used to preserve traditional modes of consensual decision making and the age-graded exercise of authority and influence. It also examines the San Juans' own tentative solutions to the membership criteria problem.

Although they have a formal Indian Reorganization Act constitution, the Kaibab Paiutes have been able to work around the formalized aspects of it to retain and foster informal consensus and kinship based authority. The Kaibabs have a system of ad hoc committees on which at one time or another all tribal members and, most prominently, the elders serve. Through these committees, elders have input in every aspect of tribal decision making. Following the Kaibabs in this manner would enable the San Juans to foreground the skills and moral authority of their own elders, giving the tribe the benefit of the elders' wisdom. Preserving the elders' role in the political system would also provide the tribal government an important source of legitimacy in members' eyes.

There are also existing precedents for formal tribal governments of the "general council" type, which most closely resembles the traditional tribal decision making processes of the San Juans and many other traditional Indian peoples. The Crows of Montana, for example, have a constitution and an elected tribal council. However, tribal officers call a General Council meeting of the tribe whenever substantive issues are to be decided (Deloria and Lytle 1983), much as the San Juans have done and continue for the moment to do under their traditional system. Such an organization if adopted by the San Juan community would have the advantage of maintaining the broad consensual basis of the traditional system and probably the traditional processes of consensus building as well. It would also provide a forum for the best speakers, once again involving the elders in the governing process.

A final point concerns present San Juan discussions on the formalization of membership criteria. The San Juan committee dealing with the formalization of the constitution has tentatively suggested--pending approval by the tribe as a whole--that descent from a San Juan as well as participation be necessary for tribal membership. Membership would be automatic if a San Juan descendent was born in the San Juan community on the reservation or if that individual lived for a certain number of years in the community. However, realizing that some flexibility must be built into the system, they are also suggesting that San Juan descendents who feel that they have demonstrated the strength of their allegiance in other ways may petition the tribal council for membership. This would put the final authority to decide on membership back into the hands of the same group in which it has always resided, although previously the group never needed to formalize the decision.

San Juan Paiute Basketry

As the recent exhibition of San Juan Paiute basketry at the Wheelwright Museum of the American Indian in Santa Fe, New Mexico, has demonstrated (see McGreevy and Whiteford 1985), San Juan Paiute contemporary basketry arts are economically viable, dynamically innovative, and certainly artistically successful. Susan McGreevy described the current variety of basketry styles produced by the San Juans as follows:

Their baskets present a fascinating portrait of continuity and change: "old-timer baskets" (weavers' term for utilitarian vessels) preserve tradition; "wedding baskets" produce revenue; and innovative "design baskets" (weavers' term) stimulate new markets and nurture artistic growth. [1985:26]

The demographics of San Juan Paiute basketmakers suggest that the craft is especially healthy in this community. Over 10% of the total population (male and female) are basketmakers and a large number are under the age of 45. The youngest exhibitor at the Wheelwright show was 9 years old. Although the weavers are primarily women, men have been fully accepted for some time as weavers of the pitch covered basketry water jars and, as we will see below, are beginning to weave other designs as well.

History of San Juan Paiute Basketry

Prior to the extensive economic changes that affected the San Juans during the last quarter of the nineteenth century and into the twentieth century, the craft of basketry was an essential component of San Juan Paiute economy. Baskets were used in both collecting and farming to harvest, transport, winnow, parch, and finally store grains and seeds. Pitch covered basketry jars were also of great importance in this semiarid region for the transportation and storage of water.

Although San Juan Paiutes continued to make baskets for their own use well into the twentieth century, basketry assumed increasing importance in the San Juan economy as a trade item. The first record of San Juan Paiutes producing baskets for trade is found in the 1870s when John D. Lee noted that they were making pitch water jugs woven from sumac to trade with the Navajos (Cleland and Brooks 1955:269). By the beginning of the twentieth century, Paiutes were also producing ritual basketry, including the so-called Navajo wedding basket, for trade to the Navajos (Franciscan Fathers 1910:291-94; George Wharton James 1972 [1909]:109-12). Production of goods, which may have no religious significance to the producers, for the purposes of exchange to cultural groups for whom such goods figure prominently in ritual is itself a long-standing tradition in the Southwest and one of greatest importance for understanding historic and even present day intertribal exchange relationships (see Richard Ford 1983).

The San Juan Paiutes' basket trade with both the Hopis and Navajos had become a major component of their economy by the 1930s. They traded Paiute-made, Hopi-style flat basketry plaques to the Moencopi Hopi during the 1930s (Humetewa 1981:70; see also Hopi Tribe 1981). Although Paiutes continued to produce some baskets of designs other than the Navajo wedding basket, they were not economically profitable until William Beaver, the trader at the Sacred Mountain Trading Post north of Flagstaff, began to take an interest in the Paiutes' work in the mid-1960s. Since then, he has assembled two collections of San Juan Paiute basketry. The first is now in the National Museum of Ethnology in Osaka, Japan, while the second collection formed the basis of the recent San Juan Paiute basketry exhibition. This second collection is of particular interest since the San Juan basketmakers worked actively with Beaver in putting it together. He encouraged the Paiutes to innovate by supplying them with pictures of baskets made by various southwestern Indian groups. At the same time, he encouraged the younger San Juans to learn all they could of traditional utilitarian baskets from the older people (McGreevy 1985).

San Juan Paiute Basketry Cooperative

Using professional advice, mainly from the Center for Indian Economic Development (CIED), funded under an Administration for Native Americans political and economic development grant, the San Juan Tribe established its basketry association, named the Yingup Weavers Association (YWA). Deborah Sick-Connelley, who recently studied decision making among San Juan Paiute weavers, noted that a major goal of this project was "to eliminate middle-man traders and allow the weavers to sell their work directly to museums, shops and other buyers" (1986:15).

The idea for such an association first emerged at a meeting between the San Juans and a CIED representative, Steven Haberfeld, during the preparation of the ANA proposal. He told the group that any economic development project that built on their prior expertise would have the best chances of working. The San Juans therefore suggested the basketry project. After the grant was awarded, organizational and marketing strategies were worked out over the course of several meetings between Haberfeld and the San Juans.

Sick-Connelley (1986:15) observed that: "According to the Association's manager only 15, the most competent weavers, [out of approximately 30 San Juan weavers] are officially members. Other weavers will be given orders according to demand for baskets and the skill of the weaver." This decision reflected tribal concerns regarding the maintenance of traditionally high standards of quality. The members of the Association must agree to perform certain duties and in turn they receive a number of benefits, such as higher prices for their work as well as help in gathering the raw materials (see Sick-Connelley 1986).

Since the association is just now becoming fully operational it is impossible to predict its social and economic consequences for the San Juan Paiute community. However, Sick-Connelley's study of the cultural and economic factors involved in San Juans' basketmaking decisions identified certain potential sources of difficulty:

> While basket making is functionally compatible in many aspects (i.e., an activity easily integrated with other daily chores), there is an indication that the high priority San Juan weavers place on social/family obligations may out-compete YWA basket weaving obligations. Study results also show that cash (derived from basket making) has a relatively low level of marginal utility among the San Juan. . . . Delays in receiving orders may well hurt the YWA economically if buyers grow weary of waiting for overdue orders. On the other hand, if San Juan baskets are well-received in the market place and demand is high, lower outputs may be economically beneficial to San Juan weavers.

> Attempting to raise economic standards through development of a crafts cooperative raises several important questions. What will be the effect of an increased cash flow on community social bonds and organization [especially if this increased cash flow is not evenly distributed among the various families]? Although basket weaving has traditionally been a woman's occupation, will the opportunity for additional income increase male participation? What effect will

this have on male/female roles and household organization? [Sick-Connelley 1986:42]

Although the cooperative may allow many San Juans to raise their standard of living significantly, the long term effects are not yet clear. Nevertheless, one consequence alluded to above has already become a reality. During the first months of operation, the association received a particularly large order and responded by inviting some of the men to make baskets. Whether this will result in a permanent entree for men into all sectors of this heretofore primarily female occupation remains to be seen.

Change and Persistence

The San Juan Tribe's constitution and basketry projects are only two of a number of factors that are likely to produce marked changes in San Juan life during coming years.

The San Juans are currently seeking reservation rights to their present holdings, which they may obtain through their current federal lawsuit. If they get their reservation, it should put an end to outside pressure on their land. It is competition with Navajos that makes land a scarce resource for San Juans, and this scarcity is the major factor giving the present ambilineage system its economic and political rationality. The ambilineage system, although it grows out of the traditional kinship system, is itself of relatively recent vintage and probably not stable as an institution. Moreover, under a reservation system, land tenure, as well as agricultural and grazing activities, will all come under the direct scrutiny of the BIA and the newly formalized tribal government. The San Juan Tribe is already making plans to improve agricultural practices under their current ANA grant. If greater capitalization in farming and grazing is encouraged, it is likely to foster individual enterprise over corporate kin group land management (see Schneider 1981). If the tribal government takes a greater hand in the management of agricultural and grazing rights, the power of the ambilineages may be reduced.

Along with reservation rights to their own lands, under the 1974 Act that sanctions the current 1934 Act Navajo Reservation lawsuit, the San Juans may also gain a share of subsurface rights in the 1934 Area. In this event, the tribe will have to decide whether to disburse money from royalties and leases as substantial per capita payments to members, to put it to some use for the tribe as a whole, or to design some combination of both. As Indian tribal history attests, negative consequences can result from any of these choices: at very least, the money can simply disappear with no permanent benefit to show for it; at worst, tribal unity can be endangered and serious social divisions created where none existed before. On the other hand, some tribes have used such money for long term benefits: they have acquired more tribal land, established tribal economic development projects, or created scholarship programs to increase educational opportunities for the young. In any event, the San Juans would face some hard decisions and risks of a sort they have not yet had to deal with, although they have successfully faced many other problems over the course of their history.

Although change will be inevitable, this does not mean that some aspects of San Juan life may not persist much as they have done historically. Indeed, we believe that much of our description of the San Juan life will continue to be accurate for some time to come. Those areas that the San Juans perceive as the most fundamental, their kinship system, their emphasis on consensual politics, their arts, and their religion, are especially likely to persevere.

Moreover, the San Juans enter their present period of change with certain important advantages. First, they have the example of the other Southern Paiute communities, which underwent similar changes at an earlier point in history. Secondly, they are politically cognizant of the choices that must be made. They are aware of the manner in which these other tribal communities--successfully and unsuccessfully-- have handled change in the past and are looking closely at Kaibab and the five Utah bands to determine in what ways they should follow their example or try a different path. At present, the San Juan Paiutes already have at least some clearly formulated goals regarding change. Perhaps the most important of these is that they wish to keep intact the traditional values and institutions of their society.

APPENDIX I

Guide to Southern Paiute Orthography and Pronunciation

Because Southern Paiute is the language of daily San Juan life, and because many historic figures in the group have only traditional San Juan names, throughout the text we have cited native linguistic forms. The orthography used is one developed for a neighboring dialect, Kaibab Paiute, by Pamela Bunte and Kaibab elder Lucille Jake. It has been modified slightly to accomodate San Juan dialectal differences.

San Juan Southern Paiute Orthography

Consonants

	Labial	Dental	Palatal	Velar	Glottal
Voiceless stops	*p*	*t*		*k/kw*	'
Affricates		*ts*	*ch*		
Voiced nasals	*m*	*n*		*ng/ngw*	
Fricatives	*v*	*s*	*sh*	*x/xw*	*h*
Liquids and semivowels	*w*	*r*	*y*		

297

Vowels

	Front		Back	
	Rounded	Unrounded	Rounded	Unrounded
High		*i/ii*	*u/uu*	*ʉ/ʉʉ*
High-Mid	*ø/øø*	*e*	*o/oo*	
Low				*a/aa*

Primary stress in Southern Paiute and Ute dialects falls almost always on the second vowel of the word, although some exceptional words stress the first vowel. Secondary stresses fall on all alternate vowels afterwards except for final devoiced vowels (which we have usually left unwritten since they can be deleted in everyday pronunciation anyway). Any unstressed vowel that precedes a voiceless consonant, e.g. a [t], must be devoiced or whispered. A good example of this last rule is the name for the San Juan's southern area plateau lands just northwest of Tuba City, *Atatsiv* ("Sands"), the first vowel of which must be whispered. Where forms are alternatively pronounced with or without a particular vowel or other sound, the optional sound is enclosed in parentheses.

APPENDIX II

Southern Paiute/Ute Kinship Terminologies

Relationship	San Juan Paiute	Kaibab Paiute	Uintah Ute	Southern Ute
FaFa/(man's)SoCh	kɨnɨ	kɨnɨ	kɨnɨ	kɨnɨ
FaMo/ (woman's)SoCh	witsi'i-	witsi-	witsi-	wichi-
MoFa/(man's)DaCh	toxo-	toxo-	toxo-	tuxu-
MoMo/ (woman's)DaCh	kaxu-	kaxu-	kaxu-	kaxu-
FaOlBr/ (man's)YrBrCh	ku'u-	ku'u-	kuu-	kuu-
FaYrBr/ (man's)OlBrCh	ai-	ai-	ai-	a'i-
FaSi/ (woman's)BrCh	paa-	pa'a-	paa-	pa-
MoOlSi/ (woman's)YrSiCh	mangwɨ-	mangwɨ'ɨ	maawu-	mawu-
MoYrSi/ (woman's)OlSiCh	nɨpwia-	nɨmpia-	nimbɨia	naapia-
MoOlBr/ (man's)YrSiCh	kukwoi-	kokwa(')i-	aku(i)-	kukwɨ-

299

MoYrBr/ (man's)OlSiCh	*shuna-*	*shuna-*	*shina-*	*china-*
Fa	*moa-*	*mua-*	***	*mua-*
Mo	*pia-*	*pia-*	***	*pia-*
Da	*pachu-*	*pachu-*	***	*pachi-*
So	*toa-*	*tua-*	***	*tua-*
OlBr (Ol Male Cousin)	*pavi-*	*pavi-*	***	*pavi-*
OlSi (Ol Female Cousin)	*patsi-*	*pasi-/ patsi-*	***	*pachi-*
YrBr (Yr Male Cousin)	*chakai-*	*chakai-*	***	*chakai-*
YrSi (Yr Female Cousin)	*nami-*	*name-*	***	*nami-*

APPENDIX III

Residential Groupings and Resource Use by Household among the Ethnographic Study Group, Summer 1983

Household	Members

Southern Area

[1]   1. Co-head; aged, widowed Mo of 2, 7, 10, and 11.
2. Co-head, Da of 1, Si of 7, 10, and 11.
3. So of 7 and 8, OlSiSo of 2.
4. Da of 7 and 8, OlSiDa of 2.
5. Da of 7 and 8, OlSiDa of 2; widow.
6. So of 5.
Current Marriages: none.
House Locations: Atatsiv.

[2]   7. Co-head, Si of 2, 10, and 11.
8. Co-head, Hu of 7, FaOlBr of 91, 105, and 108.
9. Da of 7,8.
Current Marriage: 1 San Juan=San Juan
House Locations: Hidden Spring and Willow Spring; also a dwelling at [1]'s camp, used irregularly in 1983.

[3]   10. Co-head, Si of 2, 7, and 11; unmarried.
11. Co-head, Si of 2, 7, and 10; unmarried.
12. Da of 10.
13. Da of 10.
14. Foster Da of 11, Da of 37, 38.
15. OlSiSo of 10, 11, So of 7, 8.
16. So of 61 and 62, Classificatory OlBr of 15 (2nd Cousin, once removed).
Current Marriages: none.
House Locations: Hidden Spring.

[4]   17. Co-head, Da of 7, 8 (=Navajo).
Current Marriage: 1 San Juan=Navajo
House Locations: Hidden Spring.

[5]   18. Co-head, Da of 22 (father said to have
               been Alfred Lehi).
               19. Co-head, So of 24.
               20. So of 18, 19.
Current Marriage: 1 San Juan=San Juan
House Locations: Hidden Spring and Willow Springs.

[6]   21. Co-head, YrBr of 1's deceased husband,
               Alfred Lehi.
               22. Co-head, Wi of 21, Mo of 18 (other
               children and grandchildren are live off-
               reservation).
Current Marriage: 1 San Juan=San Juan
House Locations: Willow Springs; with [5] at Hidden Spring.

[7]   23. Single older man, Classificatory YrBr of 1
               (1st Cousin).
Current Marriages: none.
House Locations: Atatsiv and Willow Springs

[8]   24. Co-head, Si of 27, 40, 53 (=Navajo,
               co-head).
               25. So of 24.
               26. So of 24.
Current Marriage: 1 San Juan=Navajo
House Locations: Willow Springs.

[9]   27. Co-head, Si of 24, 40, 53 (=Navajo, co-
               head).
               28. Da of 27.
               29. So of 27.
               30. Da of 27.
               31. So of 27.
               32. So of 27.
               33. So of 27.
               34. So of 27 (=Navajo).
               35. So of 34.
Current marriages: 2 San Juan=Navajo
House Locations: Willow Springs; Tuba City with [13], [10].

[10]   36. Co-head, So of 27.
               37. Co-head, Wi of 36, OlSiDaDa of 1,
               FaOlBrSoDaDa of 22 (Classificatory DaCh).

38. Da of 36, 37.
39. Da of 36, 37.
Current Marriage: 1 San Juan=San Juan
House Locations: Willow Springs; Tuba City with [9], [13].

[11]   40. Co-head, Si of 24, 27, 53 (=Navajo, co-
              head; ≠ non-resident San Juan living at
              Towaoc, Fa of 40's children).
Current Marriage: 1 San Juan=Navajo.
House Locations: Tuba City with [12].

[12]   41. Co-head, Adopted So of 40, So of 40's
              deceased Da (=Moenkopi Hopi, co-head).
              42. So of 41.
              43. So of 41.
              44. So of 41.
Current Marriage: 1 San Juan=Hopi.
House Locations: Tuba City with [11] and Moenkopi with
wife's family.

[13]   45. So of 40's deceased Da.
              46. Da of 40's deceased Da; unmarried.
              47. Da of 46.
              48. So of 40's deceased Da (≠Navajo?)
              49. So of 48.
              50. Da of 40's deceased Da.
              51. So of 40's deceased Da.
              52. So of 40's deceased Da.
Current Marriage: 1 San Juan=Navajo
House Locations: Tuba City with [9], [10]; this cluster of
houses is across the street from [11] and [12]'s house group,
where 40 lives.

[14]   53. Head, Si of 24, 27, 40; widow.
              54. So of 53.
              55. Da of 53; unmarried.
              56. Da of 56.
Current Marriage: none.
House Locations: Two sites on Atatsiv.

[15]   57. Co-head, classificatory Br of 2, 7, 10, 11,
              their FaYrBrSo and MoOlSiDaSo; 22's
              classificatory DaCh, FaOlBrSoDaSo; half-Br
              of 37 (=Navajo, co-head).

Current Marriage: 1 San Juan=Navajo
House Locations: Tuba City.

[16]   58. Co-head, So of 10 (=Navajo, co-head).
              59. So of 58.
              60. So of 58.
Current Marriage: 1 San Juan=Navajo.
House Locations: Hidden Spring; and with Navajo wife's
relatives in Hidden Spring area.

Northern Area

[17]   61. Co-head, Br of 71, 83; OlSiSo of 82.
              62. Co-head, Wi of 61, adopted Da (actual
              DaDa) of 8's MoSi (thus 8 and 62 are
              classificatory siblings).
              63. Da of 61, 62.
              64. So of 61, 62.
              65. Da of 61, 62 (≠73's BrSo).
              66. So of 65.
              67. So of 61, 62.
              68. Da of 61, 62.
              69. So of 61, 62.
              70. Da of 61, 62.
Current Marriage: 1 San Juan=San Juan
House Locations: By Rainbow City, Paiute Canyon part-time.

[18]   71. Co-head, Br of 61, 83; OlSiSo of 82.
              72. Co-head, Mo was Si to 8's Mo and 62's
              adoptive Mo (actual MoMo), Wi of 71.
Current Marriage: 1 San Juan=San Juan
House Locations: By Lost Mesa and Paiute Canyon part-time.

[19]   73. Co-head (Mo is off-reservation San Juan
              Paiute).
              74. Co-head, Wi of 73, Da of 72, Br of 85.
              75. So of 73, 74.
              76. So of 73, 74.
              77. So of 73, 74.
              78. Da of 73, 74.
              79. Da of 73, 74.
              80. So of 73, 74.
              81. So of 73, 74.

Current Marriage: 1 San Juan=San Juan
House Locations: By Lost Mesa with [18].

[20]   82. Co-resident, said to be adopted So and
                actual SoSo of Ruben Owl/Nasja; MoYrBr of
                84, 61, 71.
                83. Co-resident, Br of 61, 71, OlSiSo of 83.
Current Marriages: none.
House Locations: By Lost Mesa with [18]; 82 lives part-time
at dwelling north of Navajo Mountain.

[21]   84. Single man, MoYrBr of 91, 105, 108;
                classificatory Br of 104 (104 is 85's MoSiDa);
                Dora Nelson's DaSo.
Current Marriages: none.
House Locations: With [18] by Lost Mesa.

[22]   85. Co-head, So of 72 (=Navajo; co-head).
                86. So of 85.
                87. Da of 85.
                88. So of 85.
                89. So of 85.
                90. So of 85.
Current Marriage: 1 San Juan=Navajo
House Locations: Rainbow City with Navajo wife.

[23]   91. Co-head, adopted So (actual SoSo) of 8's
                Mo; adoptive Mo (FaMo) is Si of 72's Mo,
                and 62's MoMo; Mo was OlSi of 84, and
                MoSiDa of 104 (=Alaskan Native, co-head).
                92. Da of 91.
                93. Da of 91.
                94. Da of 91.
                95. So of 91.
                96. So of 91.
                97. So of 91.
                98. Da of 91.
Current Marriage: 1 San Juan=Alaskan Native.
House Locations: White Mesa Reservation, and part-time in
Paiute Canyon.

[24]   99. Co-head, Br of 72 (=White Mesa Ute, co-
                head; her family said to have originated in
                Navajo Mountain region).

100. Da of 99.
101. So of 99.
102. So of 99.
103. So of 99.

Current Marriage: 1 San Juan=Ute
House Locations: White Mesa Reservation, and part-time
with [18] at Lost Mesa and in Paiute Canyon.

[25]   104. DaDa of Dora Nelson; classificatory OlSi
              (MoSiDa) of 84 and of Mo of 91, 105, 108
              (Children from marriage to deceased Ute,
              grandchildren adopted into her Ute
              son-in-law's family, also living in White
              Mesa).

Current Marriages: none.
House Locations: White Mesa Reservation.

[26]   105. Br of 91, 108 (=White Mesa Ute).
              106. Da of 105.
              107. So of 105.

Current marriage: 1 San Juan=Ute.
House Locations: White Mesa Reservation and part-time in
Paiute Canyon.

[27]   108. Br of 91, 105 (divorced from two Ute
              marriages; children live with mothers).

Current Marriages: none.
House Locations: With [17] and in southern area, in 1983.

Resource Use by Household, Southern Area

Primary Farming or Grazing Households		Households Receiving Produce, Providing Crisis Labor Inputs
[2]	↔	[1,3,4,7,15,16]
[5,6]	↔	none
[8,9,10]	↔	[11,12,13,14]
[1]	↔	[2,3,15,16]
[14]	↔	[8,9,11]

Residence and Resource Use, Northern Area, 1983

House-hold	Primary Residence	Farm, at Paiute Canyon	Grazing, at N.M.
[17]	Camp #1 (NM)	yes	yes
[18]	Camp #2 (NM)	yes	yes
[19]	Camp #2 (NM)	yes	yes
[20]	Camp #2, and North of Mnt.	not in use	yes
[21]	Camp #2	yes	yes
[22]	Rainbow City	no	no
[23]	White Mesa Res.	yes	no
[24]	White Mesa Res.	yes	no
[25]	White Mesa Res.	yes	no

[26]	White Mesa Res.	yes	no
[27]	Camp #1; also in Southern Area.	yes	no
[27]	Camp #1; also in Southern Area.	yes	no

REFERENCES

Abbreviations:

CIA	Commissioner of Indian Affairs
CCF	Central Classified File
FARC-LA	Federal Archives and Regional Center, Los Angeles
GPO	United States Government Printing Office
M	Microfilm Publication
NARS	National Archives and Record Service
Roll	Microfilm Roll
WNA	Western Navajo Agency

Aberle, David F.
1974   Statement. *In* Navajo-Hopi Land Dispute. U.S. Senate. pp. 311-92. Washington, D.C. : GPO.

Adams, Richard N.
1975   Energy and Structure: A Theory of Social Power. Austin: University of Texas Press.

ARCIA
1865-1900, Annual Report of Commissioner of Indian Affairs.
1906-1936   Washington, D.C. : GPO.

Bartlett, Katharine
1932   Why the Navajos Came to Arizona. Museum of Northern Arizona Museum Notes 5(6):29-32.

Basso, Keith H.
1979   Portraits of "the Whiteman." Cambridge: Cambridge University Press.

Billy, Irving
1984   Letter to Irene Barrow, February 6, 1984. (Original in
             possession of DNA-People's Legal Service, Tuba City.)

Billy, Henry
1983   Deposition, January 17, 1983, Sidney vs. MacDonald.

Bolton, Herbert E., ed.
1950   Pageant in the Wilderness: The Story of the Escalante
             Expedition to the Interior Basin, 1776. Utah Historical
             Quarterly 18.

Brewer, Sally
1937   The "Long Walk" to Bosque Redondo as told by Peshlakai
             Etsidi. Museum of Northern Arizona Museum Notes 9(11).

Brooks, George R., ed.
1977   The Southwest Expedition of Jedediah S. Smith: His
             Personal Account of the Journey to California 1826-1827.
             Glendale: Arthur H. Clark.

Brooks, Juanita, ed.
1944   Journal of Thales Haskell. Utah Historical Quarterly
             12(1-2):68-98.

Brown, James S.
1971 [1900]   Life of a Pioneer: Autobiography of James S. Brown.
             Reprint ed., New York: AMS Press.

1875-1877   Journals. (Manuscript in Northern Arizona University
             Special Collections, MS No. 173.)

Brugge, David M.
1964   Vizcarra's Navajo Campaign of 1823. In Arizona and the
             West. Tucson: University of Arizona Press.

1967   Interview with Alvin Nez, Defendent's Exhibits, Sidney vs
             Zah, p. 10138.

Brugge, David M. and J. L. Correll
1973   Historic Use and Occupancy of the Tuba City-Moenkopi
             Area. In Partition of the Surface Rights of Navajo-Hopi
             Land. U.S. Senate. pp. 172-204. Washington, D.C. : GPO.

Bulletts, Dan
1984   Deposition, June 3,1984, Sidney vs. Zah vs. James.

Bunte, Pamela A.
1979   Problems in Southern Paiute Syntax and Semantics.
            Bloomington: Indiana University Ph.D. Dissertation.

1980   Birdpeople: A Southern Paiute Coyote Tale. *In* Coyote
            Stories. Martha B. Kendall, ed. pp. 111-118. International
            Journal of American Linguistics Native American Texts
            Series. Chicago: University of Chicago Press.

1985   Ethnohistory of the San Juan Paiute Tribe. *In* Translating
            Tradition: Basketry Arts of the San Juan Paiute. Susan B.
            McGreevy and Andrew Hunter Whiteford, eds. pp. 9-13.
            Santa Fe: Wheelwright Museum of the American Indian.

1986   Subordinate Clauses in Southern Paiute. International
            Journal of American Linguistics 52(3):275-300.

Bunte, Pamela A. and Robert J. Franklin
1983   San Juan Southern Paiute Numerals. The Ninth LACUS
            Forum 1982:243-52.

1984   From the Sands to the Mountain: Ethnohistory and
            Ethnography of the San Juan Southern Paiute Tribe.
            (Manuscript prepared for the San Juan Southern Paiute
            petition submitted to the BIA Branch of Acknowledgment.)

1986   San Juan Southern Paiute Numerals and Mathematics.
            (Manuscript in possession of authors).

Bunte, Pamela A. and Lucille Jake
1976   *Ampaxavaraam*: A Paiute Alphabet Book, Cedar City,
            Utah: Southern Utah State College.

Burke, Charles
1922   Burke to Secretary Albert Fall, July 10, 1922, with
            Secretary Fall's approval, July 17; NARS, RG 75, CCF
            WNA, File 17605-1922, 304, pt. 1.

Castro, Ralph
1970   Letter to the editor of the Gallup Independent, February
             13, 1970. (Manuscript in possession of DNA-People's Legal
             Service, Tuba City.)

Chavez, Fray Angelico and Ted J. Warner, eds.
1976   The Dominguez-Escalante Journal. Provo: Brigham Young
             University Press.

Cheschillige, Deshna
1932   Cheschillige to Charles J. Roads, December 11, 1932;
             NARS, RG 75, CCF WNA, File 17605-1922, 304, pt. 2.

Cleland, R. G. and Juanita Brooks, eds.
1955   A Mormon Chronicle: The Diaries of John D. Lee.
             Huntington, California: Huntington Library.

Coleman, W. S.
1919   Inspection Report, May 22, 1919; NARS, RG 75, CCF WNA
             File 48409-1919, 101.

Collier, John
1939   Collier to Fred W. Johnson, December 26, 1939; NARS, RG
             75, CCF WNA, File 17605-1922, 304.

Collier, Malcolm
1966   Local Organization among the Navajos. New Haven:
             Human Relations Area Files.

Colton, Donald B.
1930   Colton to Charles J. Rhoads, October 13, 1930; NARS, RG
             75, CCF WNA, File 17605-1922, 304.

Corbett, Pearson H.
1952   Jacob Hamblin, The Peacemaker. Salt Lake City: Deseret
             Book Company.

Coues, Elliot
1900   On the Trail of a Spanish Pioneer. New York: F. P.
             Harper.

Courlander, H.
1982   Hopi Voices. Albuquerque: University of New Mexico
             Press.

Crane, Leo
1919   Annual Report. Moqui Agency, March and August 1919.
              (Manuscript in Harry C. James Collection, Museum of
              Northern Arizona.)

Creer, Leland H.
1958   The Activities of Jacob Hamblin in the Region of the
              Colorado. University of Utah Anthropological Papers 33.
              Salt Lake City: University of Utah Press.

Crosby, A. W.
1976   Epidemic and Peace, 1918. London and Westport:
              Greenwood Press.

Cummings, Byron
[c.1950s]   Trodden Trails. (Manuscript in Arizona Pioneers' Historical
              Society, Tucson.)

1952   Indians I Have Known. Tucson: Arizona Silhouettes.

Dellenbaugh, Frederick
1962 [1908]   A Canyon Voyage. Reprint ed., New Haven and London:
              Yale University Press.

Deloria, Jr., Vine and Clifford M. Lytle
1983   American Indians, American Justice. Austin: University of
              Texas Press.

Dick's Sister
1961   Affidavit, March 23, 1961, Navajo Tribe vs. USA, Indian
              Claims Commisssion, Docket 229.

Dyk, Walter
1938   Son of Old Man Hat. New York: Harcourt Brace.

Eastman, Galen
1880   Eastman to CIA, February 6, 1880; NARS, RG 75, M234,
              New Mexico Superintendency.

1882   Eastman to CIA, June 20, 1882; NARS, RG 75, M1070,
              Inspection Reports, Roll 27.

Eggan, Fred
1950   Social Organization of the Western Pueblos. Chicago:
              University of Chicago Press.

Ellis, Florence
1951   Patterns of Aggression and the War Cult in Southwestern
              Pueblos. Southwestern Journal of Anthropology 7:177-201

Elston, Catherine
1985   Paiute Unit Asks Rank Once Again as a Tribe. Arizona
              Republic 18 November 1985.

Enders, Gordon W.
1971   An Historical Analysis of the Navajo-Hopi Land
              Disputes, 1882-1970. Provo: Brigham Young University
              Master's Thesis.

Euler, Robert C.
1966   Southern Paiute Ethnohistory. University of Utah
              Anthropological Papers 78. Salt Lake City: University of
              Utah Press.

Fogelson, Raymond D.
1977   Cherokee Notions of Power. *In* The Anthropology of
              Power: Ethnographic Studies from Asia, Oceania, and the
              New World. Raymond D. Fogelson and Richard N. Adams
              eds. pp. 185-94. New York: Academic Press.

Ford, Richard I.
1983   Inter-Indian Exchange in the Southwest. *In* Handbook of
              North American Indians 10 (Southwest). Alfonso Ortiz,
              ed. pp. 711-722. Washington, D.C. : Smithsonian
              Institution.

Fortes, Meyer and E. E. Evans-Pritchard
1940   African Political Systems. London: Oxford University
              Press.

Fowler, Don and Catherine Fowler
1971   Anthropology of the Numa. Smithsonian Contributions to
              Anthropology 14. Washington, D.C. : Smithsonian
              Institution.

Franciscan Fathers
910   An Ethnologic Dictionary of the Navajo Language. St.
             Michaels, Arizona: Franciscan Fathers.

Franklin, Robert J.
984   The Role of Structure, Agency, and Communication in the
             Development of Federal Policy towards the San Juan
             Southern Paiute Tribe. Bloomington: Indiana University
             Ph.D. dissertation.

Fried, Morton
967   The Evolution of Political Society: An Essay in Political
             Anthropology. New York: Random House.

Frigout, Arlette
979   Hopi Ceremonial Organization. *In* Handbook of North
             American Indians 9 (Southwest). Alfonso Ortiz, ed. pp.
             564-576. Washington, D.C. : Smithsonian Institution.

Fryer, S. R.
942   Fryer to Ben C. Spencer, March 16, 1942; FARC-LA, RG
             75, Window Rock Box 54-60, Folder 060, Tribal Relations.

Giddens, Anthony
977   Studies in Social and Political Theory. New York: Basic
             Books.

Gillmor, Frances and Louise W. Wetherill
934   Traders to the Navajo. Albuquerque: University of New
             Mexico Press.

Goody, Jack, Michael Cole, and Sylvia Scribner
977   Writing and Formal Operations: A Case Study among the
             Vai. Africa 47(3):289-304.

Goss, James
967   Ute Language, Kin, Myth, and Nature: A Demonstration
             of a Multi-dimensional Folk Taxonomy. Anthropological
             Linguistics 9(9):1-11.

Hafen, Leroy R., ed.
947   Armijo's Journal. Huntington Library Quarterly 11:87-101.

Hafen, Leroy R. and Ann W. Hafen
1954   Old Spanish Trail: Santa Fe to Los Angeles. Glendale:
            Arthur H. Clark.

Hagerman, H. J.
1932   Navajo Indian Reservation. Washington, D. C. : GPO.

Hauke, C. F.
1922   Hauke to Elsie Holliday, December 23, 1922; NARS, RG 7
            CCF WNA, File 17605-1922, 304, pt. 1.

Hemstreet, Rose G.
1973   Paiute Census Roll. (Manuscript in possession of
            DNA-People's Legal Service, Tuba City.)

Hieb, Louis A.
1979   Hopi World View. In Handbook of North American India
            9 (Southwest). Alfonso Ortiz, ed. pp. 577-80.
            Washington, D.C. : Smithsonian Institution.

History of Moencopi and the Hopi Land Claims
1939   Hopi Report, submitted by Moencopi Delegate to Charles
            E. Rachford, at Oraibi, December 12, 1939; NARS, RG 75,
            CCF WNA, File 8970-30, 308.2.

Hittman, M.
1973   The 1870 Ghost Dance at the Walker Reservation: A
            Reconstruction. Ethnohistory 22:247-78.

Honahni, Roger
1978   Deposition, November 9, 1978, Sekaquaptewa vs.
            MacDonald.

Hopi Tribe
1981   Interview forms submitted with [Hopi] Plaintiff's Second
            Answer to the Navajo Tribe's Interrogatories, October 1,
            1981, Sekaquaptewa vs. MacDonald.

Howard, C. H.
1882   Howard to H. M. Teller, November 29, 1882, pp. 23-24;
            NARS, RG 75, M1070, Inspection Reports, Roll 27.

Humetewa, James
1981   Deposition, October 19-21, 1981, Sekaquaptewa vs.
            MacDonald.

Information Concerning Hopi Problems
1939   Hopi Report, submitted to Charles E. Rachford at Polacca,
            December 4, 1939; NARS, RG 75, CCF WNA, File 8970-30,
            308.2.

Ivins, Anthony
1875   Journal. (Manuscript in Latter Day Saints Church
            Historical Department, Salt Lake City, MS No. F 112.)

Jake, Lucille, Evelyn James, and Pamela Bunte
1983   The Southern Paiute Woman in a Changing Society.
            Frontiers 7(1):44-49.

Jake, Merle
1977   Notes of March 12, 1977 meeting between members of San
            Juan and Kaibab tribes. (Original in possession of the
            Kaibab Paiute Tribe.)

Jake, Vivienne
1976   Letter to Arizona Bureau of Land Management, March 16,
            1976. (Copy in possession of the San Juan Paiute Tribe.)

James, George Wharton
1972 [1909] Indian Basketry. Reprint ed., New York: Dover
            Publications.

Janus, Stephen
1908   Janus to CIA, September 7, 1908; FARC-LA, RG 75, Tuba
            City Superintendent's Letters Sent, Box 6, vol. 71.

1909a   Janus to CIA, January 23, 1909; FARC-LA, RG 75, Tuba
            City Superintendent's Letters Sent, Box 6, vol. 71.

1909b   Janus to CIA, July 13, 1909; FARC-LA, RG 75, Tuba City
            Superintendent's Letters Sent, Box 6, vol. 71.

Jeffers, C. R.
1911   Annual Report, 1911; FARC-LA, RG 75, Tuba City
            Superintendent's Letters Sent, Box 2, vol. 75.

1912   Jeffers to CIA, January 29, 1912; FARC-LA, RG 75, Tuba City Superintendent's Letters Sent, Box 2, vol. 75.

Jones, W. A.
1899   Jones to Interior Secretary, July 15, 1899; NARS, RG 75, Letters Received, 1881-1907.

Jorgensen, Joseph G.
1980   Western Indians. San Francisco: W.H. Freeman.

Kaibab Paiute Tribe
1982   Resolution of the Kaibab Paiute Tribal Council. (Manuscript in possession of DNA-People's Legal Service, Tuba City.)

Kammer, Jerry
1980   The Second Long Walk. Albuquerque: University of New Mexico Press.

Kelly, Charles
1948-1949   Journal of W.C. Powell. Utah Historical Quarterly 16-17:257-478.

Kelly, Isabel T.
1934   Southern Paiute Bands. American Anthropologist 36(4):548-61.

1964   Southern Paiute Ethnography. University of Utah Anthropological Papers 69. Salt Lake City: University of Utah Press.

Kelly, Lawrence C.
1968   The Navajo Indians and Federal Indian Policy. Tucson: University of Arizona Press.

1970   Navajo Roundup. Boulder: Pruett.

Kelly, William
1964   Methods and Resources for the Construction and Maintenance of a Navajo Population Register. Tucson: Bureau of Ethnic Research, University of Arizona.

Kluckhohn, Clyde and Dorothea Leighton
1946   The Navajo. Cambridge: Harvard University Press.

Knack, Martha C.
980   Life is with People. Socorro, New Mexico: Ballena Press.

Larrabee, C. F.
907   Larrabee to Secretary of Interior, October 15, 1907, with
             First Assistant Secretary Thomas Ryan's approval; NARS,
             RG 75, CCF Kaibab Agency, 1908-1939, File 9413-1926,
             272.

908   Larrabee to Lockhart, November 7, 1908; NARS, RG 75,
             CCF WNA, File 17605-1922, 304.

Leech, A. W.
923   Leech to CIA, May 18, 1923; NARS, RG 75, CCF WNA,
             File 17605-1922, 304, pt. 1.

Lee, Joe
974   My Wonderful Life. Gladwell Richardson, ed. Frontier
             Times February-March:6-15, 29-63. (Manuscript in
             Northern Arizona University Special Collections.)

Lehi, Alfred
948   Affidavit, March 3, 1948, Office of Indian Affairs Field
             Service. (Manuscript in possession of San Juan Paiute
             Tribe.)

Lehi, La Ree [Marie]
948   Affidavit, March 3, 1948, Office of Indian Affairs Field
             Service. (Manuscript in possession of San Juan Paiute
             Tribe.)

Levy, Jerrold
962   Community Organization of the Western Navajo. American
             Anthropologist 64:781-882.

Littell, Norman M.
1967   Navajo Indians. Proposed Findings of Fact on behalf of
             the Navajo Tribe of Overall Navajo Claims (Docket number
             229). Window Rock, Arizona, Navajo Tribe.

Little, James
1971 [1881] Jacob Hamblin. Reprint ed., Freeport, New York: Books
             for Libraries Press.

Mair, Lucy
1962   Primitive Government: A Study of Traditional Political
               Systems in Eastern Africa. Bloomington: Indiana
               University Press.

McGinnies, William C.
1982   Deposition, November 23, 1982, Sidney vs. MacDonald.

McGreevy, Susan B.
1985   Translating Tradition: Contemporary Basketry Arts. *In*
               Translating Tradition: Basketry Arts of the San Juan
               Paiute. Susan B. McGreevy and Andrew Hunter Whiteford
               eds. pp. 25-31. Santa Fe: Wheelwright Museum of the
               American Indian.

McKean, E. E.
1923   McKean to A. W. Leech, November 27, 1923; NARS, RG
               75, CCF WNA, File 17605-1922, 304, pt. 1.

McKinley, William
1900   Message from the President to Congress, January 1, 1900;
               Senate Document No. 68, 56th Congress, First Session.

McLaughlin, James
1898   McLaughlin to Interior Secretary, August 15, 1898; NARS,
               RG 48, Inspection Report 6111-1898.

1899   McLaughlin to Interior Secretary, June 16, 1899; NARS,
               RG 48, Inspection Report 4314-1899.

McNitt, Frank
1962   The Indian Traders. Norman: University of Oklahoma
               Press.

1972   The Navajo Wars. Albuquerque: University of New
               Mexico Press.

Merritt, E. B.
1921a   Merritt to Paradise Oil and Refining Co., May 24, 1921;
               NARS, RG 75, CCF WNA, File 42622-1921, 337.

1921b   Merritt to Paradise Oil and Refining Co., June 4, 1921;
               NARS, RG 75, CCF WNA, File 42622-1921, 337.

Miller, D.
1959   Hole-in-the-Rock. Salt Lake City: University of Utah
              Press.

Morez, Fred
1982   Deposition, November 15, 1982, Sidney vs. MacDonald.

Murphy, Matthew
1902   Murphy to CIA, February 29, 1902; NARS, RG 75, CCF
              WNA, File 108979-1911, 341.

1907   Murphy to Frank C. Churchill, July 10, 1907; FARC-LA,
              RG 75, Tuba City Superintendent's Letters Sent, Box 1,
              vol. 67.

Navajo Tribal Council
1929   Petition of the Navajo Tribal Council, June 24, 1929;
              NARS, RG 75, CCCF WNA, File 17605-1922, 304, pt. 1.

Navajo Tribe
1985a   Second Amended and Supplemented Responses to
              Applicants' for Intervention First Interrogatories and
              Requests for Production to Navajo Tribe. Sidney vs. Zah
              vs. James. U.S. District Court for the District of Arizona.

1985b   Preliminary Response on Behalf of the Navajo Nation to
              the Petition of Evelyn James Seeking Recognition of a
              "San Juan Southern Paiute Tribe." (Manuscript in
              possession of authors).

1985c   Supplemental Response on Behalf of the Navajo Nation to
              the Petition of Evelyn James Seeking Recognition of a
              "San Juan Southern Paiute Tribe." (Manuscript in
              possession of authors.)

1986   Second Supplemental Response on Behalf of the Navajo
              Nation to the Petition of Evelyn James Seeking
              Recognition of a "San Juan Southern Paiute Tribe."
              (Manuscript in possession of authors.)

Otterbein, K. F.
1964   Comparison of Land Tenure Systems of the Bahamas,
            Jamaica, and Barbados. International Archives of
            Ethnography 50:31-42.

Page, Gordon
1983   Deposition, May 24, 1983, Sidney vs. Zah.

Paiute Canyon Band Exploration Agreement
1952   Agreement permitting mineral exploration on San Juan
            Paiute land. (Copy in possession of San Juan Paiute
            Tribe.)

Paiute Tribe of Utah
1982   Resolution of the Utah Paiute Tribal Council. (Manuscript
            in possession of DNA-People's Legal Service, Tuba City.)

Palmer, Edward
1878   Plants Used by the Indians of the United States.
            American Naturalist 12(9-10):593-606, 646-55.

Parkhill, Forbes
1961   The Last of the Indian Wars. New York: Collier Books.

Pikyavit, Ted
1946   Letter to Alfred Lehi, April 12, 1946. (Original in
            possession of San Juan Paiute Tribe.)

Qa'toqti
1974   Land Dispute Discussed by Hopis, Paiutes. Qa'toqti 4 July
            1974.

Reagan, Albert
1922   The "Flu" among the Navajos. Transactions of the Kansas
            Academy of Science 30(12):131-38.

Reay, L.
1980   Incredible Passage. Salt Lake City: Publisher's Press.

Redd, Charles
1930   Redd to Donald B. Colton, October 13, 1930; NARS, RG 75
            CCF WNA, File 17605-1922, 304.

1931   Redd to Reed Smoot, September 30, 1931; NARS, RG 75, CCF WNA, File 17605-1922, 304.

Reeve, Frank
1974   The Navajo Indians. *In* Navajo Indians, vol. 2. New York and London: Garland Press.

Roessel, Ruth
1973   Navajo Stories of the Long Walk Period. Tsaile, Arizona: Navajo Community College Press.

1983   Navajo Arts and Crafts. *In* Handbook of North American Indians 10 (Southwest). Alfonso Ortiz, ed. pp. 592-604. Washington, D.C. : Smithsonian Institution.

Rovin, Charles
1970   Letter to S. Withers, June 8, 1970. (Original in possession of DNA-People's Legal Service, Tuba City.)

Runke, Walter
1907   Runke to CIA, January 3, 1907; NARS, RG 75, Letters Received, 73473-1907.

1914   Runke to Gregory, October 27, 1914; FARC-LA, RG 75, Tuba City Superintendent's Letters Sent, Box 3, vol. 80.

1915a   Runke to CIA, March 29, 1915; FARC-LA, RG 75, Tuba City Superintendent's Letters Sent, Box 6, vol. 81.

1915b   Annual Report, 1915; NARS, RG 75, M1101, WNA Annual Reports, Roll 166.

1916a   Runke to CIA, February 3, 1916; Tuba City Superintendent's Letters Sent, vol. 82; in the J. Lee Correll Collection, Navajo Tribe, Window Rock, Arizona.

1916b   Runke to CIA, February 19, 1916; Tuba City Superintendent's Letters Sent, vol. 82; in the J. Lee Correll Collection, Navajo Tribe, Window Rock, Arizona.

1919   Runke to CIA, May 19, 1919; NARS, RG 75, CCF WNA, File 48409-1919, 101.

San Juan Paiute Tribe
1970   Minutes of Tribal Council Meeting held on May 11, 1970.
            (Original in possession of DNA-People's Legal Service,
            Tuba City).

Sapir, Edward
1913   A Note on Reciprocal Terms of Relationship in America.
            American Anthropologist 15:132- 38.

1930   The Southern Paiute Language. Proceedings of the
            American Academy of Arts and Sciences 65(2). New York.

Schapera, Isaac
1956   Government and Politics in Tribal Societies. New York:
            Schocken Books.

Schneider, Harold K.
1974   Economic Man: The Anthropology of Economics. New
            York: The Free Press.

1981   The Africans: An Ethnological Account. Englewood
            Cliffs, New Jersey: Prentice-Hall.

Schoolcraft, Henry R.
1860   Archives of Aboriginal Knowledge, vol. 4. Philadelphia:
            J.B. Lippincott and Company.

Scollon, Ron and Suzanne B. K. Scollon
1981   Narrative, Literacy, and Face in Interethnic
            Communication. Norwood, New Jersey: Ablex Publishing.

Scott, F. J.
1935   Annual Report of the WNA, September 14, 1935; NARS, RG
            75, M1101, WNA Annual Reports, Roll 167.

Service, Elman R.
1975   The Origins of the State and Civilization: The Process of
            Cultural Evolution. New York: Norton Press.

Sharp, Byron A.
1922   Sharp to CIA, June 2, 1922; NARS, RG 75, CCF WNA, File
            17605-1922, 304, pt. 1.

Shepardson, Mary and Blodwen Hammond
1970   The Navajo Mountain Community. Berkeley and Los
            Angeles: University of California Press.

Sick-Connelley, Deborah
1986   The Role of Tradition in Development: A San Juan Paiute
            Case. Las Cruces: New Mexico State University Master's
            Thesis.

Simmons, L. W., ed.
1942   Sun Chief: The Autobiography of a Hopi Indian. New
            Haven: Yale University Press.

Simonson, John S.
1859   Simonson to John D. Wilkins, September 23, 1859; NARS,
            RG 393, M1120, Department of New Mexico, Roll 10,
            Frames 786-788.

Southern Paiute Nation
[c.1982]   Proposal for an all-Paiute agency. (Manuscript in
            possession of the Kaibab Paiute Tribe.)

Spicer, Edward H.
1971   Persistent Identity Systems. Science 4011:795-800.

Spier, Leslie
1928   Havasupai Ethnography. Anthropological Papers of the
            American Museum of Natural History 29(3). New York.

Stephen, Alexander
1882a   Deposition, August 17, 1882; NARS, RG 75, M1070,
            Inspection Reports, Roll 27.

1882b   Stephen to C. H. Howard, December 13, 1882; NARS, RG
            75, M1070, Inspection Reports, Roll 27.

Steward, Julian H.
1936   The Economic and Social Basis of Primitive Bands. *In*
            Essays in Anthropology Presented in Honor of A. L.
            Kroeber. pp. 331-50. Berkeley, California.

1938   Basin-Plateau Aboriginal Sociopolitical Groups. Bureau of
            American Ethnology Bulletin 120.

Stewart, Justin
1969   Letter to Samuel Withers, October 16, 1969. Contained
            copy of letter from McKay Pikyavit to Justin Stewart. (In
            possession of DNA-People's Legal Service, Tuba City.)

Stewart, Omer C.
1938a   The Navajo Wedding Basket, 1938. Museum of Northern
            Arizona Museum Notes 10(9):25-26.

1938b   Navajo Basketry as made by Ute and Paiute. The
            American Anthropologist 40(4): 758-59.

1942   Culture Element Distributions: XVIII, Ute-Southern
            Paiute. Anthropological Records 6(4).

1984   Report on the San Juan Band of Southern Paiutes.
            (Manuscript in possession of DNA-People's Legal Service,
            Tuba City.)

Stoffle, Richard W. and Henry F. Dobyns
1982   Puaxantu Tuvip. Kenosha: University of Wisconsin-
            Parkside.

1983   Nuvagantu. Cultural Resource Series Monograph 7. Reno:
            Nevada State Office of the Bureau of Land Management.

Stoffle, Richard W., and Michael Evans
1976   Resource Competition and Population Change: A Kaibab
            Paiute Ethnohistorical Case. Ethnohistory 23(2):173-97.

Stoffle, Richard W., Merle C. Jake, Pamela A. Bunte, and Michael J.
Evans
1982   Southern Paiute People Response to Energy Proposals. In
            Indian SIA: The Social Impact Assessment of Rapid
            Resource Development on Native Peoples. C. Geisler, et
            al., eds. pp. 107-134. Ann Arbor: University of
            Michigan School of Natural Resources.

Stone, Jeff
1970   Obscure Indians Emerge. Flagstaff Sun 14 July 1970:19.

Tallsalt, Bert
1954   Navajo Mountain Paiute Census. (Manuscript in possession
            of Madeline Cameron.)

Thomas, David H.
1973   Great Basin Settlement Patterns. American Antiquity
             38(2):155-76.

Thompson, Gerald E.
1976   The Army and the Navajo. Tucson: University of
             Arizona Press.

Thrapp, Dan L.
1942   Polk and Posey on the Warpath. Desert Magazine
             5(7):9-13.

Turner, Christy G.
1962   House Types of the Navajo Mountain Community.
             (Manuscript in Museum of Northern Arizona, Flagstaff.)

Underhill, Ruth
1953   Here Come the Navaho! Washington, D. C. : U.S. BIA,
             Branch of Education.

U.S. Bureau of Census
1976   Study Plan for the Navajo Pilot Project. (Manuscript in
             possession of James Williams, New Mexico State
             University.)

1977   Report on the Findings of Special Enumeration--
             Population Register Match for Three Chapters on the
             Navajo Reservation. Washington, D. C. : U.S. Bureau of
             the Census.

U.S. BIA
1968   Southern Paiute Judgment Roll. (Manuscript in possession
             of the BIA Phoenix Area Office.)

U.S. BIA Branch of Land Operations
1974   Navajo Area Tuba City Agency Districts 2 and 8, Soil and
             Range Inventory. (Copy in Museum of Northern Arizona.)

U.S. BIA Navajo Agency
1937-66   Navajo Agency Grazing Documents, District Number Three.
             (Manuscripts in possession of Native American Rights
             Fund.)

1937-68   Navajo Agency Grazing Documents, District Number Two. (Manuscripts in possession of Native American Rights Fund.)

USDA Soil Conservation Service
1935   Summarized Annual Report for the Navajo Project, June, 1935. (Manuscript in possession of Native American Rights Fund.)

1937   Status of Surveys and Physical Work on the Navajo District, March 15, 1937. (Manuscript in possession of Native American Rights Fund.)

1940a   Livestock Census, District Number Three, February 26, 1940. (Manuscript in possession of Native American Rights Fund.)

1940b   Livestock Census, District Number Two, June 21, 1940. (Manuscript in possession of Native American Rights Fund.)

U.S. Senate
1931   Survey of Conditions of the Indians in the United States, Navajos in Arizona and New Mexico. Hearings before a Subcommittee of the Commission on Indian Affairs, U.S. Senate, Part 18, May 20, 1931, Tuba City, Arizona.

1972   Authorize Partition of Surface Rights of Navajo-Hopi Indian Land. Washington, D. C. : GPO.

1973   Partition of the Surface Rights of Navajo-Hopi Land. Washington, D. C. : GPO.

1974   Navajo-Hopi Land Dispute. Washington, D. C. : GPO.

Van Valkenburgh, Richard
1941   *Dine Bikeyah*. Window Rock: Navajo Agency.

Walker, Chester L.
1927a   Walker to CIA, March 24, 1927; NARS, RG 75, CCF WNA, File 15941-1927, 826.

1927b   Annual Reports, 1927; NARS, RG 75, M1101, WNA Annual Reports, Roll 167.

1928a   Walker to CIA, December 6, 1928; NARS, RG 75, CCF
               WNA, File 17605-1922, 304, pt. 1.

1928b   Annual Reports, 1928; NARS, RG 75, M1101, WNA Annual
               Reports, Roll 167.

1930a   Walker to H. J. Hagerman, February 5, 1930; NARS, RG
               75, CCF WNA, File 8970-1930, 308.2.

1930b   Walker to CIA, March 31, 1930; NARS, RG 75, CCF WNA,
               File 17605-1922, 304.

Walker, John G.
1859a   Walker to J. H. Edson, September 20, 1859; NARS, RG 393,
               M1120, Department of New Mexico, Roll 10, Frames
               793-806.

1859b   Walker to J. H. Edson, September 20, 1859; NARS, RG 393,
               M1120, Department of New Mexico, Roll 10, Frames
               789-792.

Ward, Martha
1970   Letter to John Smotherman, Surplus Commodities, Arizona
               State Department of Public Welfare, July 14, 1970. (Copy
               in possession of DNA-People's Legal Service, Tuba City).

1971   Case closing report, February 9, 1971 (Copy in possession
               of DNA-People's Legal Service, Tuba City).

Welton, H. S.
1888   Welton to CIA, June 17, 1888; NARS, RG 75, Letters
               Received, 15962-1888.

Western Navajo Agency Annual Reports (ARWNA)
1910-1935   Annual Reports, NARS, RG 75, M1101, Rolls 166- 67.

Western Navajo Reservation Indian Census Rolls
1937   Census Rolls, NARS, RG 75, M595, Roll 281.

Wetherill, Milton A.
1954A   Paiute Trap Corral on Skeleton Mesa, Arizona. Plateau
               26(4):116.

White Mesa Allotment Map
1939   Map, March 13, 1939; NARS, RG 75, CCF WNA, File
             17605-1922, 304.

Wilson, Leroy A.
1921a   Wilson to Charles Burke, May 7, 1921; NARS, RG 75, CCF
             WNA, File 42622-1921, 337.
1921b   Wilson to Charles Burke, May 21, 1921; NARS, RG 75, CCF
             WNA, File 42622-1921, 337.

1921c   Wilson to E. B. Merritt, May 26, 1921; NARS, RG 75, CCF
             WNA, File 42622-1921, 337.

Withers, Samuel
1969   Memorandum entitled "Paiute Hunger." (Original in
             possession of DNA-People's Legal Service, Tuba City.)

Witherspoon, Gary
1975   Navajo Kinship and Marriage. Chicago: University of
             Chicago Press.

1977   Language and Art in the Navajo Universe. Ann Arbor:
             University of Michigan Press.

1983   Navajo Social Organization. In Handbook of North
             American Indians 10 (Southwest). Alfonso Ortiz, ed. pp.
             524-535. Washington, D.C. : Smithsonian Institution.

Work, Laura
1905   Work to CIA, December 2, 1905; NARS, RG 75, Letters
             Received, 103403-1905.

1906   Work to CIA, February 20, 1906; NARS, RG 75, Letters
             Received, 18742-1906.

Wyman, Leland C.
1983   Navajo Ceremonial System. In Handbook of North
             American Indians 10 (Southwest). Alfonso Ortiz, ed. pp.
             536-557. Washington, D.C. : Smithsonian Institution.

Yazzie, Connie
1948   Affidavit, March 3, 1948, Office of Indian Affairs Field
             Service. (Manuscript in possession of San Juan Paiute
             Tribe.)

Young, Robert
1961   The Navajo Yearbook. Window Rock: Navajo Agency.

Zeh, William
1930   General Grazing Conditions of the Western Navajo
              Reservation, December 26, 1930, NARS RG 75 CCF WNA,
              File 67654-1930, 301.

INDEX

333